P9-CQV-317

The Whole Chile Pepper Book

By the same authors

The Fiery Cuisines
Fiery Appetizers
Just North of the Border

The Whole Chile Pepper Book

Dave DeWitt and Nancy Gerlach

Illustrated by Cyd Riley

Little, Brown and Company

Boston   Toronto   London

Copyright © 1990 by Dave DeWitt and Nancy Gerlach

All rights reserved. No part of this book may be reproduced in any form or by any electronic or mechanical means, including information storage and retrieval systems, without permission in writing from the publisher, except by a reviewer who may quote brief passages in a review.

First Edition

Portions of this book originally appeared in *The Whole Chile Pepper* magazine. Color photographs following page 22 are by Jeffrey Gerlach, unless otherwise noted.

Library of Congress Cataloging-in-Publication Data

DeWitt, Dave.
    The whole chile pepper book: with over 180 hot and spicy recipes
/ by Dave DeWitt and Nancy Gerlach; illustrated by Cyd Riley. —
1st ed.
      p.   cm.
    Includes bibliographical references.
    ISBN 0-316-18223-0
    1. Cookery (Hot peppers) 2. Hot peppers. I. Gerlach, Nancy.
II. Whole chile pepper. III. Title.
TX803.P46D49 1990   90-5590
641.6′384 — dc20   CIP

10 9 8 7 6 5 4 3 2 1

RRD-VA

Designed by Barbara Werden

Published simultaneously in Canada by Little, Brown & Company (Canada) Limited
Printed in United States of America

For Jeffrey and Mary Jane
with love and thanks

CONTENTS

ACKNOWLEDGMENTS

THANKS for all your help to the following chile lovers: Paul Bosland, Eleanor Bravo, Jane Jordan Browne, Ruth Cummins, Rick DeWitt, Chuck Evans, Jeffrey Gerlach, Mary Gerlach, Jo Ann Horton, Jennifer Josephy, Barbara Mitchell, Gary Nabhan, Marge Peterson, Cyd Riley, Pat Romero, Joe Sanchez, Wayne Scheiner, Keith Shepherd, Andy Smith, Robert Spiegel, Ben Villalon, Jim West, and Mary Jane Wilan.

The Whole Chile Pepper Book

INTRODUCTION

SINCE we first started researching and writing about chile peppers in 1977, we have witnessed a remarkable surge of interest in the pungent pods. In the past ten years, chiles have exploded onto the American scene. Cultivation acreage has doubled, new varieties are constantly being developed, a bewildering array of new products has been introduced, and dozens of cookbooks and hundreds of articles have been published about chiles.

Today, there is an organized industry devoted to chiles, complete with a Chile Commission, a national magazine, a trade show, dozens of festivals, and a huge bibliography (over seven thousand citations) devoted to the subject. There are even plans for a university Chile Institute.

This book is the culmination of our years of research on chiles. It was inspired by the success of *The Whole Chile Pepper* (P.O. Box 4278, Albuquerque, NM 87196; $15.95/yr.), a magazine devoted to chiles and spicy foods which has proven that far from being an esoteric fad, chiles indeed have mass-market appeal. As editors of that publication, we have witnessed its phenomenal growth as well as the near-fanatic devotion of its chile-loving readers. We should point out that although some of the material in this book first appeared in that magazine, most of it is new — or at least unpublished until now.

To prepare readers and cooks for the experience that follows, a few clarifications and explanations are in order. First, we should cover the sticky issue of nomenclature. Why do we spell *chile* with a terminal *e* instead of an *i,* as most dictionary and stylebooks do? The reason is simple: clarity. We wish to avoid confusion, so *chile,* the original Spanish spelling, refers to the plant and the pod; while *chili* refers to the dish *chili con carne,* a curious combination of the Anglicized *chili* and the Spanish *carne,* or "meat."

In this book, *chile* is used as an adjective when it describes the hot types of peppers (Capsicums), as in "chile peppers." It is also a noun when used without the word *pepper,* as in "hot chiles." To avoid confusion, the unrelated common table condiment *Piper nigrum* is called "black pepper."

Since this book is a combination of text and recipes, we should briefly explain our methods. The book begins with two chapters of important background material on the identification, usage, cultivation, and preservation of chile peppers. With Chapter 3 we begin the tale of how chile peppers conquered the world. There are recipes in every chapter except the first one.

To research the text, hundreds upon hundreds of sources were examined, and at first we were tempted to footnote all significant citations. However, that scholarly technique would not be appropriate for a work that is basically a cookbook. So we decided to attribute sources in the text as best we could and include a rather extensive bibliography, which is divided into four parts by subject for easier reference.

The recipes were created through a combination of research and kitchen testing. Over the years, we have collected a vast number of chile-related recipes, so we searched for those that were both the most traditional and the tastiest. Most of the recipes are revised versions of culinary classics from many cultures; but some, such as the pre-Columbian recipes in Chapter 3 and the New Southwest dishes in Chapter 10, are our own creations. In some cases, ingredients and cooking techniques have been adapted for American kitchens. Cooks should note that we use the generic term "ground red chile" to refer to New Mexican chile varieties, which are described in Chapter 1. Also, we have usually omitted the addition of salt to the recipes because we assume that cooks always add salt to taste.

Throughout the book, we make an attempt to estimate the

degree of chile heat in the foods we are discussing. As discussed in Chapter 8, the relative heat of the chiles themselves is measured by a laboratory process, so when we say that a Jalapeño is a "5" on the Heat Scale, it is a fairly precise statement, although heat levels can vary within varieties.

When chiles are combined with other ingredients, the heat levels can vary enormously due to a number of factors such as the cooling effects of dairy products and simple dilution. Obviously, a single raw Jalapeño will be hotter than one cooked in two gallons of stew. Thus the heat scales given in the recipes are only approximate, and cooks should constantly taste-test the recipes to determine the suitable heat level while remembering that it is much easier to add heat than to remove it from a dish.

During our research, we encountered certain regions and cities where the food is particularly fiery with chiles. But which location is the hottest? Arequipa, Peru? San Pedro Atocpan, Mexico? Santa Fe, New Mexico? Guntur, India? Bangkok, Thailand? Sichuan, China? The only conclusion we have reached is that it is best to allow readers and cooks to decide this question for themselves.

One final note. We use the word *cuisine* quite a bit in this book, so it probably needs defining. Dictionary definitions tend to be too broad, as in "the style of cooking" or "the manner of preparing food." To us, a cuisine is regional, that is, it has been developed over a period of time in a certain area and tends to reflect the geography, climate, native foods, cooking methods, favorite spices, as well as the beliefs and customs of the people of that region.

Cuisines have evolved because the world has become smaller — international commerce has been both the best stimulus for the evolution of cuisines and the greatest danger to them. For example, the early exchange of foodstuffs between the Old and New Worlds radically transformed and enriched the cuisines of both hemispheres — chiles are a perfect example of this process. Yet today, the worldwide desire for Americanized fast food threatens to replace traditional cuisines, which are now in danger of losing their identity. We hope in some small way that this book will help to preserve ancient culinary heritages.

CHAPTER ONE

A Field Guide to the Chiles

*"The tremendous variation in fruit size, shape, and color,
as well as an extremely variable plant habit in C.
annuum alone, make it impossible to devise a practical
system of classification that would cover the large
numbers of forms known to be cultivated."*

Paul G. Smith, *HortScience*, 1987

WITH all due respect to Dr. Smith, a professor emeritus at the University of California and one of the most distinguished researchers of chile peppers, a practical system for classifying chiles is not only possible, it has been accomplished. Perhaps our system is not detailed enough to satisfy botanists or horticulturists, but it will certainly serve to clarify for the general public what has become an enormously confusing issue: the identification of the myriad forms of chile peppers.

The confusion has arisen mostly because the hundreds of varieties of chile peppers have been given popular, localized, or "pet" names. When identifying chiles in order to preserve their germ plasm (seeds), botanists and horticulturists use a complicated, forty-five-step process that covers every conceivable descriptor from pedicel position at anthesis to peduncle insertion. However, for purposes of accurate nomenclature and general identification, we feel it is sufficient to organize chiles according to their pod type and then describe and discuss the important varieties within each type.

This method is based upon the organization developed by Dr. Paul W. Bosland and Jaime Iglesias-Olivas of the Department of Agronomy and Horticulture at New Mexico State University in Las Cruces with the assistance of Alton Bailey. The botanical descriptors used are based upon those recommended by the International Board of Plant Genetic Resources as modified by Dr. Bosland. Some descriptions, measurements, and pod yields are based on the authors' personal observations recorded over years of growing every type of chile included here. The Heat Scale ratings (see Chapter 8 for more information) have been determined by various tests on chiles with high-pressure liquid chromatography (HPLC) as reported by Dr. Ben Villalon at the Texas Agricultural Experiment Station in Weslaco, by New Mexico State University, and by several chile processing companies.

Please note that only pungent chile peppers are included in this guide; sweet types such as mild Bells, Pimiento, Cuban, and Squash peppers have been omitted. The hot Bells, such as Mexi-Bell, have been included. American Paprika is not a pod type but rather a powder processed from any non-pungent red pepper. All of the types belong to the species *Capsicum annuum* var. *annuum,* unless otherwise indicated.

Chile peppers are perennial subshrubs, native to South America, which are grown as annuals in colder climates. They are very closely related to tomatoes, potatoes, and eggplants, all of which are part of the large nightshade family, or *Solanaceae.* They are not related to black pepper, *Piper nigrum.*

The genus Capsicum of the family Solanaceae encompasses all peppers, from the mildest Bells to the hottest Habaneros. There are twenty to thirty separate species of Capsicums, depending upon which botanist is consulted. There are five domesticated species and literally dozens of pod types within those species. Further, each pod type has numerous varieties that are often called "cultivars."

A convenient parallel to Capsicum nomenclature is the taxonomy of dogs. Think of peppers as dogs; just as there are various species of peppers (*C. annuum, C. frutescens*), a number of dog species exist (wolves, foxes, domesticated dogs). The pod types of chiles, such as Ancho and Jalapeño, are parallel to breeds of dogs, such as collies and poodles. Finally, the varieties within the pod types, such as the New Mexico No. 6-4 and Sandia, are similar to varieties within dog breeds, such as miniature and toy poodles.

The chile plant itself is compact, herbaceous when young, and woody at maturity. Although some tropical chile plants as high as eighteen feet have been reported, the average height of the cultivated plants is under three feet. The leaves of the Capsicum genus vary between one and five inches in length. They are usually ovate (egglike) in shape, arise singly, and develop alternately. The flowers are usually pendant, and their color varies from white to purple. Pollination occurs by wind in the

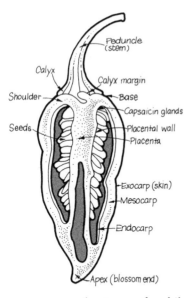

Anatomy of a chile

case of self-pollination, or by insects, which can cause cross-pollination. Fruit set is determined mostly by night temperatures, which should range between 55 and 80 degrees.

Botanically speaking, the pods are berries, but horticulturists call them fruits. When harvested in the green stage, the pods are considered to be a vegetable; when harvested red, they are termed a spice. The pods range in size from less than an inch to a foot long and are borne erect or pendant. Most varieties are ready to pick in the green stage after about 70 days and are fully ripened after about 130 days. The ripened fruits can have many colors: red, yellow, orange, or brown — and shades in between.

Ají (*Capsicum baccatum*)

Nomenclature

"Ají" is the general term in South America for chile peppers, an indication of the prevalence of this pod type. Other varieties are also called by the same name, but we think that the term most accurately applies to *Capsicum baccatum*. The pods of the Ají are yellow at some time during growth, giving rise to the common name *ají amarillo* for this species. Another common name for this type is *Escabeche*, not to be confused with the pickling method, *en escabeche*. There are three varieties of this Ají: *Capsicum baccatum* var. *baccatum*, var. *pendulum*, and var. *microcarpum*. The word *baccatum* refers to the berrylike pods of some forms. *Kellu-uchu* is the Quecha-language word for this chile, and the local Spanish-speaking population in Peru sometimes calls its dried form "cusqueño" ("from Cuzco").

Botanical Description

The plant is tall, sometimes reaching 5 feet in height, has multiple stems and an erect habit which sometimes tends toward sprawling. The leaves are dark green and large, often reaching 7 inches in length and 4 inches in width. The flowers have dark green or brown spots on the white corolla. As with the C. *annuum*s, there is a great diversity of pod size and shape, but the typical Ají pod begins its life erect and becomes pendant as it increases in size and weight. At maturity the pod is elongate in shape, between

3 and 5 inches long, and is usually colored orange-red but also can be yellow or brown.

Heat Scale

In the only known testing of this type, the immature pods of one unnamed variety from Colombia measured an 8 on the Heat Scale.

Horticultural History

Archeological evidence from Peru indicates that Ají was cultivated as early as 2500 B.C. The wild forms of this species have a narrow range of distribution from central Peru through Bolivia to southern Brazil and northern Argentina; however, it is most prevalent in Bolivia. The cultivated forms of Ají are grown in Colombia, Ecuador, Peru, and Bolivia. It has been introduced as a cultivated crop into Costa Rica (where it is called *cuerno de oro*, ("golden horn"), and into Hawaii, India, and the southern United States.

Agricultural Aspects

In South America the Ají is collected from wild plants and is also cultivated in small plots. In the United States, the plant takes at least 120 days for the pods to reach maturity, and sometimes longer. Cultivated at altitudes up to 3,400 feet, the Ají stands out in the chile patch like a small tree. It fruits well and produces 40 or more pods. No commercial cultivars of *C. baccatum* are available; seeds are obtainable only from South American travelers or from university or amateur growers who have allowed their Ajís to self-pollinate.

Legend and Lore

This species is relatively unknown outside of the Andes Mountains of South America, where it is an integral part of the diet. In fact, it is so important to the descendants of the Incas that the Indian artist who painted a mural of the Last Supper for the Cathedral of Cuzco included a dish of Ajís on the table for Christ and His Apostles. This anachronism reminds us that although chiles were undoubtedly being eaten at the time of Christ's birth, they were not discovered by European explorers for another 1,492 years.

Culinary Usage

This chile has a distinctive flavor to rival that of Habaneros. Ajís are used in *ceviche* and to make extremely hot salsas for spicing up potatoes, chicken, roasted guinea pigs, and *anticuchos*, which are marinated and grilled beef hearts.

Ancho/Poblano

Nomenclature

Literally, *chile ancho* means "wide chile pepper," an allusion to the broad, flat, heart-shaped dried pod. The fresh green form is called *Poblano* ("people" chile), and the word is descriptive of the Valley of Puebla, where large-scale production may have first begun. In the United States, the Poblano chile is the fresh green form of the dried Ancho chile; however, in Mexico, the variety is called Ancho and the Poblano is its processed green form. In Baja California both the green and dried pods are called Ancho. Further adding to the confusion are the terms *mulato* ("light brown") and *negro* ("black"), which refer to varieties of the Mexican Ancho.

Botanical Description

The plant is multiple-stemmed and compact to semi-erect in habit, semi-woody, and measures approximately 25 inches high. The leaves are dark green, shiny, and pointed in shape, measuring approximately 4 inches long by 2 1/2 inches wide. The flower corollas are off-white and appear at almost every node. The flowering period begins after 50 days and continues until the first frost. The pods are pendant, vary between 3 and 6 inches in length, are conical or truncated in appearance — often called heart-shaped — and have a marked depression at the base of the pod. The color is dark green but turns dark red when fully matured and changes to a dark, reddish-brown to almost black when dried.

Heat Scale

Poblanos are a relatively mild chile, varying between 1,000 and 1,500 Scoville Units, which places them at a level of 3 on the Heat Scale.

Horticultural History

The earliest Poblano forms were probably cultivated in pre-Columbian times, and the present varieties are at least a century old, attesting to their popularity in the cooking of Mexico. Currently, about 37,000 acres are under cultivation, particularly in the dry valleys of central Mexico in the states of Guanajuato, San Luis Potosí, Durango, Zacatecas, and Aguascalientes. They are also grown to a lesser extent in the coastal regions of the states of Sinaloa, Coahuila, and Nayarit. Popular Mexican varieties of the Poblano are Esmeralda, Verdeno, and Flor de Pabellon; the Mulato variety is represented by V-2 and Roque.

Agricultural Aspects

Anchos are fairly easy to grow in the United States because their growing period ranges from 75 to 100 days. Favorite varieties in this country are Ancho 101, Poblano, and Mulato. The major difference is that the fruit of Ancho 101 and Poblano variety is red at maturity, while that of the Mulato variety is brown. In California the Mulato is often mislabeled as Pasilla, a different type entirely. Yield is about 15 pods per plant.

Legend and Lore

The Ancho chile figures prominently in the legend of the origin of *mole poblano*. The story goes that the dish was invented in the sixteenth century by Sor Andrea de la Asuncion, a Dominican nun at the convent of Santa Rosa in the city of Puebla. (See Chapter 4 for the whole story.)

Culinary Usage

Approximately 50 percent of Mexican Ancho crop is harvested and sold as fresh green chile. These Poblano pods are often stuffed with meats and cheeses for *chiles rellenos*, or utilized in casseroles and sauces much like the New Mexican varieties of the American Southwest. Of the dried Ancho crop, about 15 percent of that is sold as powder and food coloring, and the remainder is purchased by the public in whole-pod form and is used mostly in sauces, particularly *moles*. The Ancho accounts for approximately one-fifth of all chiles consumed in Mexico.

Bell

Nomenclature

The blocky pods of this type are shaped like bells, hence the name. However, no one knows when this appellation was first applied.

Botanical Description

The plant is multi-stemmed; its habit is subcompact leaning toward prostrate, and it grows between 1 and 2 1/2 feet high. The leaves are medium green, ovate to lanceolate, smooth, and measure 3 inches long and 1 1/2 inches wide. The flowers are white with no spots. The fruit is pendant, dark green maturing to red, and bell-shaped, averaging 3 inches in diameter and 5 inches in length. The number of pods per plant is 20 or more.

Heat Scale

The hot varieties of this type are best described as Bells with a slight bite. They range between 100 and 600 Scoville Units, or a 1 or 2 on the Heat Scale.

Horticultural History

Although it is believed that Bells developed in pre-Columbian times, the first mention of the type occurred in 1681 when the English pirate Lionel Wafer wrote of them growing in Panama. Bells are mostly grown in the United States, which has about 70,000 acres under cultivation. Mexico grows about 22,000 acres of Bells for export to the United States.

Agricultural Aspects

Although the national market for sweet Bells is enormous, the cultivation of the hotter varieties seems to be limited to the home garden. The relative number of days to fruit maturity is 80 to 100. There are over 100 varieties of Bells, but only a few have any pungency: Mexi-Bell, Roumanian Hot, and Karla.

Legend and Lore

Since most Bells are bland and are used only as a vegetable, no mythology has sprung up about them. They are, however, the most commonly grown Capsicum in the United States.

Culinary Usage

The pungent varieties of Bells definitely have a "Bell" flavor rather than a "New Mexican" flavor, so they are generally not used in salsas. However, they work fairly well as a dilutant for a particularly pungent batch of fresh green New Mexican chiles, but make sure the Bells are roasted and peeled in the same manner. Bells are also stuffed with meat and cheese, used fresh in salads, sautéed as a vegetable, or added to casseroles.

Cayenne

Nomenclature

This type was named after either the city of Cayenne or the Cayenne River, both in French Guiana. However, the chile is not grown there — or anywhere in South America.

Botanical Description

The plant is treelike with multiple stems and an erect habit, often reaching 3 feet in height with foliage 2 feet in width. The leaves are ovate, smooth, and medium green in color, measuring 3 1/2 inches long and 2 inches wide. The flowers have white corollas with no spots. The pods are elongate and sharply pointed, pendant to curving erect, measuring 6 to 10 inches long by 1 inch wide, and turn red at maturity. A good-sized plant can easily produce 40 or more pods during a season.

Heat Scale

There is good reason for Cayenne's reputation as one of the hottest of the chiles. This type consistently measures between 30,000 and 50,000 Scoville Units, placing it at 8 on the Heat Scale.

Horticultural History

A mystery surrounds the origin of Cayenne. Although it seems to have originated in tropical South America, it is no longer grown in that region. Possibly this chile was transferred to Europe by the Portuguese, who later introduced it into Africa and India.

Agricultural Aspects

Cayenne is grown commercially in New Mexico, Louisiana, Africa, India, Japan, and Mexico. The growing period is 90 days or more. In 1988, 15,087 tons of dried red chiles — mostly Cayenne — were imported into the United States. Dried Cayenne pods are known as "Ginnie peppers" in world commerce. Popular varieties of the Cayenne type are Hot Portugal, Ring of Fire, and Hades Hot. They are grown only for their heat, not for color or flavor.

Legend and Lore

Legend holds that Cayenne is the hottest chile pepper of them all, but it is not — Habanero holds that honor. This chile has long been thought to have therapeutic properties. In 1832, herbalist Samuel Thompson wrote, "It is no doubt the most powerful stimulant known; its power is entirely congenial to nature, being powerful in raising and maintaining heat, on which life depends. . . . I consider it essentially a benefit, for its effects on the glands causes the saliva to flow freely and leaves the mouth clean and moist."

Culinary Usage

The two primary uses of this chile are grinding it into Cayenne powder (also called "red pepper") or processing it into hot sauces. It is quite important in spicing up Cajun dishes such as gumbos and seafood dishes, and the dried pods can be used — carefully — in Asian stir-fry dishes. The fresh green or red pods can be chopped for use in salsas or salads.

Cherry

Nomenclature

This type was so named because the pods resemble cherries.

Botanical Description

The plant has single to intermediate stems, an erect habit, and grows about 2 feet tall. The leaves are dark green, smooth, and measure 3 inches long and 1 1/2 inches wide. The flower corollas are white with no spots. The pods are round, borne erect or pendant, and measure 1 1/4 inches long by 1 3/4 inches wide. They are colored orange to red at maturity. The yield is 15 or more pods per plant.

Heat Scale

The heat levels of this type vary considerably, from zero to about 3,500 Scoville Units. Thus the pungent Cherry peppers can run from 1 to 5 on the Heat Scale.

Horticultural History

This type was mentioned in botanical literature as early as 1586 and was illustrated in Besler's *Celeberrimi Eystetensis*, an herbal published in 1613.

Agricultural Aspects

Only about 1,600 acres of Cherries are grown in the United States, but that appears to be enough to satisfy the demand of processors who pickle them. They grow well in the home garden, and the best pungent varieties are Red Cherry Hot, Large Red Hot, and Hot Apple. Some gardeners grow Cherries as ornamentals only. The growing period is 80 days or more.

Culinary Usage

These are the familiar commercial, round, pickled chile peppers that are often served with sandwiches. They also appear in salads, and, fresh from the garden they can be chopped and added to salsas.

de Arbol

Nomenclature

In Spanish, the name means "treelike," an allusion to the woody stems and erect habit of the plant. Mexican common names for this type include *pico de pajaro* ("bird's beak") and *cola de rata* ("rat's tail").

Botanical Description

The plant has multiple stems, an erect habit, and grows up to 3 feet tall. The leaves vary from smooth to very pubescent (hairy), are light green in color, and very small — 1 1/4 inches long and 3/8 inch wide. The pods are elongate, pendant (sometimes erect), and pointed, measuring 2 to 3 inches long by 3/8 inch wide. The mature pods are dark red but dry to translucent. Yield is 100 pods per plant or more.

Heat Scale

Chile de Arbol measures between 15,000 and 30,000 Scoville Units, a rating of 7 on the Heat Scale.

Horticultural History

Although a "Chile-de-Arbol" was mentioned by Francisco Hernandez in 1615, it does not resemble the type of today. The de Arbol type is believed to be derived from the Cayenne, and some references list the two types together. In Mexico, however, it is regarded as a separate type and is often called *alfilerillo* ("little pin") because of consumer preference for the thinnest pods.

Agricultural Aspects

About 6,000 acres of de Arbol are grown in Mexico, principally along the coast of Nayarit, the high plains of Jalisco, and some parts of Sinaloa, Zacatecas, and Aguascalientes. The growing period is 80 days or longer.

Legend and Lore

In Mexico, lovers of the de Arbol variety think that the thinner pods are closest in taste and appearance to the wild, undomesticated tree. The belief that the de Arbol was once wild, combined with its small, thin pods and leaves, has led to speculation that this variety may be more closely related to the Piquin than the Cayenne. Under cultivation, previously wild chile plants tend to develop larger and longer pods.

Culinary Usage

The de Arbol type is usually ground into a dry powder to give a distinctive flavor in red chile sauces. Individual pods are often added to soups and stews to increase the heat levels, and often they are the primary heat source for table sauces and chile oils and vinegars.

Exotics

Nomenclature

The name refers to land races of chiles from the Eastern Hemisphere that are sometimes grown in American gardens. All are *Capsicum annuum,* and the pod types are usually variations on Piquin or Cayenne.

Botanical Description

The exotics vary considerably botanically, so what follows is a description of the popular Thai variety. The plant has multiple stems, a compact habit, and grows only about 18 inches high. The leaves are medium green in color and are small, measuring about 2 inches long and 3/4 inch wide. The flower corollas are white with no spots. The pods are borne erect (several at each node), are elongate and pointed, and measure 2 1/2 inches long and 3/4 inch wide. The yield is 100 pods per plant or more.

Heat Scale

Most of the exotics are rated between 30,000 and 100,000 Scoville Units, rating them an 8 or 9 on the Heat Scale.

Agricultural Aspects

The Thai varieties closely resemble an ornamental called Fips, which is sold by American seed companies. The Santaka and Hontaka varieties are very similar to types of Piquins with elongate pods. Red Chili Hot is another Exotic variety. The growing period is 80 to 90 days.

Legend and Lore

A tale is told of the novice American cook who decided to prepare a spicy Sichuan stir-fry pork dish for her guests using

Santaka chiles, which she had found in an Asian market. She followed the recipe perfectly except for one minor detail: she forgot to remove the chile pods from the stir-fry before serving. Her guests innocently munched on the pods, and readers can guess the rest of the story.

Culinary Usage

The exotics are fiery chiles that are usually dried red and used in stir-fry dishes. However, they can be used green in salsas and other dishes needing extreme heat.

Habanero (*Capsicum chinense*)

Nomenclature

In Spanish, the word *Habanero* means "Havana-like," or possibly "from Havana," referring to Havana, Cuba, as a possible origin for the pod. It is the only chile pepper growing in the Yucatan that has no Mayan name, leading to speculation that it was imported there from Cuba; however, this chile is now rare in Cuba. Other names for the Habanero are "Scot's Bonnet" or "Scotch Bonnet," (commonly used in the English-speaking Caribbean islands such as Jamaica) and "Bahamian" or "Bahama Mama" in the Bahamas.

Botanical Description

This chile pepper belongs to a different species (*Capsicum chinense*) than most pods utilized in the United States. Under cultivation, the plants average between 1 and 4 1/2 feet in height, depending upon climate. In the tropics the chile grows as a perennial; Habanero trees 8 feet high have been reported growing semi-wild in Costa Rica. Generally, the plant is considerably smaller in home gardens, rarely reaching 2 feet in height. It has multiple stems and a compact habit. The leaves are large, reaching about 6 inches long and 4 inches wide, and they are characteristically highly curled. The plant sets 2 to 6 fruits per node, and the fruits are campanulate (a flattened bell shape). Some varieties of Habanero are pointed at the end, but others are flattened at the end and resemble a tam, or bonnet. They are 1 to 2 1/2 inches long and 1 to 2 inches wide and usually grow pendant on the plant. Although green when immature, the Habanero can ripen to a variety of colors: red, orange, yellow, or white. Orange is the preferred color in most areas, although some sauce manufacturers believe the bright red Habaneros make the most colorful product.

Heat Scale

According to sources who have tested Habaneros with high-pressure liquid chromatography (HPLC), these are the hottest chiles in the world, measuring between 200,000 and 300,000 Scoville Units. Not all Habaneros are this fiery, as experienced tasters of this chile will attest. Still, it registers a 10 on the Heat Scale.

Horticultural History

Although the exact origin of this chile is unknown, ethnobotanist Barbara Pickersgill suggests that since most wild species of *C. chinense* occur in South America, it makes sense to think that the Habanero originated there and then migrated into the Caribbean and Central America by way of Colombia. An intact fruit of a small domesticated Habanero was found in Preceramic levels in Guitarrero Cave in the Peruvian highlands and was dated to 6500 B.C., so it is suspected that humans have been growing these fiery fruits for at least eighty-five centuries.

Agricultural Aspects

Most of the commercial plantings of Habaneros are in the Yucatan Peninsula — mainly in Mexico but also in Belize. The cultivars most commonly grown in Mexico are called INIA and Uxmal. Seventy-five percent of the crop is consumed fresh, 22 percent is processed into sauces, and 3 percent is saved for seed. The only estimate of tonnage available is a figure of 1,500 tons for Mexico in 1981. There are some small commercial fields in Jamaica and Trinidad, but in most of the Caribbean basin the chiles are grown in family plots adjoining cornfields.

Habaneros grow well as annuals in the home garden. The seeds require quite a long time to germinate and benefit from bottom heating. The growing period varies from 80 to 120 days,

Ají (*Capsicum baccatum*) 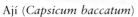   Poblano   Mexi-Bell

 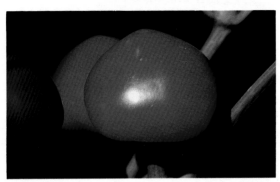

Ancho   Red Cherry Hot

Cayenne   de Arbol

Santaka

Habanero (*Capsicum chinense*)

Mirasol

Jalapeño

Cascabel

New Mexico No. 6-4

New Mexican Ristras

Peter Pepper

Dried Pasilla

Black Plum

Chinese Multi-Color

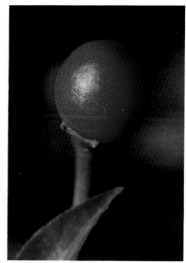

Chiltepin

Fresh Pasilla

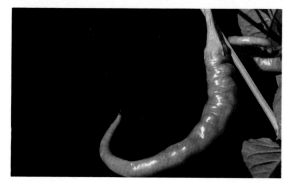

Cow Horn

Piquin

Dried Piquins

Rocoto (*Capsicum pubescens*);
photograph by D. DeWitt

Tabasco (*Capsicum frutescens*)

Serrano

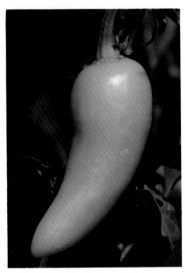

Yellow Wax Hot

depending on climate. The yield also varies considerably, but a medium-sized plant can produce over a quart of pods.

Legend and Lore

The Dominican priest Francisco Ximenez wrote in 1722 of a chile from Havana so strong that a single pod would "make a bull unable to eat." Its reputation as the hottest chile is making the Habanero both infamous and sought-after. Mexican chile expert Arturo Lomelí observes: "It is the great passion of those who love the heat because without doubt it is the hottest variety known. It has an unmistakable flavor — very characteristic. The classic recipe shows it eaten only with a little lime juice and salt." Many contemporary sources make the claim that Habaneros are a thousand times hotter than Jalapeños. A quick glance at our relative heat scale in Chapter 8 will show that, in reality, Habaneros are about a hundred times hotter.

Culinary Usage

Because of its popularity in the Caribbean, the Habanero has long been associated with barbecue. It is a principal ingredient in jerk sauces (combinations of chiles and spices such as allspice), which are literally pounded into meat before it is grilled. Most Habanero chiles that are not eaten fresh are made into bottled sauces. There are many different commercial brands: Yucateca (Mexico); Pickapeppa and Jamaica Hell Fire (Jamaica); and Melindas and Pica Rico (Belize).

The most basic use of the Habanero chiles is in fresh salsas, which differ greatly from country to country.

Jalapeño

Nomenclature

So named because of its association with the Mexican city of Xalapa in Veracruz, where the chile was grown in ancient times but is no longer found.

Botanical Description

The plant grows from 2 to 3 1/2 feet tall, has a compact single stem or upright multibranched habit, and has light to dark green foliage. The pods are conical and cylindrical, growing pendant, are very blunt to pointed, and measure about 2 1/2 inches in length. The color is medium green to red and purple, and the yield is 25 to 35 fruits per plant.

Heat Scale

Most Jalapeños rate from 2,500 to 5,000 Scoville Units, placing them at a level of 5 on the Heat Scale. The TAM Mild Jalapeño-1 variety developed by the Texas Agricultural Experiment Station is considerably less pungent.

Horticultural History

Smoked chiles (*chiles ahumados*, now called *chipotle*) were noted in Mexican markets in the sixteenth century, so Jalapeños, the chiles most commonly smoked, probably had pre-Columbian origins. Grown commercially in Mexico since the beginning of the twentieth century, Jalapeños have four recognized Mexican types: Tipico, Peludo, Espinalteco, and Morita.

The M. American Jalapeño, a basic variety from the United States, has also adapted to Mexican cultivation, as has the Early Jalapeño. Other American cultivars include San Andres, 76104 Jumbo Jal, and TAM Mild Jalapeño-1, which has greatly increased Jalapeño acreage in Texas and New Mexico.

Agricultural Aspects

In Mexico, commercial cultivation measures approximately 40,000 acres in three main agricultural zones: the Lower Palaloapan River Valley in the states of Veracruz and Oaxaca, northern Veracruz, and the area around the aptly named Delicias, Chihuahua. The latter region grows the M. American Jalapeños, which are processed and exported into the United States. Approximately 60 percent of the Mexican Jalapeño crop is used for processing, 20 percent for fresh consumption, and 20 percent in production of *chipotle* chiles (smoked Jalapeños). Jalapeño harvests in Mexico reached all-time records in the late 1980s; consequently, they sold for as little as 5 cents per pound in 1988.

In the United States, Texas is probably the leading state for Jalapeño production, followed by New Mexico. In 1988, a new

Jalapeño processing plant opened in Ciudad Juárez, Chihuahua, just across the border from the best Jalapeño market of all: Texas.

Home gardeners should remember that the U.S. varieties of Jalapeños flourish better in semi-arid climates — ones with dry air combined with irrigation. If planted in hot and humid zones in the United States during the summer, the yield of such Jalapeños decreases; thus the Mexican varieties such as Tipico should be grown instead. The growing period is 80 days, 70 for the TAM. The yield is about 2 quarts of fresh pods per plant.

Legend and Lore

Jalapeños are perhaps the most famous chile peppers. They are instantly recognizable, and a considerable mythology has sprung up about them, particularly in Texas. The ongoing popularity of Jalapeños may be attributed to their unique combination of taste and heat, and is evident in their continued use as a snack food — either pickled or as a topping for cheese nachos.

Culinary Usage

Many Jalapeños are taken straight out of the garden and made into salsas. Others are pickled *en escabeche* and sold to restaurants and food services for sale in their salad bars. Jalapeños are processed as "nacho slices" and "nacho rings," which are served as a topping for one of the fastest-growing snack foods in arenas and ballparks: nachos. Jalapeños are commonly used in both homemade and commercial salsas and *picante* sauces.

Mirasol

Nomenclature

The name in Spanish means "looking at the sun," an allusion to the erect pods on some but not all Mirasol plants. Perhaps the name is more indicative of the tendency of the pods to curl upward, like an elephant's trunk, hence the name *chile trompa*. The type is also called *chile travieso*, or "naughty" chile, although the Heat Scale does not bear out its supposedly wicked bite.

Botanical Description

The plant has an intermediate number of stems and an erect habit, although some varieties tend toward a compact habit. They grow from 2 to 3 feet high. The leaves are smooth and medium-green in color, measuring 2 inches long and 1 1/4 inches wide. The flower corollas are white with no spots. The pods are elongate and pointed, measuring 4 inches long and 3/4 inch wide. Despite the name, the pods of most varieties of Mirasol are borne pendant, not erect, and they mature to a dark red color. The pods of some varieties, such as Cascabel, are round, and, when dry, the seeds rattle inside them — hence the name. Yield is 50 pods per plant or more.

Heat Scale

The Mirasol varieties rate a 5 on the Heat Scale.

Horticultural History

It is likely that the Mirasol type was the *chilcoztli* chile first mentioned by Francisco Hernández in 1615. It appears to be a Mexico native, where it is much loved today. There are several varieties of the Mirasol type, including Cascabel, Guajillo, Loretto 74, and Real Mirasol.

Agricultural Aspects

Approximately 40,000 acres of Mirasols are cultivated in Mexico, primarily in Zacatecas. Other areas of production are Aguascalientes, Durango, and San Luis Potosí. This type grows well in American gardens; the growing period is at least 90 days.

Legend and Lore

The Cascabel variety is noted for its nutty, woody taste and its resemblance, in both appearance and sound, to a jingle bell.

Culinary Usage

The dried pods are utilized much like dried red New Mexican varieties — in sauces, stews, meat dishes, and corn dishes. The main culinary use of the Cascabel and Guajillo varieties is to crumble them into soups and stews. In the fresh green form, the chile can be a substitute for the Serrano.

New Mexican (formerly "Anaheim")

Nomenclature

For nearly a century, confusion has reigned over the proper name for the long green varieties of chiles that turn red in the fall. Originally, they were developed and grown in New Mexico; however, seeds were transported to California during the early part of this century and the pod type was given the name "Anaheim."

Since few — if any — chiles are grown near Anaheim these days, it makes little sense to use that name to describe them. Recently, chile experts at New Mexico State University have made a decision to use a more accurate descriptive term. Hence, in the future, the name of this type will be "New Mexican." Varieties within this type will include "Anaheims," California strains, as well as the numerous New Mexico–grown varieties such as Big Jim, New Mexico No. 6-4, and Española Improved. To put it simply, Anaheim has been reduced from a pod type to a variety, and the pod type has been renamed *New Mexican*.

Botanical Description

Since there are significant differences among New Mexican varieties, what follows is a description of the most commonly grown variety, New Mexico No. 6-4. The plant measures between 20 and 30 inches high, has an intermediate number of stems, and its habit varies between prostrate and compact. Corolla color is white with no spots. The leaves are ovate, medium green in color, fairly smooth, and approximately 3 inches long and 2 inches wide. The fruit is smooth, elongate, pendant, measures between 6 and 7 inches in length, and is bluntly pointed.

Heat Scale

New Mexican varieties vary between 1 and 6 on the Heat Scale, which means their Scoville Range is between 100 and 10,000. However, most New Mexican varieties are in the 500–2,500 range, or 2 to 4 on the Heat Scale. Generally speaking, New Mexico–grown chiles are hotter than those cultivated in California. See "Agricultural Aspects" for the ratings for individual varieties.

Horticultural History

The predecessors of the New Mexican varieties were cultivated at least as early as the seventeenth century. Undoubtedly, they were modified Mexican chiles, although a debate rages over whether the New Mexican chiles were introduced by earlier Spanish treasure expeditions or through trade between the Toltecs or Aztecs and the Rio Grande pueblos. Whichever is correct, there is no doubt that the Spanish settlers loved the pungent pods, planted the seeds, and adopted native fiery dishes into their cuisine.

In New Mexico, a number of land races of these chiles, adapted to specific environments, have evolved, creating a great diversity of pod shapes and heat levels. Such a diversity caused problems for farmers because they had no way to tell how large or hot the chiles might be. While Emilio Ortega was growing chiles near Anaheim, development and improvement of the modern varieties began in New Mexico. In 1907, Fabian Garcia, director of the New Mexico Agricultural Experiment Station, developed the No. 9 or College 9 variety and succeeded in his goal of standardizing chiles into recognizable varieties, so that farmers could know precisely what they were growing. By 1950 the No. 9 variety had been crossed with larger varieties to produce New Mexico No. 6-4, the most popular variety of the New Mexican type ever released. Since that time, New Mexico State University has developed most of the popular new varieties except TAM Mild Chile 2, which is a product of the Texas Agricultural Experiment Station.

Agricultural Aspects

The New Mexican varieties account for well over 50 percent of all hot chiles grown in the United States. New Mexico annually plants over 20,000 acres in New Mexican varieties, California is second with about 5,000 acres, and Arizona runs in third place with only about 350 acres. All varieties are sold in both green and red forms. Here are the most popular varieties and their descriptions:

Española Improved. This medium-hot variety was developed from the Española land race, which, along with Chimayo, Velarde, and Dixon varieties adapted to conditions in northern New Mexico. It is one of the most ancient varieties still being grown in the Southwest. Española Improved is an early variety that can be grown successfully in the northeastern United States, where the growing season is often too short for other varieties. It is primarily used in the dried red form; the fresh green form has thin pod walls and is difficult to peel. The growing period is 70 days, and the plants produce about 20 pods each, with 12 or more green pods making a pound. Heat Scale: 5.

NuMex Big Jim. The largest of New Mexican varieties (12-inch pods) is a home-garden variety and the size of the pods makes them perfect for *chiles rellenos.* The growing period is 80 days, and the yield is 5 green pods to the pound, with each plant producing at least 15 pods. Heat Scale: 2.

New Mexico No. 6-4. The most popular commercially grown New Mexican variety, the 6-4 is picked fresh and processed for "green chile" or allowed to dry after the pods turn red. The growing period is 80 days. The yield is about 7 or 8 green pods to the pound, and each plant can produce at least 20 pods during a season. Thus 6 plants can produce over 20 pounds of fresh green chiles. Heat Scale: 3.

Sandia. This hot variety is usually grown by chileheads who think the 6-4 and Big Jim varieties are too mild. The growing period is 80 days, and the yield is 12 green pods to the pound with each plant producing 20 pods or more. Heat Scale: 4.

Another popular New Mexican variety is Fresno, which was named for the California city. The short, 2-inch-long yellow or red pods (Heat Scale: 6) are used in hot pickles, in fresh salsas, and as ornamentals. Other Anaheim varieties available in the United States are NuMex Sunrise, NuMex Sunset, and NuMex Eclipse, which have been developed for making — respectively — yellow, orange, and brown *ristras.* Milder New Mexican varieties are NuMex R Naky (Heat Scale: 2) and TAM Mild Chile 2 (Heat Scale: 1).

Legend and Lore

Brilliant red *ristras* of chiles hanging in the autumn sun are such a familiar sight in New Mexico that they have become a symbol of the culture of the state. *Ristras* adorn posters, clothing, foods, note cards, T-shirts, and even college buildings; New Mexico State University students created the world's longest *ristra* in 1987. The 30-foot-long string of 15,000 pods weighed half a ton. Perhaps it is not surprising that this chile type has been designated the New Mexico "State Vegetable."

Culinary Usage

In New Mexico, Arizona, California, and parts of Texas, the New Mexican varieties are the principal chile peppers used in the American versions of Mexican cooking. Although the names of the dishes may be similar, the styles of cooking and tastes are quite different. In New Mexico red or green chiles can appear in every meal and in every dish imaginable: drinks, salsas, sauces, salads, stews, roasts, casseroles, vegetables, dressings, candies, and desserts. For a more detailed discussion, see Chapter 5.

Ornamentals

Nomenclature

So named because these diverse types were developed primarily for ornamental rather than culinary use.

Botanical Description

Since there is great diversity among the Ornamentals, what follows is a description of a typical variety called Black Plum. The plant has multiple stems, a compact habit, and grows about 12 inches tall. The leaves are dark green, smooth, and measure 2 inches long and 3/4 inch wide. The flowers have white corollas with no spots. The fruits are borne erect, are colored green in the shade, are dark purple to black in full sun when immature, and are red to dark red at maturity. Yield is 30 or more pods per plant, depending, of course, on variety.

Heat Scale

The Heat Scale of the Ornamentals is as varied as the pod types; the Peter Pepper variety rates a 2, while the Chinese Multi-Color and Black Plum varieties can easily reach 8.

Horticultural History

When chile peppers were first grown on the Iberian Peninsula after Columbus brought back the first seeds, they were grown for their beauty — lush, dark green foliage contrasting with bright, multicolored pods. Eschewing their possible culinary usage, early gardeners raised the colorful chiles for their aesthetic appeal. The miniature varieties were developed as pot plants, a purpose they still serve today — especially at Christmastime — because of their bright pods. The Ornamentals are also used to a lesser extent in landscaping as a source of color in the fall after many other flowers are spent.

Agricultural Aspects

One of the more interesting varieties of the Ornamentals is Fips, which closely resembles the Thai variety of Exotics. Many of the other variety names are self-descriptive: Cow Horn, Rat Turd, Oriental Toothpick, Bird's Eye, Black Plum, Peter Pepper, Red Missile, and Rooster Spur.

Culinary Usage

Contrary to popular belief, the Ornamentals are edible. The milder varieties such as Peter Pepper are pickled or chopped and added to salads. The hotter varieties are used to add color — and extreme heat — to fresh salsas.

Pasilla

Nomenclature

In Spanish, *pasilla* means "little raisin," an allusion to the dark brown pods and raisinlike aroma of this type. In California and other places, the Ancho is sometimes called "Pasilla," causing much confusion. In western Mexico it is sometimes called *chile negro*.

Botanical Description

The plant has an intermediate number of stems, an erect habit, and grows 2 to 3 feet high or more. The primary branches begin over 5 inches from the lowest stem portion, so the pods will not touch the ground. The leaves are ovate, smooth, medium green in color, and measure 3 inches long and 1 1/2 inches wide. The flowers have white corollas with no spots. The pods are extremely elongate, cylindrical, furrowed, and measure 6 inches long (or more) by 1 inch wide. Immature fruits are dark green, maturing to dark brown. The growing period is 90 to 100 days, and the yield is 20 pods or more to the plant.

Heat Scale

This type is not particularly pungent; measuring between 1,000 and 1,500 Scoville Units, it rates a 3 on the Heat Scale.

Horticultural History

It is likely that the Pasilla is the immediate predecessor of the New Mexican type. It has adapted particularly well to the temperate regions of Mexico.

Agricultural Aspects

About 7,500 acres of Pasillas are cultivated in Mexico, primarily in Aguascalientes, Jalisco, Zacatecas, and Guanajuato. The annual yield is approximately 3,500 tons of dried pods. The most popular Mexican varieties are Pabellon 1 and Apaseo. This type does well in the home garden, and the pods should be allowed to dry on the plant.

Legend and Lore

The Pasilla is also part of the legend of the origin of *mole* sauces — see Ancho/Poblano. Because of it is very flavorful, it is a favorite of Mexican *moleros*, cooks who specialize in preparing unique *mole* sauces.

Culinary Usage

The Pasilla is mainly used in the dried-pod or powder form in sauces such as *mole*. When eaten fresh, the Pasilla is called *chilaca*. It adds an interesting taste and color to standard red chile enchilada sauce as well.

Piquin

Nomenclature

The word "piquin," also spelled "pequin," is possibly derived from the Spanish *pequeño* ("small"), an allusion to the size of the fruits. Variations on this form place the words "chile" or "chili" before or in combination with both the words "pequin" and "tepin."

The wild form of the Piquin type, variously called "chiltepin" and "chiltecpin," may be both the nomenclatural and botanical predecessor of the Piquin. It is possible that the word "chilepequin" is derived from the Nahuatl "chiltecpin" (*chilli* + *tepectl,* "flea chile") rather than from *pequeño*. There is a botanical debate about the scientific name for the wild variety; it is either *Capsicum annuum* var. *aviculare,* var. *glabriusculum,* or var. *minimum.* Some of its common names are "chile mosquito," "bird pepper," and "chile bravo."

Botanical Description

The wild Chiltepin is a woody, perennial shrub that grows from the Andes in South America into northern Mexico and the southwestern United States. In settled regions it grows alongside ditches, fences, and roads; in the desert the Chiltepin grows along arroyos and around larger trees. Under certain conditions the wild chiles become small trees, as Chiltepin expert Dr. Gary Nabhan observed: "Near El Coyote, Sonora, saplings as tall as people form a dense, wild chile forest."

The plant has an intermediate number of stems and an erect habit. The leaves are medium green, longer and thinner than ovate, and measure 3 1/2 inches long by 1 1/2 inches wide. The flower corollas are white with no spots. Fruits of the Chiltepin are borne erect, are round or oblong, and measure between 1/4 and 1/2 inch long and wide. The domesticated Piquins have longer fruits that can be either erect or pendant and occasionally reach one inch in length. Generally speaking, the "tepin" forms are more pea-shaped and the "Piquin" types more bullet-shaped. The yield from a large, mature Chiltepin or Piquin can be over 100 pods, but 50 is more common in the home garden.

Heat Scale

The Piquin type displays a wide range of heat. The Chiltepin often registers over 70,000 Scoville Units, placing it at a 9 on the scale. In Mexico the heat of the Chiltepin is called *arrebatado* ("rapid" or "violent"), which implies that though the heat is great, it diminishes quickly. The chile Piquin is slightly milder, rating an 8 at about 40,000 Scoville Units.

Horticultural History

The Piquins were part of the prehistoric migration of *Capsicum annuum* from a nuclear area in southern Brazil or Boliva and north to Central America and Mexico. Ethnobotanists believe that birds were responsible for the spread of most wild chiles, and indeed, the Chiltepin is called the "bird pepper." In the Sonoran Desert, the Chiltepin is often found growing beneath trees where birds roost and nest. Attempts at domestication of the wild plants have led to the development of the commercial chile Piquin, which is cultivated in Mexico and Texas, where some have escaped back into the wild. A cultivated form of the Chiltepin has been grown successfully in Sonora and in the Mesilla Valley of New Mexico, where they are planted as annuals. In all cases of domestication, the cultivated forms tend to develop fruits larger than the wild varieties. Horticulturists are certain that this trait is not the result of better cultural techniques but rather the natural tendency for humans to pick the largest fruits, which contain next year's seed.

Agricultural Aspects

In Mexico a number of different varieties of Chiltepins, wild Piquins, grow wild in the mountains along both coasts: from Sonora to Chiapas on the Pacific and Tamaulipas to the Yucatan on the Gulf. The growing period is at least 90 days. They are collected and sold as fresh green, dried red, and in salsas, but the total amount of production is unknown. Some Mexican food companies bottled the Chiltepins *en escabeche* and sell them in supermarkets. In the United States, wholesale prices for wild Chiltepins reached $48 per pound in 1988.

About a thousand acres of what agriculturists call "small chili" are cultivated, mostly in Texas and New Mexico. Many of these chiles are packaged and labeled as Piquin regardless of the shape of their pods (from those resembling red peppercorns to those that look like miniature New Mexican varieties), and there is no way to tell which are cultivated and which are collected in the wild.

All of the Piquins, including the Chiltepins, grow well as perennials in pots, but make sure to bring them into a greenhouse or sunny window before the first frost.

Legend and Lore

The Tarahumara Indians of the Sonoran Desert in Mexico believe that Chiltepins were the greatest protection against the evils of sorcery. Holds one of their proverbs, "The man who does not eat chile is immediately suspected of being a sorcerer." The Papago Indians of Arizona maintain that the chiltepin "has been here since the creation of the earth."

Medical applications of Chiltepins are numerous. In Mexico they are habitually used for the relief of acid indigestion; they are crushed, mixed with garlic, oregano, and warm water. Other reputed maladies treated by Chiltepins include sore throats, dysentery, rheumatism, and tumors.

Popular folklore holds that Texans love chile Piquins so much they eat them right off the bush. In fact, their infatuation is so great that Piquin-heads rarely travel far from home without an emergency ration of the tiny pods, either whole or crushed, in a silver snuffbox or pillbox. Texans also reputedly use the chile Piquin in place of soap to punish children for using "cusswords."

Culinary Usage

Padre Ignatz Pfefferkorn, an early observer of Sonoran culinary customs, described in 1794 how Chiltepins were primarily used: "It is placed unpulverized on the table in a salt cellar, and each fancier takes as much of it as he believes he can eat. He pulverizes it with his fingers and mixes it with his food. The Chiltepin is still the best spice for soup, boiled peas, lentils, beans, and the like." Today the red dried Chiltepin is used precisely the same way — crushed into soups, stews, and bean dishes. The green fruit is crushed and used in salsas and bottled *en escabeche*.

Rocoto (*Capsicum pubescens*)

Nomenclature

The name *rocoto* seems to be derived from the Andean-Spanish word *rocín,* meaning "draft horse." No one seems to know why this chile is named after a horse, but another name for it is *chile caballo,* or "horse chile." In Mexico, it is called *chile perón* ("pear chile") and *chile manzano* ("apple chile").

Botanical Description

The plant has a compact to erect habit and the leaves are dark green, round, and quite pubescent (hairy). The corollas are distinctively purple and stand erect above the leaves. The pods are round and similar to the Cherry type, vary in size between a Cherry and a Bell, and their color at maturity is yellow, orange, or red, with yellow predominant. Unlike most chiles, the seeds of the Rocoto are black.

Heat Scale

To our knowledge this chile has not been tested with high-pressure liquid chromatography, so its heat level can only be estimated. According to most sources, it is quite hot, rating an 8 or 9 on the Heat Scale.

Horticultural History

Originally of Andean origin, the Rocoto was introduced into the mountainous regions of Chiapas and Michoacan, Mexico, in the early part of the twentieth century. The bush grows for ten or more years and becomes so large it is sometimes called the "tree chile." It is only found in cultivation in elevations from 4,500 to 21,000 feet and is the most cold-tolerant of the cultivated chiles.

Agricultural Aspects

The Rocoto needs two conditions to grow successfully: a cold climate and day lengths between 11 and 13 hours. Because these conditions are not generally found in the United States, it is difficult to grow here. It is a commercial fresh-market crop in Arequipa, Peru, and Pátzcuaro, Mexico, but is occasionally grown in northern South America and mountainous areas of Central America.

Legend and Lore

A Peruvian expression, "*gringo huanuchi*," describes this chile, meaning it is hot enough to kill a gringo (a blond or Anglo person).

Culinary Usage

This chile is consumed only in its fresh form because it is so meaty it is difficult to dehydrate. Rocotos are chopped and used in salsas and on sandwiches, and whole chiles sometimes stuffed with cheese or meat and then baked.

Serrano

Nomenclature

In Spanish, *serrano* is an adjective meaning "from the mountains." This chile was first grown in the mountains of northern Puebla and Hidalgo, Mexico.

Botanical Description

The plant varies in habit from compact to erect and grows from 1 1/2 to 5 feet tall. The leaves are diverse shades of green and are quite pubescent. The fruit grows erect or pendant, is long and slightly curved or conical, and varies between 1 and 4 inches in length. The longer Serranos, called Largo, are not as common as the shorter varieties. Immature fruits are dark green in color and ripen to red or sometimes brown, orange, or yellow.

Heat Scale

Serranos vary in heat between 10,000 and 23,000 Scoville Units, which places them at a level of a high 6 or low 7 on the Heat Scale.

Horticultural History

In addition to the Largo variety, there are two other basic Mexican varieties: Balin, so named because of its resemblance to a small-caliber bullet, and Típico, the Serrano with the biggest market demand. The most popular Mexican commercial cultivars are Altamira, Panuco, and Tampiqueño. In 1985, the Texas Agricultural Experiment Station released Hidalgo, a multiple virus–resistant strain that is becoming popular in the United States.

Agricultural Aspects

Mexico has about 38,000 acres of Serranos under cultivation, compared to 2,500 in the United States, mostly in the Southwest. The states of Veracruz, Sinaloa, Nayarit, and Tamaulipas are the biggest producers of Mexican Serrano chiles, growing about 180,000 tons of pods a year. The growing cycle varies from 80 to 240 days, producing 10 harvests in warm climates.

Amazingly enough, despite the proliferation of canned Serranos, only 10 percent of the crop is processed. The vast majority is used fresh, as "green" chile. This concept of green chile differs from that of the American Southwest, where green chile refers to New Mexican pods. A very small amount of red Serranos is dried for sale in markets.

In the home garden, Serranos thrive and produce fruit from early summer until the first hard frost. Germination of seed takes between one and two weeks, and seedlings should be started in the greenhouse, but watch out for aphids on the tender young plants.

Legend and Lore

Relatively unknown in the United States until a few years ago, Serranos have gained fame because of their fine taste when pickled. Many different brands of *serranos en escabeche,* or Serranos pickled with carrots and onions, have gained favor in the Southwest, where they are consumed as a snack or hors d'oeuvre.

Culinary Usage

By far, the most common use of Serranos is in fresh salsas. The chiles are picked fresh from the garden or purchased in produce departments, minced, and then combined with a variety of vegetables. The resulting salsas can be used as dips or as condiments for meats, poultry, seafood, and egg dishes.

Tabasco (*Capsicum frutescens*)

Nomenclature

The name of this type is derived from the Mexican city of Tabasco, which had extensive trade with New Orleans during the 1850s.

Botanical Description

The plant has an intermediate number of stems, a compact habit, and grows between 1 and 4 feet high, depending upon climate. Generally, the longer the growing season, the larger the plant. The leaves are ovate, smooth, and measure 2 1/2 inches long and 1 1/4 inches wide. The flowers have white corollas with no spots. The pods are borne erect, measure 1 1/2 inches long and 3/8 inch wide. Immature pods are yellow, maturing to orange and then turning red. Each plant can easily produce over 100 pods.

Heat Scale

Tabasco chiles measure between 30,000 and 50,000 Scoville Units, placing them at 8 on the Heat Scale.

Horticultural History

The Tabasco chile was first cultivated in Louisiana by Maunsell White, a banker who introduced the seeds from Tabasco, Mexico. He gave some pods and a sauce he had made to his friend, Edmund McIlhenny, who began to grow the type on Avery Island. The plants survived the ruin of the Avery Island plantation during the Civil War, and afterward McIlhenny began to cultivate the plants in large numbers. He began marketing a sauce from the chiles in 1869, and in 1870 he patented the now-famous brand of Tabasco sauce. (For more details on this fascinating story, see Chapter 10.)

Agricultural Aspects

Today, Louisiana cannot supply enough Tabasco chiles to meet the demand — between 200 and 1,200 acres are cultivated there. Tabascos are grown in Mexico and Colombia under contract to

Louisiana hot-sauce companies, and barrels of Tabasco mash are imported into Louisiana for bottling. Tabascos grow well in home gardens but do not grow as tall in more northern climates as they do in warmer spots such as Avery Island. The growing period is 90 days or more.

Legend and Lore

The Tabasco chile is responsible for the most famous hot sauce in the world — see Chapter 10 for the whole story.

Culinary Usage

To make Tabasco sauce, the chiles are crushed, salted, and fermented in casks, where they age for 2 1/2 to 3 years. The mash is then strained and vinegar is added. The Tabasco pulp is reserved for spices used when boiling crawfish. Although the fresh or dried Tabasco chiles are not generally used, they can be. Fresh Tabascos can be added to salsas much in the same manner as Serranos, but they are much hotter. The dried pods can be used in stir-fry dishes.

Wax

Nomenclature

The name of this type comes from the shiny appearance of the pods.

Botanical Description

The Wax type varies greatly in size, appearance, and pungency. The Santa Fe Grande variety has multiple stems and a compact habit, growing 30 inches high or more. The leaves are ovate, smooth, medium green in color, and measure 5 inches long and 3 inches wide. The flower corollas are white with no spots. The pods are borne erect to pendant (depending on size), are conical but tapering and bluntly pointed at the end. They begin as yellow, mature to orange and then red, and measure 3 1/2 to 5 inches long and 1 1/2 inches wide. The yield is 25 or more pods to the plant.

Heat Scale

This type probably has the widest heat range of any chile. Some Wax varieties have no heat at all; the pungent ones range from 3 to 8 on the Heat Scale.

Horticultural History

The pungent Wax varieties were developed from the mild Banana pepper, which was introduced into the United States from Hungary in 1932. One of the first pungent varieties was Hungarian Yellow Wax Hot (Heat Scale: 5), which became a popular garden and pickling chile. Another variety, which was first used exclusively as an ornamental, is Floral Gem (Heat Scale: 6), with its beautiful orange-red pods. This variety is commercially pickled in the yellow state as "Torrido" peppers. In 1966, Dr. Paul Smith of the University of California, Davis, crossed Floral Gem with the Fresno variety of New Mexican chile, and then crossed that hybrid with Hungarian Yellow Wax Hot to produce the Caloro variety, which was soon refined to become Santa Fe Grande (Heat Scale: 5). The most pungent variety of the Wax type is Gold Spike (Heat Scale: 8).

Agricultural Aspects

About 3,000 acres of Wax chiles are commercially cultivated in the United States, principally to produce pickled peppers. They are popular home garden varieties because of their hardiness and the beautiful colors of yellow, orange, and red fruits on the same plant. The growing period is 70 or more days.

Culinary Usage

Aside from their use in pickling, the Wax type can be used fresh in salsas or salads, or raw, stuffed with cream cheese (watch out). Also, Wax chiles are good substitutes for Jalapeños.

CHAPTER TWO

From Seed to Salsa

"When them chile pods ripen,
You gotta pick 'em before they swipe 'em,
In them old chile fields back home."

Hank and Lewie Wickham,
New Mexico troubadours

ONE of the joys of being a chile pepper aficionado is growing many different varieties and then cooking with them. Chiles are about as easy to cultivate as tomatoes, so it is relatively simple to grow enough pods for an entire year in a very small garden plot. And because chiles are actually perennials, they can be grown in pots in warm, sunny places during the winter to provide fresh chiles all year long.

In this chapter we shall not only explore gardening with chiles but also what to do with them when they ripen. The entire process requires a certain degree of planning. After all, it makes no sense to grow forty pounds of pods that might be too hot to eat or have limited culinary usage. Chile gardeners should decide which varieties to grow by considering the following criteria: culinary and ornamental uses, heat levels, climate and growing zones, and the size of the garden.

First, examine the Heat Scale in Chapter 8 for an approximate rating of relative pungencies; next, read the information on the different varieties in Chapter 1; then, select the varieties best for the individual garden. Always choose seed designated for the current year, and the germination percentages will be higher. Mail-order seed sources are listed in Appendix 2. Home gardeners should remember that chiles planted outdoors will be cross-pollinated by insects and the subsequent seed will not be true but rather a hybrid. Chiles grown in insect-free greenhouses or under netting will self-pollinate, and the seeds will remain true.

Starting Seedlings

About eight weeks before the time to transplant seedlings into the garden, start the seeds in plastic six-pack seedling growers, just as commercial greenhouses do. Use a vermiculite-based growing medium, rather than soil, and the seedlings will grow faster because their roots will receive more oxygen. A good recipe combines three parts vermiculite with two parts potting soil and one part sand.

Place the six-packs in plastic trays sitting on top of heating wire to keep the soil temperature at least 75° F, especially when starting chiles with long growing periods. The warmth of soil can radically affect the germination percentage of most chile varieties. A recent comparison of germination techniques for wild Chiltepin seeds revealed that heating the soil increased germination percentages from 10 to 80 percent.

The seedlings should be grown in full sun in a greenhouse or a window so they do not become "leggy" and topple over. Some leggy seedlings may be pinched back to make a bushier plant and to insure that leaf growth does not overwhelm stem growth. The seedlings should be kept moist but not wet, as overwatering will cause stem rot. It will also be necessary to fertilize the plants after they have put out their first true leaves. We use an all-purpose, water-soluble fertilizer (15–30–15), one-quarter teaspoon to a gallon of water, every time we water our seedlings. When growing seedlings in the house, remember that cats love to graze on the tender young plants, which will not harm the cats but will destroy the chiles!

Preparing the Patch

First, select a suitable garden area and prepare the site as for any vegetable garden. The selection criteria for the site should be a sunny location, access to irrigation water, and proper drainage. Chiles need as much sun as they can get in most parts of the country, but in the South and Southwest some partial shade in the afternoons protects the fresh chile pods from burning under intense ultraviolet rays. The plants thrive in well-drained soil but will not grow in soils heavy with clay, sand, or adobe. Adding sand, compost, peat, or manure will improve drainage.

Rototill the plot and then test the soil for pH, which should be neutral at 7.0 or barely basic, meaning a slightly higher pH.

Soil-testing kits are available at plant nurseries. Once the pH has been determined, add lime to acid soil or peat moss to overly basic soil. In the garden's first year, add about a pound of aged manure per square foot of garden area, which will both fertilize and make the soil more porous. If the garden has been used before, spread 5–10–10 fertilizer over it according to the manufacturer's instructions and then rototill it a second time.

Irrigated chile garden

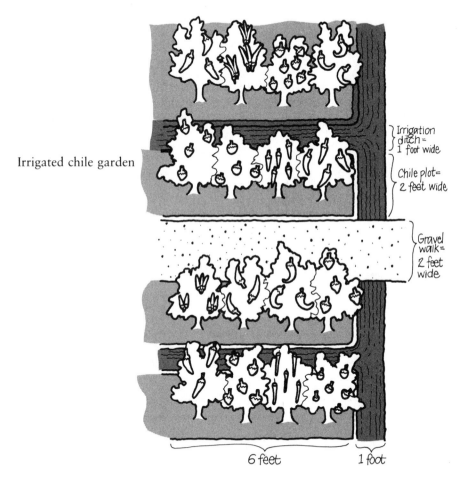

Irrigation ditch = 1 foot wide

Chile plot = 2 feet wide

Gravel walk = 2 feet wide

6 feet   1 foot

Using the accompanying diagram and a manual landscaping instrument (a shovel), sculpture the garden site into rows and ditches with a two-foot walkway down the middle. Each row should be two feet wide and each ditch one foot wide. A slight grade from one corner to its diagonal opposite makes the irrigation easier, and some chileheads even place small drainpipes under the walkway so the garden will irrigate evenly when the water hose is placed at the highest point.

Capsicum Cultivation

Chile pepper seedlings should not be set out in the garden until after the last frost, and ideally, should not be set out until the temperature of the garden soil reaches 65 degrees four inches below the surface. Before transplanting, the seedlings should be "hardened-off" by placing the plastic trays outside for a few hours each day during warm, sunny days. The constant movement of the seedlings from light breezes will strengthen the stems and prepare the plants for the rigors of the garden. Chile pepper gardeners living in particularly chilly regions should wait until the plants blossom and begin setting fruit before planting them in the garden.

Set the chile pepper plants two feet apart in the garden. It is possible to cram more plants into the garden, but this spacing has worked best for us mainly because it enables us to harvest the pods without stomping on the plants. Some gardeners place the chiles as close as one foot apart because they believe the plants will shade each other and prevent sunburn on the fruits. However, sunburn usually occurs only on fruits moved from shade into direct sunlight. If necessary, protect the young chile plants from freak frosts and cutworms by covering them with glass or plastic jars at night.

After transplanting, the garden should be thoroughly mulched. Use several layers of newspaper in hot climates or black plastic film in cool summer climates. In locations where summer temperatures are regularly in the nineties, black plastic in a garden can raise the temperature in that microclimate so high that the plants will stop flowering. Layers of newspaper weighted down with soil reflect sunlight, hold water, and provide additional organic material for the soil after they disintegrate.

Chiles need regular water and plenty of it, but overwatering is the biggest mistake of the home gardener. Well-drained soil is the key here, and the first indication of overwatering is water standing in the garden for any length of time. Some wilting of the plants in the hot summer sun is normal and is not always an indication that the plants need water.

A high-nitrogen fertilizer encourages foliage growth, but it should be discontinued after flowering. Some growers encourage root growth by adding a teaspoon of phosphate two inches below the planting hole during transplanting.

Immediately after planting, if some of the seedlings are neatly chopped down as if there were insect lumberjacks at work in the garden, cutworms are the culprits. Placing a temporary collar cut from a plastic cup around each vulnerable seedling will discourage the marauders.

Flowers and Fruit

In order to set fruit, the plants require daytime temperatures between 65 and 80 degrees and night temperatures over 55 degrees. Flowering decreases during the hottest months of the summer, and in fact, extremely hot or dry conditions will result in the blossoms dropping off the plant. However, in the early fall, flowering picks up again and usually ends after the first mild frost. The plants will survive light frosts, and the fresh chiles will still be edible. In some parts of Florida and California, the plants will become perennial and continue fruiting throughout the year. In most locations, the first hard freeze will kill the plants, and, at that point, all the remaining pods should be removed.

The pods of all varieties can be picked and eaten green as soon as they reach about an inch in length. The green fruit begins to reach maximum size about 70 to 80 days after seed germination, and another 30 to 45 days will pass before the pods mature to their vibrant reds, yellows, oranges, and browns. Remember that the more mature the green pod is, the more likely it will ripen to color after being picked.

Pepper Problems

The most common problems with growing chile peppers are directly related to watering. Underwatering chiles causes a condition known as blossom end rot, which means the chiles are growing faster than their vascular system can supply water. The apex of the pod rots, then recovers when watering is resumed, causing dried brown areas to appear near the apex, or blossom end of the fruit. The obvious solution is to avoid drying out the soil, another good reason for an irrigated garden. Some researchers believe that black plastic mulch contributes to blossom-end rot. Also, overfertilizing with nitrogen should be avoided because it promotes foliage growth instead of fruiting.

Overwatering can cause even more trouble. If water stands in the garden for longer than a few hours, the roots of the chile plants will begin to rot. They will also be susceptible to phytophthora root rot, or "chile wilt," a fungal disease. If the plants suddenly wilt with the leaves on the plant and do not recover when watered, they most probably have phytophthora root rot. The roots of these diseased plants are brown, not white as they should be. If the plants alternately wilt and recover until the leaves fall off, the problem is probably another fungal disease, verticillium wilt.

A number of other disgusting diseases can attack chile plants, such as mosaic virus, which is spread by aphids and causes leaf mottling. Anthracnose is a fungal disease that causes soft spots in the pods and makes them susceptible to rot; it is spread by spores, so avoid touching the plants and pods when they are wet. Also, do not grow beans close to chiles as both are susceptible to anthracnose.

Although there are various treatments and cures for these diseases, our advice is to destroy diseased plants and grow healthy ones from different seeds or buy new seedlings at a nursery. To avoid many diseases, rotate crops in various parts of the garden and always add fresh organic material to the soil each year.

Chile plants and pods are assaulted by a large number of insect pests including aphids, beetles, borers, bugs, flies, hoppers, miners, mites, scales, and worms. Interestingly enough, chile pods can protect chile plants when the hottest pods are transformed into an organic insecticide. Take 8 ounces of the hottest pods in the garden and liquify them in a blender with a small onion, 6 cloves of garlic, 1 tablespoon of natural soap, 3 tablespoons of pyrethrum powder, and 2 or more cups of water. Strain the mixture through cheesecloth and dilute it with water to the desired consistency for use in a sprayer. Spray the tops and bottoms of the pepper leaves every 48 hours, and most insect pests should be controlled, if not terminated.

The Truly Domesticated Chile

Most varieties of chiles can be grown as houseplants. The chiles are raised in large pots (smaller ones for *bonzai* chiles) in full sun, in well-drained organic soil. When cold weather comes, the pots are brought into a greenhouse, where the plants will continue to produce fruit all winter long. As nice as this technique sounds, it presumes the availablility of a greenhouse, or at least a solarium with full sun. Chiles are very light-demanding, and if the winter sunlight levels are too low, the plants will begin to drop leaves. However, usually the plants can be pruned back and revived in the spring by placing them outside again in full sun.

Another problem with chile houseplants is their susceptibility to whitefly, aphids, and spider mites in the winter greenhouse. Make sure to check regularly beneath leaves for infestations. For aphids, most greenhouse chile growers use insecticidal soap; we recommend that remedy, our chile insecticide (see preceding formula), or semi-weekly rinsing of the entire plant with streams of water. Most chemical insecticides are too strong for the tender young chile foliage in the winter greenhouse, although we have had success with Diazinon.

Chiles demand constant attention when they are in training to be houseplants; but properly raised, they are spectacular attention-getters when occasionally brought into the living room from the greenhouse.

Freshly Picked Pods

We recommend the technique of staggered harvesting, which means that the chiles in the garden can be used all year long. Usually the first chiles available are those that are small and used green in fresh salsas — the Serranos, Jalapeños, and the young green pods of other types such as Habanero.

It is important to continue harvesting the ripe pods as they mature. If the pods are allowed to remain on the plant, fewer new ones will form, whereas, if the pods are continuously harvested, the plants will produce greater numbers of pods. The best time to pick chiles for drying is when they start to turn red. This timing will stimulate the plant into further production, and the harvested chiles can be strung to dry and will continue to turn bright red. When harvesting, it is best to cut the peppers off the plants with a knife or scissors because the branches are brittle and will often break before the stem of the chile pod will.

Haphazard harvesting can result in waste, so careful planning is essential to ensure the maximum efficiency of the practical chile pepper patch. By studying the following preservation techniques, the gardener/cook can plan the harvest to correspond with culinary preferences.

Chiles can be picked when they are green or when fully mature. It is best to be patient because chiles picked too early have not had time to develop a full flavor. Choose pods that have smooth, shiny skins and are firm to the touch. A good rule to follow is that if the pod easily comes off the stem, the chile is ready. If it is necessary to tug on the pod, it is too early to pick it. Of course, necessity sometimes forces us to pick the chiles a bit early.

The small chiles do not have to be peeled or processed in any way before being used. They can be picked, washed, and used in any recipe, such as ours for Habanero Pepper Sauce. Even the larger pods of the New Mexican varieties such as No. 6-4, Sandia, and Big Jim do not have to be peeled if they are finely minced before being added to a recipe that will not be cooked, such as fresh salsas. However, the preferred method is to roast and peel these varieties (see following guidelines) before adding them to salsas.

The larger varieties such as Mexi-Bell and Poblano are sometimes blanched in hot water to soften their skin before being used. They can also be used without this process if a crunchier pepper texture is desired. A tasty recipe utilizing freshly picked fat chiles is ours for Stuffed Mexi-Bells.

Roasting and Peeling the Pods

The New Mexican varieties are usually blistered and peeled before being used in cooked recipes. Blistering or roasting the chile is the process of heating the fresh pods to the point that the tough transparent skin is separated from the meat of the chile so it can be removed.

Chile burns on exposed skin can be a serious problem, which is why we recommend that anyone processing or chopping chiles of any kind should wear rubber gloves. However, despite such a warning, some people will forget and end up burning their hands. In a 1986 experiment on twenty female volunteers, Leslie Jones, assistant director of the New Mexico Poison Center, determined that cooking oil worked better than water for easing burns caused by capsaicin. During the study, each volunteer placed both hands in peeled, ground green chile for forty minutes, then placed one hand in cold water and the other in vegetable oil.

During subsequent inverviews, the volunteers indicated that the vegetable oil worked better than water. Jones hinted that perhaps oil works better than water because the capsaicin is oil-soluble but is not miscible in water. Each year the poison center receives over one hundred calls from women who suffer burns while processing chile for the freezer. Jones noted that the best way to avoid chile burns is to wear rubber gloves. Incidentally, chile expert Jean Andrews has reported that she eased chile-burned hands by plunging them into common household bleach.

To roast and peel chiles, first cut a small slit in the chile close to the stem end so that the steam can escape. The chiles can be placed on a baking sheet and put directly under the broiler, or on a screen on the top of the stove. They can also be plunged into hot cooking oil to loosen the skins.

Our favorite method, which involves meditation with a six-pack of beer, is to place the pods on a charcoal grill about five to six inches from the coals. Blisters will soon indicate that the skin is separating, but be sure that the chiles are blistered all over or they will not peel properly. Although the chiles may burn slightly, take care that they do not blacken or they will be nearly impossible to peel. Immediately wrap the chiles in damp paper towels and place them in a plastic bag to steam for ten to fifteen minutes. For a crisper, less-cooked chile, plunge the chile in ice water to stop the cooking process.

Chile roasters have become commonplace in the Southwest over the past few years, and these cylindrical cages with gas jets below can roast a forty-pound sack of chile in less time than it takes to charcoal each pod. Although this method is a more convenient way to process large quantities of chile, there are some drawbacks to using a roaster. The chile is usually placed in a large plastic bag to steam after being roasted. They should be processed as soon as they have cooled enough to handle and should not be allowed to sit for too long, as bacteria growth will cause the chile to spoil.

During the charcoal-roasting process described above, the sugar and starch caramelize in the chile, which imparts a "cooked" flavor, while a rapid roasting over high heat leaves the chile tasting more "raw." And during the roasting process, why not save a few perfectly formed pods and make Chiles Rellenos, a classic spicy dish?

Freezing the Chiles

The roasted green chiles can now be frozen for future use. If they are to be frozen whole (rather than chopped), the pods do not have to be peeled first. In fact, they are easier to peel after they have been frozen.

Freeze the chiles in the form intended for use — whole, in strips, or chopped. If they are to be stored in strips or chopped, peel the pods first. A handy way to put up chopped or diced chiles is to freeze them in plastic ice-cube trays. After they are frozen, they can be "popped" out of the trays and stored in a bag. When making a soup or a stew, or a recipe such as ours for Elote con Crema, just drop in a cube! This method eliminates the problems inherent in hacking apart a large slab of frozen chiles when just a couple of ounces is needed.

The smaller chiles such as Habaneros, Tabascos, Serranos, and Jalapeños can be frozen without processing. Wash the chiles, dry them, and put them one layer deep on a cookie sheet and flash-freeze. After they are frozen solid, store them in a bag.

Frozen chiles will keep for nine months to a year at 0° F. An example of the use of these handy frozen chiles is the recipe for Picante Catsup.

Drying the Pods

Drying is the oldest and most common way to preserve chile pods and works well for most chiles — except for the very meaty ones such as Jalapeños, which are smoke-dried and called *Chipotle*. To dry chiles, select those that are starting to turn red. If the chile is picked before starting to turn, it is very likely that it will never turn red. Avoid any pods that have black spots, since these will mold and rot.

Chiles may be dried by several methods. One way is to string the chiles into *ristras* (see following guidelines), which keeps the pods whole. A quicker way to dry them is to turn the pods immediately into powders. Cut fresh chiles of any size in half, remove the seeds, chop them coarsely, and then microwave small amounts on low power until most of the moisture is removed. Place the chile pieces in a food dryer or under the sun until they break when bent. They can also be dried in a 200° F oven for six to eight hours. Remember that drying fresh chiles in the oven or under the sun for long periods of time tends to darken them.

The next step is to grind the chiles into powders. Be sure to wear a paint mask for at least some protection against inhaling the pungent capsaicin fumes. Using a food processor or chopper/grinder, puree the chiles to the desired consistency of powder. They may be ground to a fine powder called *molido*, or coarsely ground with some of the seeds, which is called *quebrado*.

Adventurous gardeners can experiment with creating powders of specific colors. For example, collect the different varieties of green, yellow, orange, red, and brown chiles and separate them into their respective colors. The colored powders can then be combined with spices, as in our recipe for Chili Powder, or stored for later use. Another use for the powders is to turn them into green, yellow, orange, red, or brown chile pastes, as in our recipe for Chile Paste. Since the colors of the powders tend to be a bit dull, they can be brightened up by adding a few drops of the appropriate food coloring when making the pastes.

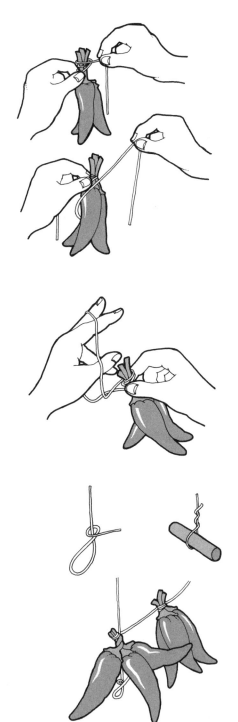

A familiar autumn sight in New Mexico is long *ristras* of brilliant red chiles hanging alongside adobe houses. They not only provide decoration, but are also the traditional method of drying red chiles for later culinary use. To make a *ristra*, a supply of freshly picked, mature red New Mexican chile pods is necessary; three quarters of a bushel of chile will make a *ristra* about three feet long. Do not attempt to make a *ristra* of green chiles with the belief they will turn red; some will be immature pods that will shrivel and turn a dull orange.

Besides the chile, a ball of lightweight cotton string and some baling wire or heavy twine will be needed. The first step is to tie clusters of three chiles with the cotton string. To do so, hold three chiles by their stems, wrap the string around the stems twice, bring the string upward between two of the chiles, and pull tight. Then make a half-hitch with the string, place it over the stems, and pull tight. Continue this process with the cotton string until there are several clusters of chiles, or until the weight of the chiles makes the string difficult to handle. At that point break the string and start again, continuing until all of the chiles have been tied into clusters of three.

The next step is to attach these clusters to a stronger length of twine or wire. Suspend the twine or wire from a rafter or the top of a door and make a loop at the end to keep chiles from slipping off the end. Starting from the bottom, braid the chiles around the twine in a manner similar to braiding hair. The twine serves as one strand and two chiles in the cluster serve as the other two strands. As the chiles are braided, keep the center pushed down to ensure a tight fit, and be sure that the chiles protrude evenly from the *ristra*.

To make a wreath, braid the chiles around a straightened-out coat hanger and then bend the wire into a circle. When the braiding is completed, hang the *ristra* or wreath in full sun from a clothesline or rafter where there is good air circulation. The chiles should dry in the sun before the *ristra* is brought inside or else they may turn moldy and rot. Do not spray the *ristra* with lacquer to make it shiny — all that will do is make the chiles inedible. Dry red chile has its own natural luster and does not need an artificial shine.

Dried whole pods can be reconstituted in a variety of ways.

Tying a ristra

They can be roasted very lightly on a griddle, they can be fried in a little oil until they puff and reconstitute slightly, or they can be soaked in hot water for 15 to 20 minutes.

Roasted, peeled, and cleaned green chiles can also be dried. Lay long strips of chiles on nylon window screening, cover them with cheesecloth, and place them in a semi-shady location with good air circulation. The moister the climate, the more sun that should be applied to the drying pods. One ounce of this *chile pasado* (dried green chile) is equivalent to ten to twelve fresh chile pods.

A Peck of Pickled Peppers

Chiles lend themselves well to pickling or preserving in a brine or solution of vinegar and other seasonings. They can be pickled in jars by themselves or in combination with other vegetables. Colorful chiles make attractive pickles, so use Habaneros, red Serranos and Jalapeños, Chinese Multicolors, Yellow Wax Hots, and even fresh red Thai peppers. Our recipes for Italian Giardiniera and Sun-Cured Pickled Jalapeños are tasty examples of recipes using pickled chiles and other ingredients.

Here are some pickling basics to follow no matter what recipes are used:

- Use only non-iodized salt and never use a salt substitute.

- Use a vinegar with an acetic acid content of 4 to 5 percent.

- Use distilled vinegar, not cider vinegar (which will discolor the food).

- Do not boil the vinegar for a long period of time, as this will reduce the acidity.

Chile Pepper Canning Techniques

Our information and recipes for canning chile and chile vegetable combinations are from the New Mexico State Cooperative Extension Service, the ultimate authority on this subject. Green chile is a low-acid fruit, and, for that reason, we do not recommend home canning of it by itself, but rather in combination with high-acid vegetables or liquids. It can be done, however, by using a pressure canner *only* and by carefully following all the manufacturer's specific instructions. Blister and peel the chiles, remove the seeds, then wash and dry. Pack the pods loosely in sealing jars, leaving one inch head space. Add one quarter teaspoon salt per pint jar and then add boiling water, again leaving one inch head space. Tighten the lids on the jars and place them in the pressure canner. Process the pint jars for thirty-five minutes.

Here are some hints about pressure-canning: let the steam escape the full 10 minutes before closing the petcock; at the end of the processing, let the pressure fall to 0 — that takes about 20 to 25 minutes; and after opening the petcock, wait 5 minutes before opening the lid of the pressure-canner. As an additional safety precaution, always boil home-canned chile for 15 minutes before eating to prevent botulism poisoning. Stir it frequently.

The pressure-canning method may also be used with salsas or the careful cook can use the water-bath method. Remember that both the chiles and tomatoes are low-acid foods, so when using the water-bath method, the acid levels of the salsas must be increased by adding vinegar or lemon or lime juice to the recipes.

Our canning recipes for Taco Sauce with Green Chile and Green Chile and Tomato Salsa are provided courtesy of the New Mexico State University Cooperative Extension Service. They utilize the water-bath — not the pressure-canning — method. Note that less chile than listed may be used, but not more or the acidity will be altered. Also, add any other seasonings such as coriander or cumin when serving the salsa rather than adding during canning.

Chile Vinegars, Oils, Butters, Mustards, and a Jelly

Herbed vinegars have a number of uses as dressings or marinades. Use your imagination to combine any herb with chiles following the basic instructions in the accompanying recipes for Hot Chile Vinegar and Chile Herb Vinegars. Red Chile Oil and Herbed Chile Oil are our two examples of powerful cooking or salad oils. Cilantro-Chile Butter makes an excellent spicy spread, while Serrano Mustard is doubly pungent with both mustard seeds and chiles. Last but not least is our recipe for a popular Southwestern cracker spread, Jalapeño Jelly.

Substitutions and Commercial Preparations

The growing popularity of fiery foods has made it considerably easier to locate chile products through gourmet shops, grocery stores, and by mail order. But cooks unable to find the exact chiles they need can make the following substitutions.

- Substitute rehydrated dried chiles for the fresh — both have approximately the same amount of heat.

- For fresh New Mexican, Serrano, or Jalapeño chiles, substitute the canned product, rinsed well.

- Substitute one quarter teaspooon ground Cayenne or one half teaspoon crushed "red pepper" in recipes calling for one small hot dried chile, such as Piquins.

- Substitute one tablespoon ground "red pepper" for one of the large dried red New Mexican varieties or one of the Mexican varieties such as Pasillas or Anchos.

Beware of commercial chile powders labeled "chili powder," which contain other spices such as oregano and garlic salt. These should not be substituted for pure chile. Finally, remember that pickled Serranos or Jalapeños, or those labeled *en escabeche,* will change the flavor of the recipe because of the pickling brine.

Habanero Pepper Sauce

Heat Scale: 9
Yield: 2 cups

12 Habanero chiles, stems removed, chopped
1/2 cup chopped onion
2 cloves garlic, minced
1 tablespoon vegetable oil
1/2 cup chopped carrots
1/2 cup distilled vinegar
1/4 cup lime juice

Cooking the chiles reduces the distinctive flavor of the Habaneros in this liquid hot sauce, so add them raw. The high percentage of both acetic and citric acids keeps the sauce from spoiling.

Sauté the onion and garlic in the oil until soft. Add the carrots with a small amount of water. Bring to a boil, reduce the heat, and simmer until the carrots are soft.

Place the mixture and the chiles in a blender, and puree the mixture until smooth.

Combine the puree with the vinegar and lime juice and simmer for 5 minutes to combine the flavors.

Strain the mixture into sterilized bottles and seal.

Stuffed Mexi-Bells

Heat Scale: 3
Serves: 6

6 Mexi-Bell chiles
1 egg
1/2 pint sour cream
2 teaspoons prepared mustard
2 tablespoons chopped onion
2 cups cooked macaroni
1 cup grated cheddar cheese

Mexi-Bells have low heat levels, so add some chopped green New Mexican chile to the macaroni mixture to increase the heat of this dish. The Mexi-Bells do not have to be parboiled if a crisper texture is desired. These chiles freeze well; when the harvest comes in, put some away for later.

Cut the tops off the chiles, remove the seeds, and parboil the chiles in salted water for 3 minutes, then drain.

Beat the egg slightly, then mix it with the sour cream, mustard, and onion.

Place the chiles in a baking dish and stuff them with half of the macaroni. Pour half of the sour cream mixture over the macaroni and sprinkle with cheese. Repeat the layers, ending with the cheese.

Bake in a 350° F oven for 30 minutes.

Serving Suggestion: A crisp garden salad complements this entrée.

Variation: Substitute fresh Poblanos for the Mexi-Bells.

Chiles Rellenos

Heat Scale: 5
Serves: 2

4 green New Mexican
  chiles, roasted, peeled, with
  stems left on
1/4 pound cheddar cheese or
  Monterey Jack, cut in
  sticks
3 eggs, separated
1 tablespoon water
3 tablespoons flour
1/4 teaspoon salt
flour for dredging
vegetable oil for frying

The Big Jim variety of New Mexican chile makes excellent chiles rellenos (stuffed chiles) because the pods are large and meaty, but any of the New Mexican varieties work well in this recipe. Top these chiles rellenos with either Classic Green Chile Sauce or Red Chile Sauce (see recipes Chapter 5).

Make a slit in the side of each chile, and stuff the chiles with the cheese sticks. Dredge the chiles with the flour.

Beat the egg whites until they form stiff peaks.

Beat the yolks with the water, flour, and salt until thick and creamy. Fold the yolks into the whites.

Dip the chiles in the mixture and fry in 2 to 3 inches of oil until they are a golden brown.

Serving Suggestions: Serve with shredded lettuce and Guacamole (see recipe Chapter 5), Spanish rice, and refried beans.

Elote con Crema

Heat Scale: 4
Serves: 4 to 6

1 cube frozen green New
  Mexican chiles, roasted,
  peeled, stems removed,
  chopped
1 small onion, chopped
1 clove garlic, minced
2 tablespoons margarine or
  bacon fat
2 cups fresh corn, cut off
  the cob and boiled in
  water for 5 minutes
1/2 cup cream
1/4 pound cheddar cheese,
  cut into cubes

Here is an excellent way to use up excess garden crops. Corn is not the only vegetable that can go into this recipe; try a combination of corn and zucchini, zucchini and crookneck squash, or even peas. It is an elegant way to serve all the garden's bounty.

Sauté the onion and garlic in the margarine until soft.

Add the chile and the corn and sauté for an additional 2 minutes.

Reduce the heat, add the cream and cheese, and simmer until the vegetables are done, the cheese has melted, and the sauce has been reduced.

Serving Suggestions: This creamy vegetable dish goes well with roasted or broiled meats or poultry.

Picante Catsup

Heat Scale: 6
Yield: 4 pints

8 Serrano or Jalapeño chiles, stems and seeds removed, chopped
1 Bell pepper, chopped
8 pounds tomatoes, peeled and seeds removed, chopped
2 stalks celery, chopped
1 large onion, chopped
1 cup brown sugar
1 1/2 cup cider vinegar
3 teaspoons ground cinnamon
3 teaspoons dry mustard
1 to 2 teaspoons salt

Use this piquant version in place of regular catsup to spice up sandwiches, meatloaf, or hamburgers. Since this catsup freezes well, it is a great way to use all those fresh tomatoes.

Cook the tomatoes for 15 minutes and then drain off the excess liquid. Add the celery, onion, Bell pepper, and chiles and simmer for 1 1/2 hours, or until it is reduced by one half.

Add the sugar, vinegar, and spices and simmer for an additional hour. Remove from the heat and puree until smooth.

Pack in freezer containers, leaving 1/2 inch head space, and freeze.

Chili Powder

Heat Scale: 7

1 part dried ground Cayenne or other red chile such as Piquin or Chile de Arbol
1 part dried ground Pasilla chile or other mild powder such as Ancho
5 parts dried ground red New Mexican chiles
2 parts garlic powder
1 1/2 parts ground cumin
1 1/2 parts ground oregano

This powder is so named because it is often used in chili con carne recipes. Try it in place of the commercial blends and experiment with the proportions of the ingredients to adjust them to individual tastes.

Combine all the ingredients together and mix well.

Variations: Collect chiles of similar colors, dry them, and use them in place of the above chiles to make variously colored powders — yellow, orange, brown, and green.

Chile Paste

Heat Scale: 9
Yield: 3 to 4 cups

1 cup small dried red chiles
  such as Piquins
2 cups dried crushed red
  New Mexican chiles, seeds
  included
1/2 cup white wine vinegar
1/4 cup finely chopped
  garlic
2 tablespoons vegetable oil
1 teaspoon kosher salt

Chile pastes are very popular throughout Southeast Asia and are used to add heat to a dish. The pastes can be added during cooking or can be used as a condiment or relish on the table. Vary the amount of garlic to suit individual tastes.

Combine all the ingredients plus 3/4 cup of water in a blender and puree for 1 minute or to the consistency of a thick paste.

Store in a glass container in the refrigerator; it will last up to three months.

 # Italian Giardiniera

fresh chiles of choice
1/2 part water
1/2 part vinegar
1 teaspoon salt per pint of
  liquid
cauliflower, broken in
  flowerets
broccoli, broken in flowerets
carrots, cut in coins or use
  baby carrots
pearl onions
garlic cloves, whole
green olives

This basic recipe can be used for pickling chiles either alone or with a combination of other vegetables. Choose the mixture of vegetables desired, the amount and type of chiles, and arrange them attractively in a jar before covering with the pickling solution.

Wash the chiles and with a toothpick poke several holes near the stem before packing in the jars.

Combine the water, vinegar, and salt in a pan and boil for a minute. Pour the hot mixture over the vegetables leaving 1/4 inch head space and cover. Allow the chiles and vegetables to pickle for 2 to 3 weeks before serving.

Sun-Cured Pickled Jalapeños

Heat Scale: 8
Yield: 1 pint

1 cup Jalapeño chiles, stems removed, cut in 1/4-inch strips
1 tablespoon coarse salt
1 tablespoon mustard seeds
1 teaspoon cumin seeds
1/4 cup oil, peanut preferred
1 teaspoon chopped fresh ginger
2 tablespoons fresh lemon juice

These pickled chiles have an East Indian flavor because of the mustard seeds and ginger. Any small green chiles can be substituted for the Jalapeños.

Sprinkle the chile strips with the salt; toss and let them sit for 10 minutes.

Toast the mustard and cumin seeds on a hot skillet, stirring constantly, for a couple of minutes until the seeds begin to crackle and "pop."

Heat the oil to 350° F, remove from the heat, stir in the ginger, and let it simmer for 2 minutes. Remove and discard.

Stir in the chiles, seeds, and lemon juice and pack in a sterilized jar.

For 5 days, set the jar in the sun in the morning on days when it is at least 70 degrees and bring it in at night. Shake the jar a couple of times each day.

Serving Suggestions: Serve these unusual chiles on sandwiches, hamburgers, or as a side relish for grilled or roasted meats.

Taco Sauce with Green Chile

Heat Scale: 4
Yield: 4 pints

3 cups green New Mexican chiles, roasted, peeled, stems removed (seeds removed, if desired), chopped
3 cups tomatoes, peeled and chopped
3/4 cup onion, chopped
1 1/2 teaspoons salt
3 cloves garlic, minced
1 1/2 cups vinegar

In addition to tacos, this simple sauce goes well with a variety of foods such as eggs and hamburgers. Before serving try adding spices such as oregano, cinnamon, cloves, or cumin.

Combine all the ingredients in a pan, bring to a boil, cover, and simmer 5 minutes.

Pack in hot, clean, sterilized jars. Use all the liquid, dividing it evenly among the jars. Adjust the lids. Process in water bath for 30 minutes. Start counting the processing time when the water returns to boiling.

Variation: Substitute Jalapeño chiles for a hotter sauce.

Note: Lemon or lime juice may be substituted equally for vinegar. If less acidic salsas are desired, freeze the salsa instead of canning it.

Green Chile and Tomato Salsa

Heat Scale: 4
Yield: 4 pints

3 cups chopped green New Mexican chiles, roasted, peeled, stems removed
3 cups tomatoes, peeled and chopped
1 1/2 teaspoons salt
1 1/4 cups vinegar

Before serving this cooked salsa, add 1 teaspoon cumin powder and stir in chopped cilantro.

Combine all the ingredients in a pan, bring to a boil, cover, and simmer 5 minutes.

Pack in hot, clean, sterilized jars. Use all the liquid, dividing it evenly among the jars. Adjust the lids. Process the jars in the water bath for 30 minutes. Start counting the processing time when the water returns to boiling.

Serving Suggestions: Serve as an all-purpose sauce with chips for a dip, with enchiladas or tacos, or as a relish or condiment with grilled meats, poultry, or fish.

Hot Chile Vinegar

Heat Scale: 9
Yield: 1 quart

1 pound hot chiles, any variety fresh green or red
1 quart distilled white vinegar

This is a chile vinegar for those recipes where heat without additional flavor is needed. Use it as a catch-all for all those excess small hot chiles from the garden.

Combine the ingredients in a pan, bring to a boil, lower the heat, and simmer for 5 minutes. Pack in clean, sterilized jars and let stand in a cool, dark place for a week. Taste for heat and remove the chiles or leave them in for a jar of liquid fire.

Chile Herb Vinegar

Heat Scale: 5
Yield: 1 quart

6 ounces fresh chiles such as
  Serrano, Cayenne, or
  Piquin
8 ounces fresh rosemary
  leaves
10 garlic cloves, whole
1 quart vinegar, either cider
  or distilled white

Herbed vinegars have a number of uses as dressings and mari-
nades. Be imaginative and substitute your favorite herbs for the
ones listed; just be sure to follow the basic instructions.

Divide the ingredients among the bottles. Cover with the vinegar,
seal, and place in a cool, dark place, and leave the bottles un-
disturbed for 3 to 4 weeks.

 Strain the mixture and place some fresh chiles and fresh rosemary stems for decorative purposes in clean jars and cover with
the vinegar.

 Variations: Try different combinations of herbs and chiles
such as oregano and dried red chile, or tarragon and fresh green
chiles.

 Note: The process may be speeded up by chopping and crush-
ing the herbs, and then heating the vinegar, which is then poured
over the herbs. Let steep for a couple of days before straining.

Red Chile Oil

Heat Scale: 9
Yield: 2 cups

1 cup dried red chiles such
  as Piquin or Cayenne
2 cups vegetable oil

Chile oil is easy to make and is a great substitute for non-pungent
oils in a variety of recipes, especially Oriental stir-fry. Use it to
make terrific hot chile popcorn.

Heat the oil in a pan to 350° F. Remove it from the heat, add
the chiles, and let the oil stand to cool.

 Cover the pan and let stand for 12 to 24 hours (the longer
it steeps, the hotter the oil). Strain the oil and use as any vegetable
oil.

Herbed Chile Oil

Heat Scale: 4
Yield: 1/2 cup

1 teaspoon dried crushed
  red chiles, seeds included
1 teaspoon chopped
  rosemary leaves
2 whole bay leaves
1/2 cup olive oil

Olive oil readily absorbs the chile flavor and heat, so it does not have to steep for as long as the chile vinegars. Flavored oils are wonderful on salads or pasta.

Combine all the ingredients, cover, and let stand for 12 to 24 hours (the longer it steeps, the hotter the oil). Remove the herbs and chiles and store the oil in a cool, dark place.

Cilantro-Chile Butter

Heat Scale: 5
Yield: 1 pound

1 tablespoon finely chopped
  green chiles such as
  Jalapeño, Serrano,
  Habanero, or New
  Mexican
1/4 cup chopped fresh
  cilantro
1 tablespoon grated lime
  peel (zest)
2 teaspoons lime juice
1 teaspoon onion powder
2 cloves garlic, finely
  chopped
1 pound unsalted butter,
  softened

Compound butters are a combination of herbs, spices, and butter that can be used in a variety of ways — on vegetables, potatoes, and pasta, with grilled meats, poultry, or fish. Use these butters for sautéing foods or even cooking an omelet. They will keep indefinitely in the freezer, so keep several variations on hand.

Mix all the ingredients together and allow to sit at room temperature for an hour to blend the flavors. Wrap in plastic or wax paper and freeze.

Variations: Try combinations such as red chile, orange zest, and orange juice or fresh basil and green chile.

Serrano Mustard

Heat Scale: 5
Yield: 1 pint

8 Serrano chiles, stems
 removed, minced
3/4 cup yellow mustard
 seeds
1/4 cup black mustard
 seeds*
1 1/4 cup flat beer
1/3 cup Chile Herb Vinegar
 (see recipe this chapter)
1/2 teaspoon salt

Replace mundane yellow mustard with this spicy version. Use pepper vinegar for a hotter mustard, and finely grind all the mustard seeds for a smoother mustard.

Grind one half of the mustard seeds to a fine powder. Coarsely grind the remainder of the seeds.

Combine the mustard seeds and powder, the beer, the vinegar, and blend well. Stir in the chiles and salt and pack into sterilized jars.

Allow the mustard to sit in a cool, dark place for 2 weeks. Refrigerate after opening.

*Available in East Indian or gourmet markets.

 # Jalapeño Jelly

Heat Scale: 7
Yield: 6 1/2 pints

10 Jalapeño chiles, stems
 removed
2 medium Bell peppers
1 1/2 cup distilled vinegar
6 cups sugar
1/3 cup lemon juice
4 ounces liquid pectin
10 drops green food
 coloring

This jelly is excellent on crackers with cream cheese and it can be used as a basting sauce for grilled poultry. For a sweet and hot flavor, add fruits such as apricots or peaches to the jelly.

Place the chiles and peppers in a blender and puree until finely chopped.

Combine the puree and vinegar, bring to a boil over high heat, and boil rapidly for 10 minutes, stirring occasionally.

Remove the pan from the heat and stir in the sugar and lemon juice.

Return the pan to the heat, bring to a boil again, stir in the pectin and food coloring and boil again, stirring constantly for a minute.

Skim off the foam and bottle in sterilized jars.

CHAPTER THREE

The Taming of the Wild Chile

"The fruit [of the Peruvian Uchu chile] is as indispensable to the natives as salt to the whites."

Friedrich Alexander von Humboldt, *Political Essay on the Kingdom of New Spain* (1814)

FOR over ten thousand years, humans have been fascinated by a seemingly innocuous plant with bright-colored fruits that bite back when bitten. Although the chile pepper has risen in our estimation from lowly weed to celebrity spice, the secrets of its domestication, its discovery by Europeans, and its subsequent spread around the world are still being uncovered. Often mistakenly thought to be of African or Indian origin, chile peppers are absolutely American; along with corn, squash, and beans they are among the earliest plants domesticated by man in the New World.

The Tolerated Weed

According to botanist Barbara Pickersgill, the genus *Capsicum*, to which all chiles belong, originated in the remote geologic past in an area bordered by the mountains of southern Brazil to the east, by Bolivia to the west, and by Paraguay and northern Argentina to the south. Not only does this location have the greatest concentration of wild species of chiles in the world, but here, and only here, grow representatives of all the major domesticated species within the genus. Another chile botanist, W. Hardy Eshbaugh, believes that the location for the origin of chile peppers was further east, in central Bolivia along the Rio Grande.

Scientists are not certain about the exact time frame or the method for the spread of both wild and domesticated species from the southern Brazil–Bolivia area, but they suspect that birds were primarily responsible. The wild chiles (like their undomesticated cousin of today, the Chiltepin) had erect, red fruits that were quite pungent and were very attractive to various species of birds which ate the whole pods. The seeds of those pods passed through their digestive tracts intact and were deposited on the ground encased in a perfect fertilizer. In this manner, chiles spread all over South and Central America long before the first Asian tribes crossed the Bering land bridge and settled the New World.

When humans arrived in the Americas over 10,000 years ago, about twenty-five species of the genus *Capsicum* existed in South America. Five of these species were later domesticated; however, some of the other wild species were and still are occasionally utilized. Two of the five domesticated species of chiles, *C. baccatum* and *pubescens,* never migrated beyond South America. *Baccatum,* known as "Ají," merely extended its range from southern Brazil west to the Pacific Ocean and became a domesticated chile of choice in Bolivia, Ecuador, Peru, and Chile. Likewise, *C. pubescens* left Brazil to be domesticated in the Andes, where it is known as "Rocoto." Its range today is primarily in the higher elevations of Bolivia, Peru, and Ecuador, although it was introduced during historical times into mountainous areas of Costa Rica, Honduras, Guatemala, and Mexico.

Three other Capsicum species that were later domesticated are *annuum, chinense,* and *frutescens.* These closely related species shared a mutual, ancestral gene pool and are known to botanists as the *annuum-chinense-frutescens* complex. They seem to have sprung up in the wilds of Colombia and later migrated individually to Central America and Amazonia. These three species were all in place when humans arrived on the scene, and, apparently, each type was domesticated independently — *annuum* in Mexico, *chinense* in Amazonia (and, possibly, Peru), and *frutescens* in southern Central America. These three species have become the most commercially important chiles, and the story of their domestication and further spread is revealed in the archaeological record.

The earliest evidence of chile peppers in the human diet is from Mexico, where archaeologist R. S. MacNeish discovered chile seeds dating from about 7500 B.C. during his excavations at Tamaulipas and Tehuacán. This find and an intact pod from Peru's Guitarrero Cave dated 6500 B.C. seem to indicate that chiles were under cultivation approximately 10,000 years ago.

However, that date is extremely early for crop domestication and some experts suggest that these specimens are chiles that were harvested in the wild rather than cultivated by man. The common bean (*Phaseolus vulgaris*) was also found in the same excavation levels, and scientists cannot be certain if they were wild or domesticated varieties. Experts are certain, however, that chile peppers were domesticated by at least 3300 B.C.

Ethnobotanists — scientists who study the relationship of plants to man — have theorized that during the domestication process, chiles were first accepted as "tolerated weeds." They were not cultivated but rather collected in the wild when the fruits were ripe. The wild forms had erect fruits that were deciduous, meaning that they separated easily from the calyx and fell to the ground. During the domestication process, whether consciously or unconsciously, early Indian farmers selected seeds from plants with larger, non-deciduous, and pendant fruits.

The reasons for these selection criteria are a greater yield from each plant and protection of the pods from chile-hungry birds. The larger the pod, the greater will be its tendency to become pendant rather than to remain erect. Thus the pods became hidden amid the leaves and did not protrude above them as beacons for birds. The selection of varieties with the tendency to be non-deciduous ensured that the pods remained on the plant until fully ripe and thus were resistant to dropping off as a result of wind or physical contact. The domesticated chiles gradually lost their natural means of seed dispersal by birds and became dependent upon human intervention for their continued existence. Because chiles cross-pollinate, hundreds of varieties of the five domesticated chiles developed over thousands of years. The color, size, and shape of the pods of these domesticated forms varied enormously. Ripe fruits could be red, orange, brown, yellow, or white. Their shapes could be round, conic, elongate, oblate, or bell-like, and their size could vary from the tiny fruits of Chiltepins or Tabascos to the large pods of the Anchos and New Mexican varieties. However, no matter what the size or shape of the pods, they were readily adopted into the customs and cuisines of all the major civilizations of the New World.

Pre-Columbian Chile Customs and Kitchens

Chiles were the major spice of the New World and played a role similar to that of black pepper in the Old World; ancient New World cultures from Mexico to South America combined the pungent pods with every conceivable meat and vegetable. Our knowledge of the pre-Columbian culinary uses of chile peppers is derived from many sources: archaeological finds, Indian artifacts and illustrations of the period, Spanish and Portuguese explorers of the sixteenth and seventeenth centuries, botanical observations, and studies of the cooking methods of the modern descendants of the Incas, Mayas, and Aztecs.

Our examination of the culinary uses of chiles begins in one of the major regions where they were first cultivated, the Andes. It was there that the great Inca civilization came to depend upon the chiles as their principal spice and a major crop. At the heart of the Incan Empire was farming, which determined nearly every aspect of society: the calendar, religion, law, and even war. The Incas were farmer-soldiers, likely to be called out of their elaborately terraced and irrigated fields at any time to defend the empire or extend its boundaries. But farming took precedence over fighting, and some later uprisings against the Spanish failed because the Inca soldiers left the battlefront to return to their fields. It has been estimated that more kinds of foods and medicinal plants were systematically cultivated in the Andes than anywhere else in the world at any time. The result of the Incan agricultural expertise included 240 varieties of potatoes, nearly as many kinds of beans, twenty types of maize, plus sweet potatoes, peanuts, pineapples, chocolate, avocados, papayas, tomatoes, and — of course — several varieties of the beloved chile pepper.

The Incan historian Garcilaso de la Vega, known as El Inca, wrote in detail about chile peppers and their place in Incan culture. In his *Royal Commentaries of the Incas* (1609), he noted that chiles were the favorite fruit of the Indians, who ate it with everything they cooked, "whether stewed, boiled, or roasted." He traced the nomenclature of the plant: the pods were called "Uchu" by the Incas, "Pimiento de las Indias" by the Spaniards, and "Ají" by the people of the West Indies, a name that became quite common in the Andes in later times.

The Incas worshiped the chile pepper as one of the four brothers of their creation myth. "Agar-Uchu," or "Brother Chile Pepper," was believed to be the brother of the first Incan king. Garcilaso de la Vega observed that the chile pods were perceived to symbolize the teachings of the early Incan brothers. Chile peppers were thus regarded as holy plants, and the Incas' most rigorous fasts were those prohibiting all chiles.

According to El Inca, the Incas raised three types of chiles. The first was called *rocot uchu,* "thick pepper," which described the long, thick pods that matured to yellow, red, and purple. The most likely identification of these chiles would be the Ají type, *Capsicum baccatum.* El Inca forgot the name of the next type but wrote that it was used exclusively by the royal household. The third chile he described was *chinchi uchu,* which "resembles exactly a cherry with its stalk." This type, with its name and cherrylike pods both still intact, has survived to this day in Peru and Bolivia; it is *rocotillo,* a variety of *Capsicum chinense* and a cousin to the Habanero. El Inca noted that the *chinchi uchu* was "incomparably stronger than the rest and only small quantities of it are found."

El Inca also collected some chile anecdotes. Chiles were reputedly good for the sight, were avoided by poisonous creatures, and had been offered as one of the gifts to appease Pizarro and his invading soldiers. As a final culinary note, El Inca unconsciously predicted the spread of chile around the world when he noted, "All the Spaniards who come to Spain from the Indies are accustomed to it and prefer it to all Oriental spices." Thus the invaders were conquered by the fiery foods of the Incas!

Most Incan dishes were vegetarian because fish and meat were luxuries — at least for the commoners. The Incan royalty, however, did consume fish caught in the rich coastal waters and Lake Titicaca, and also ate deer, wild llama, guanaco, and viscacha, a large rodent. But the royalty would not consume dogs, domesticated ducks, and *cui* (guinea pigs) — meat sources beloved of the peasants when they could obtain them.

The Incas' morning meal was extremely simple: leftovers

from the previous evening and a cup of *chicha,* a mildly intoxicating beverage made from fermented corn. Around noon, an Inca family would gather for the midday meal, which was prepared by boiling or baking because cooking oils and frying were unknown. Corn was often boiled with chile peppers, potatoes, and herbs to make a stew called *mote.* (A similar dish that has survived the test of time and is still prepared in the Andes is our recipe for Corn and Potatoes with Two Chiles.) Another midday meal of the Incas was *locro,* a stew made from sun-dried llama meat, dehydrated potatoes, and chiles.

The evening meal was eaten at about five o'clock in the afternoon and was usually a soup or stew similar to the midday feast. Potatoes were ubiquitous, as we see in our recipe for Papas Con Tomates. Another popular Incan dish was Squash Soup with Chile Sauce, but in deference to today's taste preferences we have taken the liberty of substituting chicken for the guinea pig it usually contained.

But food was not the only use for the beloved chiles. According to historian L. E. Valcárcel, chile peppers were so highly valued in Inca society that they were probably used as currency. Since there were no coins or bills in those days, certain preferred products like chiles became part of a rudimentary monetary system. He noted that until the mid twentieth century, shoppers in the plaza of Cuzco could buy goods with *rantii,* a handful of chiles.

The Incas decorated bowls and dishes with chile pepper designs, as shown in the accompanying photograph of an exquisite dish painted with fish swimming amid two types of chiles. It was found near Cuzco and is dated from 1400 to 1532. The fish appear to be catfish, and the chiles closely resemble Garcilaso de la Vega's description of *rocot uchu* and *chinchi uchu,* mentioned earlier.

Chiles also were the subject of embroidery designs. One example of textile art of the early Nazca period is a yarn-embroidered cotton cloth showing the figures of twenty-three farmers carrying their crops. One of the farmer figures is wearing chile pods around his neck and is carrying a plant bearing pods.

About A.D. 900, a sculptor of the Chavín culture in Peru carved elaborate designs into a sharp-pointed granite shaft mea-

Peru, probably vicinity of Cuzco, Incan, Dish with fish and peppers, ca. 1400–1532. Photograph by Robert Hashimoto. © 1989 The Art Institute of Chicago. All rights reserved.

suring eight feet long and a foot wide that has become known as the Tello Obelisk. The principal figure on this obelisk is a mythical creature, the black caiman. The sharp point of the stone corresponds to a real caiman's narrow snout, and the end of the stone is carved with the feet and claws of the reptile, which are holding the leaves and pods of a chile plant. As yet, no scholar has deciphered the meaning of a magical caiman grasping chile peppers in its claws, but the image is suggestive of the magical powers that the people of the Andes Indians believed were inherent in the powerful pods.

As chile peppers spread north through Central America and Mexico, they gained the reputation of being not only a spicy condiment but also a powerful medicine. The pre-Columbian tribes of Panama used chile in combination with cacao and tobacco (and probably other plants) to enter into hallucinatory trances. According to scientist Mary Helms, these Indians used chile to "travel" to the heavens or to the underworld to negotiate with the good and evil spirits on behalf of mankind. Today, the Cuna Indians of Panama burn chiles so the irritating smoke will drive away evil spirits during a girl's puberty ceremony. They also trail a string of chiles behind their canoes to discourage sharks from attacking. (We should caution modern sportsmen that the efficacy of chiles as a shark repellent has never been verified.)

In southern Mexico and the Yucatan Peninsula, chile peppers have been part of the human diet since about 7500 B.C. and thus their usage predates the two great Central American civilizations, the Mayas and the Aztecs. From their original usage as a spice collected in the wild, chiles gained importance after their domestication, and they were a significant food when the Olmec culture was developing, around 1000 B.C.

About 500 B.C., the Monte Alban culture, in the Valley of Oaxaca, began exporting a new type of pottery vessel to nearby regions. These vessels resembled the hand-held *molcajete* mortars of today and were called Suchilquitongo bowls. Because the *molcajetes* are used to crush chile pods and make salsas today, the Suchilquitongo bowls are probably the first evidence we have for the creation of crushed chile and chile powders. Scientists speculate that chile powder was developed soon after the Suchilquitongo bowls were invented, and both the tool and the product were then exported.

Glyph from Monte Alban

A carved glyph found in the ceremonial center of Monte Alban is further evidence of the early importance of chile peppers. It features a chile plant with three pendant pods on one end and the head of a man on the other. Some experts believe that the glyph is one of a number of "tablets of conquest" that marked the sites conquered by the Monte Alban culture.

By the time the Mayas reached the peak of their civilization in southern Mexico and the Yucatan Peninsula, around A.D. 500, they had a highly developed system of agriculture. Maize was their most important crop, followed closely by beans, squash, chile peppers, and cacao. Perhaps as many as thirty different varieties of chiles were cultivated. They were sometimes planted in plots by themselves but more often in fields already containing tomatoes and sweet potatoes. The Mayas also cultivated cotton, papayas, vanilla beans, manioc, and agave. They kept domesticated turkeys, ducks, and dogs, and their main game animals were deer, birds, and wild boar. Armadillos and manatees were considered delicacies.

For breakfast the Mayas ate a gruel of ground maize spiced with chile peppers, which is usually called *atole* but is sometimes known as *pozol*. A modern equivalent would be cornmeal or *masa* mixed with water and ground red chiles to the consistency of a milk shake.

For the main, or evening meal, stews of vegetables and meats heavily spiced with chiles were served. Our recipe for Chicken in Red Pipian Sauce is a good example of a Mayan stew; it is an early form of the *mole* sauces to come and uses two common Mexican chiles, Ancho and Pasilla. Of course, the Mayas would have served turkey rather than chicken (which was introduced by the Spanish), but either fowl is acceptable in this recipe and also in Tlaloc-Chile Stew, which is a predecessor of the Green Chile Stew served today in the American Southwest (see recipe Chapter 5).

Because corn tortillas were a staple in Mayan cookery, we have also included a recipe for Tamales Negros, which shows the influence of another important Mayan crop: cacao, or chocolate. In the recipe for Mayan Chile Sauce, tomatoes, another significant New World food, are combined with Habanero chiles, spices, and pumpkin seeds, which also make their appearance in our basic Mayan vegetarian dish, Lima Beans with Chiles and Pepitas.

The Mayan civilization had declined considerably by the time the Spanish arrived in Mexico, so there are no Spanish observations about the height of their culture. All that exist today are Mayan hieroglyphics, which are slowly being transliterated, and ethnological observations of the present Maya Indians, whose food habits have changed little in twenty centuries.

According to the Ethnology volume of the *Handbook of Middle American Indians,* chiles are highly visible today in areas with a Mayan heritage. Today in the Yucatan Peninsula, descendants of the Mayas still grow chiles, tomatoes, and onions in boxes or hollowed-out tree trunks that are raised up on four posts for protection against pigs and hens. These container gardens are usually in the yard of the house, near the kitchen.

Despite the passage of centuries, the most basic Mayan foods have changed little. Still common are tortillas with bean paste, chiles, and a little squash. Meat, usually chicken or pork, is only consumed about once a week.

The Tzeltal Indians of central Chiapas plant chile in plots about fifty feet on a side, alternating cotton every other year. Interestingly enough, the seeds are planted by women, but only after the men have punched holes in the ground with a planting stick — a ritual with obvious symbolism. The only difference between this method and that used by the Mayas is that planting sticks today have metal tips.

Among the descendants of the Maya, chile is regarded as a powerful agent to ward off spells. For the Tzotzil Indians of the Chiapas highlands, chile assists in both life and death. The hot pods are rubbed on the lips of newborn infants and are burned during the funeral ceremonies of *viejos* ("old ones") to defeat evil spirits that might be around. The Huastec tribe of San Carlos Potosí and Veracruz treat victims of the "evil eye" with chile peppers. An egg is dipped in ground chile then rubbed on the victim's body to return the pain to the malefactor. The Cicatec Indians of the southern Mexican highlands prepare *tepache,* a drink of fermented sugar-cane juice, with cacao and chile, for use in various rituals. Such a concoction vividly recalls a similar combination of chiles and chocolate consumed by the Aztecs.

In 1529, a Spanish Franciscan friar living in Nueva España (present-day Mexico) noted that the Aztecs ate hot red or yellow chile peppers in their hot chocolate and in nearly every dish they prepared! Fascinated by the Aztecs' constant use of a previously unknown spice, Bernardino de Sahagún documented this fiery cuisine in his classic study, *Historia General de las Cosas de la Nueva Espana*, now known as the *Florentine Codex*. His work proves that of all the pre-Columbian New World civilizations, it was the Aztecs who loved chile peppers the most.

The marketplaces of ancient Mexico overflowed with chile peppers of all sizes and shapes, including, according to de Sahagún, "hot green chiles, smoked chiles, water chiles, tree chiles, beetle chiles, and sharp-pointed red chiles." In addition to some twenty varieties of *chillis*, as the pungent pods were called in the Nahuatl language, vendors sold strings of red chiles (modern *ristras*), pre-cooked chiles, and "fish chiles," which were the earliest known forms of *ceviche*, a method of preserving

Father Bernardino de Sahagún

fish without cooking. This technique places the fish in a marinade of an acidic fruit juice and chile peppers.

Other seafood dishes were common as well in ancient Mexico. "They would eat another kind of stew, with frogs and green chile," de Sahagún recorded, "and a stew of those fish called *axolotl* with yellow chile. They also used to eat a lobster stew which is very delicious." Our recipe for Shrimp Tenochtitlan is a typical Aztec seafood dish; it combines Ancho chiles, Chipotles, dried shrimp, and tomatoes.

Apparently the Aztecs utilized every possible source of protein. The friar noted such exotic variations as maguey worms with a sauce of small chiles, newt with yellow chiles, and tadpoles with *chiltecpitl*. De Sahagún classified chiles according to their pungency, as evidenced by the following chart:

NAHUATL	SPANISH	ENGLISH
cococ	*picante*	sharp
cocopatic	*muy picantes*	very sharp
cocopetzpatic	*muy muy picantes*	very, very sharp
cocopetztic	*brillantmente picantes*	brilliantly sharp
cocopetzquauitl	*extremadamente picantes*	extremely sharp
cocopalatic	*picantisimos*	sharpest

Father de Sahagún, one of the first behavioral scientists, also noted that chiles were revered as much as sex by the ancient Aztecs. While fasting to appease their rather bloodthirsty gods, the priests required two abstentions by the faithful: sexual relations and chile peppers.

Chocolate and chiles were commonly combined in a drink called *chicahuatl,* which was usually reserved for the priests and the wealthy. De Sahagún also discovered the earliest examples of dishes that have since become classics of Mexican cuisine: tamales and *moles.* The early versions of tamales often used banana leaves as a wrapper to steam combinations of *masa* dough, chicken, and the chiles of choice. De Sahagún wrote that there were two types of *chilemollis:* one with red chile and tomatoes, and the other with yellow chile and tomatoes. These *chilemollis* eventually became the savory *mole* sauces for which Mexican cuisine is justly famous (see Chapter 4).

Aztec cookery was the basis for the Mexican food of today, and, in fact, many Aztec dishes have lasted through the centuries virtually unchanged. Since oil and fat were not generally used in cooking, the foods were usually roasted, boiled, or cooked in sauces. Like the Mayas, the Aztecs usually began the day with a cup of *atole* spiced with chile peppers. We prefer another Aztec breakfast, Nopales con Huevos y Serranos, or cactus and eggs spiced with Serrano chiles.

Aztecs living close to either coast were fond of drinking *chilote,* a liquor made with pulque (fermented agave pulp), Ancho chiles, and herbs. Our recipe for Loin of Pork Pulque shows another use for the combination of pulque and chiles. Since pork was not available until the Spanish arrived, the Aztecs would have used peccary (wild pig) meat.

The main meal was served at midday and usually consisted of tortillas with beans and a salsa made with chiles and tomatoes. The salsas were usually made by grinding the ingredients between two hand-held stones, the *molcajetes.* Even today, the same technique is used in Indian villages throughout Central America. A remarkable variety of tamales were also served for the midday meal. They were stuffed with fruits such as plums, pineapple, or guava; with game meat such as deer or turkey; or with seafood such as snails or frogs. Whole chile pods were included with the stuffing, and after steaming, the tamales were often served with a cooked chile sauce such as our Pasilla-Tomato Sauce. A variation on the Aztec tamales is our recipe for Pumpkin Blossom Quesadillas.

It was this highly sophisticated chile cuisine that the Spanish encountered during their conquest of the New World.

Capsicum-Conqueror Contact

Christopher Columbus "discovered" chile peppers in the West Indies on his first voyage to the New World. In his journal for 1493, he wrote, "Also there is much Ají, which is their pepper, and the people won't eat without it, for they find it very wholesome. One could load fifty caravels a year with it in Hispaniola."

Dr. Diego Chanca, the fleet physician for Columbus on his second voyage, wrote in his journal that the Indians seasoned manioc and sweet potatoes with Ají, and that it was one of their principal foods. Of course, both Columbus and his doctor be-

lieved that they had reached the Spice Islands, or East Indies. Not only did Columbus misname the Indians, he also mistook chiles for black pepper, thus giving them the inaccurate name "pepper." But he did one thing right — he transported chile seeds back to Europe after his first voyage, which began the chile conquest of the rest of the world.

Explorers who followed Columbus to the New World soon learned that chiles were an integral part of the Indians' culinary, medical, and religious lives. In 1526, just thirty-four years after Columbus's first excursion, El Capitán Gonzalo de Oviedo noted that on the Spanish Main, "Indians everywhere grow it in gardens and farms with much diligence and attention because they eat it continuously with almost all their food."

Bernabe Cobo, a naturalist and historian who traveled throughout Central and South America in the early seventeenth century, estimated that there were at least forty different varieties. He wrote that there were "some as large as limes or large plums; others, as small as pine nuts or even grains of wheat, and between the two extremes are many different sizes. No less variety is found in color . . . and the same difference is found in form and shape." In Peru, he noted that next to maize, Ají was the plant most beloved of the Indians.

Chile peppers were such a novelty to the explorers that rumors were rampant about their medical properties. Wrote the Jesuit priest, poet, and historian José de Acosta in 1590, "Taken moderately, chile helps and comforts the stomach for digestion." The priest had undoubtedly heard about the reputed aphrodisiac qualities of chiles because he continued his description of chile with the following warning: "But if they take too much, it has bad effects, for of itself it is very hot, fuming, and pierces greatly, so the use thereof is prejudicial to the health of young folks, chiefly to the soul, for it provokes to lust." Despite the good father's suspicions, the only thing lustful about chiles was the desire everyone, including the Spanish, had to devour them.

When the Spanish forces under Cortez arrived in Tenochtitlán (now Mexico City) in 1519, they were astounded by the size and complexity of the market at the great plaza of Tlatelolco. According to descriptions by Bernal Díaz del Castillo, it resembled a modern flea market, with thousands of vendors hawking every conceivable foodstuff and other products. The noise of the market could be heard three miles away, and some of the soldiers who had traveled to such places as Rome and Constantinople said it was the largest market they had ever seen. Every product had its own section of the market, and chiles were no exception; they were sold in the second aisle to the right. Sometimes chiles were used as a form of money to buy drinks or other small items.

Most of the chiles sold in the market had been collected as tribute, a form of taxation used by the Toltecs and Aztecs and later adopted by the Spanish. The payers of the tribute were the *macehuales,* the serfs or commoners; the collectors were Indian officials, or later on, Indian officials who worked for the Spanish. The tribute consisted of locally produced goods or crops that were commonly grown, and the tribute of each village was recorded in boxes on codices of drawn or painted pictographs.

According to many sources, chiles were one of the most common tribute items. The chiles were offered to the government in several different forms: as fresh or dried pods, as seed, in two-hundred-pound bundles, in willow baskets, and in Spanish bushels. After the chile and the rest of the produce was moved to the capital, it was stored in warehouses and closely guarded, and then sold. Chile peppers were considered to be the most valuable of the tributes.

One of the most famous tribute codices is the *Matricula de Tributos,* which is part of the *Mendocino Codex.* This codex was compiled for the first viceroy of New Spain, Antonio de Mendoza, who ordered it painted in order to inform the Emperor Charles V of the wealth of what is now Mexico. Glyphs on the codex indicate the tribute paid to the Aztecs by conquered towns just before the Spanish conquest; the towns on one tribute list (what is now San Luis Potosí) gave sixteen hundred loads of dry chile to the imperial throne each year!

The *Mendocino Codex* also reveals an early use of chile peppers in punishment. One pictograph shows a father punishing his eleven-year-old son by forcing him to inhale smoke from roasting chiles. The same drawing shows a mother threatening her six-year-old daughter with the same punishment. Today, the Popolocán Indians who live near Oaxaca punish their children in a similar manner.

Wherever they traveled in the New World, Spanish explorers, particularly nonsoldiers, collected and transported chile seeds and thus further spread the different varieties. And not only did they adopt the chile as their own, the Spanish also imported foods that they combined with chiles and other native ingredients to create even more complex chile cuisines.

In the recipes in this chapter, post-Columbian ingredients are indicated as such to give cooks the option of preparing "pure" pre-Columbian recipes.

 # Corn and Potatoes with Two Chiles

Heat Scale: 6
Serves: 4

4 Ají or 5 Serrano chiles, stems removed, chopped
2 dried Mirasol chiles, stems removed, crushed
1 1/2 cups "corn milk"
4 cups fresh corn, cut from the cob
1 teaspoon ground allspice
2 medium potatoes, cooked, peeled, thinly sliced
2 hard-cooked eggs, sliced

Potatoes played a very important role in diet throughout the Andes. In the lower elevations, they were combined with corn and served as a vegetarian entrée. Fresh corn cut off the cob, along with "corn milk" (the liquid or juice that results from cutting the kernels of corn off the cob, mixed with cream) and chiles, provide the basis of the sauce for this pre-Columbian casserole.

Combine the corn, "corn milk," chiles, and allspice and simmer for 5 minutes until the mixture is hot and has thickened.

Place alternate layers of potatoes and eggs in a casserole, top with the sauce and heat in a 350° F oven for 10 minutes until thoroughly heated.

Serving Suggestion: Serve as a side dish with Loin of Pork Pulque (see recipe this chapter) and a tossed green salad.

Papas con Tomates

Heat Scale: 6
Serves: 4 to 6

6 dried Mirasol chiles, stems
  and seeds removed,
  crushed
2 medium tomatoes, peeled
  and diced
1/2 teaspoon ground cumin*
1 large potato, cooked,
  peeled, and diced
1 medium sweet potato,
  cooked, peeled, and diced
chopped fresh culantro† for
  garnish

The Incas cultivated potato varieties for thousands of years and they even invented a freeze-dried potato called "chuñu." They would spread the potatoes on the ground and let them freeze overnight, which was easy in the high Andes. After thawing them out, they would then squeeze out any remaining moisture by walking on them. This recipe includes two different potatoes grown by the Incas, as well as tomatoes and hot chiles; all are New World crops.

Simmer the chiles, tomatoes, and cumin for 15 minutes to form a thick sauce.

Pour the sauce over the potatoes, toss to coat, garnish with the culantro and serve.

Serving Suggestions: Roast pork and green beans go well with these colorful potatoes.

*A post-Columbian ingredient.
†A variety of cilantro indigenous to the Americas. Substitute cilantro if not available.

Squash Soup with Chile Sauce

Heat Scale: 6
Serves: 6

6 Ají, Rocoto, or Serrano
  chiles, stems removed,
  chopped
2 tablespoons chopped fresh
  culantro*
1 2-pound chicken, cut in
  pieces
1 medium onion†, coarsely
  chopped
1/2 pound squash
  (butternut, Hubbard, or
  turban), peeled, cut into
  2-inch cubes

Stews and hearty soups were commonly served by the Incas. A native herb called palillo *was used to impart a yellow color to dishes, but we have substituted turmeric, as palillo is difficult to find. Since the Incas ate a wide variety of squash, cooks should select their favorite for this recipe.*

Combine the chiles and chopped culantro with 1/2 cup water, bring to a boil, reduce the heat, and simmer for 10 minutes. Puree the ingredients to form a sauce, adding more water if necessary.

*A variety of cilantro indigenous to the Americas. Substitute cilantro if not available.
†Post-Columbian ingredients.

1 small potato, peeled, cut
  into 2-inch cubes
1 small yam, peeled, cut
  into 2-inch cubes
1/4 teaspoon ground
  turmeric†
fresh culantro or cilantro for
  garnish

Cover the chicken and onions with water, bring to a boil, reduce the heat and simmer, skimming off any foam that forms, until the chicken is tender and starts to fall from the bone. Remove the chicken, reserving the broth, and, using two forks, shred the meat.

Place the squash, potato, yam, and turmeric in the chicken broth. Add additional water to bring the liquid to about a quart. Bring to a boil, reduce the heat, and simmer for 20 minutes or until the squash is tender. Add the chicken and heat.

To Serve: Place the soup in bowls, put a tablespoon of the hot sauce to each bowl, top with the chopped culantro, and serve. The sauce can also be served on the side.

Serving Suggestions: Serve with Ceviche (see recipe Chapter 4) and hot rolls.

 # Chicken In Red Pipian Sauce

Heat Scale: 1
Serves: 4

1 large dried Ancho chile,
  stem and seeds removed
2 dried Pasilla chiles, stems
  and seeds removed
4 chicken breasts
1 cup pumpkin seeds
1 cup chopped onions*
3 cloves garlic, chopped*
2 tablespoons vegetable oil
1 large tomato, peeled and
  seeded
1 teaspoon ground
  cinnamon*
1/2 teaspoon ground allspice
1/2 teaspoon *achiote*†
  (optional)

Pipian sauces are both flavored and thickened by seeds and can probably be classified as the earliest moles. *This Mayan recipe uses* pepitas *(pumpkin seeds) as its base, but if they are not available, nuts such as almonds can be substituted. Although this recipe has not changed since pre-Hispanic times, we advise pureeing the sauce in a blender rather than by hand in a mol-cajete.*

Cover the chicken with water, bring to a boil, reduce the heat, and simmer until the chicken is tender, skimming off any foam that rises. Remove the chicken and reserve the broth.

Soak the chiles in a cup of the chicken broth to soften.

Toast the pumpkin seeds on a hot skillet, stirring constantly until browned, being careful that they do not burn. Grind the seeds to a fine powder.

Sauté the onions and garlic in the oil until softened.

*Post-Columbian ingredients.

†The red seeds of the annatto tree. Used as a seasoning and to impart a yellow coloring. Available in Latin markets.

Combine the chiles along with the broth they were soaking in, pumpkin seeds, tomato, cinnamon, allspice, onion mixture, and *achiote* in a blender and puree until smooth. Use more of the chicken broth to thin if necessary.

Simmer the sauce for 15 minutes. Add the chicken and simmer for an additional 15 minutes.

Serving Suggestions: Serve with black beans, baked pumpkin, chopped tomatoes with cilantro, and corn tortillas.

Tamales Negros

Heat Scale: 3
Yield: 12 tamales

3 dried Mirasol chiles, stems and seeds removed
2 dried Pasilla chiles, stems and seeds removed
2 small tomatoes, peeled
1 ounce bitter chocolate, melted
2 tablespoons pumpkin seeds, toasted and coarsely ground
1 teaspoon ground cinnamon*
2 boneless chicken breasts

Tamale dough:

2 cups *masa*
1 1/2 cups water
1/2 cup shortening
corn husks, soaked in warm water

This recipe incorporates many of the staples of the Mayan diet — chiles, tomatoes, seeds, chocolate (cacao), and corn. These tamales would have been wrapped and cooked in banana leaves, a practice still followed today in the coastal regions. We substitute corn husks, also an authentic Mayan tamale wrap.

Cover the chiles with hot water and let them sit for 15 minutes until softened. Combine the chiles, the water they were soaking in, the tomatoes, chocolate, pumpkin seeds, and cinnamon in a blender and puree until smooth.

Simmer the chicken in the sauce for 15 to 20 minutes or until tender. Remove the chicken and, using two forks, shred the meat and mix it with the sauce.

Mix the *masa* with the shortening and water and knead to the consistency of a solid dough.

To Assemble: Spread the center of a corn husk with 2 tablespoons of the *masa* dough and top with 2 tablespoons of the meat and sauce. Fold the sides of the husk toward the center, then fold in the bottom and the top, and tie with a thin strip of corn husk.

Add 2 cups of water to a large kettle, place the tamales on a rack, and steam them for an hour.

*A post-Columbian ingredient.

Tlaloc-Chile Stew

Heat Scale: 4
Serves: 6 to 8

4 dried Pasilla chiles, stems and seeds removed
5 Jalapeño chiles, stems removed, chopped
3 medium tomatoes, peeled
1 medium onion, chopped*
1 teaspoon *achiote*†
1/4 cup chopped fresh culantro‡
1/4 cup chopped fresh *yerba buena* or mint
1 8-pound turkey, skin removed, cut in serving pieces
1 quart water

The turkey was the Mayan god of rain and fertility and was called Tlaloc. A meal to the Mayas consisted of a stew, either with meat and vegetables or vegetables alone in a broth base. This stew also uses mint, or native yerba buena, *as well as culantro for flavoring.*

Cover the Pasilla chiles with hot water and let them sit for 15 minutes until softened.

Combine the chiles, tomatoes, onions, *achiote,* and the water in which the chiles were soaking, in a blender and puree until smooth. Stir the culantro and mint into the sauce.

Place the turkey pieces and water in a pan. Add the sauce and water, bring to a boil, reduce the heat, and simmer until the turkey is tender, about 1 1/2 hours. Add more water if necessary.

Serving Suggestions: Serve with an avocado salad and corn tortillas.

   *A post-Columbian ingredient.
   †The red seeds of the annatto tree. Used as a seasoning and to impart a yellow coloring. Available in Latin markets.
   ‡A variety of cilantro indigenous to the Americas. Substitute cilantro if not available.

Mayan Chile Sauce

Heat Scale: 7
Yield: 1 to 1 1/2 cups

4 Habanero chiles or 8 Serrano chiles, stems removed, chopped
1/2 cup pumpkin seeds
2 large tomatoes, peeled and chopped
1 tablespoon chopped fresh culantro*

There are a number of variations of this basic Mayan sauce still served today; however, this recipe includes only pre-Columbian ingredients.

Toast the pumpkin seeds in a hot skillet, stirring constantly until they brown, being careful that they do not burn. Grind them coarsely.

Combine all the ingredients in a blender and puree to desired consistency.

Serving Suggestions: Serve as a dipping sauce with toasted corn chips or as a relish with grilled poultry or fish.

   *A variety of cilantro indigenous to the Americas. Substitute cilantro if not available.

Lima Beans with Chile and Pepitas

Heat Scale: 4
Serves: 4

4 Jalapeño chiles, stems removed, chopped
2/3 cup lima beans, either fresh or frozen
1/2 cup pumpkin seeds
1 medium tomato, peeled and chopped
2 tablespoons chopped onion*
1 teaspoon chopped fresh culantro†

The Mayas attributed divinity to seeds, so it is logical that seeds should appear in one form or another in many of their recipes. This recipe was probably eaten as a snack rather than as part of a main meal, but it does make a good side dish on a modern menu.

Cook the lima beans in water until done, then drain.

Toast the pumpkin seeds on a hot skillet, stirring constantly until browned, taking care that they do not burn. Coarsely grind or crush the seeds.

Simmer the beans, pumpkin seeds, chile, tomato, onion, and culantro for 10 minutes, taking care not to mash the beans.

Serving Suggestions: Serve with a grilled fish, Pasilla-Tomato Sauce (see recipe this chapter), and fried plaintains.

*A post-Columbian ingredient.
†A variety of cilantro indigenous to the Americas. Substitute cilantro if not available.

Shrimp Tenochtitlán

Heat Scale: 5
Serves: 4 to 6

3 small dried Ancho chiles, stems and seeds removed
3 dried Chipotle chiles, stems removed
2 dried Piquin chiles, stems and seeds removed
2 ounces dried shrimp*
1 medium onion†, chopped
4 cloves garlic†, chopped
3 tablespoons vegetable oil
2 medium tomatoes, peeled and seeds removed, chopped
1 pound shrimp, shelled and deveined

The combination of different varieties of chiles was commonplace with the Aztecs (as evidenced by this stew), and that influence can still be seen in modern Mexican cookery. The oil used was extracted from the popular pumpkin seeds and can still be purchased today in some parts of the Yucatan Peninsula.

Toast the Ancho chiles in a hot skillet for a minute, taking care that they do not burn. Cover the Anchos, Chipotle, and Piquin chiles with hot water and let them sit for 15 minutes until softened.

Toast the dried shrimp in the skillet for a couple of minutes and then grind them to a powder.

*Available in Latin or Asian markets.
†Post-Columbian ingredients.

Sauté the onions and garlic in one half of the oil until softened.

Combine the chiles, the water they were soaking in, tomatoes, and onions in a blender and puree until smooth. Fry the sauce in the remaining oil for 10 minutes, stirring constantly.

Add the fresh and dry shrimp and an additional cup of water. Bring to a boil, reduce the heat, and simmer for 10 minutes or until the shrimp is done.

Serving Suggestions: Although originally eaten as a stew, this dish is also great served over rice and accompanied by green beans (which were also served by the Aztecs).

 # Nopales con Huevos y Serranos

Heat Scale: 3
Serves: 4

4 Serrano chiles, stems removed, chopped
2 tablespoons chopped onion*
2 tablespoons vegetable oil
2 small tomatoes, peeled and seeds removed, chopped
1 cup cooked *nopales*, cut into small strips, or 1 small jar *nopalitos*, rinsed well
1 teaspoon chopped fresh culantro†
6 eggs, well beaten
grated Monterey Jack cheese*

Nopales *are the meat from the fleshy pads of the nopal or prickly pear, an edible variety of Opuntia cactus. Preparing the cactus for eating, including the removal of the skin and spines, can be a tedious job. Instead, look for* nopales *pickled in brine in Latin markets and gourmet shops. Although not quite as tasty as fresh, they are a good substitute — just be sure to rinse them well.*

Sauté the chiles and onions in the oil until soft. Add the tomatoes, cactus, and culantro, and simmer until the moisture is absorbed.

Add the eggs to the mixture and sprinkle the cheese on the top. Cover, and cook over a low heat until the eggs are set.

Serving Suggestions: Serve for breakfast with papaya and banana slices, toast with guava jam, and hot chocolate.

*Post-Columbian ingredients.
†A variety of cilantro indigenous to the Americas. Substitute cilantro if not available.

Loin of Pork Pulque

Heat Scale: 4
Serves: 6

Note: This recipe requires advance preparation.

2 small dried Ancho chiles, stems and seeds removed
2 dried Pasilla chiles, stems and seeds removed
1 dried Chipotle chile, stem removed
1 medium onion, chopped*
2 cloves garlic, chopped*
2 tablespoons vegetable oil
2 tablespoons brown sugar*
1 teaspoon ground cinnamon*
1/2 teaspoon allspice
1/4 cup pulque or tequila
3 to 4 pound pork loin
roasted pumpkin seeds or *pepitas*, chopped for garnish

The Aztecs used peccary (wild pig), but domesticated pork works equally well. The highly alcoholic and sweet liquor called pulque is the fermented drink made from the agave, or century, plant and is used to marinate the meat. Pit-roasting was the method the Aztecs used to cook such meats, but an oven is more convenient and less destructive to the lawn.

Cover the chiles with hot water and let sit for 15 minutes until softened. Remove the chiles and drain.

Sauté the onions, garlic, and chiles in the oil. Stir in the sugar, cinnamon, allspice, and the pulque and simmer for 10 minutes. Put the mixture in a blender and puree until smooth, adding water if necessary.

Marinate the pork in the mixture for 24 hours in the refrigerator.

Bake the pork in a covered pan along with the marinade in a 350° F oven for 2 hours or until done. Let the roast sit for 15 minutes and then slice thinly. Strain the marinade, pour it over the pork, and top with the pepitas and serve.

Serving Suggestions: Rice, zucchini and corn, and pumpkin muffins go well with this dish.

*Post-Columbian ingredients.

Pasilla-Tomato Sauce

Heat Scale: 3
Yield: 1 cup

5 dried Pasilla chiles, stems
  and seeds removed
1 small dried Chipotle chile,
  stem removed
8 green tomatoes
chopped fresh culantro* for
  garnish

Although very basic, this tasty Aztec sauce goes well with broiled meats and poultry or as a sauce over enchiladas.

Cover the chiles with hot water and let them sit for 15 minutes until softened.

Roast or blister the tomatoes by placing in a 200° F oven until the skin blackens or secure on a fork and place over the flame of a gas burner. Peel the tomatoes.

Simmer tomatoes for 10 minutes or until soft.

Combine the chiles and tomatoes in a blender and puree until smooth. Thin with the water the chiles were soaking in, if necessary.

Garnish with the culantro and serve.

*A variety of cilantro indigenous to the Americas. Substitute cilantro if not available.

Pumpkin Blossom Quesadillas

Heat Scale: 4
Serves: 4

4 Serrano chiles, stems
  removed, chopped
1 medium Poblano chile,
  stem and seeds removed,
  cut in strips
1 tablespoon vegetable oil
1 cup whole kernel corn,
  cooked
20 squash blossoms, stems
  and green sepals removed,
  chopped
4 corn tortillas

The Aztecs used a variety of flowers in their cooking. They were especially fond of pumpkin blossoms, which they utilized in soups and puddings as well as in stuffings for quesadillas and tacos. The large male blossoms are considered the choicest. Pick the blossoms early in the morning before they start to open.

Sauté the chiles in the oil until soft. Add the corn and continue to cook for an additional 5 minutes.

Add the blossoms and continue to cook, uncovered, until the moisture is absorbed.

Warm slightly dampened tortillas in the oven to soften. Place some of the mixture on one half of the tortilla, fold over, moisten with water, and press the edges together. Toast on a hot griddle to heat.

Serving Suggestions: Serve with Black Bean Soup (see recipe Chapter 4) and sliced avocados.

CHAPTER FOUR

New World Chile Cuisines

*"Chile, they say, is the king, the soul of the Mexicans —
a nutrient, a medicine, a drug, a comfort. For many
Mexicans, if it were not for the existence of chile, their
national identity would begin to disappear."*

Arturo Lomelí, *El Chile y Otros Picantes* (1986)

LATIN America and the Caribbean are enigmas when it comes to chile peppers. Since the fiery fruits originated and proliferated there for thousands of years before the Spanish arrived, it would stand to reason that chiles would have permeated all of the cuisines of this vast area. Yet in South America, Peru is hot while Venezuela is not. In the Caribbean, one island such as Jamaica may love fiery foods while nearby Cuba has only a few dishes considered truly hot. Even on a single island such as Hispaniola, Haitian food is fairly spicy, while in adjoining Santo Domingo meals rarely, if ever, contain chiles.

Thus there are definite pockets of heat scattered about Latin America and the Caribbean, especially in those countries where the indigenous population had a greater influence on the cuisine than the European settlers. Generally speaking, these pockets are the regions where the great civilizations of the Incas, Mayas, and Aztecs arose: Peru and adjoining Andean countries, Yucatan and Central America, and Mexico. Although the Caribbean Islands had no single culture to rival those civilizations, both the Arawak and Carib Indians had adopted chile peppers into their diets and that legacy remains today.

It is in these four areas that the peoples' fanatic fondness for chile peppers created what we call a "fiery cuisine." This is not to say that chiles do not appear in other regions; they do, but only sporadically at best. Countries such as Argentina and the Bahamas have some wonderful chile-spiced dishes, but true fiery cuisines have not evolved.

The arrival of Europeans greatly assisted the development of the chile-dominated cuisines of the New World. It is difficult to imagine the cuisines of the Americas today without the foods introduced by the Spanish, Portuguese, and Africans: grains such as rice, oats, and wheat; fruits such as apples, peaches, grapes, mangoes, limes, oranges, olives, and bananas; meats such as chicken, beef, pork, and lamb; vegetables such as onions, garlic, carrots, okra, and lettuce; and spices such as cumin, black pepper, cinnamon, mustard, and horseradish.

These new foods were adopted by the indigenous civilizations in varying degrees depending upon region, climate, and local preference. In many cases — especially with the grains, meats, vegetables, and spices — they were combined with chile peppers for the first time in history.

The Legacy of the Incas

It is ironic that the chile cuisines of the countries of South America, where the chile pepper originated, are not as complex as those of Mexico, or even Thailand, for that matter. The people of the Andean region of Peru, Ecuador, and Bolivia still eat basically Incan food that has been only slightly modified by the meats and vegetables introduced by the Spanish. But despite the basic nature of the cuisine of this region, chiles are used extensively, and they are among the hottest in the world.

There are several chiles of choice in the Andes, where they are generically called "Ají" or "Uchu." The first and foremost chile is the specific Ají, *Capsicum baccatum,* which is often called "Ají amarillo" because of its yellow fruits. One variety of Ají, *puca-uchu,* grows on a vinelike plant in home gardens because Ajís are rarely commercially cultivated in South America. The Ajís are extremely hot, rating an 8 on the Heat Scale.

Another favorite chile in the Andes is Rocotillo, a variety of *Capsicum chinense* and a close relative of the Habanero — though it is considerably milder. It is used in a similar manner to Bells and is sometime called a Squash pepper. Such terminology is confusing because there is a variety of *Capsicum annuum* called "Tomato" or "Squash" that is cultivated in the United States. The Rocotillo is served fresh as a condiment or garnish, or is cooked with beans and stews, or is spread over grilled meat.

Another species, *Capsicum pubescens,* is beloved in the region and is called Rocoto. The cherrylike pods of the Rocoto are as dangerously hot as the Ajís — also rating an 8 on the Heat Scale. In fact, they are so pungent that there is a Peruvian expression about them, *"llevanta muertos,"* meaning they are hot enough to raise the dead.

In addition to their culinary uses, the various South American chiles are employed in other ways. Mothers who are descendants of the Inca in Peru coat their nipples with chile juice or powder to discourage their babies from suckling during the weaning process. Perhaps the oddest usage of the Ajís is in southern Colombia, where Indians mix powdered chile with cocaine before snorting it. Supposedly, the chile increases the mucus secretions and somehow heightens the stimulating properties of the drug. Both practices sound remarkably painful, especially considering the pungency of most South American chiles, and neither is recommended. However, they do give an indication of just how pervasive chiles are in Andean culture.

Such pervasiveness is also illustrated by the reputation of certain cities for having particularly fiery cuisines. Arequipa, in southern Peru, is probably the hottest city in South America and is in the competition for the title of hottest city in the world. There, the dishes are so hot that restaurants in Lima list menu items as "arequipeño," meaning they are from Arequipa and diners should use caution when eating them.

Some examples of fiery dishes from Arequipa include *ocopa,* potatoes covered with a hot cheese and peanut sauce plus a yellow Ají chile paste; Rocoto chiles stuffed with cheese or sausage; and our recipe for Papas a la Huancaina, another dish with an Ají-spiced cheese sauce. The use of peanuts in hot chile dishes in Arequipa is interesting because it anticipates some African dishes with similar ingredients. The peanut, like the chile pepper, is a native of South America (a similar nut, the Bambara groundnut, is a native of Africa) and has been found in Peruvian mummy graves in Ancón. The combination of the two is a classic example of the addition of chile to spice up an essentially bland food.

In the Andes, Ajís or Ají salsas are used to add heat to other bland foods such as potatoes and manioc. There are several kinds of Ají salsas, but the most important of them is Ají *molida*, which is prepared by mixing the fresh chiles with ground herbs, onions, and water. On the coast, Peruvian fishermen mix the Ajís with olives, olive oil, and chopped onions, or add them to raw fish to create *ceviche*, a dish that now appears, with variations, all over the world. Our recipe for Ceviche with Ajís combines native fish and Ají chiles with bitter oranges and onions imported from the Old World.

Other Andean dishes also demonstrate the influences of both the Spanish and Incan cultures. Chickens spiced with Ajís reflect the combination of native chiles with European-introduced chickens. It is probable that a pre-Columbian version of this dish combined the chiles with birds such as the *macuca*, a large jungle fowl. Another famous Andean dish is illustrated by our recipe for Peruvian Anticuchos, marinated and grilled beef hearts, which are as common in Lima as hot dogs are in the United States.

In Chile, various sauces are used to spice up bean, potato, and chicken dishes. One simple sauce is *color*, which is made by sautéing garlic, paprika, and dried red chiles in cooking oil. Its name alludes to its bright red-orange — well, color. Another sauce is *pebre*, which combines a red chile paste with olive oil, vinegar, cilantro, onions, and garlic.

In other parts of South America, where European influences had a greater impact upon the cuisines, chile peppers are combined with a wider variety of Old World foods.

Collisions of Cultures and Cuisines

After the Andean region, chiles are most prevalent in Brazilian cookery and occur in many dishes. The popularity of chiles in Brazil is the result of three factors: the prevalence of chiles in the Amazon Basin, their combination with foods introduced by the Portuguese, and the fact that the first African slaves readily adopted the native chiles.

The Amazon Basin is one of the greatest areas of genetic diversity of *Capsicum chinense*, the Habanero-type chile. Most probably, the Habaneros found today in the Caribbean Islands and Central America migrated from the Amazon region. However, they are not the only chiles in the region. Varieties of both *C. annuum* and *C. frutescens,* the Tabasco type, also appear in Brazil, and pickled Tabascos are often called for in Brazilian dishes. One type of *annuum* is known as the *malagueta* pepper, an allusion to the pods, which resemble miniature versions of the famed grapes of Malaga, Spain. Some experts believe that additional *annuum* varieties were re-introduced by slaves into Brazil in the eighteenth century after the chiles had become established in Africa.

Indeed, Brazilian cuisine was influenced more by African sources than its own native Indian tribes. In colonial times, the Portuguese were totally dependent upon African cooks, who began as slaves and utilized both Brazilian and West African foods. A good example of such cooking is Vatapá de Camarão e Peixe, a Bahian dish which combines shrimp, chiles, coconut, peanuts, ginger, and tomatoes. In the coastal city of Salvador de Bahia, the dish is very spicy, with either dried or fresh chiles added. In more tourist-influenced areas such as Rio de Janeiro, Vatapá is generally much blander.

Salsa Carioca is a Brazilian variation on Mexican guacamole, featuring the ever-popular and native avocado, a Tabasco-type sauce, tomatoes, eggs, and hot chiles. Also popular in Brazil are the *moquecas,* or native stews, and our recipe for Bahian Moqueca features the combination of Serrano chiles and fish. Other Brazilian dishes are often seasoned Caribbean-style with hot sauces. One such sauce is *molho de pimenta e limao,* which combines Habanero chiles with limes.

In southern Brazil and Argentina, spicy barbecues called *churrascos* are enormously popular, especially where large cattle ranches are located. Beef cuts and sausages are marinated in various chile barbecue sauces and are then skewered on large "swords" and grilled. Some cuts of meat are drenched in sauces, wrapped in papaya leaves, and buried in hot coals. The papaya leaves contain papain, which tenderizes the meat. Our recipe for Grilled Flank Steak with Chimichurri Sauce is an example of a fiery *churrasco.* Another popular Argentine dish is Spicy Empanadas.

Moving north, another region with a collision-of-cultures chile cuisine is the Caribbean, where chile peppers are the dominant spice in a region filled with other spices such as ginger, nutmeg, mace, cloves, and allspice. Although there is little doubt that the Indians of the Caribbean Islands were cultivating and cooking with chile peppers for centuries before Columbus happened upon the hot fruits, they left little evidence of their cuisine. First, the Arawak Indians were wiped out by the ferocious Carib Indians, and then smallpox and swine flu, imported by European colonists, rendered the Caribs extinct. So, the main culinary influences upon the islands were from the Old World, with the exception of the chiles, which were adopted into the new foods and styles of cooking imported from Europe and Africa.

European influences in the Caribbean included Dutch, Spanish, English, and French styles of cooking that adopted native ingredients such as fruits, seafood, and of course, chiles. The arrival of slaves from West Africa and immigrants from India added even more exotic influences to the incredible mixture of cuisines that abounded in the Caribbean region. The combination of chiles with peanuts, for example, is typically both Peruvian and African (see Chapter 6) but occurs commonly in Caribbean dishes such as groundnut soup. Many Indian-style curry dishes are found in the West Indies, particularly in Jamaica and Trinidad.

As in Brazil, the main source of heat is the Habanero, although Chiltepin varieties still grow wild in Jamaica, Barbados, and other islands, where they are called "bird peppers" or "country peppers." Varieties of Habaneros from Jamaica and Belize have measured as high as 300,000 Scoville Units, making them by far the hottest chiles in the world. With heat like that, it's no wonder that these chiles are generally sliced, chopped, or crushed into tiny pieces before adding them to foods. The most common use of the Habaneros is to prepare sauces with them, such as our Haitian Hot Pepper Sauce. These hot sauces are sprinkled over seafood, poultry, and meat dishes, or are added to soups and stews. Habaneros are also the primary ingredient in commercially prepared hot sauces, and nearly every island has at least one brand of Habanero-based hot sauce.

In 1988, we traveled to the Caribbean country of Belize to investigate Habanero usage, and we soon became fascinated by the extremely hot sauces produced there utilizing Habanero chiles — including Habanero Five Drops, Pica Rico, Hi-Taste, and Melinda's. We visited the tiny town of Melinda in the foothills of the Maya Mountains in the southern part of Belize and met Marie and Gerry Sharp, who have a hot-sauce bottling operation.

Marie Sharp began bottling Melinda's hot sauce in 1983 after she became frustrated with the local produce markets. A lover of Habanero chiles, she had grown about a hundred plants among citrus groves on the Sharp's 400-acre plantation. After the initial harvest, she carried the chiles to the local market, where buyers insulted her by offering one dollar Belize (fifty cents U.S. currency) for a *gallon* of pods.

"I will not give away my peppers," Marie vowed, and from that point on she knew that a bottled sauce was the answer to marketing the Habaneros. But there was one problem — her friends told her that the other Habanero sauces were so hot that a single bottle often lasted six months or more. Since she wanted her customers to buy more than two bottles of sauce a year, Marie experimented with numerous recipes until she found one with more flavor and less heat than the competition.

Next it was necessary to find a dependable source for the Habanero chiles, since in Belize they are grown only in limited quantities for the local market or under contract to other sauce producers. The Sharps contacted various growers and began horticultural experimentation with the Habaneros, which, like other peppers, are susceptible to wilt and viral diseases in the tropics, where the rainfall can be one hundred inches per year or more.

In order to standardize the color in their Habaneros, which can vary from orange to purple at maturity, only the reddest pods were selected, and those seeds were spaced for plants three feet apart in rows four feet apart. The Habanero plants grow about one year before producing pods and reach a height of four feet or more. They are perennial and produce pods constantly for about three years before yields are reduced. Then the plants are removed and the rows replanted with seeds from the reddest pods available. In 1988, the Sharps had about five acres of Habaneros under cultivation but expected to double that as export demand for Melinda's sauce increased. It takes about seven pounds of Habaneros to produce about five gallons of hot sauce.

Bottled Habanero sauces are readily available on the Caribbean islands as well as the mainland regions such as Belize and the Yucatan Peninsula, but homemade sauces are also common. The hot sauces *piquante* and *chien* from Martinique and *timalice* from Haiti all combine shallots, lime juice, garlic, and the hottest Habaneros available. On Saint Kitts and Jamaica, a mango chutney is made with chiles, unripe mangoes, raisins, cashews, ginger, garlic, brown sugar, and vinegar. Puerto Rico has two hot sauces of note: one is called *pique* and is made with acidic Seville oranges and Habaneros; the other is *sofrito*, which combines small Piquins with annatto seeds, cilantro, onions, garlic, and tomatoes.

In the Caribbean Islands, most of the meat dishes are prepared by stewing or braising because tough cuts such as goat legs and pork shoulders must be tenderized by cooking until the meat breaks down. One example is our Stoba recipe from the Netherlands Antilles: a goat or lamb stew with Habaneros, cucumbers, olives, capers, garlic, ginger, and lime juice. Another is our recipe for Picadillo Picante from Cuba.

Martinique has similar stews, its *colombo* dishes, which were introduced in the mid-1800s by Hindu workers from Bengal. *Colombos* are curry variations that combine Habanero chiles, coriander, turmeric, saffron, black mustard, and garlic in a paste that is added to stews along with tamarind pulp. A legend in Martinique bemoans the lack of ingredients to prepare the *colombos*.

The story goes that a poor woman discovered that her kitchen was bare of the above ingredients except for chiles, so she decided all she could prepare for dinner was a soup made solely of Habaneros and water. Her unsuspecting children ate one spoonful of the soup and then ran to the river to try to douse the heat, where they drank so much water they drowned. Obviously, the apocryphal children were unaware that water is the least effective cool-down for chile heat — see Chapter 8 for the best ones.

Incidentally, the French-speaking islands of the Caribbean have some picturesque names for their chiles. In Guadeloupe, small, wrinkled chiles are known as "Bonda Man Jacques" (Madame Jacques's behind) and the purplish-black chiles are called "Piment Negresse."

One exception to the rule of braising and stewing meats is Jerk Pork with Pimento Season-Up. This Jamaican favorite features pork chops that have had a paste of spices and chiles pounded into them. They are marinated in this spice mixture and then are grilled over wood or charcoal. The word *jerk* is thought to have originated from the word *charquí,* a Spanish term for jerked or dried meat, which, in English, became known as "jerky."

The technique of jerking was originated by the Maroons, Jamaican slaves who escaped from the British during the invasion of 1655 and hid in the maze of jungles and sinkholes known as the Cockpit Country. The Maroons cooked the pork until it was dry and would preserve well in the humidity of the tropics. During the twentieth century, the technique gained enormous popularity in Jamaica and today "jerk pork shacks" are commonly found all over that island. The method has evolved, however, and the pork is no longer overcooked. In addition to pork, heavily spiced chicken, fish, and beef are grilled to juicy perfection.

An interesting variation on the concept of using a spicy paste is the *bajan* seasoning of Barbados. Hot Bajan Chicken is made from minced fresh Habaneros, green onions, lime juice, thyme, parsley, garlic, marjoram, chives, paprika, and cloves. The fiery paste is inserted into cuts in boiled chicken pieces, which are then breaded and deep fried. Two other fiery recipes from Barbados are a vegetarian soup called Spicy Pumpkin Bisque and a famous Carib Indian dish known as Pepperpot Stew.

We should not leave the Caribbean without mentioning the seafood dishes that are also combined with chiles. In addition to the fresh fish caught daily, imported salt cod is still a favorite ingredient on the islands with a British heritage such as Jamaica. There it is combined with chiles and the nutty-tasting fruit of the *ackee* tree. Spiny lobsters also make an appearance in chile-spiced stews and salads. The tough but tasty conch can be found combined with chiles and vegetables in Bahamian salads. One of the most famous Bahamian dishes is Conch and Chile Fritters, which makes a delicious appetizer.

The Spicy Soul of a Nation

Central America also has its pockets of heat. As is true of South America and the Caribbean, some countries have embraced chile peppers with more fervor than others. Panama and Costa Rica, for example, have some spicy dishes, but the overall cuisine is not as spicy as that of Belize or Guatemala. Perhaps because of its Mayan heritage, Guatemala has a fiery cuisine second only to Mexico in terms of chile usage.

The most popular chile in Guatemala is the *chile de Coban,* a variety of Chiltepin with round to slightly elongated pods that are smoke-dried over wood and have a powerful, smoky taste. Our recipe for Guatemalan Jocon utilizes these chiles, or if they are unavailable, the similarly smoky Chipotles. Jocon is a perfect example of a Mayan recipe that has resisted European influences; the only non–New World ingredients are the garlic, onions, and chicken. The Mayas, of course, would have substituted duck or turkey for the chicken. Another Central American recipe from the Yucatan Peninsula features chiles combined with black beans, as evidenced by our Black Bean Soup with Jalapeños.

The Old World influence was greater in Mexico than Central America and the arrival of the Spanish in Mexico had a profound effect on the cuisine of the country. The Old World foodstuffs the explorers brought with them soon transformed the eating habits of the Indians. However, the Aztecs and their descendants did not give up their beloved staples such as chiles, corn, and chocolate; they combined them with the new imports and thus created the basis for the Mexican cuisines of today.

Throughout the centuries, an astonishing variety in Mexican cooking developed as a result of geography. From the Yucatan Peninsula, Mexico stretches over two thousand miles to the deserts of the north, so the length and size of Mexico, combined with the fact that mountain ranges separate the various regions, led to the development of isolated regional cuisines. This geographical variety is the reason that the cooking of tropical Yucatan differs significantly from that of the deserts of Chihuahua and Sonora.

One common factor, though, in Mexican cookery is the prevalence of chile peppers. Unlike South America, where chiles are still consumed mostly by the Indian population, in Mexico everyone fell in love with the pungent pods. Chile peppers are Mexico's most important vegetable crop; they are grown all over the country from the Pacific and Gulf coasts to mountainous regions with an altitude above 8,000 feet. Approximately 200,000 acres of cultivated land produce 500,000 tons of fresh pods and 30,000 tons of dry pods. Although over ten different varieties are grown or collected in Mexico, Anchos/Poblanos, Serranos, Mirasols, and Jalapeños account for 75 percent of the crop. In 1988 Mexico exported 2,529 metric tons of fresh or dried chiles worth $4.6 million into the United States.

In 1985, each Mexican consumed about fourteen pounds of green chile and nearly two pounds of dried chile. In fact, the Mexicans eat more chile per capita than onions or tomatoes. The favorite chiles are about evenly divided between those harvested fresh and those utilized in the dry form.

The Serranos and Jalapeños are grown for processing and the fresh market, where they are the chiles of choice for salsas. Over 90 percent of the Serrano crop is used fresh in homemade salsas such as our version of Pico de Gallo, which is known by quite a few other names. Serranos are also used in a popular cooked sauce, Tomatillo Sauce.

About 60 percent of the Jalapeño crop is processed, either by canning or pickling or as commercial salsas. Of the remainder, 20 percent is used fresh and 20 percent is used in the production of *chipotles*, the smoked and dried form of the Jalapeño.

The use of another favorite Mexican chile, the Ancho/Poblano, is equally divided between fresh (Poblano) and dried (Ancho). Some Mexican chiles, such as Pasilla, Mirasol, and de Arbol are used almost exclusively in the dried form as the basis for a number of cooked sauces. These sauces, which are nearly identical to those in the American Southwest, are discussed in Chapter 5 — except for the *moles*.

The word *mole* means "mixture" in Spanish, as in *guacamole*, a mixture of vegetables *(guaca)*. The word used by itself embraces a vast number of sauces utilizing every imaginable combination of meats, vegetables, spices, and flavorings — sometimes up to three dozen different ingredients. Not only are there many ingredients, there are dozens of variations on *mole* — red *moles,* green *moles,* brown *moles,* fiery *moles,* and even mild *moles.*

In Mexico today, cooks who specialize in *moles* are termed *moleros,* and they even have their own competition, the National Mole Fair held every year in October at the town of San Pedro Atocpan, just south of Mexico City. At the fair, thousands of people sample hundreds of different *moles* created by restaurateurs and *mole* wholesalers. This fair is the Mexican equivalent of chili con carne cookoffs in the United States; the *moleros* take great pride in their fiery creations and consider each *mole* a work of art in the same way that chili-cookoff chefs regard their chili con carne. Their recipes are family secrets not to be revealed to others under any circumstances. Often the preparation of a family *mole* recipe takes as long as three days.

The color of a particular *mole* depends mostly upon the varieties of chiles utilized. A green *mole* consists mostly of Poblano chiles while a red *mole* could contain three or four different varieties of dried red chiles, such as chiles de Arbol, or Cascabels. The brown and black *moles* owe their color to Pasillas and Anchos, both of which are often called "chile negro" because of their dark hues when dried.

Other than chiles, there are literally dozens of other ingredients added to the various *moles,* including almonds, anise, bananas, chocolate, cinnamon, cilantro, cloves, coconut, garlic, onions, peanuts, peppercorns, piñons, pumpkin seeds, raisins, sesame seeds, toasted bread, tomatillos, tomatoes, tortillas, and walnuts. Undoubtedly, some *moleros* add coriander, cumin, epazote, oregano, thyme, and other spices to their *moles.*

On the basis of the devotion of its people to the fiery chiles used in their *moles,* it is evident that San Pedro Actopan is also in the running to be named the hottest city in the world. No wonder — it is located in the state of Puebla, renowned for the most famous *mole* of all, *mole poblano.*

This is the sauce traditionally served on special occasions such as Christmas that combines chiles and chocolate, a popular and revered food of the Aztecs. Moctezuma's court consumed fifty jugs of chile-laced hot chocolate a day, and warriors drank it to soothe their nerves before going into battle. However, the story of how chocolate was combined with chile sauces does not involve warriors, but rather nuns.

Legend holds that *mole poblano* was invented in the sixteenth century by the nuns of the convent of Santa Rosa in the city of Puebla. It seems that the archbishop was coming to visit, and the nuns were worried because they had no food elegant enough to serve someone of his eminence. So, they prayed for guidance and one of the nuns had a vision. She directed that everyone in the convent should begin chopping and grinding everything edible they could find in the kitchen. Into a pot went chiles, tomatoes, nuts, sugar, tortillas, bananas, raisins, garlic, avocados, and dozens of herbs and spices. The final ingredient was the magic one: chocolate. Then the nuns slaughtered their only turkey and served it with the *mole* sauce to the archbishop, who declared it the finest dish he had ever tasted.

It is a nice story, but more likely *mole* was invented by the Aztecs long before the Spaniards arrived. Since chocolate was reserved for Aztec royalty, the military nobility, and religious officials, perhaps Aztec serving girls at the convent gave a royal recipe to the nuns so they could honor their royalty, the archbishop. At any rate, the recipe for *mole poblano* was rescued from oblivion and became a holiday favorite. Our recipe for Classic Mole Poblano Sauce should be considered as a basis for experimentation with additional ingredients mentioned above. Another popular holiday chile dish unites chiles and walnuts and is called Chiles en Nogada.

Visitors to Mexico are often surprised to discover that chiles and seafood often appear in the same dish. Chile aficionados realize, however, that dishes such as Shrimp in Adobo Sauce merely reflect a culinary tradition thousands of years old. Chiles both spice up usually bland fish and also assist in the preservation process. Our recipe for Huachinango a la Vera Cruz is a perfect example of the elegance of some of these chile-seafood dishes.

Although chiles are grown and consumed all over Mexico, they are particularly evident in the cooking of northern Mexico, which is termed ''Norteño-style'' Mexican food, or the food of *La Frontera*, the frontier. In fact, in Mexico City the fiery cooking of the states of Chihuahua and Sonora is termed *platillos* nortenses, or "northern plates." A good example of such cooking is our recipe for Chile Carnitas, in which little pieces of pork are marinated in red chile powder and spices and then are baked or sometimes fried.

The combination of chile with corn — particularly corn tortillas — is traditional in Norteño-style cooking, and takes many forms. The tortillas can be rolled into flutelike shapes, as in our recipe for Chicken Flautas with Avocado Sauce, or cut in strips for Chilaquiles. Other corn tortilla and chile combinations are popular on both sides of the border and are discussed in Chapter 5. The lore of Mexican cuisine holds that Norteño-style cooking is the hottest of them all, and that level of heat is a tradition that migrated to the American Southwest.

 # Papas a la Huancaina

Heat Scale: 4
Serves: 4 to 6

6 dried ground Mirasol chiles, stems and seeds removed
2 Ají or 3 Jalapeño chiles, stems and seeds removed, chopped
1/2 cup lemon juice
1 medium onion, thinly sliced and separated into rings
6 potatoes, boiled and diced
1 cup *queso blanco* or Munster cheese
1 cup heavy cream
2 tablespoons olive oil
8 black olives
2 hard-cooked eggs, cut in wedges

This dish of potatoes, cheese, and hot chile sauce is from Huancayo in the highlands of Peru. It probably evolved from an Incan recipe after the Spanish introduced cheese to the Indians. A regional herb called palillo *(which imparts a bright yellow color to food) is hard to find, but turmeric makes an acceptable substitute.*

Mix the Mirasol chiles and the lemon juice. Add the onion rings and toss until coated. Marinate, at room temperature, for an hour, then drain.

Combine the Ají or Jalapeño chiles, cheese, and cream in a blender and puree until smooth. Heat the oil and slowly add the cheese mixture, stirring constantly. Simmer the sauce for 5 minutes or until it thickens.

To Serve: Place the hot potatoes on a platter, pour the sauce over the top, and garnish with the marinated onion rings and olives. Arrange the egg wedges around the potatoes and serve.

Serving Suggestions: This rich dish is best when served with broiled meat, poultry, or fish. A simple vegetable and salad make a complete meal.

Ceviche with Ajís

Heat Scale: 4
Serves: 4

Note: This recipe requires
advance preparation.

4 Ají or Serrano chiles,
  stems and seeds removed,
  cut in strips
1 pound firm white fish
  (snapper, pompano,
  flounder, or bass), cut into
  1 1/2-inch cubes
1 small red or Bermuda
  onion, thinly sliced and
  separated into rings
1 cup bitter orange juice*
1 large sweet potato
2 ears corn, cut in half

There are many ceviche (or "seviche") dishes throughout all of Latin America, but the original recipe for this tasty appetizer is credited to Peru. The acid in the orange or lemon juice "cooks" the fish, and the recipe probably began out of a need to preserve fish before refrigeration. Be sure to use a ceramic or glass dish; never use a metallic one!

Cover the chiles, fish, and onions with the juice and refrigerate for 4 hours, turning occasionally until the fish loses its translucency and turns opaque.

Cook the sweet potatoes until done. Peel and cut them into 4 slices. Cook the corn until done.

To Serve: Arrange the fish and onions on a bed of lettuce and place a sweet potato slice on one side and a corn portion on the opposite side.

Variation: Substitute whole kernel corn for the corn on the cob. Either marinate the corn with the fish or mix with the fish before serving.

*Bitter, or Seville, oranges are found in Latin markets. If not available, substitute 1/2 cup orange and 1/2 cup lemon juice.

Peruvian Anticuchos

Heat Scale: 6
Serves: 8 to 10
Note: This recipe requires advance preparation.

Marinade:

3 Ají or Jalapeño chiles, stems and seeds removed, chopped
3 tablespoons dried crushed red chiles such as Piquins, seeds included
1 tablespoon *achiote**
1 1/2 teaspoons cumin seeds
2 tablespoons olive oil
4 cloves garlic, chopped
3/4 cup red wine vinegar
1 teaspoon salt
freshly ground black pepper

3 to 4 pounds sirloin beef, cut into 1-inch cubes

Anticuchos are commonly sold by street vendors in Peru as a snack, but they also make a good party hors d'oeuvre. Traditionally, they are made only with beef heart, but other cuts of meats can be successfully substituted.

Simmer the annatto and cumin seeds in the oil for 5 minutes. Strain the oil and discard the seeds.

Place all the ingredients for the marinade in a blender and puree until smooth. Marinate the beef cubes in the mixture overnight in the refrigerator.

Thread the beef on skewers and grill over charcoal or under the broiler until medium-rare, basting frequently with the marinade.

Variation: Substitute boneless chicken breasts for the beef.

*The red seeds of the annatto tree. Used as a seasoning and to impart a yellow coloring. Available in Latin markets.

Vatapá de Camarão e Peixe

Heat Scale: 4
Serves: 6

3 teaspoons dried ground red New Mexican or Cayenne chile
1 teaspoon ground Paprika
1 pound shrimp, peeled and deveined
1 pound firm white fish (snapper, flounder, or pompano), cut in 2-inch pieces
2 tablespoons vegetable oil

Famous throughout the world, this dish reflects African influences (possibly Sudanese) as well as the abundance of shrimp in Brazil. Combining coconut milk and nuts produces a very rich, creamy sauce, and the addition of peixe *(fish) creates a dish that is very popular in Bahia, where this recipe originated. Dende oil, which is made from the* dende *palm, is traditionally used, but since it is difficult to find and high in saturated fat, vegetable oil is an acceptable substitute.*

Lightly brown the shrimp and fish in the oil, adding the shrimp a few at a time. Remove and drain.

Add the onion to the pan and sauté until soft and transparent.

1 medium onion, finely
  chopped
3 teaspoons ground ginger
2 small tomatoes, peeled
  and seeds removed,
  chopped
1 1/2 cups milk
1 cup unsweetened coconut
  milk
1/2 cup ground almonds
1/2 cup ground cashew nuts
1 cup ground dried shrimp*

Reduce the heat and add the chiles, Paprika, ginger, and tomatoes. Cover and cook over medium heat for 5 minutes.

Stir in the milk, coconut milk, almonds, cashews, and dried shrimp. Simmer over a low heat for 15 minutes. Put the sauce in a blender and puree until smooth.

Return the sauce to the heat and cook, stirring constantly, until thickened. Add the fish and shrimp and simmer until thoroughly heated, about 5 minutes.

Serving Suggestions: Serve over rice, accompanied by slices of fresh orange and a green vegetable.

Variation: Substitute chicken for the white fish.

*Available Latin or Asian markets.

Salsa Carioca

Heat Scale: 4
Serves: 4

The Dressing:

3 teaspoons hot pepper
  sauce, such as a Lousiana-
  type Tabasco sauce or a
  Caribbean-type Habanero
  sauce
3 tablespoons olive oil
1 tablespoon white vinegar
1 tablespoon chopped fresh
  parsley
1/4 teaspoon ground
  coriander
1/2 teaspoon freshly ground
  black pepper

The Salad:

2 Serrano chiles, stems
  removed, finely chopped
1 small onion, finely
  chopped
1 small tomato, chopped
1 avocado, peeled and
  chopped
2 hard-cooked eggs,
  chopped

This recipe could probably be called the South American version of guacamole. It is served in Brazil and Venezuela in individual glasses as a salad or as an accompaniment to grilled or roasted meats.

Combine all the ingredients for the dressing and allow it to sit for an hour or more to blend the flavors.

Mix the ingredients for the salad and toss with the dressing until well coated.

Bahian Moqueca

Heat Scale: 4
Serves: 4

4 Serrano chiles, stems and
  seeds removed, chopped
1 small Bell pepper, stem
  and seeds removed,
  chopped
2 medium tomatoes, peeled
  and seeds removed,
  chopped
1 medium onion, chopped
2 cloves garlic, chopped
2 tablespoons chopped fresh
  cilantro
3 tablespoons lime juice
2 tablespoons peanut oil
2 pounds fish fillets (sole,
  cod, haddock, or snapper)

Unlike other areas of Central and South America, Brazil had no great Indian civilization, so much of the cuisine of the country originated with the Portuguese and the slaves they brought from West Africa. Nowhere are these influences more evident than in the cooking of Bahia. This dish probably began as a mixture cooked in a banana leaf, and, when the Europeans provided cooking pots, stews emerged. The Africans added the dende *oil that is traditionally used in the preparation. We have substituted the healthier peanut oil. A hot sauce of tiny "malagueta" peppers in* dende *oil mixed with manioc is served on the side to increase the heat.*

Combine the chiles, Bell pepper, tomatoes, onion, garlic, cilantro, and lime juice in a blender and puree until smooth. Sauté the sauce in 1 tablespoon of the oil for 10 minutes, stirring frequently.

Allow the sauce to cool, pour over the fish, and marinate for an hour.

Place the fish, marinade, the remainder of the oil, and a cup of water in a pan. Simmer the fish in the sauce until done, about 5 to 8 minutes.

Serving Suggestions: A traditional meal includes white rice or a side of black beans and okra with peanuts.

Grilled Flank Steak with Chimichurri Sauce

Heat Scale: 3
Serves: 6
Note: This recipe requires advance preparation.

Chimichurri Sauce:

4 Jalapeño chiles, stems and seeds removed, finely chopped
1/2 cup finely chopped onion
4 cloves garlic, minced
1/4 cup chopped fresh parsley
1 teaspoon chopped fresh oregano
1 teaspoon freshly ground black pepper
1/2 cup olive oil
1/4 cup red wine vinegar
2 tablespoons lemon juice
1/4 cup water

1 2-pound flank steak

Argentines love a barbecue, or churrasco, cooked on a parrilla or grill over coals. A gaucho would not even bother with a fork when eating a churrasco on the pampas. He would secure the piece of meat with his teeth, cut off bite-size pieces of meat with his knife, and eat the pieces with his fingers. In the United States, forks are used and the meat is served with the popular parsley-based Chimichurri Sauce.

Combine all the ingredients for the Chimichurri Sauce.

Score each side of the steak about 1/8 to 1/4 inch deep and rub in the sauce, reserving some sauce to serve with the meal. Place the meat and the marinade in a ceramic or glass pan and marinate overnight in the refrigerator. Remove the meat and extra sauce from the refrigerator and allow to sit at room temperature before grilling.

Grill the meat over charcoal or under a broiler until medium-rare. Carve the steak immediately across the grain into strips about 1/4 inch wide and serve with the extra sauce. If the meat is allowed to sit before carving, it will toughen.

Serving Suggestions: Serve with crusty French bread, fried potatoes, carrots, and a green salad.

Spicy Empanadas

Heat Scale: 3
Yield: 12

The Pastry:

2 cups flour
2 teaspoons baking powder
1/2 teaspoon salt
2/3 cup solid shortening
1/3 cup cold water
1 egg, beaten

The Filling:

2 tablespoons small dried chiles such as Piquins, crushed, including the seeds
1 small onion, finely chopped
2 tablespoons olive oil
3/4 pound lean ground beef
1 medium potato, peeled, parboiled 5 minutes, finely grated
1 teaspoon ground cumin
1 tablespoon finely chopped walnuts
2 hard-cooked eggs, chopped

Variations on this all-time Argentine favorite can be found in every Spanish-speaking country around the world. Similar pastries are made in other countries, such as Cornish pasties, Polish pierogis, Jamaican patties, and Indian samosas. Any type of filling can be used, from meats, potatoes, or vegetables to fruits and nuts. Large empanadas are eaten as a light meal, and smaller versions called empanaditas *make excellent appetizers.*

Sift the dry ingredients together.

Using a pastry blender, cut the shortening into the dry ingredients until the flour has the texture of fine crumbs. Add just enough of the water so that the mixture holds together. Chill for 1 hour.

Sauté the onion in the oil until softened. Add the meat and cook until the meat has browned. Pour off all except 2 tablespoons of the remaining oil. Add the chiles, potatoes, and cumin. Continue to cook until the potatoes are done. Set aside and cool before adding the walnuts and hard-cooked eggs.

Roll the dough out 1/8 inch thick and cut into circles 5 inches in diameter. Place 2 tablespoons of the filling on one half of each circle and fold over. Moisten the edges with water and crimp with a fork to seal.

Brush the top of each half circle with beaten egg and bake in a 400° F oven for 15 to 20 minutes or until golden brown. Or, deep-fry in 365° F oil until golden brown. Remove and drain.

Serving Suggestions: Serve with a crisp garden salad for a light lunch.

Variations: Vary the fillings by using pork and green chile, chicken and broccoli, or apricots, peaches, and chile.

Haitian Hot Pepper Sauce

Heat Scale: 6
Yield: 2 cups

3 Habanero or 6 Serrano
  chiles, stems removed,
  chopped
1/2 cup papaya, chopped
1/2 cup raisins
1 cup finely chopped onions
3 cloves garlic, minced
1/2 teaspoon turmeric
1/4 cup malt vinegar

Nearly every island in the Caribbean has its own version of a hot pepper sauce. In fact, pepper sauces can be found on the table of virtually every Caribbean restaurant. This Haitian version combines fruits, as well as chiles, to produce a hot and sweet sauce.

Combine all the ingredients in a sauce pan and bring to a boil, stirring constantly. Reduce the heat and cook for an additional 5 minutes. Put the mixture in a blender and puree until smooth.

Serving Suggestions: This sauce goes well with fish, poultry, and pork. It can be added to soups and chowders.

Stoba

Heat Scale: 5
Serves: 6

3 Habanero or 6 Jalapeño
  chiles, stems removed,
  chopped
1 small Bell pepper,
  chopped
2 pounds boneless lamb, cut
  into 2-inch cubes
2 tablespoons vegetable oil
2 medium onions, chopped
4 cloves garlic, chopped
1/2 cup chopped celery
1 teaspoon finely chopped
  fresh ginger
2 medium tomatoes, peeled
  and chopped
3 tablespoons lime juice
1 teaspoon ground cumin
1 teaspoon ground allspice
1 tablespoon vinegar
1 large cucumber, peeled
  and chopped
1/4 cup pitted green olives
1 tablespoon capers

On the island of Curaçao in the Netherlands Antilles, where hundreds of goats roam free, this dish would be prepared with goat instead of lamb, which is more commonly available in the United States. The cucumbers in this recipe are the small round tropical variety, called lemon cucumbers, but any cuke works well.

Brown the lamb in the oil. Remove and drain. Add the onions, garlic, celery, ginger, chiles, and Bell pepper to the pan and sauté until the onions are soft.

Combine the lamb, onion mixture, tomatoes, lime juice, cumin, allspice, and cover with water. Simmer the mixture until the meat is very tender and starts to fall apart, about 1 1/2 hours. Add more water if necessary.

Add the vinegar, cucumber, olives, and capers and simmer for an additional 15 minutes.

Serving Suggestions: A crisp garden salad and some crusty rolls are all that is needed to complete a meal.

Picadillo Picante

Heat Scale: 6
Serves: 4

6 green New Mexican
  chiles, roasted, peeled,
  stems and seeds removed,
  chopped
1 teaspoon ground Cayenne
1 pound pork, cut in
  1 1/2-inch cubes
2 tablespoons vegetable oil
1 cup chopped onions
3 cloves garlic, chopped
2 cups chicken broth
2 small tomatoes, peeled,
  seeded, chopped
2 tablespoons raisins
2 tablespoons red wine
  vinegar
1/4 teaspoon ground
  cinnamon
1/4 teaspoon ground cumin
1/4 teaspoon ground cloves
1/8 teaspoon ground allspice
1/4 cup stuffed green olives,
  chopped
1/4 cup blanched almonds,
  chopped

This famous Cuban dish is Spanish in origin, and variations can be found in most Latin American countries. Picadillo is a kind of Latin "hash" and is made with either shredded or ground meats. Serve it as an entree or as a filling for burritos or tacos.

Brown the pork in the oil. Add the onion and garlic and sauté until soft.

Add the remaining ingredients, except the olives and almonds, and simmer for an hour or until the meat is tender and most of the liquid is absorbed.

Before serving, add the olives and almonds.

Serving Suggestions: Traditionally served with white rice, black beans, and fried plantains.

Variation: Use beef in place of the pork and add bananas and chopped pineapple in place of the raisins and olives. Shred the meat instead of leaving it in cubes and use as a filling for burritos or tacos.

Jerk Pork with Pimento Season-Up

Heat Scale: 5
Serves: 4

4 Habanero or 7 Jalapeño
  chiles, stems and seeds
  removed, chopped

The "jerk" in jerk pork is a spice mixture that was used to preserve meat before refrigeration. It was developed in Jamaica by runaway slaves known as Maroons. These days, the spices are used to season meats for barbecue and to tenderize rather than to preserve. In Jamaica, jerk pork is one of the most popular

2 ounces fresh pimento
  berries, or substitute 1/4
  cup powdered allspice
3 tablespoons lime juice
2 tablespoons chopped
  scallions
1 teaspoon ground
  cinnamon
1 teaspoon ground nutmeg
4 center-cut pork chops

entrées, and features fresh pimento (allspice) berries, which should not be confused with pimiento, the mild pepper used to stuff olives.

Pound or puree all the ingredients, except the pork, to make a thick paste. Spread the paste over the chops and marinate for one hour or longer.

Grill the chops over a hot charcoal fire until done. The seasonings will cause the chops to char on the outside, which is natural for this dish.

Serving Suggestions: A tomato and cucumber salad and coconut rice complement jerk pork.

Variations: Substitute lamb chops, chicken, or rib steaks for the pork.

 # Hot Bajan Chicken

Heat Scale: 4
Serves: 4

3 Habanero chiles, stems
  and seeds removed, finely
  chopped
1 tablespoon Louisiana-type
  Tabasco sauce or
  Caribbean-type Habanero
  sauce
4 chicken breasts
6 scallions, finely chopped,
  including the greens
3 cloves garlic, minced
2 tablespoons lime juice
2 tablespoons chopped fresh
  parsley
1/2 teaspoon ground cloves
1/2 teaspoon freshly ground
  black pepper
1 egg
1 tablespoon soy sauce
flour for dredging
3 cups dry breadcrumbs
vegetable oil for frying

This fried chicken, Barbados-style, is prepared with a spice blend called bajan *that is stuffed in slits or pockets cut into the chicken meat. Bajan blends are common on the island and cooks keep their own private blends in the refrigerator to use in a variety of recipes.*

Cover the chicken with water and simmer for 30 minutes or until tender, skimming off any foam that forms. Remove and drain.

Combine the chiles, scallions, garlic, lime juice, parsley, cloves, and ground pepper. Cut deep gashes in the chicken and fill with the mixture.

Beat together the egg, soy sauce, and pepper sauce. Lightly dust the chicken with the flour, dip in the egg mixture, and roll in the bread crumbs.

Heat the oil to 375° F and fry the chicken until golden brown, about 3 to 4 minutes on each side.

Serving Suggestions: This chicken goes well with au gratin potatoes and minted peas.

Spicy Pumpkin Bisque

Heat Scale: 5
Serves: 4

1 1/2 teaspoons dried
    ground small red chiles
    such as Piquins
1 large onion, chopped
2 garlic cloves, chopped
1 tablespoon butter or
    margarine
1 16-ounce can pumpkin
    puree
4 cups chicken stock
1/2 teaspoon freshly ground
    black pepper
1/4 teaspoon ground allspice
1/2 teaspoon sugar
1 cup half-and-half or light
    cream
1/4 cup dry sherry
grated nutmeg

Calabaza is a very popular pumpkin-like squash that appears in many Caribbean recipes, including soups such as this one from Barbados. The Caribbean pumpkin is much smaller than those we carve for Halloween. Cooked and pureed butternut or Hubbard squash can be substituted for the pumpkin; although the taste is slightly different, it is still delicious.

Sauté the onion and garlic in the butter until they are soft and transparent.

Add the pumpkin, stock, chile pepper, ground pepper, allspice, sugar, and sherry. Bring to a boil and cover. Simmer the soup for 30 minutes. Place the mixture in a blender and puree until smooth.

Return the soup to the pot, add the half-and-half, and simmer until heated. Garnish with the nutmeg and serve.

Serving Suggestions: This soup can be served either hot or cold. Serve it hot with grilled fish and seasoned green beans or cold as a luncheon entrée with a crisp garden salad.

Pepper Pot Stew

Heat Scale: 4
Serves: 6 to 8

5 green New Mexican
    chiles, roasted, peeled,
    stems and seeds removed,
    chopped
1 2 1/2-pound chicken, cut
    into serving pieces
1 pound lean pork or beef,
    cut into 1 1/2- to 2-inch
    cubes
2 tablespoons vegetable oil
1 large onion, coarsely
    chopped

This stew should not be confused with the soup of the same name; it is a modern adaptation of a very old recipe handed down from the Carib Indians in Trinidad, Tobago, Saint Kitts, and Barbados. This stew plays the sweet against the bitter and in the islands obtains its unique flavor from cassareep, *which is raw cassava juice that has been boiled down with salt, brown sugar, cinnamon, and cloves. We have made appropriate substitutions. It is said in the islands that a pepper pot is always cooking, with fresh meats and other vegetables added daily and that some of these "pots" have been going for generations.*

Cover the chicken with water, bring to a boil, reduce the heat, and simmer for 45 minutes, skimming off any foam that forms.

3 tablespoons brown sugar

2 teaspoons ground cinnamon

2 teaspoons ground cloves

2 tablespoons vinegar

Remove the chicken and reserve the broth. Remove the chicken meat from the bone and chop.

Brown the pork or beef in the oil. Add the onions and sauté until soft.

Combine all the ingredients, except the vinegar, in the broth and simmer for an hour or until the meat is very tender and the stew is thick. Stir in the vinegar and serve.

Serving Suggestions: Boiled potatoes, seasoned greens, and fresh pineapple chunks go well with this spiced stew.

Conch and Chile Fritters

Heat Scale: 4

Serves: 4 to 6

4 Habanero or 6 Jalapeño chiles, stems and seeds removed

1/4 teaspoon ground Cayenne

1 package dry yeast

1 cup warm milk (110° F)

1 pound canned or fresh conch

1 large onion, finely chopped

2 teaspoons finely chopped fresh parsley

2 teaspoons Worcestershire sauce

1/2 teaspoon freshly ground black pepper

1 egg, beaten

2 cups all-purpose flour

vegetable oil for frying

Conch is a mollusk that lives in those large spiral pink shells that are so common throughout the Caribbean. Their meat is tough and needs to be tenderized by pounding, but this recipe makes it easier by processing it in a blender. If canned conch is unavailable, substitute clams.

Dissolve the yeast in the warm milk and let sit for 15 minutes.

Place the conch in a blender and chop into small pieces.

Mix all the ingredients together, adding the flour last. When the mixture is well combined, cover and let sit for an hour.

Heat the oil to about 350° F. Drop the fritter mix into the oil by the teaspoonful and cook until golden brown, about 3 to 5 minutes. Remove and drain.

Serving Suggestions: Serve as an appetizer with Haitian Hot Pepper Sauce for dipping (see recipe this chapter).

Guatemalan Jocon

Heat Scale: 3
Serves: 4

4 dried Chipotle chiles, stems removed
1 3-pound chicken, cut in serving pieces
1 small onion, chopped
2 cloves garlic, chopped
1 quart water
1 tablespoon pumpkin seeds
1/2 cup chopped fresh cilantro
1 tablespoon vegetable corn oil
1 cup chopped scallions, including the greens
1/2 cup canned tomatillos, drained and chopped

There are many versions of this chicken in green sauce throughout Guatemala. The concept is Mayan, and, after the Spanish introduced onions and cilantro, this recipe evolved. Coban chiles are traditionally used in this dish, but since they are difficult to find outside of Guatemala, Chipotle chiles have been substituted.

Cover the chicken, onion, and garlic with water, bring to a boil, reduce the heat, and simmer until done — about 30 minutes — skimming off any foam that forms. Remove the chicken, strain and reserve the broth.

Cover the chiles with boiling water and allow them to sit for 15 minutes to soften.

Toast the seeds in a hot skillet until they start to brown, taking care not to let them burn. Grind the seeds in a blender or mortar and pestle.

Combine the chiles, toasted seeds, cilantro, scallions, and tomatillos in a blender along with 2 cups of the chicken broth and puree until smooth.

Remove the skin and brown the chicken in the oil.

Combine the sauce with 1 cup of the reserved broth and pour over the chicken. Simmer for 15 minutes before serving.

Serving Suggestions: Serve with fried rice and black beans, corn tortillas, and sliced papaya.

Black Bean Soup with Jalapeños

Heat Scale: 7
Serves: 8

Note: This recipe requires advance preparation.

8 Jalapeño chiles, stems and seeds removed, chopped
1 tablespoon dried crushed red chile, seeds included

Black beans, also called "turtle" beans, are a favorite in the Yucatan Peninsula and other parts of Central America. This hearty soup can be either a first course or an entrée.

Cover the beans with water and soak them overnight.

Sauté the onion and garlic in the bacon fat until soft.

Combine all the ingredients, except the tequila and sour cream, in a large pot and bring to a boil. Reduce the heat and simmer for 2 to 3 hours or until the beans are soft.

2 cups black beans, sorted
and rinsed
2 tablespoons bacon fat or
vegetable oil
2 medium onions, chopped
4 cloves garlic, minced
1 large ham hock
1 cup canned tomatoes,
chopped
2 teaspoons ground cumin
1 teaspoon ground epazote
(optional)
1 teaspoon ground
coriander
1/4 teaspoon ground cloves
1 tablespoon red wine
vinegar
6 to 8 cups water
3 tablespoons tequila
(optional)
sour cream for garnish

Remove the ham hock and shred the meat.

Divide the soup in half, puree half of it and add back to the remaining soup. Add the shredded meat and simmer for 15 minutes or until thickened to the desired consistency.

Remove from the heat, stir in the tequila, garnish with the sour cream, and serve.

Serving Suggestions: Serve as a lunch entrée with warmed flour tortillas and a citrus salad.

 # Pico de Gallo Salsa

Heat Scale: 6
Yield: 2 cups

6 Serrano or Jalapeño chiles,
stems and seeds removed,
finely chopped
1 large onion, finely
chopped
2 medium tomatoes, finely
chopped
3 cloves garlic, finely
chopped
1/4 cup finely chopped fresh
cilantro
1/4 cup oil
3 tablespoons red wine
vinegar

This blend of hot chile and fresh vegetables is known by a number of names — salsa fría, salsa cruda, salsa fresca, and salsa Mexicana, to name a few. Variations of this salsa can be found on tables with tostada chips from Tapachula to Chihuahua to the American Southwest. It is excellent as a dip and also as a salsa on tacos, enchiladas, grilled meats or poultry, and on any dish where the addition of tasty heat is desired. The important thing to remember is to chop all the ingredients finely by hand.

Mix all the ingredients together. Allow the salsa to sit at room temperature for an hour before serving.

Tomatillo Sauce

Heat Scale: 6
Yield: 1 1/2 cups

8 Serrano chiles, stems
  removed, chopped
1/2 pound tomatillos
1 small onion, chopped
4 cloves garlic, chopped
1 tablespoon vegetable oil

Tomatillos are small, hard green fruits that are covered with a paper-like husk. They are not green tomatoes, although they are called tomate verde *in Mexico. If they are not available fresh, there are a number of canned brands available in markets. They are very easy to grow and, in fact, reseed themselves and can become invasive if left alone. There are a number of variations of this sauce, some being* cruda *(uncooked), or, as with this recipe,* cocida *(cooked). This sauce complements poultry, pork, or beef. It can also be served with carnitas, enchiladas, and tacos.*

Remove the husks from the tomatillos and rinse well. Cover with water, bring to a boil, reduce the heat, and simmer for 5 minutes or until soft and transparent.

Place the tomatillos and a little of the cooking water, chiles, onion, and garlic in a blender and puree until smooth.

Heat the oil and sauté the sauce for 5 minutes.

Serving Suggestions: This sauce is used with Chile Carnitas (see recipe this chapter).

Variations: For a sauce with a "toasted" taste, heat the tomatillos on a heavy skillet, turning frequently, until the husks are quite brown and the fruit is soft. Remove the husk and use the tomatillos. Do not puree the sauce for a chunkier, salsa-type sauce.

Classic Mole Poblano Sauce

Heat Scale: 4
Yield: 2 cups

4 dried Pasilla chiles, stems and seeds removed

4 dried red New Mexican chiles, stems and seeds removed

1 medium onion, chopped

2 cloves garlic, chopped

2 medium tomatoes, peeled and seeds removed, chopped

2 tablespoons sesame seeds

1/2 cup almonds

1/2 corn tortilla, torn into pieces

1/4 cup raisins

1/4 teaspoon ground cloves

1/4 teaspoon ground cinnamon

1/4 teaspoon ground coriander

3 tablespoons shortening or vegetable oil

1 cup chicken broth

1 ounce bitter chocolate (or more to taste)

This subtle blend of chocolate and chile is unusual but quite tasty. It is called the "National Dish of Mexico" when it is served over turkey, and the sauce can also be used in a number of other ways, such as with enchiladas. Descended from the Aztec chi-lemolli *dish, this version is probably the richest.*

Combine the chiles, onion, garlic, tomatoes, 1 tablespoon of the sesame seeds, almonds, tortilla, raisins, cloves, cinnamon, and coriander. Puree small amounts of this mixture in a blender until smooth.

Melt the shortening in a skillet and sauté the puree for 10 minutes, stirring frequently. Add the chicken broth and chocolate and cook over a very low heat for 45 minutes. The sauce should be very thick. The remaining sesame seeds are used as a garnish.

Serving Suggestions: This sauce is excellent with poultry; serve it over a turkey or chicken breast. It is also excellent as a sauce over shredded chicken or over turkey enchiladas.

Chiles en Nogada

Heat Scale: 2
Serves: 6

6 Poblano chiles, roasted
  and peeled
3/4 pound ground pork
1 small onion, chopped
3 cloves garlic, minced
1 tablespoon vegetable oil
1 small tomato, peeled and
  seeds removed, chopped
1 apple, peeled and chopped
1/2 cup raisins, soaked in
  water to plump
1/2 cup blanched almonds,
  chopped
1 teaspoon sugar
1 teaspoon ground
  cinnamon
1/2 teaspoon ground cloves
3/4 cup flour
2 eggs, beaten
vegetable oil for frying

Nogada Sauce:

1 cup walnuts, chopped
1 3-ounce package cream
  cheese
1 tablespoon sugar
1 cup half-and-half
1/4 cup pomegranate seeds
chopped fresh cilantro for
  garnish

This elegant dish originated in the town of Puebla to commemorate Mexican independence and is served throughout the country on special patriotic holidays such as Cinco de Mayo (the anniversary of the beginning of independence from the French), the sixteenth of September (commemorating the beginning of the fight against the Spanish), and St. Augustine Day (the anniversary of the day that General Augustin defeated the French). The chiles are served warm rather than hot, covered with a white sauce, and garnished with red pomegranate seeds and green chopped cilantro — the colors of the Mexican flag.

Brown the pork, onion, and garlic in the oil until the pork is no longer pink. Add the tomato, apple, raisins, almonds, sugar, cinnamon, and cloves. Simmer the mixture until almost dry.

Make slits in the chiles and stuff them with the pork mixture. Dust the chiles with the flour, dip them in the egg, and then again in the flour. Fry the chiles in 375° F oil until browned. Remove and drain.

To Make the Sauce: Place all the ingredients in a blender and puree until smooth. Add enough of the half-and-half to make an easy-to-pour sauce.

To Serve: Place the chiles on a plate, pour the sauce over them, and garnish with the seeds and cilantro.

Serving Suggestions: Serve with Low-Sodium Caldillo (see recipe Chapter 8) and avocado and grapefruit slices.

Variations: These chiles can be stuffed with a variety of fillings such as Picadillo Picante (see recipe this chapter) or white cheese and chicken.

Shrimp in Adobo Sauce

Heat Scale: 3
Serves: 6

3 large dried Ancho chiles,
  stems and seeds removed
1 dried Pasilla chile, stem
  and seeds removed
1 large onion, chopped
2 cloves garlic, chopped
1/2 teaspoon dried oregano
1/4 teaspoon ground cumin
1/4 cup vegetable oil
1/4 cup distilled white
  vinegar
1 1/2 teaspoons sugar
1 1/2 pounds large shrimp,
  shelled and deveined

Adobo is a sauce made with chiles, vinegar, herbs, and garlic that is popular in the Phillipines as well as in Mexico. This type of sauce was also used to preserve meats before refrigeration. Mixed with shrimp, it makes an unusual entrée — but be sure to use large shrimp so that their flavor is not lost in the sauce.

Cover the chiles with hot water and let them sit for 15 minutes until softened. Combine the chiles and 1/4 to 1/2 cup of the water they were soaking in, onion, garlic, oregano, and cumin in a blender and puree to a smooth paste.

Sauté the chile mixture in the oil for 5 minutes, add the vinegar and sugar, and bring to a boil. Reduce the heat and simmer until the sauce is very thick, about 5 to 8 minutes.

Add the shrimp to the sauce and toss to coat, then simmer for 5 to 8 minutes until the shrimp are done.

Serving Suggestions: Serve on a bed of cilantro rice with an Apple-Jicama Salad (see recipe Chapter 8).

Huachinango a la Vera Cruz

Heat Scale: 4
Serves: 4 to 6

4 pickled Jalapeño chiles,
  stems and seeds removed,
  cut into strips
1 large onion, chopped
3 cloves garlic, chopped
4 tablespoons olive oil
2 medium tomatoes, peeled
  and seeds removed,
  chopped
1/4 cup pimiento-stuffed
  green olives
2 tablespoons lemon juice
2 bay leaves
1/2 teaspoon sugar
1/2 teaspoon ground thyme
1/4 teaspoon ground
  cinnamon
1/4 teaspoon ground cloves
2 tablespoons capers
1 whole red snapper or 2
  pounds snapper fillets
flour for dredging
chopped fresh parsley or
  cilantro for garnish

Legend holds that Montezuma loved fresh fish so much that he had teams of relay runners bring them from the coast to his palace in Mexico City. Today, Mexicans are equally fond of fish and this dish from the city of Vera Cruz is probably one of the most famous. Huachinango refers to red snapper, but any firm white fish can be used. The pickled chiles, called jalapeños en escabeche (available in Latin markets), add a distinctive taste to the dish, but if these are not available, substitute fresh ones.

Sauté the onion and garlic in 2 tablespoons of the oil until soft. Add the chiles, tomatoes, olives, lemon juice, bay leaves, sugar, thyme, cinnamon, and cloves; bring to a boil, reduce the heat, and simmer for 15 minutes. Add the capers to the sauce and keep the sauce warm.

Lightly dust the fish with the flour and sauté the fish in the remaining oil until browned on both sides and flakes easily.

Place the fish on a platter, cover with the sauce, garnish with the chopped cilantro, and serve.

Serving Suggestions: Start the meal with an appetizer of Guacamole (see recipe Chapter 5) and chips; serve the fish on a bed of rice accompanied with green beans and corn tortillas.

Chile Carnitas

Heat Scale: 3
Serves: 6

1 tablespoon dried ground
  red New Mexican chile
1/4 teaspoon freshly ground
  black pepper
1 teaspoon ground cumin

These "little pieces of meat" are served throughout Mexico and make a very tasty antojito (snack or appetizer). The meats should be crisp on the outside and moist on the inside. Serve them with a variety of sauces for dipping, warm flour tortillas, and ice-cold Mexican beer.

Combine all the spices and rub the pork cubes with the mixture.

3 cloves garlic, minced
2 teaspoons finely chopped
  fresh cilantro
3/4 teaspoon salt
1 pound boneless pork,
  trimmed and cut into
  1-inch cubes

Let the meat marinate at room temperature for an hour.

Bake the cubes on a rack over a baking sheet for 1 1/2 hours at 250° F, or until the meat is quite crisp.

Serving Suggestions: Serve in a chafing dish with toothpicks accompanied by Pico de Gallo Salsa (see recipe this chapter), Tomatillo Sauce (see recipe this chapter), Guacamole (see recipe Chapter 5) for dipping, sour cream, chopped onions, and chopped cilantro together with flour tortillas, and allow guests to assemble their own burritos.

Chicken Flautas with Avocado Hot Sauce

Yield: 12

1 cup Avocado Hot Sauce
  (see following recipe)
1 medium onion, chopped
3 cloves garlic, chopped
2 tablespoons oil
2 chicken breasts, poached,
  skin removed, shredded
1/4 cup chopped fresh
  cilantro or 1/4 teaspoon
  ground cumin
1/4 cup sour cream
1 cup grated Monterey Jack
  cheese
24 corn tortillas
vegetable oil for frying

Flautas, or "flutes," are rolled, fried tortillas similar to taquitos except that two tortillas are rolled together to form a long flute that is dipped into avocado sauce or salsa after frying.

Sauté the onion and garlic in the oil until soft.

Mix the onion, chicken, cilantro, and sour cream.

Heat the oil and heat the tortillas, one at a time, for 5 seconds to soften, being careful they do not become crisp.

Overlap two tortillas (cover one half of one with the other) and place on it a couple of tablespoons of the filling, sprinkle with cheese, roll tightly, and secure with toothpicks. Deep-fry until crisp and browned, then drain. Remove the toothpicks and serve with avocado sauce on the side for dipping.

Avocado Hot Sauce

Heat Scale: 6
Yield: 3/4 to 1 cup

4 Serrano chiles, stems,
  seeds removed, chopped
3 teaspoons liquid hot sauce
2 avocados, pitted and
  peeled
2 tablespoons chopped
  onion
1/2 teaspoon chopped garlic

Place all the ingredients in a blender and puree until smooth.

Chilaquiles

Heat Scale: 6
Serves: 4

6 dried red New Mexican
  chiles, stems and seeds
  removed
1 dried Chipotle chile, stem
  removed (optional)
1 small onion, chopped
2 cloves garlic, chopped
2 tablespoons vegetable oil
1 medium tomato, peeled
  and seeds removed,
  chopped
1/2 teaspoon ground cumin
1 dozen corn tortillas, cut in
  strips
vegetable oil for frying
1 pound chorizo sausage,
  cooked and crumbled
1 cup cooked pinto beans
1 cup chicken broth
1/2 pound crumbled *queso
  fresco* or Monterey Jack
  cheese
1/2 cup chopped onion, for
  garnish

Chilaquiles is an idiom that translates into "broken-up sombrero" and refers to the "stale or dry" corn tortilla strips in this casserole simmered in a chile sauce. Actually, it is a tasty way to use any tortillas that have become stale. The following recipe adds chorizo (a spicy Mexican sausage) and beans for additional flavor, but they can be omitted for a simpler entrée.

Cover the chiles with hot water and let them sit for 15 minutes until softened. Place the chiles in a blender with one cup of the water in which they were soaked and puree until smooth.

Sauté the onion and garlic in the oil until soft. Stir in the chile sauce, tomato, and cumin and simmer the sauce for 10 minutes. Put the sauce in a blender and puree until smooth.

Fry the tortilla strips in the oil until chewy but not crisp.

Combine the chile sauce, chicken broth, chorizo, and the beans, and simmer for an additional 5 to 10 minutes.

Stir in the tortilla strips, top with the cheese and chopped onion, and serve.

Serving Suggestions: Serve with refried beans, seasoned corn, and avocado slices.

Variations: Substitute shredded chicken for the chorizo and beans and garnish with sour cream.

CHAPTER FIVE

The Spicy Southwest

"You can keep your dear old Boston,
Home of bass and cods;
We've opted for New Mexico and chile,
The food of the Gods!"

Miles Standish IV, 1842

A vast majority of Americans believe that the standard fare of the Southwest is Mexican food. They are wrong on two counts. First, the term "Mexican food" in the United States generally means tacos and beans and is far too sweeping to define the marvelous diversity of highly spiced meals served south of the border. Second, although some of the names of the dishes may be the same, the Mexican-*influenced* food of the American Southwest has, through time, been transformed into several distinct cuisines that can stand quite well on their own.

Fortunately, in recent years there has been a greater awareness among food lovers that some of the most exciting and delicious food in America is being prepared and served in the Southwest, as evidenced by the flood of cookbooks and restaurants devoted to the subject. And although there are significant differences among the Southwestern dishes served from Texas to California, there is one common denominator: chile peppers.

The Fiery Invasion of the USA

According to most accounts, chile peppers were introduced into what is now the United States by Capitán General Juan de Oñate, who founded Santa Fe in 1598. But that generally accepted theory could be completely wrong, and it is possible that the ancestors of the Pueblo Indians may have been collecting or even growing chiles prior to the Spanish colonization of the Southwest.

Over twelve thousand years before Europeans arrived in the New World, immigrants from Asia had crossed the land bridge across the Bering Strait. These new Native Americans then settled the two American continents from Alaska to Tierra del Fuego.

During the long process of migration and settlement, these native peoples developed agriculture in Central and South America independent of the Old World, and based their cookery on four staple foods uniquely American in origin: corn, beans, chile peppers, and squash.

As we have seen, chile peppers were well established in Mexico by the time of the Spanish invasion in the early 1500s. But how far north were they cultivated? In the course of our research for this book, we have found contemporary citations suggesting that Indians utilized chiles before the arrival of the Spanish. One source claimed chile seeds were found in New Mexico excavations dating to pre-Columbian times. Another source quoted Coronado's historian Pedro de Castañeda as describing Indians of New Mexico sprinkling chile on *carne seca*.

One final report on possible pre-Hispanic chiles is particularly important. Adolph Bandelier, the noted Southwest historian, quoted the Spanish explorer Antonio de Espejo as noticing chiles under cultivation in 1583 in the southern Rio Grande district, near what is now Las Cruces, New Mexico. Previous expeditions to the region by Fray Marco and Francisco Vázquez de Coronado had military and treasure-hunting purposes, not agricultural aims, so it seems unlikely that any of these conquistadors would have taken time to teach the Indians how to grow chile peppers.

Coronado left New Mexico in 1542, and thirty-eight years passed before the Spanish returned to New Mexico. In 1581, the northernmost Spanish settlement in the western New World was Santa Barbara, Chihuahua. In that year Father Augustine Rodriguez's ecclesiastical expedition to New Mexico perished at the hands of the Tigua Indians.

The next Spanish expedition was Espejo's in 1583, which Bandelier said reported the cultivated chiles along the Rio Grande. Spanish padres often carried both Old World and New World seeds with them while exploring the Americas. In fact, they embraced the chile pepper as fervently as the Indians. But it is implausible that the Spanish introduced chile peppers into New Mexico; it is more likely that they were already under cultivation there earlier. The rumor giving chile pepper—cultivation credit to the Spanish was probably a result of the fact that the only written records of the era were kept by the conquerors.

One of two scenarios is likely: that the Pueblo Indians utilized the wild Chiltepins, as did their brothers to the south, or that chile pepper seeds were introduced into the Southwest through inter-Indian trade between the Pueblos and early Mexican civilizations.

By studying ancient American trade routes, a theory can be proposed for how chile peppers moved north from Mexico. From the time of the height of the Mayan civilization (the first century A.D.) until the Aztecs were conquered by the Spanish (ca. 1500), long-distance traders called *pochteca* traveled far and wide from southern Mexico. The *pochteca* were a hereditary class, similar to a guild, which had their own rites, insignia, and gods. They were also foreign agents of expansionist empires.

The *pochteca* established what anthropologists call a down-the-line trading system that connected the Mexican civilizations with what is now the American Southwest. In this system, the Toltecs, for example, would not have a great amount of direct trade with the Anasazi, but rather the commerce, directed by the *pochteca,* would proceed down the line from one culture to another.

The connection between the Southwest civilizations and the Mexicans was through Casas Grandes in Chihuahua. From about A.D. 1050, regular trade routes were established between Casas Grandes and the ancestors of the Rio Grande Pueblo people, the Hohokam and Anasazi. The people of the Southwest traded turquoise and salt for copper bells, seashells, parrots, macaws, cotton, and presumably at some point in time, dried chiles containing seeds.

This hypothetical scenario does not assume that chiles were commonly grown in the Southwest before the arrival of the Spanish, because it is likely that chiles and their seeds would be less common the farther north they traveled. The colder climate of the Southwest would necessitate growing the chiles as annuals rather than as perennials — except for the wild Chiltepin.

Intrigued by such a scenario, we decided to investigate more deeply. We contacted Dr. Joseph Sanchez, director of the National Park Service's Spanish Colonial Research Center at the University of New Mexico. He graciously consented to read, in the original Spanish, all of the Spanish colonial documents pertaining to the settlement of New Mexico and Arizona. He also checked the Castañeda, Bandelier, and Oñate citations mentioned above, as well as the archaeological record.

Dr. Sanchez's report was uniformly negative in the sense that he found no chile citations in the original documents, and no evidence of chiles or their seeds in pre-Hispanic archaeological excavations. The Castañeda and Bandelier quotes could not be verified, and neither could the legend attributing New Mexico chiles to Juan de Oñate! In other words, we have only theories, not facts.

However, another possibility for pre-Hispanic chile usage in the Southwest is the presence of the Chiltepin, which grows wild in parts of southern Arizona, New Mexico, and Texas. These tiny chiles have been ingrained in the customs of the Papago Indians, an Arizona tribe directly descended from the Hohokam. Since we know that Chiltepins were spread by birds such as cardinals and pyrrhuloxias, it makes sense that at least these chiles were in culinary use long before the Spanish arrived.

Many Southwest Indian chile dishes have been passed down through the oral tradition, indicating extensive pre-Hispanic culinary usage. Perhaps the simplest of these recipes is one from the Pimas of Arizona: *chile pasado,* or green chile pulp made into pancake shapes and dried in the sun. Another basic recipe calls for red chile pods to be crumbled and cooked in oil or lard, which is what the Rio Grande Pueblo people call "Indian bacon." More sophisticated Native American chile dishes combine green chiles and mutton in stews, and lamb with *chicos* (dried corn) and red chile.

Even if the Spanish did not introduce chiles into the Southwest, they certainly assisted in their spread and usage during colonization. The Spanish settlers embraced the fiery fruits with a proper passion, and that love led to the development of the unique cuisines of the Southwest.

New Mexican Cuisine: Chiles, Chiles, and More Chiles

The cuisines of the Southwest were strongly influenced by the Norteño style of Mexican cooking popular in Chihuahua and Sonora. Although many of the dishes have identical names, they are made with slightly different methods and ingredients — various chiles, for example. After the Spanish began settlement, however, the cultivation of chile peppers exploded, and they were grown all over New Mexico. Several different varieties were cultivated, including Poblanos, Serranos, and Jalapeños, but the "long green" chile pepper (now known generically as "New Mexican") reigned supreme. This particular variety, which dries to a bright red color, was cultivated with such dedication that several land races developed in New Mexico. (A land race is a spontaneous hybrid that has adapted particularly well to a certain area.) These land races, called "Chimayo" and "Española," are varieties that are still planted today in the same fields in northern New Mexico where they were grown centuries ago.

The earliest cultivated chiles in New Mexico were small and were more a heat source than an actual food; indeed, they were (and still are, in some cases) considered a spice. But as the land races developed and the size of the pods increased, the food value of chiles became evident. There was just one problem — the bewildering sizes and shapes of the chile peppers made it very difficult for farmers to determine which variety of chile they were growing from year to year. And, there was no way to tell how large the pods might be, or how hot. For centuries after the Spanish arrived, chile farming in the United States, Mexico, and South America was a product of chance. But the advent of the modern era of selective breeding changed all that. (See chapters 1 and 10 for more details.) The taming of the chile pepper has transformed it from a tolerated weed with fruit the size of a pea to a hardy, cultivated plant with fruits a foot long.

Today, New Mexico is by far the largest producer of chile peppers in the United States, with nearly 24,000 acres under cultivation, producing about 36,000 dry tons of chile peppers each year. California is in second place, Texas is third, and Arizona is fourth in chile pepper production. Also, about 10,000

Chiles hanging at Zia Pueblo, 1884; photograph by E. A. Bass (Library of Congress)

metric tons of chiles are imported into the United States from major foreign producers such as Mexico, Pakistan, the Peoples Republic of China, Korea, India, and Costa Rica.

All of the primary dishes in New Mexican cuisine contain chile peppers: sauces, stews, *carne adovada*, enchiladas, *posole*, tamales, *huevos rancheros*, and many combination vegetable dishes. Through our recipes, we will give a brief tour of New Mexican cuisine.

New Mexico chile sauces are cooked and pureed, while salsas utilize fresh ingredients and are uncooked. (See our recipe for Pico de Gallo Salsa in Chapter 4, which is identical to salsas prepared in New Mexico.) Debates rage over whether tomatoes are used in cooked sauces such as red chile sauce for enchiladas. Despite the recipes in numerous cookbooks (none of whose authors live in New Mexico), traditional cooked red sauces, such as our Classic Red Chile Sauce, do *not* contain tomatoes. They are, however, optional in the green sauces such as our Classic

Green Chile Sauce and Green Chile Sauce with Beef. The stews usually follow the same pattern as the sauces. Traditional Red Chile Stew does not contain tomatoes, and they are optional in the Green Chile Stew.

Carne Adovada, pork marinated in red chiles and then baked, is one of the most popular New Mexican entrées. Another is enchiladas; in fact, there are so many variations on enchiladas that cooks soon determine their favorites through experimentation. In our recipe for Sour Cream Enchiladas with Chile Verde, the sour cream cuts the heat of the chile, so cooks desiring a hotter version should add Serrano chiles to the green sauce.

Other traditional New Mexican ingredients that are not as common in other parts of the Southwest include blue corn, a type of native Indian corn used in tortillas and corn chips; piñon nuts, which are one of the few crops in the world harvested in the wild rather than cultivated; and *posole*, corn that has been treated with lime.

Posole is one of the easiest and most basic methods of preparing corn and chile. This ancient dish is probably the earliest form of stew developed in the New World and is an ancestor of the chili con carne we know and love today. The name seems to be a variation of *pozo*, Spanish for "puddle," and in Mexico the dish is spelled *pozole*.

One of the more interesting aspects of its history is the fact that *posole* prevents the disease pellagra among people who are heavy corn consumers. After corn was transferred around the world, many cultures became dependent upon the grain as a major food source. Unfortunately, such dependence resulted in the onset of pellagra, a disease that causes skin lesions and mental and physical degeneration because of protein and niacin deficiencies. But in the Americas, where corn originated, there was no pellagra.

It seems that the so-called primitive cultures of the New World had developed a sophisticated technique that anticipated the findings of science. By some sort of unknown trial and error method, the Mayas, Aztecs, and North American Indians determined that boiling corn in a solution of water and ashes from the fire improved it as a source of vitamins. Of course, they had never heard of vitamins or pellagra, but their cooking method removed the hull more easily, making the corn more digestible. The corn also reacted chemically with the lime in the ashes to make amino acids more readily available to the body, and the lime also released chemically bound niacin, which the body could now utilize.

Thus was born alkaline processing to produce what is now called hominy corn. Corn is boiled in a 5 percent lime solution and then is washed and drained before further processing. In Mexico and the Southwest, the treated corn is ground to produce cornmeal and masa; in the southern United States it is ground to produce grits, which are in turn rolled and toasted to make corn flakes. The most common use of whole hominy corn these days is in that simple corn stew called *posole*.

The combination of treated hominy corn with other foods such as chile and beans made the early versions of *posole* even more nutritious. All that was needed in the dish was more protein, generally supplied by wild pigs, called peccaries, in pre-Hispanic days, but now usually provided by pork.

Posole has become so commonplace during the holiday season in the Southwest that some restaurants and households have reduced this dish to a crockpot favorite. They simply buy a bag of *posole* corn, throw in some chiles and pork, and boil it down to an unappetizing orange mush. The proper way to prepare Posole with Chile Caribe is to separate the corn and pork from most of the chile, which allows the diner to adjust the spiciness of the dish and keeps the heat of the chile distinct from the texture and flavor of the hominy corn.

There are many variations on another traditional New Mexican dish with obvious Mexican roots, Classic Tamales. Sometimes sweet fillings are substituted for the chile sauce and they become dessert tamales.

Another Southwestern favorite, Huevos Rancheros, is prepared in New Mexican cuisine by poaching eggs in red or green chile sauce. The eggs are then placed over softened corn tortillas, covered with more chile sauce, and garnished with fresh tomatoes. Pinto beans, part of the legacy of Old Mexico, are cooked, mashed, and then refried in oil or lard and spiced with red chile.

The sensations of sweet and heat combine in Feast Day Chile

Balls, another holiday favorite that is served during the feast days of the Rio Grande Pueblos. Breads, too, can be spiced up with chiles, as evidenced in the recipe for Jalapeño Corn Bread. An interesting vegetable side dish that goes well with any of the entrées described in this chapter is Chile Quelites, in which Piquin chiles heat up spinach and pinto beans.

New Mexican cuisine today is a rich mixture of traditions that have evolved from Native American, Mexican, and Anglo sources, plus variations that reflect the influence of modern restaurant chefs and innovative home cooks. Despite its uniqueness, only recently has it achieved the fame it justly deserves.

Arizona and California Variations

Although Father Eusebio Francisco Kino introduced cattle, sheep, horses, and wheat into Arizona in 1691, Arizona remained sparsely settled (as compared to New Mexico and Texas) until the arrival of cattlemen and miners during the 1800s. There was no *Camino Real* connecting the region with Mexico City, so the Spanish influence upon cuisine was not as pervasive, except around Tucson, which was settled by migration from the Mexican state of Sonora. Early frontier and territorial cookbooks have an abundance of Anglo recipes such as sourdough biscuits, rhubarb pie, beef stew, and roast turkey.

The Arizona version of Mexican cooking is often referred to as "Sonoran style" and shows many Native American influences such as fry bread and mutton stew. Cactus fruits are commonly used, especially saguaro and prickly pear. One aboriginal Pima Indian recipe calls for cholla cactus buds with green chile, and a traditional Navajo meal uses chicos (dried roasted corn) in a stew with lamb and red chiles. One of the most popular Native American recipes is Navajo Tacos made with Indian Fry Bread.

Generally speaking, Arizona cuisine is not as fiery as that of New Mexico or Texas; the chiles used are mostly mild New Mexican types and some Sonoran recipes call for no chiles at all. Mexican Poblanos and Anchos are surprisingly uncommon. These general rules are often contradicted when the fiery Chiltepin enters the picture. This untamed ancestor of the modern chile pepper grows wild in Sonora and southern Arizona on perennial bushes, as in Texas. The red, berrylike pods are harvested and dried and then crushed and sprinkled over soups, stews, and salsas.

However, as is true for the entire country, Jalapeños and the New Mexican varieties of chiles are steadily invading both Arizona and California. Growers are increasing the size of fields, and more of the fiery fruits are being imported from both Mexico and New Mexico.

In the westernmost part of the Southwest, wheat tortillas are more popular than corn, primarily because farmers in both Sonora and Arizona grow more wheat than corn. These tortillas are usually quite large — as much as sixteen inches across — and are stuffed with meat, beans, or cheese. When stuffed, they are called *burros* and *burritos,* which are more popular there than enchiladas. Burritos are simply sandwiches, so there is no need to give a recipe here — simply roll up wheat tortillas with any stuffing desired.

Perhaps the most famous Arizona specialty dish is the *chimichanga,* a dish whose name is translatable only as "thingamajig." It is a burrito (usually stuffed with beans or ground meat, chiles, and cheese) that is deep-fat fried and served with guacamole and a *pico de gallo*–type salsa. Our recipe for Chimichangas with Carne Machaca uses the famous shredded meat stuffing, which is traditional. Two other popular Arizona chile dishes are Chalupa Compuesta and Chile Corn Chowder.

Similar styles of Southwest cuisine prevail in Southern California, where Mexican cooking is often called "Cal-Mex" and has been influenced by an abundance of fruits, vegetables, and seafood. The chiles used most often here are New Mexican varieties, but Mexican Poblanos also make their appearance, especially in New Southwest dishes (see Chapter 10). Goat cheeses, similar to traditional Mexican *asadero,* are used in enchiladas and to stuff mild chiles. Tomatillos, avocados, and fresh cilantro are widely utilized in Cal-Mex dishes.

Coauthor Nancy Gerlach moved from California to New Mexico in the early 1970s and remembers the differences in cuisines. The only chiles used in California cooking were large, mild New Mexican varieties or Jalapeños in salsas; dried red chiles were rarely utilized and tomatoes were usually added to both salsas and sauces in Cal-Mex cooking. She was surprised not only by the amount of red chile used in New Mexico but also by the greatly increased heat levels.

Like that of most Southwest states, California cuisine has been influenced by cultures other than Mexican, particularly Anglos during the gold rush days and Asian peoples such as the Chinese and Japanese. The Mediterranean climate of California — and the fruits and vegetables that thrive in it — has led to variations on Italian, French, and Spanish dishes. Especially popular are dates, olives, grapes, figs, oranges, and avocados.

The Californians have found ways to simplify basic Mexican-influenced dishes such as tacos, tamales, and *chiles rellenos*. Although not particularly traditional, the recipes for Chorizo Taquitos, Tamale Pie, and Chiles Rellenos Casserole show the West Coast knack for easy-to-cook variations.

Tex-Mex Cuisine: Chili Con Carne and Barbecue Reign Supreme

Like the cuisine of New Mexico, Texas cuisine was influenced mostly by the Norteño style of cooking from Mexico, and Texans love their versions of enchiladas and tamales. As Texas food writer Richard West explains,

> The standard Tex-Mex foods existed in Mexico before they came here. What Texas restaurant cooks did was to throw them together and label them Combination Dinner, Señorita Dinner, and the hallowed Number One. In so doing, they took a few ethnic liberties and time-saving short cuts. For example: Tex-Mex tacos as we know them contain ground, instead of shredded, meat.

The chile peppers most commonly used in Tex-Mex cuisine are the Poblanos from Mexico, which are tasty, mild, and usually served *relleno*-style; the Serranos for fresh salsas; the chile Piquin, or Chiltepin, for soups and stews; and, of course, the ubiquitous Jalapeño. This fat and fiery pepper is popular everywhere, is served raw, pickled, stuffed, chopped up in salsas (such as in our recipe for Guacamole), and is even utilized in cooked sauces for topping enchiladas and *huevos rancheros,* which are served Tex-Mex–style with fried eggs and *salsa ranchera* over corn or wheat tortillas. New Mexican chile varieties are gradually making an appearance in Tex-Mex cooking, especially in the dried red form.

A fairly recent innovation in Tex-Mex cooking are *fajitas*, which are prepared with "skirt steak," or beef diaphragm muscle. *Fajitas* have their roots in the Mexican dish *carne asada*, thin beef steaks that are roasted or grilled until well-done. But fajita skirt steak is marinated first in Jalapeño juice and red wine. Its name means "little belts," an allusion to the fact that after grilling, the steak is cut across the grain into thin strips. These strips are placed on flour tortillas and topped with fresh salsa, cheese, tomatoes, and sometimes guacamole.

It is believed that fajitas originated on the vast *ranchos* surrounding Monterrey, Mexico, and gradually worked their way north. In the early 1960s, Sonny "Fajita King" Falcon established the first fajita stand in Kyle, Texas. Twenty years later, the Austin Hyatt-Regency was serving 13,000 orders of fajitas a month.

Our recipe for Texas Fajitas was served to the staff of NBC's *Today* show and received rave reviews. And nowadays, fajitas are not limited to skirt steak; they are made from flank and sirloin steaks and variations upon the theme include chicken and lamb fajitas.

Perhaps the most famous Tex-Mex creation is that bowl o' red, chili con carne, a dish that most writers on the subject say did *not* originate in Mexico. Even Mexico disclaims chili; one Mexican dictionary defines it as "a detestable dish sold from Texas to New York City and erroneously described as Mexican."

Despite such protestations, the combination of meat and chile peppers in stewlike concoctions is not uncommon in Mexican cooking. Elizabeth Lambert Ortiz, in her *Complete Book of Mexican Cooking*, has a recipe for chili con carne made with Ancho chiles that she describes as "an authentic northern Mexican style of cooking . . . as distinct from the version that developed in Texas." Mexican *caldillos* (thick soups or stews), *moles*, and *adobos* (thick sauces) often resemble chili con carne in both appearance and taste because they all use similar ingredients: various types of chiles combined with meat (usually beef), onions, garlic, cumin, and occasionally tomatoes.

But chili con carne fanatics are not satisfied with such a mundane culinary evolution, and some recount a strange tale about the possible origin of chili. The story of the "lady in blue" tells of Sister Mary of Agreda, a Spanish nun in the early 1600s, who never left her convent in Spain but nonetheless had out-of-body experiences during which her spirit would be transported across the Atlantic to preach Christianity to the Indians. After one of the return trips, her spirit wrote down the first recipe for chili con carne, which the Indians gave her: chile peppers, venison, onions, and tomatoes. Less fanciful is another account suggesting that Canary Islanders, transplanted to San Antonio as early as 1723, used local peppers and wild onions combined with various meats to create early chili combinations.

E. De Grolyer, a scholar, chili aficionado, and multimillionaire, believed that Texas chili con carne had its origins as the "pemmican of the Southwest" in the late 1840s. According to De Grolyer, Texans pounded together dried beef, beef fat, Chiltepins, and salt to make trail food for the long ride out to San Francisco and the gold fields. The concentrated, dried mixture was then boiled in pots along the trail as sort of an "instant chili."

A variation on this theory holds that cowboys invented chili while driving cattle along the lengthy and lonely trails. Supposedly, range cooks would plant oregano, chiles, and onions among patches of mesquite to protect them from cattle. The next time they passed along the same trail, they would collect the spices, combine them with beef (what else?), and make a dish called "trail drive chili." Undoubtedly, the chiles used with the earliest incarnations of chili con carne were the wild Chiltepins, called "chilipiquins" in Texas, that grow wild on bushes, particularly in the southern part of the state.

Probably the most likely explanation for the origin of chili con carne in Texas comes from the heritage of Mexican food combined with the rigors of life on the Texas frontier. Most historians agree that the earliest written description of chili came from J. C. Clopper, who lived near Houston. He wrote of visiting San Antonio in 1828: "When [the poor families of San Antonio] have to pay for their meat in the market, a very little is made to suffice for the family; it is generally cut into a kind of hash with nearly as many peppers as there are pieces of meat — this is all stewed together."

Except for this one statement, which does not mention the dish by name, historians of heat can find no documented evidence of chili in Texas before 1880. Around that time in San Antonio, a municipal market — El Mercado — was operating in Military Plaza. Historian Charles Ramsdell noted that "the first rickety chili stands" were set up in this marketplace, with the bowls of red sold by women who were called "chili queens."

"The legendary chili queens," wrote Ramsdell, "beautiful, bantering, but virtuous, made their first appearance. All night long they cooked, served, and flirted in the picturesque flare from hand-hammered tin lanterns, in the savory haze rising from clay vessels on charcoal braziers."

A bowl o' red cost visitors like O. Henry and William Jennings Bryan a mere dime and was served with bread and a glass of water. O. Henry later wrote a short story about the chili stands entitled "The Enchanted Kiss." In it, a young San Antonio drugstore clerk eats chili in the *mercado* and hallucinates that he is a former captain of the Spanish army in Mexico who has remained immortal since 1519 by eating chili con carne!

The fame of chili con carne began to spread, and the dish soon became a major tourist attraction, making its appearance in Mexican restaurants all over Texas — and elsewhere. At the 1893 World's Fair in Chicago, a bowl o' red was available at the "San Antonio Chili Stand." Given the popularity of the dish, some commercialization of it was inevitable. In 1898, William Gebhardt of New Braunfels, Texas, produced the first canned chili con carne, which appeared in San Antonio under the Gebhardt brand, a name still in existence today.

In 1937 the chili queens were banned from San Antonio for health reasons — public officials objected to flies and poorly washed dishes. Though they were restored by Mayor Maury Maverick (a real name) in 1939, their stands were closed again shortly after the start of World War II. But Texans have never forgotten their culinary heritage, and, in 1977, the Texas legislature proclaimed chili con carne to be the "Official Texas State Dish."

Recently, San Antonio has been staging what they call "historic reenactments" of the chili queens, complete with some of the original queens such as songstress Lydia Mendoza, who would serenade the chili eaters. The "Return of the Chili Queens Festival," held each year in Market Square, re-creates the era of the chili queens and celebrates the dish that, no matter what its origin, will live forever in the hearts, minds, and stomachs of Texans.

Today chili con carne is enormously popular in Texas and other states, and large chili cookoffs are held. Teams of cooks use highly secret recipes to compete for thousands of dollars in prizes while having a good old time partying — see Chapter 10 for the history of cookoffs. Some traditionalists, however, scorn the cookoff-style chili con carne as too elaborate and are promoting a return to the classic, "keep it simple, stupid" café-style chili. Our recipe for Chili con Carne is based on the old San Antonio–style recipes.

It should be pointed out that Tex-Mex cuisine is not just Mexican-oriented. It has also been influenced greatly by the basic foods of the East and Midwest and by Southern cooking — especially barbecue. Texas ranch barbecues are legendary for their huge size, with whole goats and pigs and sides of beef being cooked for days over low heat. The differences between grilling and barbecuing are important to remember: grilling utilizes high heat and quick cooking, while barbecuing is more akin to smoking and is done over low or indirect heat for a long time. Another important distinction is that barbecue sauces are used to baste barbecued or smoked meats but are generally not placed on grilled meats because their sugar content causes them to burn easily.

The final four recipes in this chapter can be served together as a kind of Tex-Mex feast. The Three-Chile Barbecue Sauce is combined with beef brisket for a Traditional Texas Barbecue. With the barbecue, serve the Red Chile Cheese Enchilada Casserole and the Frijoles Borrachos as tasty — and fiery — side dishes.

Other influences prevail as well in Texas. Along the Gulf Coast, seafood is quite important, and although it is not usually included in the category of Tex-Mex cuisine, fish and shrimp are often combined with Jalapeños to create the spiciest seafood dishes imaginable. The closer one travels to Louisiana, the more prevalent are influences from the hot Tabasco and Cayenne cuisines of Louisiana — see Chapter 10 for details.

 # Classic Red Chile Sauce

Heat Scale: 6
Yield: 2 cups

10 dried red New Mexican
 chiles
1 medium onion, chopped
2 cloves garlic, chopped
2 tablespoons bacon
 drippings or vegetable oil
1/2 teaspoon ground cumin
 (optional)
3 cups water

This famous sauce can be used in any recipe calling for a "red sauce," and is also used with traditional foods such as beans, tacos, tamales, and enchiladas.

Arrange the chiles on a baking pan and place in a 200° F oven for 5 minutes or until the chiles smell like they are toasted. Take care that they do not burn. Remove the stems and seeds.

Sauté the onions and garlic in the oil until soft.

Place all the ingredients in a blender with a cup of the water and puree to a smooth sauce.

Stir in the additional water, bring to a boil, reduce the heat, and simmer for an hour. The sauce should be smooth and thick.

Variations: To make sauce from powder, use 1/2 to 3/4 cup powdered red chile, 4 tablespoons shortening, 3 tablespoons flour, 1 medium onion (chopped), 2 cloves garlic, and 2 to 3 cups water. Melt 2 tablespoons of the shortening, stir in the flour, and cook the roux over a medium heat until browned, stirring constantly. Add the onions, garlic, 1 tablespoon oil, and sauté until the onion is soft. Stir in the chile powder and heat for 1 minute. Add the water, bring to a boil, reduce the heat, and simmer for an hour.

Classic Green Chile Sauce

Heat Scale: 6
Yield: 2 cups

8 green New Mexican
   chiles, roasted, peeled,
   stems and seeds removed,
   chopped
1 medium onion, chopped
2 cloves garlic, chopped
2 tablespoons vegetable oil
1 medium tomato, peeled
   and chopped (optional)
1/2 teaspoon ground cumin
   (optional)
2 cups water

When a "green chile sauce" is called for in Southwestern recipes, this is the standard. It is also known as chile verde.

Sauté the onion and garlic in the oil until softened. Add the remaining ingredients, bring to a boil, reduce the heat, and simmer for 30 minutes.

Serving Suggestions: Use with recipes calling for green chile sauce, such as our recipe for Sour Cream Chicken Enchiladas with Chile Verde (see recipe this chapter).

Variations: Puree in a blender for a smoother sauce. Eliminate the tomato for a "purist's" sauce.

Green Chile Sauce with Beef

Heat Scale: 5
Yield: 2 cups

2 cups chopped green New
   Mexican chiles, roasted,
   peeled, stems, seeds
   removed
3/4 pound ground beef or
   diced pork
1 large onion, chopped
3 cloves garlic, minced
1 small tomato, peeled and
   chopped
1 teaspoon ground cumin
2 to 2 1/2 cups chicken
   broth or water
1 tablespoon flour
1 tablespoon vegetable oil

This all-purpose sauce has its roots in the southern part of New Mexico, where green chile is the main agricultural crop and is used more commonly than the red form. Pour the sauce over chiles rellenos, *enchiladas, beans, or simply eat it from a bowl — it tastes so good. The beef and pork are optional and can be omitted for a vegetarian version.*

Sauté the beef or pork until browned. Add the onions and garlic and continue to sauté until soft. Pour off the excess fat.

Stir in the chiles, tomato, cumin, and broth. Bring to a boil, reduce the heat, and simmer for 20 minutes.

Mix the flour with the oil and simmer in a small skillet for 3 minutes to cook the flour. Stir the roux into the sauce and simmer until thickened.

Traditional Red Chile Stew

Heat Scale: 6
Serves: 6

8 dried red New Mexican chiles
2 pounds pork or beef stew meat, cut in 1 1/2-inch cubes
2 tablespoons vegetable oil
4 cups beef broth

When ordering a bowl of "chili" in New Mexico, this is what will be served. Cooks here use the chiles from their ristras (strings of red chile) to make this spicy stew.

Arrange the chiles on a baking pan and place in a 200° F oven for 5 minutes or until they smell like they are toasted. Take care that they do not burn. Remove the stems and seeds. Cover the chiles with 2 cups of the beef broth and let sit for 15 minutes until they are softened. Place the chiles and the broth in a blender and puree until smooth.

Brown the meat in the oil and remove from the pan. Add 1 cup of the broth to the pan to deglaze it.

Combine all the ingredients in a Crockpot or a stockpot, bring to a boil, reduce the heat, and simmer for 2 hours, or until the meat is very tender and starts to fall apart, and the stew is thickened, adding more water if necessary.

Serving Suggestions: Serve with tostadas, Pico de Gallo Salsa (see recipe Chapter 4), and warmed flour tortillas.

Green Chile Stew

Heat Scale: 6
Serves: 6

8 green New Mexican
  chiles, roasted, peeled,
  stems and seeds removed,
  chopped
2 pounds lean pork, cut into
  1 1/2-inch cubes
2 tablespoons vegetable oil
2 large onions, chopped
2 cloves garlic, chopped
2 small tomatoes, peeled
  and chopped (optional)
1 large potato, diced
  (optional)
1 quart beef broth

This traditional dish from New Mexico can be made with just chiles and meat, or a variety of other ingredients and seasonings can be added. So, cooks should experiment with the recipe until they find the perfect combination and then keep a pot of stew in the refrigerator for cold winter days! The addition of tomatoes and potatoes transforms this stew into caldillo, *popular in El Paso.*

Brown the pork in the oil, then remove and drain. Add the onion and garlic to the oil and sauté until soft.

Place all the ingredients in a kettle or Crockpot and simmer for 2 or more hours, or until the meat is very tender and starts to fall apart.

Serving Suggestions: Serve as an entrée with warm flour tortillas as a side dish, or use as a basis for other dishes such as the following: place a serving of the stew on fried corn tortillas, top with poached eggs and grated cheddar cheese and serve as an entrée for a Southwestern brunch.

 # New Mexico Carne Adovada

Heat Scale: 6
Serves: 6
Note: This recipe requires
advance preparation.

1 1/2 cups crushed dried red
  New Mexican chiles, seeds
  included
4 cloves garlic, minced
3 teaspoons dried oregano
3 cups water
2 pounds pork, cut in strips
  or cubed

This simple but tasty dish evolved from the need to preserve meat without refrigeration since chile acts as an antioxidant and prevents the meat from spoiling.

Combine the chiles, garlic, oregano, and water and mix well to make a *caribe* sauce.

Place the pork in a glass pan and cover with the *chile caribe* sauce. Marinate the pork overnight in the refrigerator.

Bake the Carne Adovada in a 300° F oven for a couple of hours or until the pork is very tender and starts to fall apart.

Serving Suggestions: Place the Carne Adovada in a flour tortilla to make a burrito, use it as a stuffing for *sopaipillas,* or use it as filling for enchiladas.

Sour Cream Chicken Enchiladas with Chile Verde

Heat Scale: 4
Serves: 4

2 cups Classic Green Chile
  Sauce (see recipe this
  chapter)
1 3-pound chicken, cut into
  pieces
2 onions, chopped
3 cloves garlic, chopped
1 cup sour cream
8 corn tortillas
vegetable oil for frying
  (about 1/4 inch in pan)
1/4 cup black olives,
  chopped
2 cups grated Monterey
  Jack cheese

Enchiladas are probably the most varied of all Southwestern dishes and are very easy to prepare. The secret is to have all the ingredients ready before assembling. The tortillas can be rolled or stacked, and any type of red or green chile sauce can be used. Also, any combination of fillings is permissible — chicken, beef, pork, cheese, and even shrimp. After mastering the basics, let the imagination run free. Below is our favorite version.

Cover the chicken pieces, one half of the onions, and garlic with cold water, bring to a boil and simmer for 30 to 45 minutes or until tender. Remove the chicken, strain, and reserve the broth for future use. When the chicken is cool enough to handle, remove the skin and the bones and shred the meat.

To Assemble: Have all the ingredients prepared and ready. Heat the oil and sauté the tortillas in the oil, one at a time, for a few seconds until they are softened, turning once with tongs. Do not overcook or the tortillas will toughen. Dip the tortillas in the sauce and place in a casserole dish or pan. Put a small amount of the chicken, onions, olives, sour cream, and grated cheese in the middle of the tortilla and roll up, making sure that the open end of the tortilla is on the bottom of the casserole (so they will stay together). Continue the process for each of the tortillas until the dish is filled.

Pour the chile sauce over the enchiladas and top with more grated cheese. Heat in a 350° F oven just long enough to heat through, about 15 minutes.

Garnish with shredded lettuce and radishes, chopped tomatoes, avocado slices, chopped cilantro, and chopped olives and serve.

Serving Suggestions: These enchiladas go well with a typical dinner of refried beans, Spanish rice, and flour tortillas.

Posole with Chile Caribe

Note: This recipe requires
advance preparation.

The Posole:

2 dried red New Mexican
  chiles, stems and seeds
  removed, crumbled
8 ounces frozen posole or
  dry posole that has been
  soaked in water overnight
1 medium onion, chopped
1 teaspoon garlic powder
1 teaspoon dried oregano
6 cups water
1 pound pork loin, cut in
  1-inch cubes

The Chile Caribe:

8 dried red New Mexican
  chiles, stems and seeds
  removed
2 teaspoons garlic powder

Posole *refers to the lime-dried corn as well as the stew itself.
The* chile caribe *in this recipe is served as a side dish and each
person can add as much as desired. Posole is traditionally served
for Christmas and New Year's Day feasts by all three cultures
in New Mexico — Native American, Hispanic, and Anglo.*

To Make the Posole: Combine all the ingredients, except the
pork, in a pot and boil at medium heat for about 3 hours, or
until the posole is tender, adding more water if necessary.

Add the pork and continue cooking for 1/2 hour, or until
the pork is tender but not falling apart.

To Make the Chile Caribe Sauce: Cover the chiles with hot
water and let them sit for 15 minutes until softened. Place the
chiles with 1 cup of the water they were soaking in and the garlic
in a blender and puree to a sauce.

To Serve: Serve the posole in soup bowls accompanied by
warm flour tortillas. Three additional bowls of garnishes should
be provided, the Chile Caribe, freshly minced cilantro, and
freshly chopped onion. Each guest can then adjust the pungency
of the posole according to individual taste.

Variation: The Chile Caribe sauce can be added to posole
during the last hour of cooking.

Note: For a really hot Chile Caribe, add dried Piquins, Cayennes, or Chiles de Arbol to the New Mexican chiles.

Classic Tamales

Heat Scale: 5
Yield: 2 1/2 to 3 dozen

1 cup Classic Red Chile
Sauce (see recipe this
chapter)
1 2-pound pork roast
dried corn husks
6 cups *masa*
1 cup shortening
2 1/2 to 3 cups meat broth

Tamales consist of masa — *flour made from ground dried corn and available in Latin markets — spread on a corn husk and filled with almost anything: from meat or poultry to fruits and nuts. They have been a staple in Mexico and the Southwest for hundreds of years and can be very time-consuming to prepare; however, they do freeze well. Many a Christmas Eve has been spent with friends making the tamales that are kept warm for guests who stop by on Christmas Day. The following is a traditional recipe, but cooks should use their imaginations to create variations.*

Cover the pork roast with water, bring to a boil, reduce the heat, and simmer until the pork is very tender and starts to fall apart, about 2 1/2 hours. Remove the roast and save the meat broth. With 2 forks or fingers, shred the meat finely.

Combine the pork with the chile sauce and simmer for 15 minutes, adding more water if necessary.

Soak the corn husks to soften.

Mix the *masa* with the shortening and meat broth and knead to the consistency of a solid dough.

To Assemble: Spread the center of a corn husk with 2 tablespoons of the masa dough and top with 1 tablespoon of the meat. Fold the sides of the husk toward the center, then fold the bottom and the top and tie with a thin strip of corn husk.

Put 2 cups of water in the bottom of a large kettle, place the tamales on a rack, and steam one hour for each dozen tamales.

Serving Suggestions: Prepare a combination plate with cheese enchiladas, Chiles Rellenos (see recipe Chapter 2), rice, and refried beans.

Variations: Fill the tamales with the Sour Cream Chicken Enchilada filling (see recipe this chapter).

Huevos Rancheros

Heat Scale: 5
Serves: 4

2 cups Green Chile Sauce
   with Beef (see recipe this
   chapter)
4 to 8 eggs
4 corn tortillas
vegetable oil for frying
1/2 cup grated cheddar
   cheese

There are many variations of this Southwest classic, ranch-style eggs. It is delicious for breakfast as well as for brunch, and the dish can be varied by using different sauces and cheeses.

Heat the sauce in a shallow frying pan. Crack the eggs into the sauce, cover with a lid, and poach to the desired firmness.

Fry each tortilla in the hot oil for only a few seconds until soft, then drain.

Place the eggs and sauce on the tortillas. Mound additional sauce around the edges. Top with the grated cheese and serve immediately.

Serving Suggestions: Serve with chilled orange juice, refried beans or hashed brown potatoes, and chorizo sausage.

Variations: Substitute Classic Red Chile Sauce (see recipe this chapter), Classic Green Chile Sauce (see recipe this chapter), or even Green Chile Stew (see recipe this chapter).

Feast Day Chile Balls

Heat Scale: 2
Yield: 20 to 24

1 cup chopped green New
   Mexican chile, roasted,
   peeled, stems and seeds
   removed
1 pound lean ground pork
1/4 cup chopped onion
1/2 cup raisins
1/2 cup sugar
2 eggs, separated
3 tablespoons flour
2 teaspoons salt
flour for dredging
vegetable oil for deep-frying

This recipe has been popular with the Pueblo Indians of New Mexico for centuries. The Chile Balls are served as a dessert for weddings and feasts but are also great as appetizers.

Brown the pork, add the onions, and sauté until the onions are soft. Pour off the extra fat as it accumulates. Stir in the chile, raisins, and sugar.

Beat the egg whites until they form peaks. Combine the flour and egg yolks and mix thoroughly. Fold the egg-yolk mixture into the whites until combined to form a batter.

Take about 1 teaspoon of the meat mixture, roll it in the flour, and shape it into 1-inch balls. Dip the chile balls into the batter and deep-fry in 350° F oil until golden. Drain on paper towels.

Jalapeño Corn Bread

Heat Scale: 3
Serves: 6

4 tablespoons finely
  chopped Jalapeño chiles
1 cup blue cornmeal
1 cup all-purpose flour
2 teaspoons sugar
1 teaspoon baking soda
1 teaspoon baking powder
1 teaspoon salt
1 1/2 cups buttermilk
2 cloves garlic, finely minced
1 cup finely chopped onions
2 eggs, beaten
1 cup grated cheddar cheese
3 tablespoons bacon
  drippings or shortening,
  melted

The heat of this bread can be decreased by reducing the amount of Jalapeños or by substituting peeled and chopped green New Mexican chiles. We suggest using blue cornmeal in place of the yellow for a real northern New Mexico speciality.

Combine all the dry ingredients in a large bowl.

Heat the buttermilk with the chiles, garlic, and onions just until small bubbles form around the edges, remove from the heat, and let cool.

Combine the eggs, cheese, buttermilk, and shortening and blend well. Add the liquid ingredients to the dry ingredients and stir until smooth.

Pour into a greased 9-inch-square pan and bake in a 425° F oven for 40 to 50 minutes, or until the corn bread is done.

Serving Suggestions: Serve this bread with any of our chili con carne recipes or with our Traditional Texas Barbecue (see recipe this chapter), coleslaw, and pork and beans for a real Texas cookout.

 # Chile Quelites

Heat Scale: 3
Serves: 6

2 teaspoons dried crushed
  Piquin chiles, seeds
  included
1 1/2 pounds fresh spinach
  or substitute one 10-ounce
  package frozen spinach
5 slices bacon
1/4 cup chopped onion
2 cloves garlic, minced
1/2 cup cooked pinto beans

This traditional dish from New Mexico combines chile with quelites, which are wild greens or wild spinach, to make a dish that would give Popeye both a vitamin and chile charge. This vegetable dish adds color as well as taste to any meal.

Steam the spinach until done. Drain well and chop.

Cook the bacon until crisp. Remove the bacon, drain, and crumble.

Add the onion and garlic to the bacon drippings and sauté until soft. Add the chile, spinach, bacon, and pinto beans and continue to cook for 5 to 10 minutes.

Serving Suggestions: Serve with New Mexico Carne Adovada (see recipe this chapter), refried beans, and tortillas.

Navajo Tacos

Heat Scale: 4
Serves: 8

4 dried red New Mexican
chiles, stems and seeds
removed
1 small onion, chopped
2 tablespoons vegetable oil
3/4 pound ground beef
3 cups cooked pinto beans
8 pieces Indian Fry Bread
(see following recipe)
grated cheddar cheese
shredded lettuce
chopped tomatoes

These tacos are very popular on the Navajo reservation in northern Arizona — hence the name. The basis for these "sandwiches" is fry bread instead of the usual tortillas. Unlike commercial tacos, these are traditionally huge and definitely a meal in themselves! We have cut the size in half to provide a more manageable taco.

Sauté the onion in the oil until soft, then add the chiles and 3 cups of water. Bring to a boil, reduce the heat and simmer for 30 minutes. Place the mixture in a blender and puree until smooth.

Sauté the beef until browned and drain off any excess fat. Add the chile sauce and beef to the beans and heat.

To Assemble: Place the bean mixture on the fry bread, top with the cheese, lettuce, and tomatoes, and serve.

Indian Fry Bread

Yield: 8 pieces

3 cups flour
1 1/2 teaspoons baking
powder
1/2 teaspoon salt
1 1/3 cup warm water
vegetable oil for frying

Mix the flour, baking powder, and salt together.
Add the water and knead the dough until soft.
Roll the dough until 1/4 inch thick, then cut out rounds 4 inches in diameter.
Fry the bread in 2 to 3 inches of hot oil until puffed and browned on both sides.

Chimichangas with Carne Machaca

Heat Scale: 4
Serves: 10

6 small dried red chiles such
  as Piquins or Chiltepins
1 cup salsa, either
  commercial or homemade
1 pound boneless pork roast
1 large onion, coarsely
  chopped
6 cloves garlic, chopped
1 cup refried beans (see
  recipe for Frijoles
  Borrachos this chapter)
10 small flour tortillas
1 cup grated Monterey Jack
  cheese (optional)
vegetable oil for deep-frying

Chimichanga, *freely translated, means "thingamajig" and is really a deep-fried burrito, a sort of a Southwestern egg roll. Carne machaca, sometimes called carne seca, is dry shredded meat. Very popular in Arizona, the Carne Machaca reflects the Sonoran influence. Historical accounts have described the Southwest Indians as sprinkling chile on beef as it dried, and this recipe approximates the texture of the carne seca.*

Place the chiles, pork, onion, and garlic in a pot. Cover with water and simmer for 1 1/2 hours, or until the meat starts to fall apart. Remove the meat, allow to cool slightly, and shred using two forks.

Spread some of the refried beans on each tortilla. Place 2 tablespoons of filling in the middle, then top with the salsa and cheese. Fold up the top and bottom and sides much like an eggroll. Secure with toothpicks if necessary.

Deep-fry wrapped tortillas in 375° F oil, turning constantly, until browned, about 1 1/2 to 2 minutes. Remove the chimichangas, drain, and serve.

Serving Suggestions: Top with salsa, Guacamole (see recipe this chapter), sour cream, and serve with Spanish rice and refried beans.

Chalupa Compuesta

Heat Scale: 4
Serves: 4
Note: This recipe requires
advance preparation.

The Salad:

2 teaspoons ground
  Cayenne
2 tablespoons vegetable oil
2 tablespoons red wine
  vinegar

Chalupa compuesta *means "adorned little boat," and that is what this popular and fancy dish from Arizona is served in — a flour-tortilla boat. This salad is a meal in itself, and after the salad has been eaten, the bowl can be consumed as well.*

Combine the Cayenne, oil, vinegar, onion, cilantro, and garlic. Toss the chicken in the mixture and marinate in the refrigerator overnight.

To Make the Dressing: Mix all the ingredients together and allow them to sit for a couple hours to blend the flavors.

3 tablespoons finely
  chopped onion
1 tablespoon finely chopped
  fresh cilantro
2 cloves garlic, minced
2 cups cooked chicken,
  either diced or shredded
chopped lettuce — iceberg
  or romaine
4 flour tortilla bowls*
2 cups Frijoles Borracho (see
  recipe this chapter)
1 medium tomato, chopped
1 small red onion, sliced in
  thin rings
1 cup grated Monterey Jack
  cheese
1/4 cup sliced black olives
1 avocado, seeded, peeled,
  and chopped or 1/2 cup
  Guacamole (see recipe this
  chapter)
sour cream

The Dressing:

1/4 cup salsa such as Pico
  de Gallo (see recipe,
  Chapter 2)
1/4 cup red wine vinegar
1/4 cup vegetable oil
2 tablespoons lime juice
1 tablespoon chopped
  cilantro
1/2 teaspoon ground cumin

To Make the Salad: Place the mixed greens in the tortilla bowl. Place the Frijoles Borracho on the lettuce, then add the chicken, arrange the tomatoes around the outside, top with the onion rings, cheese, olives, and avocado or guacamole, and garnish with the sour cream. Serve the dressing on the side.

Serving Suggestions: This entrée is a meal in itself.

*These can be made by deep-frying flour tortillas in a "tortilla fryer," a double-cup tool made especially for this purpose, or by using a small can to push the tortilla down into 375° F oil.

Chile Corn Chowder

Heat Scale: 5
Serves: 6

6 green New Mexican
  chiles, roasted, peeled,
  stems and seeds removed,
  chopped
3 cups chicken broth
1 potato, peeled and diced
1 medium onion, chopped
2 cups corn, whole kernel or
  creamed
1 cup grated cheddar cheese
1 cup heavy cream

This soup, which combines two native Southwestern ingredients, chile and corn, is easy to prepare and can be made in a Crockpot. For a heartier soup, add either diced or shredded chicken before adding the cheese.

Combine all the ingredients, except the cheese and cream, in a large pot and cook over a low heat or until the potatoes are done.

Add the cream and cheese and heat until the cheese is melted.

Serving Suggestions: Serve with Red Chile Cheese Enchilada Casserole (see recipe this chapter), sautéed squash, and corn tortillas.

Chorizo Taquitos

Heat Scale: 4
Serves: 4 to 6

1 pound chorizo sausage, or
  substitute 1 pound mild
  sausage mixed with 2
  tablespoons crushed red
  New Mexican chile, seeds
  included
1 small onion, chopped
1/4 cup tomato sauce
1 small cooked potato,
  peeled and cubed
1 cup grated cheddar cheese
12 corn tortillas
vegetable oil for deep-frying

Taquitos are rolled tacos, or "taco fingers," that are deep-fried and served with a salsa. They can be stuffed with any number of fillings; we prefer a mixture of chorizo, which is a spicy Mexican sausage, and a sharp cheddar cheese.

Remove the sausage from the casing and cook until crumbly. Add the onion (and crushed chile, if needed) and sauté until soft.

Add the tomato sauce and cook until the mixture thickens. Stir in the cooked potato.

Place a few tablespoons of the chorizo mixture in the center of a tortilla and sprinkle the cheese over the top. Roll the tortilla tightly and secure with a toothpick.

Fry the *taquitos* in 365° F oil until crisp, then drain and serve.

Serving Suggestions: Serve with accompaniments for dipping, such as Guacamole (see recipe this chapter) or Pico de Gallo Salsa (see recipe Chapter 4).

Tamale Pie

Heat Scale: 1
Serves: 6 to 8

3 tablespoons Chili Powder
  (see recipe Chapter 2)
3/4 cup yellow cornmeal
1 1/4 cups milk
1 egg, beaten
1 pound ground beef
1 small onion, chopped
2 cloves garlic
1 16-ounce can of tomatoes
2 cups whole kernel corn
1 cup cooked pinto or
  kidney beans
1/2 cup ripe black olives,
  drained
1 cup grated cheddar cheese

Leave it to the Californians to make tamales easy to prepare! This popular casserole is as simple as it is tasty. Serve it for a brunch, lunch, or as a dinner entrée.

Mix together the cornmeal, milk, and egg.

Brown the meat and add the onions and garlic. Continue to sauté until the onions are soft. Stir in the Chili Powder, tomatoes, corn, beans, and olives. Heat for an additional 5 minutes.

Stir in the cornmeal mixture, place in a 2 1/2-quart casserole and bake for 1 hour 15 minutes at 350° F. Sprinkle the cheese on top and bake for 5 more minutes, until the cheese melts.

Serving Suggestions: Serve with a wilted-spinach salad, broccoli spears, and avocado slices.

 # Chiles Rellenos Casserole

Heat Scale: 4
Serves: 4 to 6

8 whole green New
  Mexican chiles, roasted,
  peeled, stems removed
1/2 pound Monterey Jack
  cheese, cut in strips
1 cup grated cheddar cheese
3 eggs
1/4 cup flour
3/4 cup milk
1/4 teaspoon salt

This method of preparing chiles rellenos is easier than the traditional method (see recipe Chapter 2), though equally delicious. Poblano chiles can be substituted for the New Mexican ones, and different cheeses and fillings can be used.

Cut a slit down the side of each chile and carefully remove the seeds, if desired. Gently stuff each chile with the Monterey Jack cheese strips. Lay them side by side in a greased 9- by 13-inch pan. Sprinkle with the cheddar cheese.

Beat the eggs with the flour until smooth. Add the milk and salt.

Carefully pour the egg mixture over the chiles and bake, uncovered, at 350° F for 35 minutes or until a knife inserted in the custard comes out clean and the casserole is lightly browned.

Let the casserole cool for 5 to 10 minutes before cutting.

Texas Fajitas

Heat Scale: 4
Serves: 8
Note: This recipe requires
advance preparation

1/2 cup canned Jalapeño
  chiles, chopped
1/3 cup Jalapeño juice (from
  canned Jalapeños)
1/3 cup soy sauce
1/3 cup port wine
2 tablespoons tequila
  (optional)
2 pounds skirt steak
4 onions, cut in half
8 flour tortillas

Fajitas have been a popular party staple in Texas and the Southwest for a long time and now are being served everywhere. They are great for an outdoor barbecue party because they are so easy to prepare. Marinate the meat overnight and then grill when guests arrive. It is important to carve the meat as soon as it is done, as this cut of steak will toughen as it sits.

Combine the chiles, juice, soy sauce, wine, and tequila for the marinade, and marinate the meat for 12 to 24 hours in the refrigerator.

Grill the onions and meat over charcoal to desired doneness. Carve the steak diagonally across the grain in thin strips as for London broil. Coarsely chop the grilled onions. Serve with flour tortillas, chopped onions, grated cheese, sour cream, diced avocados, and a variety of sauces and salsas. Guests can make burrito-like sandwiches with the fajitas and the garnishes.

Serving Suggestions: Serve with a crisp tossed salad or coleslaw, frijoles, and Jalapeño Corn Bread (see recipe this chapter).

 # Guacamole

Heat Scale: 4
Yield: 2 cups

3 Jalapeño or Serrano chiles,
  stems and seeds removed,
  chopped
2 ripe avocados, pitted and
  peeled, mashed (save the
  pit)
1/2 cup finely chopped
  onion
1 small tomato, chopped
1/4 teaspoon garlic powder
juice of 1 lime or lemon

Guacamole is popular in one form or another wherever avocados are grown. The heat sources include Serranos, Jalapeños, New Mexican green chiles, or liquid hot sauces. Be sure to add lemon or lime juice to keep the avocados from turning black, and place the pit back in the sauce and cover the surface with plastic wrap to prevent oxidation.

Combine all the ingredients, place the pit back in the sauce, cover, and let sit for an hour to blend the flavors.

Serving Suggestions: Remove the pit and serve this sauce with toasted tortilla chips as a dip, with chopped lettuce as a salad, or as a garnish or topping on a variety of dishes such as tacos and enchiladas.

Chili con Carne

Heat Scale: 5
Serves: 6 to 8

6 dried Ancho chiles, stems
  and seeds removed
6 dried red New Mexican
  chiles, stems and seeds
  removed
2 teaspoons ground
  Cayenne
2 pounds ground beef (chili
  or coarse grind, if
  available)
1 pound ground pork (chili
  or coarse grind, if
  available)
2 medium onions, chopped
1 tablespoon chopped garlic
3 teaspoons ground cumin
3 teaspoons dried oregano
1 teaspoon sugar
1 cup tomato sauce
3 cups beef broth

There must be as many recipes for "chili" as there are cooks in Texas, New Mexico, Arizona, California, and even Cincinnati! Cooks seem to guard their recipes as if they were classified information. This recipe is our version of the classic San Antonio chili. Health-conscious cooks should prepare it the day before, chill it, and skim off any fat that rises.

Cover the chiles with hot water and let them sit for 15 minutes to soften. In a blender, place the chiles and the water they were soaking in and puree until smooth.

Sauté the beef and pork until browned. Add the onions and garlic and continue to cook for 10 minutes.

Stir in the cumin, oregano, sugar, tomato sauce, and the beef broth and simmer for an hour.

Add the pureed chile paste and continue to simmer for 30 minutes. Add the ground Cayenne to increase the heat and additional water, if necessary.

Serving Suggestions: Serve with coleslaw and corn bread.

Three-Chile Barbecue Sauce

Heat Scale: 5
Yield: 2 1/2 cups

6 dried red New Mexican chiles, stems and seeds removed
4 dried Chiltepin chiles, or substitute small dried hot chiles such as Piquin or Cayenne
1/2 cup commercial bottled "chili" sauce
1 large onion, chopped
2 cloves garlic, chopped
2 tablespoons bacon drippings or vegetable oil
1 cup catsup
5 tablespoons distilled white vinegar
4 tablespoons brown sugar
2 teaspoons dry mustard
2 teaspoons Worcestershire sauce
2 teaspoons Liquid Smoke

Spicy barbecue sauces were invented in the South by simply adding hot sauces to a tomato-based sauce; however, this one is definitely a Southwestern invention. Because of high sugar content, the catsup and the brown sugar tend to burn, so apply this sauce toward the end of the grilling.

Cover the chiles with hot water and let them sit for 15 minutes until softened. Place the chiles in a blender with 1 cup of the water they were soaked in and puree until smooth.

Sauté the onion and garlic in the oil until soft, then add all the rest of the ingredients, including the chili sauce. Bring to a boil, reduce the heat, and simmer for 30 minutes. Place the sauce in a blender and puree until smooth.

Serving Suggestions: This sauce complements beef, pork, poultry, and it can also be served as a condiment.

Traditional Texas Barbecue

Heat Scale: 5
Serves: 6 to 8

Three-Chile Barbecue Sauce (see preceding recipe)
1 3- to 4-pound beef brisket

The earliest barbecues were meats cooked in a pit lined with hot rocks and coals. Brisket should be cooked with a similar slow, moist heat to achieve the best flavor. Plan to start the barbecue early in the morning.

Start the fire with a large amount of charcoal. When it has burned down to coals, place a drip pan in the center of the coals and fill it with water. Place the brisket over the pan with the fat side down. Cover the barbecue and adjust to provide a slow heat.

After the meat has been cooking for an hour, baste with the sauce. Repeat the basting and turn the meat, so that it cooks evenly. The total process should take about 4 to 5 hours.

Soak mesquite or hickory chips in water for an hour. Spread a couple of cups of the chips over the coals, cover, and smoke for 45 minutes.

Remove, carve, and serve with extra sauce.

Serving Suggestions: This barbecue can be made into sandwiches on sourdough rolls. Serve with steak fries, roasted corn on the cob with Cilantro-Chile Butter (see recipe Chapter 2) and Three-Bean Salad (see recipe Chapter 8).

 # Red Chile Cheese Enchilada Casserole

Heat Scale: 6
Serves: 4

4 cups Classic Red Chile Sauce (see recipe this chapter)
1 pound ground beef (optional)
12 corn tortillas
vegetable oil for frying
1 pound cheddar cheese, grated
2 medium onions, chopped
shredded lettuce and chopped tomatoes for garnish

This West Texas enchilada casserole is traditionally served topped with fried or poached eggs. Other ingredients can be added, including shredded chicken or pinto beans.

Sauté the beef, if used, until browned and drain off the fat.

Fry the tortillas, one at a time, in the hot oil until softened but not crisp, then drain.

To Assemble: Place a small amount of sauce on the bottom of a casserole pan, place a tortilla on top, then more sauce, then the beef, 1/4 cup of the cheese, and the onions. Repeat the procedure for 2 more layers, ending with the cheese.

Bake in a 350° F oven for 15 minutes, or until the cheese melts. Garnish with the lettuce and tomatoes and serve.

Serving Suggestions: Serve with Elote con Crema (see recipe Chapter 2) and refried beans.

Frijoles Borrachos

Heat Scale: 4
Serves: 6

Note: This recipe requires advance preparation

4 Jalapeño chiles, stems and
  seeds removed, cut in half
2 cups pinto beans, cleaned
  and rinsed
12 ounces beer
1 large onion, quartered
1 tablespoon vegetable oil
6 cups water
vegetable oil for refrying

These borracho, *or* "drunken" *beans, go well with any Southwest or Mexican entrée. The beans absorb the chile flavor and have a smoother texture if they are soaked overnight with the beer and the Jalapeños — a tip that was passed on to us from a chile vendor in Ciudad Juárez. Adjust the number of chiles depending on heat preference.*

Combine the chiles, beans, beer, onion, 1 tablespoon oil, and water in a large pot and soak overnight.

The next day, bring the mixture to a boil, reduce the heat, and simmer until the beans are done — that is, when they start to fall apart. Add more water if necessary.

Remove the onion and chiles and either serve the beans whole with the cooking liquid or mash the beans and then fry with additional oil for refried beans.

CHAPTER SIX

Paprika and Africa

*"The person who has once acquired a taste in
the tropics for . . . African chiles becomes an addict."*

Laurens van der Post, *African Cooking* (1970)

SHORTLY after Christopher Columbus brought back the first chile pods with seeds from the West Indies, the word was out about the pungent pods. Peter Martyr, a cleric in the service of the Spanish court at Barcelona, wrote in 1493 that the new hot pepper was called "caribe, meaning sharp and strong," and that "when it is used, there is no need of black pepper." From that point on, chiles spread like wildfire across the globe.

At any time after 1493, chile seeds from the West Indies were available to the Spanish and Portuguese for transmittal to ports anywhere along their trade routes. Spanish and Portuguese ships returning home were not only loaded with gold and silver, they also carried packets of the seeds of the New World plants that were destined for monastery gardens. Monks and amateur botanists carefully cultivated the Capsicums and provided seed to other collectors in Europe.

In 1494, Papal bulls of demarcation divided the world into Spanish and Portuguese spheres of influence; Portugal controlled Africa and Brazil, while Spain effectively ruled the remainder of the colonies of the New World. Thus Spanish and Portuguese traders spread chiles from both the Iberian Peninsula and their major colonies throughout the Eastern Hemisphere by way of their extensive trade routes.

In Search of a European Chile Cuisine

Considering the fact that chiles arrived so early in Spain and Portugal, it is something of a mystery that these countries never became hotbeds of fiery cuisines. Why did Spaniards and Portuguese in the New World fall in love with chiles, while their countrymen back home virtually ignored them? The most probable answer is that the colonists were literally inundated by chiles and chile dishes; in Spain and Portugal the seeds were scarce, the pods were rare and exotic, and cultivation was not extensive.

Although the Spanish and Portuguese never embraced chiles with the fervor of other cultures, a few fiery foods caught on and are still served today on the Iberian Peninsula. Perhaps the most unusual dish is *anguilas*, which are baby eels boiled in olive oil and water with chiles and garlic.

Less exotic but more tasty is our recipe for Salsa Romesco, a Catalan sauce that combines two of the most popular horticultural imports from the New World — chiles and tomatoes. A favorite dish of the Spanish-held Canary Islands is a blending of chiles, potatoes imported from Peru, and an Old World cheese; it is known as Papas Canary Island–Style. In Portugal, the combination of crushed hot red chile, garlic, onions, carrots, and fish cooked in wine is popular and is called Pescado en Escabeche.

From Portugal and Spain and into central Europe, the pattern of expansion of chile peppers is similar to that in South America — they appear in pockets of heat. In other words, the cooks of some European countries utilized the pungent pods in certain dishes, but the cuisine was not dependent upon them. Chile peppers first appeared in Italy in 1526, yet their influence on Italian food has only been significant in the south.

In southern Italy, Cayenne chiles are commonly combined with tomatoes to make sauces for pasta dishes. Chile is regarded as a spice to be added to taste and to raise the heat level by the individual chef; thus, southern Italian cuisine does not have the reputation as being particularly fiery because such recipes rarely appear in cookbooks.

However, lurking beneath the surface of tomato-dominated sauces, as natives of such towns as Bari will attest, is a tradition of extremely pungent chiles. In the Catanzaro region of Calabria, a favorite dish is *morseddu*, pig or calf livers and hearts seasoned with tomatoes and hot red chiles and served on bread. Two examples of fiery southern Italian pastas are our recipes for Spaghetti alla Carrettiera and Pasta with Chile and Cauliflower.

The arrival of chiles in the New World coincided with the

invasion of the Ottoman Turks and resulted in their spread throughout Central Europe. The armies of Süleyman the Magnificent conquered Syria and Egypt in 1516–17, Yugoslavia in 1521, and Hungary in 1526. The year 1526 is the date usually given for the introduction of the chile now known as Paprika into Hungary by the Turks, but this date is only plausible if the Turks had somehow acquired chiles from either Spanish, Italian, or Greek traders in the Mediterranean.

Writes Zoltan Halasz, author of *Hungarian Paprika Through the Ages:* "Most probably the Turks got into the possession of Paprika through Italian intermediaries, and since a great many nations fond of gardening lived on the Balkan Peninsula, which was under Turkish occupation, the cultivation of the spice, winning favor among all these peoples, soon became widespread." At any rate, the Hungarians called it *paparka,* a variation on the Bulgarian *piperka,* which in turn was derived from the Latin *piper,* for "pepper." Of course, *paparka* later became the Paprika of today.

A more likely scenario holds that the Turks first became aware of chile peppers when they besieged the Portuguese colony of Diu, near Calicut, in 1538. This theory suggests that the Turks learned of chile peppers during that battle and then transported them along the trade routes of their vast empire, which stretched from India to central Europe. According to Leonhard Fuchs, an early German professor of medicine, chiles were cultivated in Germany by 1542, in England by 1548, and in the Balkans by 1569. Fuchs knew that the European chiles had been imported from India, so he called them "Calicut peppers." However, he wrongly assumed that chiles were native to India.

So, sometime between 1538 and 1548, chiles were introduced into Hungary, and the first citizens to accept the fiery pods were the servants and shepherds who had more contact with the Turkish invaders. Zoltan Halasz tells the tale:

Hungarian herdsmen started to sprinkle tasty slices of bacon with Paprika and season the savoury stews they cooked in cauldrons over an open fire with the red spice. They were followed by the fishermen of the Danube . . . who would render their fish-dishes more palatable with the red spice, and at last the Hungarian peasantry, consuming with great gusto the meat of fattened oxen and pigs or tender poultry which were prepared in Paprika-gravy, professed their irrevocable addiction to Paprika, which by then had become a characteristically Hungarian condiment.

From that point on, the landed gentry, the aristocracy, and the royal courts readily adopted the hot spice, and the Danube region developed Europe's only genuine chile cuisine. In the sunny south of Hungary, the brilliant red pods decorated gardens everywhere, and even today, that part of the country is the heart of Paprika country. In 1569, an aristocrat named Margit Szechy listed the foreign seeds she was planting in her garden in Hungary. On the list was "Turkisch rot Pfeffer" (Turkish red pepper) seeds, the first recorded instance of chiles in Hungary. Upon Mrs. Szechy's death and the subsequent division of her estate, her daughters fought bitterly over the valuable Paprika plots.

The famous "Hungarian flavor," which is unique to the cuisine of that country, is created by the combination of lard, Paprika, and spices. Chopped onions are always cooked to translucency in the lard; Paprika and sour cream are added to pan drippings after meats have been browned to make a rich sauce, which is then served over meat and peppers. There are many versions of hot and spicy recipes with the generic terms of *gulyas* ("goulash") and *paprikas* ("paprikash"). An example of a *gulyas* dish is our recipe for a famous goulash soup, Gulyásleves. Two of our favorite *paprikas* recipes are Chicken Paprikás and Paprikash Potatoes.

In the Hungarian countryside, Paprika peppers are threaded onto strings and are hung from the walls, porches, and eaves of farmhouses, much like the chile *ristras* in the American Southwest. Today Hungary produces both pungent and sweet Paprikas, but originally all Hungarian Paprika was aromatic and quite hot. It was evidently too hot for some tastes, for by the turn of this century other countries were requesting that Hungary develop a non-pungent variety. By accident, farmers produced a sweet variety in their fields when they planted milder "eating" Paprika with hotter "seasoning" Paprika in proximity, and in-

Paprika being strung for drying, Sarkoz, District of Tolna, Bulgaria (The Bettmann Archive)

sects cross-pollinated the two. The resulting hybrid reduced the pungency of the Paprika pods and probably led to the non-pungent varieties now grown in Spain.

Hungarian Paprikas range from the faintly pungent kind called "half-sweet" to a variety known as "rose," which is paler in color and tastes definitely hot. There is also a variety named "brown" for its brownish-red color; it is extremely pungent and is generally used in small quantities only. The mildest of the Paprikas are those with the generic name "Delicatessen." Cooks should remember that labeling varies considerably on Paprikas and the only reliable determination of pungency is the taste test.

175 ■ *Paprika and Africa*

When preparing the accompanying Paprika recipes, cooks should remember that in Europe Paprika is a distinctive pepper type, while in the United States it is not. Here, "Paprika" is simply any non-pungent red pepper powder, and the product is not well liked by American cooks. As food authority Craig Claiborne has noted, "The innocuous powder which most merchants pass on to their customers as Paprika has slightly more character than crayon or chalk. Any Paprika worthy of its name has an exquisite taste and varies in strength from decidedly hot to pleasantly mild but with a pronounced flavor." We recommend that cooks use imported Hungarian Paprika such as Szeged, and if it is too mild, they should heat it up with ground Cayenne.

Bright red Paprika pods are not the only chiles popular in central Europe. Also proliferating in the region are yellow Wax varieties, which appear both fresh and pickled. The mild or sweet variety is the Banana pepper, as it is known in the United States; its fiery cousin is called Hungarian Yellow Wax Hot. These yellow peppers, which run from pale yellow to red-orange at maturity, are particularly devious because their gorgeous golden appearance can signal either heat or sweetness to the shopper, and it is impossible to tell them apart without tasting. Another nearby region where chiles are appreciated is the Moldavian Republic, where Bells are mated with hot Wax chiles as in our recipe for Moldavian Stuffed Chiles.

Moldavia and Hungary are not the only countries in central Europe that appreciate hot chiles; they are beloved as well in Serbia, Croatia, and Dalmatia — all in Yugoslavia. At farmers' markets, a common Saturday social event in central Serbia, pepper purveyors sit gossiping at long tables behind piles of Paprika powder. The potential buyer is invited to sample the powder for pungency or sweetness, and may wish to take a few Paprika grains on the tip of a pocket knife and place them gently on the tongue for a heat and taste test.

Peasant cooking from Serbia is simple and hearty. Serbian dishes often contain hot ground Paprika, tiny chiles, and a touch of mild Paprika as well, and Serbia's spicy recipes for fish, grilled meats, and tangy stews are most renowned. A spicy vegetarian recipe from this area is Zucchini with Sour Cream and Dill.

Paprika has exerted a great influence on the culture of the

people of central Europe. There is a Paprika Museum in Kalocsa, Hungary, a city that also holds an annual Paprika Festival each October. Hungarians believe that the passion of a woman is reflected in her capacity to consume the fiery, Paprika-spiced food, and ill humor is often blamed on Paprika considered too pungent. Paprika also has its own very popular folkloric figure, Jancsi Paprika. Often represented as a puppet, Jancsi resembles a red chile, complete with a large chile hat and a pod-shaped nose. Jancsi Paprika is the prototype of the folk hero, being at once valiant, generous, knowledgeable, humorous, and ingenious. He is often called the Hungarian Sancho Panza — an appropriate personification of the pungent Paprika pod so loved by people of the region of the Danube.

Jancsi Paprika

In Hottest Africa

The cooking of a continent reflects the influences of its explorers, its conquerors, and its commercial contacts. Such is the history of chiles in Africa, which were unknown before 1500 but conquered a continent in less than half a century. Unlike the Spanish and Portuguese, Africans embraced the imported Capsicums with a fervor unmatched except, perhaps, by the East Indians.

Since the Arabic countries north of the Sahara are linked culturally, economically, and gastronomically more closely with the Mediterranean region than with the rest of Africa, there is little doubt that chiles first appeared in North Africa. In the first place, the Strait of Gibraltar separates the Iberian Peninsula and North Africa by only a few miles, so it is a logical assumption that chiles would filter southward from Cádiz to Tangier by at least the early 1500s. Secondly, the Turks completed their conquest of North Africa in 1556, and since they had already introduced chiles into Hungary, it makes sense that they also carried them to Tunisia, Algeria, and Libya.

The first chiles to appear in North Africa were probably small, extremely hot *annuums* closely related to Cayennes, which were and still are used mostly in the dried red pod form or are ground into powders. By examining the chile recipes that exist today, we can taste dishes that are centuries old because the cuisines of North Africa have hardly changed at all.

Harissa is a classic North African sauce that combines Cayenne or other dried red chiles with cumin, cinnamon, coriander, and carraway. It is extremely hot and is used as a condiment, a marinade, a basting sauce, and as a salad dressing. It may also be served on the side as a dipping sauce for grilled meats such as kabobs. Our recipe for Chicken Baked with Orange-Spiced Harissa Sauce is an example of its use simultaneously as a marinade and a basting sauce.

In Morocco, couscous is king, a "national dish." As kings are likely to do, it has invaded the rest of North Africa also. In most servings, it not only has its own chiles but is "married" to Harissa Sauce, that is, they are inseparable. The name of the dish is onomatopoeic, meaning that it emulates the sound the steam makes as the grains of semolina cook. Our recipe combines the semolina with lamb, chiles, *and* Harissa Sauce.

Another Moroccan specialty is Lamb and Cayenne Kefta, which combines those two ingredients with a bewildering array of spices such as mint, cloves, allspice, ginger, cardamom, nutmeg, and cumin. North African stews — and the earthenware pots they are cooked in — are called *tajines* and are represented here in our almond and apricot–laced recipe for Tajine Tafarout.

We do not usually think of salads as being spicy, but they are in Tunisia. Salata Mechouia is an unusual salad utilizing small green chiles, Bells, tomatoes, and garlic, which are grilled and then crushed together.

Although chiles probably appeared first in North Africa, they did not spread into the rest of Africa from that region but rather were brought by Portuguese explorers and traders. Even before Columbus, Portuguese exploration of Africa had proceeded down the west coast of the continent between 1460 and 1488. When Vasco da Gama rounded the Cape of Good Hope, crossed the Indian Ocean, and landed in India in 1498, he established the trade route for spices and other goods that the Portuguese controlled for over a century.

By 1482, the Portuguese had settled the western Gold Coast of Africa, and by 1505 they had colonized Mozambique on the east coast. By 1510 they had seized Goa in India and had established a colony there. During this time, it is suspected chile peppers were introduced by way of trade routes between Lisbon

A load of red chiles arrives at the market, Nabeul, Tunisia (The Bettmann Archive)

and the New World. By 1508, Portuguese colonization of the Pernambuco region of Brazil meant that both the *annuum* and *chinense* chiles prevalent there were made available for importation into Africa. The introduction of sugarcane into Brazil in the 1530s and the need for cheap labor was a cause of the trade in slaves, and an active passage of trade goods between Brazil and Africa sprang up.

The most likely scenario for the introduction and spread of chile peppers into Africa south of the Sahara is as follows. Varieties of *C. annuum* and *C. chinense* were introduced into all West and East African Portuguese ports during the forty years between 1493 and 1533, with the introduction into West Africa logically preceding that of East Africa. The chiles were first grown in small garden plots in coastal towns by the Portuguese settlers and later by the Africans. Although it has been suggested that chiles were spread throughout Africa by Europeans during their search for new slaves, the simplest answer is the best: the Portuguese may have been responsible for the introduction of chiles into Africa, but spreading them was for the birds. History — and evolution — repeated themselves. Precisely in the same manner that prehistoric chiles spread north from South to Central America, chiles conquered Africa.

African birds fell in love with chile peppers. Attracted to the brightly colored pods, many species of African birds raided the small garden plots and then flew farther inland, spreading the seeds and returning the chiles to the wild. Chiles thus became what botanists call a *subspontaneous* crop — one newly established outside of its usual habitat, and only involuntarily spread by man.

From West Africa, birds moved the peppers steadily east, and at some time chiles either reached the coast of East Africa or met the advance of bird-spread chiles from Mozambique and Mombasa. They also spread chiles south to the Cape of Good Hope. We must remember that these chiles were being dispersed by birds centuries before the interior of Africa was explored by Europeans. So when the early explorers encountered chiles, it was only natural for them to consider the pods to be native to Africa.

The German explorer G. Schweinfurth reported that the natives of West Africa concocted a magic potion from wild chiles that ensured eternal youth! Other explorers observed that chiles were used to spice up dried locusts, which were considered a tasty snack in some parts of Africa. In 1871, when the American Henry Stanley finally found the "lost" David Livingstone, he discovered that the Scottish explorer had lived on meat and gravy seasoned with wild chiles. Livingstone also told him that the native women would sometimes bathe in water to which chile powder had been added in order to increase their attractiveness.

Now as then throughout Africa, the names for the pungent pods vary according to the language being spoken. The Portugeuse call chile *pimento,* the English refer to it as *chilli,* the Muslim words for it are *shatta* or *felfel,* and the French word is *piment.* The Swahili words for chile are *piripiri, pilipili,* or *periperi,* which are regional variations referring to both chiles and dishes made with particularly pungent pods. Tribal names vary greatly: chile is *mano* in Liberia, *barkono* in northern Nigeria, *pujei* in Sierra Leone, and *foronto* in Senegal.

In much of Africa today, chiles remain tolerated weeds. Birds deposit the seeds in peanut or cotton fields, and the plants that sprout are cultivated by the farmers, only in the sense that they do not chop them down. The chiles become associated with the cotton or peanut crops and thrive from the maintenance of those fields. The chile plants are perennial and ripen year-round in the tropical regions. They are expensive to handpick yet have become an important wild-harvested crop in some regions.

Pierre de Schlippe, a senior research officer at the Yambio Experimental Station in the Congo, reported in 1956 that chiles had become the most important cash crop after cotton in the Zande district with, as he put it, "very little encouragement and no supervision whatsoever." When he asked a Zande tribesman whether he preferred chiles to cotton as a cash crop, the farmer replied, "Do the birds sow my cotton?" De Schlippe noted in his book on the Zande system of agriculture that the tribesman was suggesting that one should never do for oneself what others will do. "It is safe to assume that chiles as a cash crop had no influence on agricultural practice whatever," wrote de Schlippe.

In Nigeria, chiles are grown in patches near houses and as field crops under the shade of locust bean trees. They are planted in late May, and the chiles are ripe and ready for picking by November. One source reports that soon after Nigerian farmers began planting chiles, they were getting a four- to eight-thousand-pound yield per acre and, as early as 1938, were exporting one hundred tons a year.

Besides chiles, an important Nigerian food crop is peanuts, or groundnuts, as they are called there. They combine very nicely with chiles, as evidenced by our recipe for Fiery Groundnut Soup, which is sometimes called "groundnut chop" in Nigeria when chopped vegetables such as okra or spinach are added. Another delicious combination of those two ingredients occurs in Pepper-Peanut Beef Kabobs, which are grilled over charcoal and make an excellent appetizer.

Rice is another important West African foodstuff, and it is not surprising to see it combined with chiles. Our recipe for Joloff Rice, a sort of African *paella,* combines both green and red chiles with three kinds of meat plus rice, cabbage, and to-matoes.

In addition to their heavy application in foods, chiles have medicinal uses in West Africa. Fresh green and red pods are eaten whole as a cold remedy, undoubtedly to clear out the sinus cavities. In 1956, L. Stevenel, a French Army officer, noted an interesting medicinal usage of chiles in Africa. Writing in the *Bulletin of the Society of Exotic Pathology,* Stevenel attributed the absence of varicose veins and hemorrhoids in the natives to the constant use of red chile in their diets. "Native workers on the railroad always carry a supply with them and consider them as a panacea necessary for good health," he wrote. Stevenel claimed that he had cured his own hemorrhoid problem and that of his fellow officers by adding red chile pulp to their food. The cure worked quickly — in a matter of days — but only with red chiles; green chiles were ineffective. Although Stevenel did not state why red chiles worked and green did not, we suspect the reason could be connected with the high concentration of vitamin A in red chiles.

Chiles in many East African countries are cultivated on plantations amid banana trees, and a chile export industry began in Uganda in the early 1930s. During the same period of time in Kenya, Europeans as well as Africans took to the chiles so much that local consumption caused exports to drop dramatically. Thus it is not surprising to learn that East African foods are as heavily spiced with chiles as are the West African dishes.

East African cooking has also been greatly influenced by Indian curries, which are usually not prepared powders but rather combinations of chiles and curry spices that are custom-mixed for each particular dish. In Kenya, a stew called *kima* is served in which chopped beef with red chile powder and curry spices are combined. Tanzanians are fond of adding goat or chicken to curried stews, or simply charcoal-broiling the meats after they have been marinated in a mixture of curry spices and chiles. Our recipe for Curried Chicken and Banana Soup is a variation on a popular Tanzanian dish locally called *ndizi na nyama*.

One of the most famous East African dishes is *piripiri*, Mozambique's "national dish." The same word describes small, hot, dried red chiles; a sauce or marinade made with those chiles; and the recipes combining shrimp, chicken, or fish with the *piripiri* sauces. In our recipe for Shrimp Piripiri, after marinating, the *piripiri*-coated shrimp are skewered and grilled over charcoal. Such fiery combinations are so popular in Beira and Maputo that *piripiri* parties are organized. The dish has even been introduced into Lisbon, Portugal, where it is served with less chile heat.

Ethiopians prepare a condiment called *berbere*, which is made with the hottest chiles available, plus other spices, and is served as a side dish with meat or is used as an ingredient in other hot and spicy recipes. According to legend, the more delicious a woman's *berbere* is, the better chance she has to win a husband.

Our recipe for Berbere Paste, believe it or not, is not as hot as some versions we encountered in our research. In Ethiopian cookery, chiles in several forms are indispensable ingredients in the "national dish" known as *wat*, a stew to which a *berbere* paste is added. Our recipe for Doro Wat combines the paste, Paprika, spices, and hard-cooked eggs.

These days, chiles are primarily cultivated in Ethiopia, Kenya, Nigeria, Sierra Leone, Sudan, Tanzania, and Uganda. Interestingly enough, the African countries with the largest exports of red chile pods and powders to the United States are Morocco and Ethiopia. Reputedly, the hottest African chiles are those called "Mombassa" and "Uganda," which are *Capsicum chinense,* probably introduced from Brazil. In some parts of Africa, these Habanero-type chiles are called "crazy-mad" peppers, and, reputedly, they were reintroduced into the Caribbean Islands during the slave trade. However, there were probably two species of chiles already extant in the West Indies, *C. annuum* and *C. chinense.*

It is safe to say that chiles were adopted with relish into most African cuisines, except in those countries in the south with Dutch and British influence, though they do appear there occasionally in chutneys. Most cookbooks published for American palates reduce the amount of chiles in African dishes; however, we have refrained from that dubious practice in our recipes because we believe chile-loving cooks want authenticity and are intelligent enough to make their own adjustments.

We have one final observation before leaving hottest Africa. There is still much to learn about chiles there given the continent's diversity of nations, languages, cultures, and culinary arts. We request that readers with knowledge of African chiles share this information by sending it to us in care of the publisher.

Salsa Romesco

Heat Scale: 2
Yield: 2 cups

1 small dried Ancho chile,
  stem and seeds removed
2 dried red New Mexican
  chiles, stems and seeds
  removed
1/2 cup blanched, slivered
  almonds
5 large cloves garlic,
  unpeeled
2 tomatoes, unpeeled
1/2 cup red wine vinegar
1/2 cup water
1/2 cup olive oil
freshly ground pepper

Romesco is a famous Catalan sauce from the region of Tarragona in Spain. The name comes from a pepper called "Romesco," but since they are not available outside of Spain, the combination of Ancho and New Mexican chiles approximates the taste. Originally it was used to flavor a seafood stew, but now it is served with fish, shrimp, and grilled meats such as rabbit, as well as hard-cooked eggs, and vegetables.

Place the almonds, garlic, and tomatoes on a roasting pan in a 200° F oven. Remove the nuts when toasted, about 5 minutes, and the tomatoes and garlic when the skins are blistered, about 30 minutes. Grind the almonds. Place the chiles in a saucepan with the vinegar and water. Bring to a boil, reduce the heat, and simmer for 5 minutes.

After removing the skins from the tomatoes and garlic, put them in a blender along with the nuts, chiles, and vinegar and puree to a smooth paste.

Transfer the paste to a bowl and slowly whisk in the oil 1 teaspoon at a time until half of the oil is absorbed. Gradually add the remaining oil. Season with the salt and pepper.

Allow the sauce to sit for a couple of hours to blend the flavors.

Eggs with Romesco Sauce

Heat Scale: 2
Yield: 12 stuffed eggs

3 Serrano chiles, stems and
  seeds removed, minced
2 tablespoons Salsa
  Romesco (see preceding
  recipe)
6 hard-cooked eggs, peeled
  and halved
1 tablespoon mayonnaise
stuffed green olives, sliced
  for garnish

Most of the "hot" food in Spain is served as a tapa, *or hors d'oeuvre, such as this recipe for stuffed eggs. These are served in "tapa bars" where, with a glass of sherry or wine, one can sample a wide array of appetizers. Since chile stimulates the appetite, this is an excellent way to launch a meal.*

Grate the egg yolk into a bowl. Add the other ingredients, mix well, and salt to taste.

Using a pastry bag, pipe the filling back into the egg whites. Garnish with the olives and serve.

Papas Canary Island–Style

Heat Scale: 3
Serves: 4

2 medium potatoes
salted water

Sauce:

4 dried Piquin chiles, stems
  and seeds removed
4 cloves garlic, chopped
2 tablespoons red wine
  vinegar
1 tablespoon olive oil
1/2 teaspoon ground cumin
Parmesan cheese

In the Canary Islands, these potatoes would be boiled in sea-water, but since seawater is not always readily available, heavily salted water can be substituted. These are reminiscent of twice-baked potatoes, only with a "spicy bite" from the sauce.

Boil the potatoes with skins in heavily salted water, for 15 to 20 minutes, until done. Cut the potatoes in half, lengthwise, and scoop out the meat, saving the skins.

Cover the chiles with hot water and let sit for 15 minutes until softened. Place the chiles, garlic, vinegar, oil, and cumin in the blender and puree until smooth.

Mash the potatoes with the sauce and put them back into the potato skins. Top with the cheese and bake for 5 minutes in a 400° F oven until hot.

Pescado en Escabeche

Heat Scale: 2
Serves: 8 as an appetizer

Note: This recipe requires advance preparation.

1 tablespoon dried crushed
  red New Mexican chile,
  seeds included
1 pound halibut, or other
  firm fish, cut in 1 1/2-inch
  cubes
3 tablespoons olive oil
6 cloves garlic
1 small carrot, peeled and
  sliced in rings
1 medium onion, sliced and
  separated into rings
3/4 cup olive oil
3/4 cup red wine vinegar
3/4 cup white wine
10 whole peppercorns

The Portuguese, who can take most of the credit for spreading chiles around the world, do not appear to have incorporated them into their cuisine. The following recipe is an exception. Escabeche is a method of preserving fish in a spicy vinegar-based sauce. In Portugal, sardines are most commonly used, but any firm white fish will produce good results.

Sauté the fish in 2 tablespoons of the olive oil until browned, then remove and drain. Add the garlic, carrot, and onion and sauté until soft. Remove and drain.

Combine the remaining oil, chiles, vinegar, wine, and peppercorns. Simmer for 10 minutes to blend the flavors and reduce the sauce.

Arrange the chiles, garlic, carrots, and onions on the fish in a ceramic or glass pan. Pour the sauce over the top and marinate in the refrigerator for at least 2 days.

Drain and bring to room temperature before serving.

Spaghetti alla Carrettiera

Heat Scale: 3
Serves: 4 to 6

4 teaspoons dried ground
  red chile
1 pound tomatoes, peeled,
  seeds removed, chopped
3 cloves garlic, chopped
2 tablespoons olive oil
3/4 cup heavy cream
2 tablespoons vodka
10 sprigs fresh Italian
  parsley, coarsley chopped
1 pound spaghetti

This fresh tomato sauce from southern Italy was named after the mule carts, or carretti, *that were used to bring wine and produce to Rome. Because the drivers had to prepare their meals from inexpensive ingredients that were in season, there are many variations on this theme.*

Combine the chile, tomatoes, garlic, and olive oil. Simmer the sauce for 30 minutes. Add the cream and vodka and simmer until the sauce is thickened and reduced.

Cook the spaghetti in 4 quarts of boiling salted water until tender but still firm, or al dente.

Mix the sauce with the spaghetti, top with the parsley, and serve.

Pasta with Chile and Cauliflower

Heat Scale: 4
Serves: 6

1 tablespoon dried crushed
  red chile, seeds included
1 medium cauliflower,
  broken into flowerets
1/4 cup olive oil
2 tablespoons butter
6 cloves garlic, minced
1 pound *caveatelli* or
  pennette pasta, cooked al
  dente
1/4 cup grated Romano
  cheese
1 tablespoon chopped
  parsley

Chiles have found their way into Italian cooking and not just in shakers of crushed red chiles in pizza parlors in the United States. This dish from southern Italy does not have a sauce; the pasta and cauliflower are tossed with the spices.

Steam the cauliflower until almost done.

Heat the oil and butter and add the cauliflower and garlic. Sauté, stirring frequently, until the cauliflower is browned. Stir in the chile and heat for an additional 5 minutes.

Toss the cauliflower mixture with the pasta and parsley. Top with the cheese and serve.

Gulyásleves

Heat Scale: 5
Serves: 6

6 small dried red chiles such as Cayenne or Piquin
5 tablespoons hot Hungarian Paprika
1 cup flour
1 pound cubed, boneless beef chuck
2 tablespoons bacon fat or oil
1 medium onion, cut in thin slices
1 large carrot, peeled and diced
4 cups beef broth
1 tablespoon fresh black pepper, coarsely ground
3/4 teaspoon caraway seeds

Best described as Hungarian goulash soup, this dish probably had its roots with the roving Magyar tribes of central Europe who cooked their meat and vegetables over campfires in large kettles. Since "hot" paprika is hard to find, bring up the heat by adding small dried red chiles, rather than adding more paprika, which can make the soup too sweet.

Mix 4 tablespoons of the Paprika with the flour. Add the beef, toss to coat, and shake off excess flour. Brown the beef cubes in the bacon fat, remove and drain.

Add the onions to the oil and sauté until they are browned.

Place all the ingredients in a large pot or Crockpot, bring to a boil, reduce the heat, and simmer until the vegetables and meat are very tender and start to fall apart. Add more water if necessary to thin to desired consistency.

Variation: Add diced potatoes and tomatoes that have been peeled and seeds removed for a heartier soup or stew.

Chicken Paprikás

Heat Scale: 4
Serves: 4 to 6

2 tablespoons hot Hungarian Paprika
2 teaspoons ground Cayenne
1 large onion, finely chopped
2 tablespoons oil
1 3- to 4-pound chicken, cut in serving pieces
1 cup chicken stock
1 cup dry white wine
1 cup sour cream

This classic Hungarian dish uses sour cream to produce a creamy, rich sauce. The Cayenne is added to boost the heat of the Paprika if the hot variety is not available.

Sauté the onions in the oil until browned. Add the Paprika, Cayenne, and the chicken and brown.

Stir in the chicken stock and wine. Cover and simmer over a very low heat for an hour until the chicken is very tender.

Stir the sour cream into the pan and heat for a couple of minutes and serve with the sauce.

Serving Suggestions: Serve over egg noodles.

Paprikash Potatoes

Heat Scale: 4
Serves: 6

3 tablespoons hot
  Hungarian Paprika
2 teaspoons ground
  Cayenne
1 small Bell pepper, stems
  and seeds removed, diced
1 large onion, sliced into
  rings
3 cloves garlic, minced
2 tablespoons bacon
  drippings or vegetable oil
1/2 teaspoon caraway seeds
2 large potatoes, peeled and
  sliced
1 cup white wine
freshly ground black pepper
1 cup sour cream

The addition of sour cream to the sauce in this potato dish is typically Hungarian. It is a hearty side dish that goes well with roast pork and sauerkraut.

Sauté the onion and garlic in the bacon drippings until soft. Add the chiles, Bell pepper, and caraway seeds and sauté for an additional 1 to 2 minutes.

Add the potatoes, wine, black pepper, and enough water to cover. Simmer, covered, for 20 minutes or until the potatoes are done.

Stir in the sour cream and simmer until heated through.

Zucchini with Sour Cream and Dill

Heat Scale: 1
Serves: 4 to 6

2 teaspoons hot Hungarian
 Paprika
1 medium zucchini,
 julienned
1/2 teaspoon salt
2 tablespoons distilled white
 vinegar
1 small onion, chopped
2 tablespoons butter or
 vegetable oil
2 tablespoons finely
 chopped fresh dill, or 2
 teaspoons of dried dill
2 tablespoons flour
3 tablespoons zucchini
 water (see recipe for
 directions)
1/3 cup sour cream

Vegetables from the regions of the Hungarian Plain are rarely served plain. Instead, herbs and various seeds such as dill or caraway are added, or they are cooked in a creamy sauce as in this recipe.

Sprinkle the zucchini with the salt and vinegar, toss to coat, and let stand for 15 minutes. Drain off the liquid that accumulates and save.

Sauté the onion in the oil until softened. Add the zucchini, Paprika, and dill. Cover the pan and cook until the squash is done but still crisp.

Mix the flour and reserved zucchini water together, add to the zucchini, and heat for a couple of minutes to cook the flour. Stir in the sour cream and stir gently until the sauce has thickened.

Serving Suggestions: These vegetables go well with veal or roast pork.

Moldavian Stuffed Chiles

Heat Scale: 2
Serves: 4

3 Yellow Wax Hot chiles, stems and seeds removed, chopped
4 Bell peppers, tops cut off, seeds removed
1 large onion, chopped
1 cup chopped cabbage
2 carrots, peeled and chopped
1/2 cup cauliflower, broken into flowerets
1/2 cup green peas
3 tablespoons olive oil
1 cup sour cream
1 tablespoon chopped dill
1 cup grated cheddar cheese

This is an interesting version of stuffed peppers from the Moldavian Republic, which borders Romania. The Moldavians love their chiles — be they sweet or hot — and along with a love of peppers, they also have a great fondness for vodka. If there are any chiles left from making this dish, they are thrown in the vodka bottle to steep.

Parboil the Bell peppers for 3 minutes. Remove and drain. Sauté the Wax chiles and the vegetables in the olive oil until soft but still slightly crisp. Stir in the sour cream and dill.

Stuff the peppers with the vegetable mixture, top with grated cheese, and place in a baking dish with a cup of water. Bake for 15 minutes until hot and the cheese has melted.

Serving Suggestions: Serve as a vegetarian entrée with roast potatoes and cucumbers in sour cream.

 # Harissa Sauce

Heat Scale: 7
Yield: 1 to 1 1/2 cups

10 dried red New Mexican chiles, stems and seeds removed
2 tablespoons olive oil
5 cloves garlic
1 teaspoon ground cumin
1 teaspoon ground cinnamon
1 teaspoon ground coriander
1 teaspoon ground caraway
water

This sauce is thought to be of Tunisian origin but is used throughout all of North Africa to flavor couscous and grilled dishes such as brochettes. It is also used as a relish with salads. The sauce reflects the region's love of a combination of spices with a definite cumin taste. Cover this sauce with a thin film of olive oil and it will keep up to a couple of months in the refrigerator.

Cover the chiles with hot water and let them sit for 15 minutes until they soften.

Place the chiles and remaining ingredients in a blender and puree until smooth using the chile water to thin it. The sauce should have the consistency of a thick paste.

Chicken Baked with Orange-Spiced Harissa Sauce

Heat Scale: 4
Serves: 4

Note: This recipe requires advance preparation.

1/4 cup Harissa Sauce (see preceding recipe)
1/2 cup orange juice
1 tablespoon grated orange peel
1/4 cup cider vinegar
2 tablespoons vegetable oil
2 teaspoons sugar
1 teaspoon ground cinnamon
1 3-pound chicken

This entrée borrows its flavors from the popular Harissa Sauce and wonderful Moroccan oranges. The sweet taste of the fruit complements the spicy heat of the chiles in the sauce. Placing the sauce under the skin of the chicken allows the flavors to penetrate deeply into the meat.

Combine all the ingredients, except the chicken, to make a smooth sauce. Thin with orange juice if necessary.

Carefully separate the skin from the breast of the chicken, being careful not to cut the skin. Place some of the sauce between the skin and meat. Cover the chicken with the remainder of the sauce and marinate the chicken for 3 to 4 hours in the refrigerator.

Bake the chicken in a 350° F oven for 2 hours until done, basting frequently with the sauce. Cover the chicken with aluminum foil if the chicken starts to brown too much.

Serving Suggestions: Serve with rice pilaf, fried baby eggplants, and tomato and chick-pea salad.

Variations: Substitute other citrus fruits such as tangerines or lemons for the orange.

Couscous Lamb Stew

Heat Scale: 5
Serves: 6 to 8

Note: This recipe requires advance preparation.

6 dried Piquin chiles, stems removed
1/4 cup Harissa Sauce (see recipe this chapter)
1 pound lamb, cut in 1 1/2-inch cubes

This "national dish" of Morocco should be called the national dish of all of North Africa since it is popular all the way to Egypt. It is Berber in origin and is a classic dish served on Fridays as well as for special holidays and weddings. Couscous is made from semolina, a wheat grain that has been steamed to form separate tiny grains. Stews served with couscous are prepared with lamb, chicken, fish, or with vegetables only and can be sweet and spicy, as well as hot, and are served as both an entrée and a dessert. It is traditionally prepared in a couscousiere (similar to a double boiler), which allows the stew to be cooked in

4 tablespoons olive oil
1 large onion, chopped
4 cloves garlic, chopped
2 teaspoons ground cumin
1 teaspoon ground ginger
1 teaspoon ground
   cinnamon
1/2 teaspoon allspice
1/2 teaspoon turmeric
1 cup chick-peas, soaked
   overnight
3 cups beef broth
4 medium tomatoes
2 medium carrots, julienned
2 small zucchini, julienned
1 small eggplant, cubed
1/2 pound couscous

the bottom while the couscous is steamed on the top. We have adapted this recipe to American kitchens.

Brown the lamb in the olive oil. Add the onion and garlic and sauté until soft. Stir in the chiles and spices and simmer for 10 minutes.

Add the chick-peas and broth, bring to a boil, reduce the heat, cover, and simmer for an hour.

Add the tomatoes and carrots and cook for an additional 20 minutes. Add the zucchini, eggplant, and Harissa Sauce and continue to cook until the vegetables are done.

Combine equal amounts of couscous and boiling water. Cover and let stand for 5 minutes.

To Serve: Pile the couscous on a platter, top with the stew, and serve with additional Harissa Sauce on the side.

Lamb and Cayenne Kefta

Heat Scale: 5
Serves: 4

2 teaspoons ground
   Cayenne
1 pound ground lamb
1 medium onion, finely
   chopped
2 tablespoons chopped fresh
   mint
1 teaspoon ground cloves
1 teaspoon ground allspice
1 teaspoon ground ginger
1 teaspoon ground
   cardamom
1/2 teaspoon ground nutmeg
1/2 teaspoon ground
   cinnamon
1/2 teaspoon ground cumin
freshly ground black pepper

Keftas are meatballs prepared with ground lamb or beef and a number of different herbs and spices. They appear in a variety of dishes, such as stews, and also as brochettes hot off the charcoal grill served on flat Arab or pita bread. The seasonings range from chile peppers to cinnamon and usually include another Moroccan favorite, fresh mint.

Combine all the ingredients and allow to sit for an hour to blend the flavors.

Shape into 1-inch meatballs and thread on skewers. Either slightly flatten them to make sausage-shapes or leave as balls. Grill over charcoal or under the broiler to desired doneness.

Serving Suggestion: Remove from the skewers, place in a split piece of pita bread, and serve as a sandwich.

Tajine Tafarout

Heat Scale: 3
Serves: 4

4 teaspoons ground
Cayenne
1 3- to 4-pound chicken, cut
in serving pieces
4 tablespoons oil, olive
preferred
1 large onion, finely sliced
1 teaspoon ground ginger
1 teaspoon ground
coriander
1/2 teaspoon ground cumin
1/2 teaspoon ground
cinnamon
1/4 teaspoon ground
turmeric
2 cups water
1 cup dried apricot halves
2 tablespoons butter or
margarine
1 cup whole, blanched
almonds

The word tajine *refers to both the well-known North African stew and the cone-shaped clay pot in which it is cooked. These stews are slowly simmered for long periods of time so that the meat literally falls off the bone. They are then placed in the center of the room and everyone eats out of the communal bowl by using small pieces of unleavened bread to pick up the stew. This* tajine *comes from Tafarout, Morocco, home of an annual celebration in honor of the flowering of the almond trees, and the dish reflects the cuisines of both North Africa and Andalusia, Spain, in the combination of meats and fruits and the interplay of sweet and spicy flavors.*

Brown the chicken in the olive oil and remove when evenly browned. Pour off all but a few tablespoons of the oil.

Add the onion and sauté until browned. Add the spices and sauté for 2 minutes. Add the water and bring to a boil.

Reduce the heat, add the chicken pieces and apricots, and simmer for 45 minutes, turning the chicken frequently, until the chicken is very tender and starts to fall from the bone. Add more water if necessary.

Brown the almonds in the butter, remove and drain.

To Serve: Arrange the chicken on a platter, top with the sauce, and garnish with the almonds.

Serving Suggestions: Serve with a carrot salad, couscous, and pita bread.

Variation: Use lamb cubes, brown, and stew for 2 hours. Add the apricots for the last half hour.

Salata Mechouia

Heat Scale: 3
Yield: 2 to 2 1/2 cups

4 Jalapeño chiles, stems
removed, or 5 green New
Mexican chiles (do not
peel)

Some of the best known Tunisian foods are the grilled salads. The vegetables are roasted before they are combined, giving a "cooked" taste to the salad. It is traditionally prepared over a brazier, then pulverized in a mortar and served spread on chunks of French baguettes or as a relish or salsa with fish and meats.

1 medium Bell pepper (do
    not peel)
4 medium tomatoes (do not
    peel)
4 cloves garlic (do not peel)
2 tablespoons olive oil
1 tablespoon lemon juice
1/4 teaspoon ground cumin
1 tablespoon capers
    (optional)

*Prepare this dish when fresh tomatoes are available and exper-
iment with combinations of vegetables.*

Grill the chiles, tomatoes, Bell pepper, and garlic on a charcoal
grill, over an open gas flame, or under the broiler until the skins
blacken and crack. Remove, cool, peel, and remove the stems
and seeds.

Either coarsely chop or blend the vegetables, depending on
the consistency you desire. Add the remaining ingredients and
let sit for 30 minutes at room temperature to blend the flavors.

Serving Suggestions: Serve with bread or chips as a dip, as a
relish to accompany grilled fish or poultry, or on shredded lettuce
as a salad.

Variation: Add a small can of drained tuna to the salad after
chopping and garnish with 2 hard-cooked egg wedges.

Fiery Groundnut Soup

Heat Scale: 6
Serves: 4

8 dried Piquin chiles, stems
    removed
1 medium onion, chopped
2 carrots, diced
1 tablespoon peanut oil
3 cups chicken broth
1 cup smooth peanut butter

*The use of peanuts, also called groundnuts, in soups and stews
is common over all of Africa but is especially popular in the
west. This recipe can be turned into a stew or Groundnut Chop
("chop" is African slang meaning food or meal) with the addition
of chicken and vegetables such as okra, tomatoes, and yams.
The important step to remember in preparing this soup or stew
is to mix some of the broth with the peanut butter before adding
to the soup to keep it from curdling and breaking apart.*

Sauté the onion and carrots in the oil until softened, about 5
minutes. Add the broth and chiles and bring to a boil, reduce
the heat, and simmer for 30 minutes.

Remove the chiles and puree the soup in a blender until
smooth, strain if necessary, and then return to the pan.

Mix the peanut butter with 1/2 cup of the soup until smooth.
Stir this mixture into the soup and simmer for an additional 10
minutes until hot.

Serving Suggestions: This soup makes an excellent beginning
to a meal of grilled pork chops, yams, and seasoned spinach.

Variation: Add cooked, diced chicken to the soup.

Pepper-Peanut Beef Kabobs

Heat Scale: 8
Serves: 4 to 6

Note: This recipe requires advance preparation.

2/3 cup dried crushed Piquin chile, seeds included
1 1/2 pounds beef, cut in 1 1/2- to 2-inch cubes
12 ounces beer
1 1/2 cups crushed peanuts

The combination of two ingredients native to tropical America, peppers and peanuts, occurs again in these kabobs. In Nigeria, where they are served hot off the grill, they are very, very, hot.

Marinate the beef in the beer for 3 to 4 hours.

Roll the beef cubes in a mixture of the peanuts and chile until they are completely covered. Put the cubes on skewers and grill over charcoal until done.

Serving Suggestions: These hot kabobs are eaten as a snack or appetizer.

 # Jollof Rice

Heat Scale: 4
Serves: 6 to 8

5 green New Mexican chiles, roasted, peeled, stems and seeds removed, chopped
3 teaspoons ground Cayenne
1 2-pound chicken, cut into serving pieces
4 tablespoons vegetable oil, peanut preferred
1/2 pound stew beef, cut in 1 1/2-inch cubes
2 large onions, chopped
3 medium tomatoes, peeled, seeds removed, chopped
2 teaspoons ground ginger
2 bay leaves
2 cups beef broth
1/2 pound smoked ham, cut in 1 1/2-inch cubes
1 small cabbage, cut in wedges
1/4 cup tomato paste
1 1/2 cups long grain rice

One-dish dinners are standard fare in Africa, and this one is popular in Ghana, Sierra Leone, The Gambia, and all of West Africa. The rice is served with many different kinds of meats, depending on expense and availability, or it is also served with no meat at all. The name is said to be derived from an ancient tribe called the "Wollofs."

Brown the chicken pieces in the oil, then remove, drain, and keep warm. Add the beef and brown, then remove and keep warm.

Sauté the onions in the oil until browned, and then stir in the chiles, Cayenne, tomatoes, ginger, and bay leaves. Simmer for 5 minutes. Add the broth and the meat to the mixture, bring to a boil, reduce the heat, and simmer for 1 hour.

Add the chicken, ham, and cabbage and simmer for an additional 15 minutes.

Mix the tomato paste with the rice. Add the rice to the mix and stir in 3 cups of water. Bring to a boil, reduce the heat, and simmer for 20 minutes or until the rice is done. Let the dish sit for 10 to 15 minutes before serving.

Serving Suggestions: A meal in itself, this stew needs only a simple salad such as marinated cucumbers and chiles and sourdough rolls.

Curried Chicken and Banana Soup

Heat Scale: 5
Serves: 6

1 tablespoon dried ground red chile
1 3-pound chicken, cut in pieces
4 tablespoons peanut oil
1 small onion, chopped
2 cloves garlic, chopped
2 tablespoons Madras Curry Powder (see recipe Chapter 7)
1 large tomato, peeled and chopped
1 cup shredded coconut
2 teaspoons freshly ground black pepper
1 quart chicken broth
1 banana, sliced

Although soups and stews are the most commonly eaten dishes in all of Africa, this soup from Tanzania is an unusual and tasty blend of ingredients from the East. The curry powder reflects the Indian influence and also the love of the spices that are grown there.

Brown the chicken pieces in the oil, then remove and drain. Add the onions and garlic and sauté until soft. Add the chile and curry powder and sauté for an additional 2 minutes.

Combine the chicken, onion mixture, tomato, coconut, black pepper, and broth. Bring to a boil, reduce the heat, and simmer for 30 minutes until the chicken starts to fall off the bone.

Remove the chicken pieces and shred the meat. Return the chicken to the soup, add the banana, and simmer for 10 minutes.

Shrimp Piripiri

Heat Scale: 6
Serves: 4 to 6
Note: This recipe requires advance preparation.

Marinade:

2 tablespoons dried crushed red chile, seeds included
1/4 cup butter or margarine
1/4 cup peanut oil
4 cloves garlic, minced
3 tablespoons lime or lemon juice, fresh preferred
1 pound shrimp or prawns, shelled and deveined

Piripiri is the name of a chile as well as the name of this shrimp dish from Mozambique. Shellfish are abundant off the coast, and the prawns are so large that a couple will make a meal. The marinade not only goes well with shrimp or prawns, but also with fish and chicken.

Melt the butter and add the oil and the remaining marinade ingredients. Simmer for a couple of minutes to blend the flavors.

Toss the shrimp in the marinade and marinate for a couple of hours.

Thread the shrimp on skewers and grill over charcoal or broil, basting with the marinade, until done.

Heat the marinade and serve on the side.

Berbere Paste

Heat Scale: 9
Yield: 1 cup

14 dried Piquin chiles, stems removed
2 tablespoons ground Cayenne
2 tablespoons ground Paprika
4 whole cardamom pods
2 teaspoons cumin seeds
1/2 teaspoon black peppercorns
1/2 teaspoon fenugreek seeds
1 small onion, coarsely chopped
4 cloves garlic
1 cup water
1/2 teaspoon ground ginger
1/4 teaspoon ground allspice
1/4 teaspoon ground nutmeg
1/4 teaspoon ground cloves
3 tablespoons oil

Berbere *is the famous, or should we say, infamous, scorching Ethiopian hot sauce, as well as the offical language of Ethiopia. One recipe we ran across called for over a cup of powdered Cayenne! This highly spiced sauce is used as an ingredient in a number of dishes, a coating when drying meats, and as a side dish or condiment. Tribal custom dictated that it be served with* kifto, *which are raw-meat dishes that are served warm. Recipes for* berbere *are closely guarded, as the marriageability of women is often based on the quality of their* berbere. *This sauce will keep for a couple of months under refrigeration.*

Toast the cardamom, cumin, peppercorns, and fenugreek in a hot skillet, shaking constantly, for a couple of minutes, until they start to crackle and "pop." Grind these spices to form a powder.

Combine the onions, garlic, and 1/2 cup water in a blender and puree until smooth. Add the chiles and the spices and continue to blend. Slowly add the remaining water and oil and blend until smooth.

Simmer the sauce for 15 minutes to blend the flavors and thicken.

Serving Suggestions: Serve sparingly as a condiment with grilled meats and poultry or add to soups and stews.

 # Doro Wat

Heat Scale: 8
Serves: 4

1/4 cup Berbere Paste (see preceding recipe)
2 tablespoons Paprika
1 3-pound chicken, cut into small pieces
3 tablespoons lemon juice
1 large onion, chopped
2 cloves garlic, chopped
2 tablespoons butter or margarine
2 teaspoons ground ginger
1 teaspoon ground black pepper
1/4 teaspoon ground cardamom
1/4 teaspoon ground nutmeg
2 cups water
4 hard-cooked eggs, peeled, left whole

The most well known of the "national dishes" of Ethiopia is doro wat, or chicken stew. This dish is served over injera, *a sourdough bread. The serving dish is a brightly colored woven straw basket three feet high that is placed in the center of the room and around which everyone sits and eats the "wat" with their fingers.*

Remove the skin and score the chicken so that sauce will penetrate the meat. Rub the chicken with the lemon juice and let it marinate for 30 minutes.

Sauté the onion and garlic in the oil until browned. Add the spices, *berbere*, and Paprika and cook for 2 to 3 minutes.

Add the chicken to the pan and toss to coat. Stir in enough water to form a thick sauce. Bring to a boil, reduce the heat, cover and simmer for 45 minutes or until the meat starts to fall off the bone.

Using a fork, poke holes all over the eggs, then add them to the stew. Cover again and simmer for an additional 15 minutes.

CHAPTER SEVEN

Favoring Curry

*"Chile is so ingrained in the culture of Guntur, India,
that an event like a chile-eating contest would be
a silly redundancy."*

Anthony Spaeth, *Wall Street Journal*, 1988

IT is a Hindu belief that food was created for humans by the gods. Because of this conviction, cookery on the Indian subcontinent over the centuries became not only an art but a sacred ceremony. Certain prayers were said before preparation began and ritual methods were observed during the cooking. For example, Indians ate two meals a day and believed that each meal should consist of precisely thirty-two mouthfuls. Under the doctrine of karma, with its successive states of existence, and in an adherence to the caste systems, various foods were considered either clean or unclean. For example, one could not eat food prepared by a murderer or one might become one in the next life. Likewise, to eat food prepared by someone of lower caste would cause the diner to be reduced to that caste.

Religion and superstition pervade Indian cookery even today, and many early customs, rituals, and food prohibitions are still observed. Hindus, who compose 80 percent of the population, will not eat beef because the cow is sacred to them; Muslims eat beef and lamb but abhor pork; and Buddhists and Jainists will not take any animal life and so will not even crack an egg. Considering such attitudes, it is no wonder that highly spiced vegetarian cooking is so popular all over India.

In the fifth century A.D., all of the references to food found in the Vedas and Upanishads, the holy books of the Hindus, were collected by the Brahmin Khema Sharmin. He determined that the three classical elements of food were nutrition, flavor, and aesthetic appeal. The belief that food should consist of these three qualities has persisted throughout the centuries as cooking became an honored and skilled art.

It was this world of cookery that chile peppers invaded, late-comers to the development of Indian cuisines. Yet despite the complicated customs and rituals of cookery in India, chiles eventually dominated the cuisines and even became the principal spice of the region.

The Four Hundred-Year-Long Invasion

When the Portuguese arrived in India, the west coast of the subcontinent, known as the Malabar Coast, was one of the most important trading centers of the Old World. Huge camel caravans and shipping fleets were drawn to the Malabar Coast by an abundance of spices that were eagerly sought after in Europe. Vasco da Gama was the first European to visit the Malabar Coast, landing in Calicut in 1498. He brought back to Portugal an offer from the ruler of Calicut to trade spices and gems for gold, silver, and scarlet cloth.

Such temptations were more than the Portuguese could bear. They were eager to wrest the spice trade from Arab sailors, while at the same time outmaneuvering the Spaniards to the lucrative business; so they did what most powerful European countries did to less-powerful nations: they took what they wanted.

Under the leadership of Afonzo de Albuquerque, the Portuguese conquered the city of Goa on the Malabar Coast in 1510 and gained control of the spice trade. Goa was rich in spices — cloves, cinnamon, cardamom, ginger, and black pepper —which were shipped to Lisbon in return for silver and copper. These spices were essential to Indian *kari* cooking. *Kari* is a Tamil, or South Indian, word for sauce — or, more correctly, the combination of spices that are added to meat, fish, or vegetables to produce a stew. It was the word *kari* that was Anglicized to become the famous "curry." Before chiles, Indian cooks used white pepper and mustard seed to "heat up" their *kari* mixtures.

Shortly after the fall of Goa to the Portuguese, it is suspected chile peppers were introduced there by way of trade routes with Lisbon. Because of their familiarity with all kinds of pungent spices, the Indians of the Malabar Coast were undoubtedly quite taken with the fiery pods, and planted seeds that had been imported from monks' gardens on the Iberian Peninsula.

By 1542, three varieties of chiles were recognized in India, according to Dutch botanist Charles Clusius, and by the middle

Capsicum, India, Cayenne
type (The Bettmann
Archive)

Capsicum (India)
CAYENNE PEPPER.

of the century chiles were extensively cultivated and exported.
One variety of Indian chile was called "Pernambuco," after a
town in Portuguese Brazil, giving rise to speculation that the
chiles had passed from Brazil to Lisbon and then round the Cape
to Goa.

The difficulty with such a theory is the fact that the principal
chile of Brazil was *Capsicum chinense* yet that species is rare

today in India if it exists at all. The *chinense* growing in India may actually be an extreme form of *frutescens,* the Tabasco chile. A more likely scenario is that the chiles introduced into India were *annuums* from the West Indies, the first chiles grown in Spain and Portugal. This theory is supported by the fact that *Capsicum annuum* became the most extensively cultivated chile in India and its main Capsicum of commerce.

Unlike Africa, where chiles were dispersed primarily by birds, in India they were spread by more deliberate cultivation. The Capsicums became known as *achar,* a term probably derived from the Native American name *Ají,* and as *mirch* in northern India, and *mulagay* in the southern regions of the country and in Sri Lanka. Incidentally, *achar* is also the name of a spicy pickle.

No matter what they were called, chiles eventually appeared in such a variety of ways in Indian cookery that the diversity and intensity of their use rivals that of Mexico, the southwestern United States, and some parts of Asia. Four hundred years after chiles first entered India, the degree of their penetration into the various Indian cuisines was vividly illustrated by the cooking experiences of Robert H. Christie.

Christie, a British Army officer, collected recipes from India and used them to prepare elaborate banquets for his fellow members of the Edinburgh Cap and Gown Club in Scotland. In 1911, he published his landmark book on Indian cookery, *Twenty-two Authentic Banquets from India,* which contained recipes for dishes from all parts of India and from neighboring regions that are today separate countries. An examination of the ingredients of these recipes reveals that fully two thirds of the nondessert and nonbread recipes contained some form of hot chiles!

In some regions, chiles totally dominated the food. In Christie's chapter on Bengal, for example, twenty-two of twenty-three entrées contained chile peppers. In the Madras chapter, the count was eleven of thirteen, and in the Kashmir chapter, seven of eight recipes called for hot chiles in various forms, including fresh green and red plus dried red pods and powders.

Christie's recipes from some regions, such as Punjab, were not nearly so hot, but still it is evident that in 400 years chiles had completely conquered the cuisines of India, a land already rich in spices. They became an essential ingredient in both vegetarian and nonvegetarian cooking — imparting color, flavor, heat, and nutrients.

Chiles Conquer a Subcontinent

Today in India, chile is even more prevalent than it was in Christie's time, primarily because of increased agricultural acreage devoted to growing them. The most recent figures we could find for Indian chile production were for the year 1981, when 206,000 acres were devoted to growing chiles and total production was 48,500 tons. Their cultivation is widely scattered throughout the country and the amount of consumption varies from state to state. The central and southern states of Andhra Pradesh, Maharashtra, and Tamil Nadu grow and consume the most chiles. India exports nearly a thousand metric tons of red chile pods and thirty-five metric tons of ground red chile to the United States each year.

The most commonly grown chile is *Capsicum annuum,* of which the New Mexican and Cayenne types are most common. Farmers in some locales plant and harvest the Chiltepin-like *C. annuum* var. *glabrisculum,* known locally as "Bird's Eye" chile. The Tabasco-like *frutescens* species is grown primarily for green chile in India. Some chiles are harvested in their green stage and are taken directly to produce markets, but most are allowed to dry to their red stage, are harvested, and then are spread out over sand to dry. Near Madurai in southern India, red chiles in the process of drying can be seen covering a vast area of dozens of acres. After they are sun-dried, the chiles are tossed into the air to allow the wind to blow away sand and straw. Then they are bagged and taken to spice markets where they are sold as whole pods or as various grinds of chile powder.

Spices in general and chiles in particular are so important to the Indian kitchen that they are purchased in *monds,* a unit of ninety pounds. Once in the kitchen, they are stored until the cook is ready to use them in freshly ground spice mixtures called *masalas,* which vary greatly from region to region and are designed for specific applications. The *masalas* generally combine red chile with cardamom, cinnamon, cloves, cumin, coriander, and black pepper. However, ginger, mustard seed, fennel, mace, poppy seeds, nutmeg, and saffron also make an appearance in various incarnations of *masala*.

Whichever spices are chosen to blend with the chiles, they are first roasted separately and then ground together in a *chakki*, a stone mill, or in a *kootani*, an iron mortar and pestle. The dry *masala* can then be stored in airtight containers or used immediately in cooking. When the dry *masala* is mixed with water, garlic, and fresh ginger, it becomes a "wet" *masala*. This paste is generally cooked by itself before adding the vegetables, meat, or fish to the pan.

If the *masalas* and their culinary use seem familiar, it is because Western cooks often use such spices but substitute commercial curry powder for the freshly made *masala*. However, such commercial curry powders are not recommended. According to Indian-food expert Dharamjit Singh, "Curry powders are anathema to Indian cookery, prepared for imaginary palates, having neither the delicacy nor the perfume of flowers and sweet-smelling herbs, nor the savour and taste of genuine aromatics."

In India, homemade *masala* preparations vary from region to region, cook to cook, and dish to dish. They usually contain chiles, but occasionally do not. Variations may be thick or watery, or colored white, yellow, green, or red. Whatever kind the cook prepares, it will always be made from freshly ground and mixed spices. We believe that commercially prepared blends of curry spices mask the natural taste of the dishes and make all "Indian" dishes taste the same. So, in recipes calling for curry powder, we recommend not using prepared commercial blends but rather our recipe for Madras Curry Powder. In other dishes, such as Curried Split-Pea Soup, spices should be freshly ground and mixed according to the specific instructions. Cooks should remember that the word "currying" describes the technique of stewing rather than the use of a prepared powder.

Chile peppers not only transformed the *masalas* of India but also the chutneys, the primary condiments of the country. Chutney is an Anglicized version of the Hindi *chatni*, a word that refers to licking the fingertips, which were the utensils originally used to eat this mixture of chiles, fruits, various vegetables, and spices. Originally, the making of *chatni* was a method of preserving ripe fruits in the tropical climate. Today, Indian cooks prepare fresh chutney just hours before each meal by mixing fresh ingredients and then chilling them before serving.

Indian cooks are not impressed with Major Grey, the famed brand of bottled relish. They say that this commercial mango preserve bears no resemblance to homemade chutneys because it is too sweet and not hot enough. Also, the prepared chutneys contain too much vinegar and ginger but not enough of the other ingredients that make homemade chutneys superior: mixtures of different chiles and "exotic" ingredients (for bottled chutneys) such as tamarind, bananas, chopped green tomatoes, fresh coriander, coconut, and freshly ground spices.

Despite these complaints, the British and now the Americans are quite fond of the commercial chutneys and serve them with dishes prepared with commercial curry powders. Such a practice is mystifying, especially considering how easy it is to prepare much better-tasting chutneys from scratch. Our two chutney recipes, Classic Mango Chutney and Coconut-Mint Chutney, are not only properly hot but they also combine other pungent ingredients, such as ginger, with fresh herbs such as mint and coriander.

In addition to their use in *masalas* and chutneys, chiles also appear as part of various styles of cooking such as *vindaloo* and *tandoori*. In *vindaloo* cooking, meats such as pork, goat, lamb, shrimp, or chicken are marinated for hours or even days in a mixture of vinegar, fiery chiles, fruit pulp, and spices. Then the meat is simmered in the same marinade, a process that melds the marinade with the meat juices and the chiles and reduces the entire mixture to an extremely powerful sauce. Our recipe for Pork Vindaloo with Bird's Eye Chile illustrates this technique and utilizes the small, Chiltepin-like chiles occasionally grown in India.

The other style of cooking, *tandoori*, is very popular in Punjab and also uses chiles as a marinade ingredient; however, the method of cooking the meat is quite different. Instead of being stewed, it is baked in the intense heat generated in a *tandoor*, a clay oven that is sunk vertically into the ground. The chicken is first scored and then slathered with a yogurt-chile-lime paste. Then the bird is marinated for at least twelve hours in the mixture before it is skewered and inserted into the *tandoor*.

Cooking the chicken in the intense heat of the *tandoor* causes two delicious things to happen. The marinade dripping onto the coals below produces an aromatic and pungent smoke, and the dry heat of the oven causes the skin of the chicken to become very crisp while the meat beneath becomes succulent. Cooking a whole skewered chicken in a *tandoor* takes only twenty minutes. Since most American backyards do not contain a *tandoor*, we have adapted our recipe for Tandoori Chicken to baking or to smoke-grilling, the technique most similar to using a *tandoor*.

Combining chiles with yogurt tempers the heat of the chiles while improving the taste of the yogurt. This combination occurs in another of the Indian recipes we have selected, Tamatar Raita, which is served cold like a salad and provides a similar contrast to the more highly spiced main dish.

Chiles are also incorporated into the most basic appetizers and side dishes, such as Ekoori Curry. Since India produces over a thousand kinds of rice, it is not surprising to see this staple combined with chiles and lemons in our recipe for Hot Lemon Cashew Rice. Spicy Samosas are chile-stuffed, deep-fried turnovers that are sold all over India. Chile Chat is another vegetarian snack that is also used as a salad; it combines the heat of Cayenne with the chewy texture of radishes, onions, and cashew nuts.

During festival times in India, chiles take center stage — virtually every important dish from every region contains them in great amounts. In Bengal, a whole fish is covered with a paste of chiles, turmeric, and mustard and then baked; a variation on that idea is our recipe for Broiled Fish in Fiery Lemon-Coriander Sauce. By the way, seafood-chile combinations also figure prominently in festival foods of the state of Kerala; *meen vevichathu*, fish in a hot red chile sauce, is a favorite there as is *meen molee*, fish in a creamy green chile–coconut sauce. A leg of lamb roasted with chiles and coriander is a popular festival dish in Rajasthan.

The Hottest City in the World Competition, Continued

The fact that chiles occur in the majority of Indian entrées, side dishes, snacks, and festival specialties is not really surprising. In India it is said, "The climate is hot, the dishes are hotter, and the condiments are the hottest." This saying supports the legendary Indian tolerance for hot chiles. In southern India, a typical meal for four persons can include the following amounts and types of chiles: a handful of soaked and drained whole red chiles, two tablespoons of Cayenne powder, two tablespoons of freshly chopped green chiles, and a bowl of whole green chiles on the table for snacking. These chiles are, of course, in addition to the *masalas* and chutneys that are also used.

In fiery south India, there is another saying, "Heat plus heat equals cool," an allusion to the gustatory sweating caused by hot chiles. The southern state of Andhra Pradesh is the chile capital of the entire country, and, according to the *Wall Street Journal,* the city of Guntur is the hottest city of that state and is another location competing for the title of the hottest city in the world. In 1988, the *Journal* sent reporter Anthony Spaeth to India to investigate rumors that chile peppers had completely conquered the local cuisine. His report was shocking, to say the least.

"In Guntur," he wrote, "salted chiles are eaten for breakfast. Snacks are batter-fried chiles with chile sauce. The town's culinary pride are fruits and vegetables preserved in oil and chile, particularly its *karapo* pickles: red chiles pickled in chile." Another popular snack is deep-fried chiles dipped in chile powder.

Hot and spicy food is so predominant in Guntur that the agricultural market in town sells a single commodity: chile in its myriad forms. Legend and lore about chiles figure prominently in the culture of Guntur. The people often dream about them, and they believe that hot tempers arise from heavy chile eating and that chiles increase sexual desire. Children begin to eat chile at age five and quickly build up an incredible tolerance. In addition to culinary usage, the burning of red chile pods is said to ward off evil spells.

In Guntur, as in other worldwide hotbeds of chile consumption, those who do not eat chile are viewed with concern, if not suspicion. The people of Guntur attribute the abnormal avoidance of chile to several causes: the offenders have lived abroad, are from out of town, or have married someone from a less-fiery state.

Since it would not be difficult to imagine eating chiles in a chile sauce in Guntur, we offer *murgh salan,* Chile Peppers in Spicy Cream Sauce, which features two types of chiles combined with virtually every important Indian flavor.

The Migration of Heat

Southern India was the starting point for the dissemination of chile peppers north to Nepal, Tibet, and western China; northwest to Pakistan and Afghanistan; west to the Middle East and central Europe; and east to the Spice Islands and Asia. There is little doubt that the spread of chiles throughout the Indian subcontinent and beyond was along established spice trade routes. However, chiles were unique among the spices traded — they could grow virtually anywhere. Other spices such as black pepper, ginger, cardamom, nutmeg, and cloves were restricted to certain climactic and geographic zones.

The adaptability of the Capsicums led to their quick adoption into the cuisines of the other regions surrounding India. To the north, mountainous Nepal and Tibet adopted not only chiles but another important Andean-mountain food crop combined with them from ancient times: potatoes. An example of such parallel cooking, continents apart, is our recipe for Tibetan Potato Curry.

Nepalese food tends to be spicy as well; a popular breakfast chile dish is *khuras ko anda,* eggs scrambled with green chile, onions, tomato, cilantro, and ginger. In another example of parallel cookery, *khuras ko anda* is virtually identical to our Ekoori Curry and the Mexican scrambled egg dish *huevos revueltos.* Our vegetarian recipe for Curried Lentil Stew shows the importance of grains; in Nepal and northern India, dozens of different kinds of lentils are grown and other popular sources of starch are rice and wheat, which are usually served with a fiery dish such as *masma,* a mixed vegetable curry, or *songor ko tarkari,* curried pork with chiles.

The Pakistanis' love affair with chiles would seem to be never ending. By 1979 Pakistan was producing 124,000 tons of pods per year on 77,000 acres of cultivated land — a fivefold increase in just 24 years. Undoubtedly, much of that increase was due to increased chile exports. Today, Pakistan exports more red chile pods to the United States than any other country, 2,700 metric tons per year, plus about 70 metric tons of ground red chile.

There is no vegetarian tradition in that Muslim country, so chiles are most often served with the meat, fowl, and fish of choice, which is grilled, roasted, curried, or steamed; lamb, chicken, and beef are the main meats served. The cooking of Pakistan is as closely related to the Middle East as it is to India, so grilled kabob dishes are very popular. Our example of this country's spicy-meaty tradition is Korma Lamb Curry. A variation on this style of cooking is Pistachio Pillau of Lamb, from nearby Afghanistan.

In the Middle East, chiles appear only occasionally in the main dish itself but often as condiments. In Yemen, a powerful sauce called *zhoug* is considered to be not only a condiment, it is said to ward off disease, warm the people in the winter, and burn off calories. *Zhoug* is made with small green chiles, garlic, fresh parsley and coriander, cumin, and olive oil. Our recipe is traditional and is served over salads or used as a marinade and basting sauce for grilled meats. Speaking of salads, an unusual chile-based one from the Middle East is our Spicy Sautéed Apple Salad from Iraq.

Since chile heat on the Indian subcontinent is greater in the south than the north, perhaps it is not surprising that Sri Lanka has gained the reputation for the hottest cuisine of the region — although the people of Guntur would surely protest this claim. In this island nation south of India, it is not uncommon for cooks to use as many as thirty large dried red chiles to heat up a dish that serves between six and eight people!

Sri Lanka's reputation for heat rests with its red, white, and black curries. The color of the red curry is derived, not surprisingly, from a preponderance of red chile pods of varying shades. White curries are considerably milder because the chiles are tempered with coconut meat and milk. But it is the "black curries," dark roasted curry spices, that give, according to Sri Lankan cooks, better aroma and flavor.

Typically, a Sri Lankan black curry is made as follows: coriander, cumin, fennel, and fenugreek seeds are roasted separately then combined with whole cinnamon, cloves, cardamom seeds, and leaves from the curry tree. This mixture is then finely ground with mortar and pestle. The finishing touch is the addition of no fewer than three types of chiles. Medium-hot Yellow Wax chiles are ground together with bush-ripened dried red chiles called *valieche miris* plus the tiny but deadly hot "Bird's Eye" chile, a form of Chiltepin. The result is our recipe for Sri Lankan Black Curry. Another unusual Sri Lankan recipe, Tamarind Chicken in White Curry Sauce, combines the tartness of tamarinds with the heat of chiles and the pungency of shallots, garlic, and spices.

From India, chiles also spread east to Bangladesh and Burma, where they are often combined with seafood and poultry. In Bangladesh, whole fish are coated with a hot red chile *masala,* then fried in hot mustard oil. In Burma, a dish known as *naga pi yet,* our Burmese Spiced Duck, has both Indian and Chinese influences. The spices and the curry cooking style are Indian; the addition of the soy sauce is an adaptation from Asia. Another Burmese recipe is Ginger Noodle Salad.

In addition to their culinary usage, chile peppers have worked their way into the customs and traditions of the region to an unusual degree. Many people on the Indian subcontinent believe that the smoke of roasting or even burning chile peppers protects the house and gives a feeling of warmth and security. On the other hand, chiles can be an instrument of terrorism. In 1988, a gang of hoodlums boarded a train in India and began robbing the passengers. Anyone who dared to resist got a handful of chile powder thrown in the face and eyes.

On a lighter note, as our final example of how ingrained chiles are in the cuisines of India, we present the kitchen of the Taj Majal Hotel in Bombay, which now serves Mexican food! Because this famous hostelry must cater to tastes of international guests, it now experiments with a cross-cultural cuisine known as Indian-Mexican food.

In this cross-cultural cuisine, corn *masa* is replaced with yellow corn flour for making tortillas and tacos. In the tacos, lamb meat is spiced with ginger and turmeric, is laced with a *panir* salsa made with Serrano-like chiles, and is sprinkled with distinctive Indian cheeses. Nachos, the familiar snack of the American Southwest, are transformed with the addition of spiced garbanzo beans covered with a red chile sauce made with a combination of New Mexican–type chiles and the far hotter Japanese Santaka variety.

Such a collision of cultures recalls that of Latin America, where totally dissimilar foodstuffs were combined with spectacular results to produce coherent cuisines. At the Taj Mahal Hotel, five hundred years after chiles were first introduced into India, history repeats itself. However, this time it is two completely different *chile-based* cuisines that have collided.

Cross-cultural cuisines are inevitable as the world becomes more cosmopolitan, but that fact does not prevent a feeling of disappointment when we travel to an exotic city halfway around the world and are confronted by a Kentucky Fried Chicken franchise. We can only hope that the adoption of foreign foods such as tacos in India and hamburgers in Pakistan does not cause the ethnic cuisines to be spoiled or completely lost.

Madras Curry Powder

Heat Scale: 5
Yield: 1/2 cup

5 tablespoons dried ground
   red New Mexican chile
2 teaspoons ground
   Cayenne
4 tablespoons ground
   coriander seeds
4 tablespoons ground cumin
   seeds
1/2 teaspoon ground ginger
1 teaspoon ground
   fenugreek seeds
1 teaspoon freshly ground
   black pepper
1 tablespoon cardamom
1 teaspoon ground cloves

The British took the name "curry powder" from the Indian kari podi, which refers to a turmeric-based powder used in the south of India. There is no single recipe for "curry," as each dish requires its own spice mixture to produce its own unique taste. However, there are many recipes that call for "curry powder," and the following all-purpose mix is a welcome change from commercial products.

Mix all the ingredients together and grind in a blender or mortar and pestle until fine. Store in a tight-fitting jar.

Curried Split-Pea Soup with Apples

Heat Scale: 4
Serves: 4 to 6

Note: This recipe requires
advance preparation.

5 small green chiles such as
   Jalapeños, stems and seeds
   removed, chopped
1 cup yellow split peas,
   soaked in water overnight
1 teaspoon ground
   cinnamon

One of the staples of the Indian diet are legumes — dried beans and peas. In fact, there are over sixty different varieties grown in India, and they supply a major portion of the daily protein requirement. Beans are used in soups, sauces, stews, curries, pancakes, breads, and even in chutneys. The following soup is an unusual combination of fruit and peas.

Combine all the ingredients, except the cream, in a quart of water. Bring to a boil, reduce the heat, and simmer for 60 to 90 minutes or until the peas are done and start to fall apart. Add more water if necessary.

1 teaspoon ground cumin
1/2 teaspoon ground ginger
1/2 teaspoon ground cloves
1/2 teaspoon ground
  turmeric
freshly ground black pepper
1 medium Granny Smith
  apple, cored and chopped
1/2 cup heavy cream

Place the mixture in a blender and puree until smooth. Return the mixture to the heat and simmer for an additional 15 minutes or until hot.

Stir in the cream and serve.

 # Classic Mango Chutney

Heat Scale: 6
Yield: 1 1/2 cups

2 teaspoons ground
  Cayenne
5 small green chiles such as
  Serranos, stems and seeds
  removed, chopped
1 large ripe mango, peeled
  and chopped
3 dried apricots, soaked in
  water until soft, chopped
2 tablespoons orange or
  lime juice
2 teaspoons ground
  coriander
1 teaspoon ground cumin
1 teaspoon ground ginger
1/4 teaspoon ground cloves
1/4 teaspoon ground nutmeg
2 teaspoons honey or sugar

The word chutney *comes from the Hindi word* chatni, *and this fruit version is a favorite during the summer months in northern India. It is not unusual to find a couple of chile heat sources in one recipe.*

Place all the ingredients in a blender and puree until smooth. Allow the chutney to sit for a couple of hours to blend the flavors.

Serving Suggestions: This chutney makes a nice dip or a glaze and can be served with grilled chops or chicken.

Variation: For a chunkier chutney, leave the fruits diced.

Coconut-Mint Chutney

Heat Scale: 3
Yield: 1 cup

4 small green chiles such as
    Jalapeños, stems and seeds
    removed, chopped
1 cup grated fresh coconut
2 tablespoons blanched
    almonds
2 tablespoons chopped
    onions
2 tablespoons fresh lime
    juice
1 tablespoon chopped fresh
    ginger
1 tablespoon vegetable oil
1/2 cup chopped fresh mint

Chutneys are relishes that are used to accent other dishes. Usually prepared daily, they can be made with everything from chick-peas to fruits and can be sweet, sour, hot, or mild. This chutney uses coconut from the south of India and will keep a couple of days in the refrigerator before it darkens.

Combine all the ingredients in a blender, in small batches, and puree. Add just enough water to make a smooth paste.

Serving Suggestions: Usually served with vegetable fritters, this chutney also goes well with fish and shrimp.

Pork Vindaloo with Bird's Eye Chile

Heat Scale: 7
Serves: 6

8 small dried red chiles such
    as Piquins, stems removed
5 tablespoons distilled white
    vinegar
freshly ground black pepper
1 2- to 3-pound boneless
    pork roast, cut in 1 1/2- to
    2-inch cubes
1/4 cup tamarind pulp
1/2 cup boiling water
2 teaspoons ground turmeric
1 2-inch whole cinnamon
    stick
6 whole cloves
6 cloves garlic

Vindaloo describes the cooking method of marinating with a mixture of vinegar and spices and then cooking the meat in the marinade with additional seasonings. This dish is traditionally made with pork, and although not generally eaten by Hindus and Muslims, the Christians from Goa love it. There are a number of variations of this hot curry that also use lamb, beef, and shrimp.

Mix the vinegar and black pepper and toss the pork in the mixture until well coated. Marinate the pork for 2 hours, stirring occasionally. Drain and reserve the liquid.

Cover the tamarind with boiling water and soak for 30 minutes. Strain and reserve the liquid.

Combine the vinegar liquid with the chiles, cinnamon, cloves, garlic, ginger, coriander, cumin, mustard, and fenugreek in a blender and puree until smooth.

3 teaspoons finely chopped
   fresh ginger
2 tablespoons coriander
   seeds
1 tablespoon cumin seeds
1 teaspoon mustard seeds
1/2 teaspoon fenugreek
   seeds
3 tablespoons vegetable oil
1 large onion, chopped
1 small tomato, peeled and
   seeds removed, chopped

Brown the pork in the oil. Add the onions and sauté until soft. Stir in the turmeric and the spice mixture and heat for 2 to 3 minutes. Add the tomatoes and tamarind liquid. Bring to a boil, reduce the heat, and simmer for 2 hours or until the pork is very tender and starts to fall apart. Add water if necessary.

Serving Suggestion: This curry is traditionally served with rice, Tamatar Raita (see recipe this chapter), fried cauliflower, and almonds.

 # Tandoori Chicken

Heat Scale: 4
Serves: 4
Note: This recipe requires advance preparation.

4 teaspoons ground
   Cayenne
3 teaspoons ground Paprika
1 small onion, chopped
5 cloves garlic
1 tablespoon chopped fresh
   ginger
2 teaspoons coriander seeds
1 teaspoon cumin seeds
1/2 teaspoon turmeric
1/2 cup lime juice, fresh
   preferred
1 cup plain yogurt
red food coloring (optional)
1 3-pound chicken, skin
   removed

This famed chicken "barbecue" from northern India is historically prepared in a tandoor, an underground jar-shaped clay oven that is believed to have originated in Persia. The oven can be heated to very high temperatures, which quickly sears the chicken and seals in the juices, but equally delicious results can be obtained in a conventional oven or on a grill. Paprika is added for color as this dish should be a reddish-orange color; red food coloring can also be used to produce the characteristic color.

Combine the chiles, onion, garlic, ginger, coriander, cumin, and turmeric in a blender and add enough lime juice to puree to a smooth paste. Stir in the remainder of the lime juice, yogurt, and a couple of drops of red food coloring.

Make deep gashes in the flesh of the chicken and stuff with the yogurt mixture. Rub the remaining mixture over the chicken and marinate for 24 hours in the refrigerator.

Bake the chicken, with the marinade, at 350° F for an hour or until the juices run clear when pierced with a fork. Or smoke-grill the chicken over charcoal until done.

Serving Suggestion: Serve this chicken with Hot Lemon Cashew Rice (see recipe this chapter).

Tamatar Raita

Heat Scale: 3
Serves: 4

4 green New Mexican
  chiles, roasted, peeled,
  stems and seeds removed,
  chopped
1 teaspoon black mustard
  seeds*
1/2 teaspoon cumin seeds
1 cup plain yogurt
1/4 cup sour cream
1 small onion, finely
  chopped
1/4 teaspoon white pepper
1 tablespoon chopped fresh
  cilantro
2 medium tomatoes,
  chopped

Yogurt salads are made with raw or cooked vegetables, fruits, and, of course, yogurt. Some Indians do not think a meal is complete without a yogurt dish, and that is probably why some version of this dish is served at virtually every meal. Tamatar, or tomatoes, are very popular in these salads; rai means black mustard seeds, and so naturally this recipe contains both. The sour cream is added to give extra body, since Indian yogurt is made from buffalo milk, which is thick and high in fat.

Toast the mustard and cumin seeds on a hot griddle until they start to crackle and "pop."

Combine the chiles, mustard and cumin seeds, yogurt, sour cream, onion, white pepper, cilantro, and mix well. Gently stir in the tomatoes and allow the mixture to sit for an hour or more to blend the flavors.

Garnish with cilantro leaves and serve.

Serving Suggestions: This raita goes well with lamb or beef dishes such as Pistachio Pillau of Lamb (see recipe this chapter).

*Available in East Indian or gourmet food stores.

Ekoori Curry

Heat Scale: 4
Serves: 4

3 small green chiles such as
  Serranos, stems removed,
  chopped
3 scallions, chopped
  including the greens
2 teaspoons finely chopped
  fresh ginger
3 tablespoons ghee* or
  vegetable oil
1/4 teaspoon ground
  turmeric
1/4 teaspoon ground cumin

Ekoori is the Parsi word for scrambled eggs. Originally from Persia, the Parsis brought their love of eggs and omelets when they settled in the Bombay area over a thousand years ago. The shrimp are optional and can be omitted for vegetarians.

Sauté the chiles, scallions, and ginger in 2 tablespoons of ghee until the onions are soft. Stir in the turmeric, cumin, coriander, and shrimp. Simmer for 5 minutes or until the shrimp is done. Remove and keep warm.

Combine the eggs, milk, and yogurt and beat until smooth. Add the remainder of the ghee to the pan and pour in the egg mix. Stir the eggs gently, add the shrimp mixture, and continue to stir gently over a low heat until the eggs are firm and done.

1 tablespoon chopped fresh
  coriander
1/2 cup shrimp, shelled and
  deveined
6 eggs
2 tablespoons milk
2 tablespoons plain yogurt

Serving Suggestions: These eggs make a wonderful brunch entrée with honeydew melon, oven-roasted potatoes, toasted French bread with Classic Mango Chutney (see recipe this chapter), and hot spiced tea.

*Ghee is a clarified butter commonly used in Indian recipes.

Hot Lemon Cashew Rice

Heat Scale: 5
Serves: 4

5 small Yellow Wax Hot
  chiles, stems removed,
  sliced into rings
2 cups cooked *basmati* or
  other long-grained rice
3 tablespoons lemon juice
1/2 teaspoon mustard seeds
1 tablespoon finely chopped
  fresh ginger
2 tablespoons ghee* or
  vegetable oil
1/2 cup chopped cashew
  nuts
2 tablespoons finely
  chopped fresh cilantro or
  parsley

Basmati, *the long-grained Indian rice, will give the most authentic taste in this recipe, but any long-grained rice can be used. The trick to producing the best rice is to rinse it until the water runs clear, and, if possible, let the rice soak for 20 minutes before cooking. Another method of removing the starch before cooking is to fry the rice in a little oil until the grains become opaque.*

Toss the rice with the lemon juice and let sit for 10 minutes.

Fry the mustard seeds and the ginger in the ghee until the seeds start to darken. Add the chiles, cashews, and the rice. Stir and toss until heated.

Garnish with the cilantro and serve.

Serving Suggestions: This rice goes well with any chicken or meat dish and is best served with a vegetable such as broiled eggplant.

Variation: For a creamier rice, gently stir in plain yogurt.

*Ghee is a clarified butter commonly used in Indian recipes.

Spicy Samosas

Heat Scale: 5
Yield: 16

Pastry:

2 cups all-purpose flour
1/2 teaspoon salt
2 tablespoons shortening
1/2 to 3/4 cup water

Filling:

6 to 8 small green chiles
  such as Serranos, stems
  and seeds removed,
  chopped
1 teaspoon coriander seeds
1 teaspoon cumin seeds
1 small onion, finely
  chopped
1 tablespoon finely chopped
  fresh ginger
1 tablespoon vegetable oil
1/2 teaspoon ground
  turmeric
2 cups diced cauliflower,
  steamed until tender
1 cup peas, steamed until
  tender
2 tablespoons chopped
  cilantro or parsley
2 tablespoons lemon juice
vegetable oil for deep-frying

These classic Indian turnovers are popular snacks in all areas of the country from the big cities to the smallest villages. These fried turnovers are filled with a variety of ingredients, the most popular being green chile. Serve these samosas with a sauce on the side for dipping.

To Make the Pastry: Combine the flour and salt. Cut in the shortening until the mixture resembles coarse cornmeal. Slowly add the water and mix until it can be gathered into a ball. Knead the mixture until smooth, about 10 minutes. Cover and let the dough stand for 30 minutes.

To Make the Filling: Toast the coriander and cumin seeds on a hot skillet until they begin to crackle and "pop," then grind the seeds.

Sauté the onion and ginger in the oil until soft. Stir in the chiles and spices and sauté for an additional 2 minutes. Add the cauliflower and peas and cook for a couple of minutes until heated. Remove and toss the mixture with the cilantro and lemon juice.

Knead the dough for a couple of minutes and divide it into 8 balls. Roll out the balls to a 5-inch diameter. Keep the dough covered with a towel when not working with it to keep it from drying out. Cut each of the circles in half. Moisten the straight edge of the semicircle with water and fold in half to form a cone. Place a portion of the filling into the cone. Close the top of the cone and stick together with a little water. Using a fork, crimp the edges of the cone to seal.

Fry the *samosas* in 350° F oil, turning frequently, for about 5 minutes or until golden brown. Remove the *samosas* and drain.

Serving Suggestion: Serve with Classic Mango Chutney (see recipe this chapter).

Variations: Substitute potatoes for the cauliflower in the above recipe.

Chile Chat

Heat Scale: 3
Serves: 4 to 6

3 teaspoons ground
  Cayenne
2 medium carrots, peeled
  and shredded
1/2 cup shredded radishes
1/4 cup finely chopped
  onions
1/4 cup toasted cashews or
  peanuts, chopped
1 tablespoon chopped fresh
  cilantro or parsley
1/4 teaspoon cumin seeds
1/4 teaspoon celery seeds
2 tablespoons ghee* or
  vegetable oil

Chat *refers to the dish that is a type of salad, as well as the stands or houses that sell them in northern India. They are eaten cool but not cold as a snack or an appetizer, or with a meal as a side dish. They can be made with fruits or vegetables and commonly have coriander and cumin seeds as an ingredient.*

Combine the Cayenne, carrots, radishes, onions, nuts, and cilantro.

Heat the oil to 250° F, add the seeds, and heat until they darken.

Pour the oil over the salad, toss, and allow to sit for an hour to blend the flavors.

*Ghee is a clarified butter commonly used in Indian recipes.

Fish in Fiery Lemon-Coriander Sauce

Heat Scale: 4
Serves: 4
Note: This recipe requires
advance preparation.

5 green New Mexican chiles
  roasted, peeled, stems and
  seeds removed, chopped
1 teaspoon garlic, minced
1/4 cup lemon juice
4 tablespoons chopped fresh
  cilantro
1/2 teaspoon ground
  coriander seeds
1 1/2 pounds firm white fish
  such as halibut
4 tablespoons ghee* or
  vegetable oil
lemon slices for garnish

This is a relatively simple fish dish, at least by Indian standards. The acidic marinade helps to cook the fish and reduces the cooking time.

Mix the chiles, garlic, lemon juice, cilantro, and coriander and use to marinate the fish overnight in a glass or ceramic dish.

Remove the fish and combine the marinade with the melted ghee.

Grill or broil the fish, basting with the marinade mixture.

Garnish with lemon slices and serve with the butter on the side.

*Ghee is a clarified butter commonly used in Indian recipes.

Chile Peppers in Spicy Cream Sauce

Heat Scale: 5
Serves: 4

6 green New Mexican chiles roasted, peeled, stems and seeds removed, cut in strips
1 teaspoon ground Cayenne
2 tablespoons ghee* or vegetable oil
1 large onion, finely chopped
1 tablespoon finely chopped fresh ginger
2 teaspoons ground coriander
1 teaspoon dry mustard
1 teaspoon ground cumin
1/2 teaspoon ground cinnamon
1/2 teaspoon ground turmeric
1/4 teaspoon ground cloves
1 cup unsweetened coconut milk
3 tablespoons heavy cream

Since vegetables are an important part of Indian cuisine, they, are not treated as side dishes but are found in every course of a meal. The following recipe can be served as an entrée or as an accompaniment to curried dishes. Other vegetables can be substituted for the chiles, such as cauliflower, potatoes, or green beans.

Sauté the onions and ginger in the oil until the onions are browned. Add the Cayenne, coriander, mustard, cumin, cinnamon, turmeric, and cloves. Heat for another minute.

Add the chiles to the pan along with the coconut milk. Simmer for 10 minutes, stirring constantly, until the sauce thickens. Stir in the cream and simmer for an additional 5 minutes.

*Ghee is a clarified butter commonly used in Indian recipes.

Tibetan Potato Curry

Heat Scale: 5
Serves: 4

1 tablespoon chopped small green chile such as Jalapeño chiles
1/2 teaspoon fenugreek seeds

Although the cuisine of Tibet is somewhat mysterious to Westerners, we do know that Tibetans eat yak meat and drink a lot of tea. This recipe shows that they also eat chiles. Serve these potatoes as an accompaniment to lamb or beef dishes.

Heat the fenugreek seeds in the oil until they brown. Stir in the chile, onion, garlic, and ginger and simmer until the onions are

2 tablespoons vegetable oil
1 small onion, chopped
2 cloves garlic, minced
1 teaspoon finely chopped
  fresh ginger
1 medium tomato, peeled
  and diced
1/4 teaspoon turmeric
1 pound potatoes, peeled,
  diced, and cooked

soft. Add the tomatoes and turmeric and heat. Place the mixture in a blender and puree until smooth.

Gently mix the sauce with the potatoes and serve.

 # Curried Lentil Stew

Heat Scale: 5
Serves: 4 to 6
Note: This recipe requires advance preparation.

3 teaspoons ground
  Cayenne
4 small green chiles such as
  Serranos, stems removed,
  chopped
2 cups lentils, sorted and
  rinsed
1 tablespoon coriander seeds
1 teaspoon cumin seeds
1 cup chopped onions
2 tablespoons cooking oil
3 teaspoons ground turmeric
1/3 cup lime juice
6 scallions, chopped
  including the greens
cilantro sprigs for garnish

Dals, or legumes, are as popular in Nepal as they are in India and constitute a major part of the daily diet. This popular, hearty dish is served throughout the country at rest houses for hikers and climbers of the Himalayas.

Cover the lentils with water and soak overnight, then drain and rinse.

Toast the coriander and cumin seeds on a hot griddle until they begin to crackle and "pop." Remove and grind.

Sauté the onions in the oil until soft. Add the Cayenne, chiles, coriander, cumin, and turmeric. Heat for a couple of minutes.

Add the onion mixture to the lentils and cover with water. Bring to a boil, reduce the heat and simmer for 30 minutes or until the beans are done, adding more water if necessary.

Stir in the lime juice and scallions and heat. Garnish with the cilantro and serve.

Serving Suggestion: Serve over rice and accompany with broiled chicken and tossed green salad.

Korma Lamb Curry

Heat Scale: 2
Serves: 4 to 6

Note: This recipe requires advance preparation.

5 teaspoons ground
   Cayenne
2 medium onions, chopped
4 cloves garlic, chopped
2 tablespoons finely
   chopped fresh ginger
2 tablespoons ghee* or
   vegetable oil
2 teaspoons ground
   coriander
2 teaspoons ground
   cardamom
1 teaspoon ground cumin
1 teaspoon ground cloves
1 cup plain yogurt
2 pounds boneless lamb, cut
   into 1 1/2-inch cubes
1/2 cup cream
1 teaspoon freshly ground
   black pepper

Korma curries were brought to Pakistan and northern India by the Moghuls in the sixteenth century. These curry dishes characteristically involve marinating the meat to tenderize it and then braising the meat in the marinade. Yogurt or cream is used as the braising medium, which produces the rich and creamy sauce that is characteristic.

Sauté the onions, garlic, and ginger in the ghee until soft. Add the Cayenne, coriander, cardamom, cumin, and cloves. Sauté for an additional 2 minutes. Put the mixture in a blender and puree to a paste. Stir the paste into the yogurt until well mixed. Add the lamb and toss to coat.

Marinate the lamb overnight in the refrigerator.

Bring the lamb to room temperature before cooking. Place in a heavy pan, along with the marinade and 2 cups of water. Bring to a boil, reduce the heat, and simmer until the meat is tender, about 2 hours, stirring occasionally.

Mix the cream with 1/2 cup water and stir into the lamb. Add the pepper and simmer until heated and the sauce is creamy.

Serving Suggestion: Serve with pilaf, broccoli with garlic-lemon butter, and Tamatar Raita (see recipe this chapter).

*Ghee is a clarified butter commonly used in Indian recipes.

Pistachio Pillau of Lamb

Heat Scale: 3
Serves: 4 to 6

4 green New Mexican
   chiles, roasted, peeled,
   stems and seeds removed,
   chopped
2 medium onions, chopped
2 pounds boneless lamb, cut
   in 1 1/2-inch cubes
4 tablespoons ghee or
   vegetable oil
6 dried apricots
1/2 cup pistachio nuts
1 teaspoon ground turmeric
1 teaspoon ground cumin
1 teaspoon ground
   coriander
1/2 teaspoon ground cloves
1 cup yogurt

This lamb dish from Afghanistan involves a cooking method different from the previous dish, as the meat is not marinated but simmered until tender. It takes longer, but the slow cooking blends the flavors. The foods and cooking methods of this area are related more to those of the Middle East and Asia than to those of southern India and the subcontinent.

Sauté the onions and lamb in the ghee until the lamb is browned.

Add the remaining ingredients along with 2 cups of water. Simmer for 4 hours or until the meat is very tender, adding more water if necessary.

Serving Suggestions: Tibetan Potato Curry (see recipe this chapter), seasoned spinach, and unleavened bread such as pita go well with this lamb dish.

Zhoug

Heat Scale: 5
Yield: 1 1/2 cups

8 small green chiles such as
   Jalapeños, stems and seeds
   removed, chopped
1 cup chopped fresh cilantro
1/2 cup chopped fresh
   parsley
2 tablespoons chopped
   garlic
2 teaspoons ground cumin
1/2 to 3/4 cup olive oil

Yemenites often live to be over a hundred years of age. Perhaps it is due to the daily consumption of zhoug, *a chile condiment that is served with meat, fish, and poultry — and just about anything else.*

Place all the ingredients in a blender and add enough oil to puree to a smooth paste.

Spicy Sautéed Apple Salad

Heat Scale: 2
Serves: 4 to 6

2 tablespoons finely
  chopped green New
  Mexican chile, roasted,
  peeled, stems and seeds
  removed
1 small onion, thinly sliced
2 cloves garlic, minced
1 tablespoon vegetable oil
2 green apples, cored and
  cut in wedges
2 small tomatoes, quartered
2 tablespoons lime juice,
  fresh preferred
1 tablespoon finely chopped
  fresh parsley
1 teaspoon caraway seeds

This unusual salad from Iraq combines green chile with fruits and vegetables.

Sauté the chiles, onions, and garlic in the oil until softened. Add the apples and sauté until just browned but still slightly crisp. Add the tomatoes and heat through. Remove and cool.

Before serving, toss with the lime juice. Garnish with the parsley and caraway seeds and serve.

Sri Lankan Black Curry

Heat Scale: 8
Serves: 4 to 6

4 Yellow Wax Hot chiles,
  stems and seeds removed,
  chopped
4 small dried red Piquin
  chiles, stems removed
5 small dried red Chiltepin
  chiles
1 tablespoon ground
  coriander seeds
2 teaspoons cumin seeds
1 teaspoon fennel seeds
1 teaspoon fenugreek seeds

Some Sri Lankan curries are black because the various seeds that are used are toasted or roasted to a dark brown color. Sri Lanka is famous for its hot cuisine, and this is one of the hottest of all Sri Lankan dishes.

Toast the coriander, cumin, fennel, and fenugreek seeds on a hot griddle until they turn dark and begin to crackle and "pop."

Grind together the Piquins, Chiltepins, toasted seeds, cinnamon, cloves, and cardamom. Place the spice powder and 1/2 cup of water in a blender and puree to a smooth paste. Toss the lamb cubes in the mixture and marinate for an hour.

Sauté the onion and Yellow Wax Hot chiles in the oil until soft. Add the lamb and the marinade, and 2 cups of water. Bring

1 2-inch stick whole
  cinnamon
6 whole cloves
1 tablespoon cardamom
  seeds
1 pound lamb, cut in 1 1/2-
  inch cubes
1 medium onion, chopped
2 tablespoons vegetable oil

to a boil, reduce the heat, and simmer until the lamb is tender,
about 2 hours. Add more water if necessary.

Serving Suggestion: Serve the lamb over rice.

Tamarind Chicken in White Curry Sauce

Heat Scale: 7
Serves: 4

8 small green chiles such as
  Jalapeños, stems removed,
  sliced into rings
4 green New Mexican
  chiles, roasted, stems and
  seeds removed, chopped
1 teaspoon ground Cayenne
1/2 cup tamarind pulp
1 cup chopped shallots or
  scallions
5 cloves garlic, minced
2 tablespoons finely
  chopped fresh ginger
3 tablespoons vegetable oil
1 3-pound chicken, skinned,
  cut into 1 1/2-inch cubes
1 1/2 cups unsweetened
  coconut milk

*White curries with a coconut-milk base are the mildest of the
Sri Lankan curries — but still rate a 7 on the Heat Scale!*

Soak the tamarind in 3/4 cup boiling water for 2 hours. Mash
the tamarind and then strain. Throw away the pulp and reserve
the juice.

Sauté the chile rings, shallots, garlic, and ginger in the oil
until soft. Stir in the Cayenne and chicken and mix well.

Add the coconut milk, bring to a boil. Reduce the heat, and
simmer covered, stirring occasionally, for 30 minutes. Add the
chopped chile and cook for an additional 5 minutes. Stir in the
tamarind and cook, uncovered, for 10 minutes or until thickened, stirring occasionally.

Serving Suggestion: Serve over rice with stir-fried green beans.

Burmese Spiced Duck

Heat Scale: 4
Serves: 4 to 6

2 tablespoons dried crushed
  red chile, seeds included
1 4-pound duck, cut into
  serving pieces
4 tablespoons soy sauce
1 tablespoon Red Chile Oil
  (see recipe Chapter 2)
1 teaspoon sesame oil
1 large onion, thinly sliced
4 tablespoons finely
  chopped fresh ginger
2 tablespoons vegetable oil
12 cardamom pods, crushed
2 teaspoon ground
  cinnamon
1 teaspoon ground cloves
1/4 teaspoon ground mace
2 cups water

The cooking of Burma reflects the influence of its two large neighbors — India and China — but still retains a taste all its own. Hot chiles are liberally used, along with large amounts of ginger. A typical meal would consist of a salad, clear consommé, rice, and a type of curry dish. If duck is not available, chicken can be successfully substituted in this recipe.

Remove as much fat as possible from the duck. Mix the soy sauce, Chile Oil, and sesame oil, and coat the duck with the mixture. Let it sit for an hour or more to marinate.

Sauté the onion and ginger in the vegetable oil until browned. Add the chiles, cardamom, cinnamon, cloves, and mace. Heat for a couple of minutes. Add the duck and brown on all sides.

Pour in the water, bring to a boil, reduce the heat. Cover and simmer for 1 to 1 1/2 hours, basting frequently with the sauce. Add more water if necessary.

Serving Suggestion: Serve the duck on a bed of rice, accompanied with a cucumber salad and lime pickle.

Ginger Noodle Salad

Heat Scale: 5
Serves: 4 to 6

4 small green chiles such as
   Jalapeños, stems and seeds
   removed, sliced thin
1/4 cup oil, peanut preferred
4 tablespoons finely
   chopped fresh ginger
4 cloves garlic, minced
3 tablespoons distilled white
   vinegar
1 tablespoon Red Chile Oil
   (see recipe Chapter 2)
1 teaspoon sesame oil
2 teaspoons fish sauce (*nam
   pla* or *nuoc nam**) or
   substitute soy sauce
2 tablespoons vegetable oil
1/2 cup flaked coconut
2 cups cooked linguini or
   other thin noodles
1 medium cucumber, thinly
   sliced
1 cup finely shredded
   cabbage
1/2 pound cooked shrimp,
   shelled and deveined

Salads play an important role in the diet of Burma, but they differ from those of the West, the typical salad containing fish sauce, noodles, meat or shellfish, garlic, onions — and, of course, chiles.

Heat the peanut oil to 350° F and simmer the chiles, ginger, and garlic in it for a couple of minutes. Allow the oil to cool and stir in the vinegar, Red Chile Oil, sesame oil, and fish sauce. Let the mixture sit for an hour to blend the flavors.

Heat the additional oil and add the coconut. Stir-fry the coconut until golden, about 5 minutes. Remove and drain.

Toss the noodles, cucumber, and cabbage with the dressing. Top with the coconut and shrimp and serve.

Serving Suggestion: Serve with the Burmese Spiced Duck (see recipe this chapter).

*Available in Asian markets

CHAPTER EIGHT

Hot and Healthy

*"A single drop of capsaicin diluted in 100,000 parts of water
will produce a persistent burning of the tongue. Diluted
in one million drops of water, it still produces a
perceptible warmth."*

Science News, 1988

PITY the poor maligned pods! Ever since their first usage in prehistoric South America, chile peppers have gained a reputation for being both a remedy for some ailments and an aggravation of others. The first warning was issued in 1590, when the Jesuit priest and historian José de Acosta warned of the reputed aphrodisiac qualities of chiles, saying the fruit of the pepper plant was "prejudicial to the health of young folks, chiefly to the soul, for it provokes to lust." Unfortunately, this assertion was never proven to be true.

Today, chiles are sometimes cited as being both the cure and the cause of the same ailment! For example, chiles have a reputation in the United States for irritating the digestive tract, yet a popular Mexican stomach-ache cure is to chew up and swallow a whole Serrano chile. Such a contradiction begs for resolution, and the only way to proceed is to examine the historical record and compare it to modern experiments — a tedious and frustrating task, since all the research has not been completed.

Since we began researching chile peppers in 1977, we have maintained a list of the maladies supposedly treated or cured by the use of chile peppers both topically applied and eaten. The efficacy of chile as a treatment for most of these conditions has not been scientifically verified and thus remains on the level of a folk remedy. However, as we shall see, some of the following conditions have been successfully treated with capsaicin, the chemical that gives chiles their heat: acid indigestion, acne, ague, alcoholism, anorexia, apoplexy, arteriosclerosis, arthritis, asthma, blood clots, boils, bronchitis, cancer, catarrh, cholera, colic, colds, congestion, conjunctivitis, coughs, cramps, croup, dropsy, dysentery, ear infections, epilepsy, fever, gout, headache, hemorrhoids, herpes, liver congestion, malaria, migraine, night blindness, phantom-limb pain, low blood pressure, rheumatism, seasickness, scurvy, sore throats, stomach aches, tonsilitis, tooth-aches, tumors, ulcers, vascular problems, venereal disease, vertigo, and wounds.

One of the first real breakthroughs to prove the efficacy of chile peppers occurred when vitamin C was determined to be a link between chiles and scurvy prevention.

Wholesome Heat: Vitamins C and A

Chile peppers were responsible for the awarding of a Nobel Prize. In 1928, Albert Szent-Györgyi, a professor at the University of Szeged in Hungary, was experimenting with a then-mysterious chemical he called "God-knows," because no one knew what its uses were. At first he produced small quantities of the chemical from the adrenal glands of cattle and eventually named it ascorbic acid.

Since Szent-Györgyi lived in the heart of Paprika country, it was only natural that his wife would prepare a dish made from those chiles, but the professor did not care for her meal and joked that if he could not eat it, he could at least experiment with it! He took the Paprika to his laboratory and made history by discovering that the pods were an excellent source of ascorbic acid, which we now call vitamin C.

In 1937, Szent-Györgyi was awarded the Nobel Prize in physiology and medicine for his work with vitamim C. In 1978, he wrote, "I strongly believe that a proper use of ascorbic acid can profoundly change our vital statistics, including those for cancer. For this, ascorbic acid would have to cease to be looked upon as a medicine, sold in milligram pills by the druggist. It would have to become a household article, like, sugar and salt and flour." Of course, today vitamin C is both a medicine and a household article!

One of the earliest uses of the vitamin C in chile peppers was, like citrus fruits, in preventing that scourge of the high seas, scurvy. The historian and naturalist Bernabe Cobo wrote in 1653 that after the Spanish sailors discovered chiles in Mexico, they took *Ají en escabeche* with them on voyages. Today, chile peppers are used as an excellent source of both vitamins C and A.

Vitamin C promotes growth and tissue repair and is important for healthy blood vessels, bones, and teeth. Undoubtedly, vitamin C is essential in resisting diseases, but the way it functions is not clear despite claims by some promoters that large doses will prevent colds and other maladies.

Green chiles are quite high in vitamin C, with twice the amount as citrus, while dried red chiles contain more vitamin A than carrots. In this way the two chile pepper vitamins are complete opposites. Vitamin C is one of the least stable of all the vitamins; it will break down chemically through heat, exposure to air, solubility in water, and by dehydration. Vitamin A, however, is one of the most stable vitamins and is not affected by canning, cooking, or time.

Despite its tendency to break down, a high percentage of vitamin C in fresh green chiles is retained in canned and frozen products; however, the vitamin C content drops dramatically in the dried red pods and powder. Each 100 grams of fresh ripe chile pods contains 369 milligrams of vitamin C, which diminishes by more than half to 154 milligrams in the dried red pods. Red chile powder contains less than 3 percent of the vitamin C of ripe pods, a sorry 10 milligrams.

However, in an incredible turnabout, vitamin A dramatically increases as the pod turns red and dries, from 770 units per 100 grams of green pods to 77,000 in freshly processed dried red pods. This hundredfold rise in vitamin A content is the result of increasing carotene, the chemical that produces the orange and red colors of ripe peppers. Vitamin A helps maintain normal vision in dim light, is important for skeletal growth and tooth structure, and is necessary for proper birth and lactation.

The recommended daily allowances for these vitamins are 5000 International Units for A and 60 milligrams for C. These allowances could be satisfied daily by eating about a teaspoonful of red chile sauce for vitamin A and about one ounce of fresh green chile for vitamin C.

Instead of eating the chile raw, however, we suggest preparing our "vitamin" recipes for High "C" Salsa, Walnut-Grapefruit Salad with Yellow Chiles, and Monkfish with Chile Orange Oil. We have also included Apple-Jicama Salad with Green Chile Dressing as an example of one of the healthiest dishes possible.

Capsaicin, the Power Chemical

The heat source of chile peppers, capsaicin, is produced by glands at the junction of the placenta and the pod wall. The capsaicin spreads unevenly throughout the inside of the pod and is concentrated mostly in the placental tissue. The seeds are *not* sources of heat, as commonly believed. However, because of their proximity to the placenta, the seeds do occasionally absorb capsaicin through the processing procedure. For every hundred parts of capsaicin in the placental tissue, there are six parts in the rest of the fruit tissue, and four parts in the seeds.

Capsaicin is an incredibly powerful and stable alkaloid seemingly unaffected by cold or heat, which retains its orginal potency over time, cooking, or freezing. Because it has no flavor, color, or odor, the precise amount of capsaicin present in chiles can only be measured by a specialized laboratory procedure known as high-pressure liquid chromatography (HPLC), sometimes called high-*performance* liquid chromotography.

Capsaicinoids are the chemical compounds that give chile peppers their bite. Scientists have identified and isolated six naturally occurring members of this fiery family and one synthetic cousin, which is used as a reference gauge for determining the relative pungency of the others.

The synthetic capsaicinoid vanillylamide of n-nonanoic acid (VNA), was administered to sixteen trained tasters by researchers Anna Krajewska and John Powers at the University of Georgia. The tasters compared the heat of VNA to the four natural capsaicinoids and the results were as follows.

The mildest capsaicinoid was nordihydrocapsaicin (NDHC), which was described as the "least irritating" and "fruity, sweet, and spicy." Next was homodihydrocapsaicin (HDHC), a compound described as "very irritating" and one that produced a "numbing burn" in the throat, which also was the most prolonged and difficult to rinse out.

The two most fiery capsaicinoid compounds were capsaicin (C) and dihydrocapsaicin (DHC), which produced burning everywhere from the mid-tongue and palate down into the throat. Evidently, all of the capsaicinoids work together to produce the pungency of peppers, but capsaicin itself is still rated the strongest.

The sensation of heat created by capsaicin is caused by the irritation of the trigeminal cells, which are pain receptors located in the mouth, nose, and stomach. They release substance P, a chemical messenger that tells the brain about pain or skin inflamation. Repeated consumption of chile peppers confuses the substance P receptors, which is the reason people eventually build up a tolerance to capsaicin and can eat hotter and hotter foods.

When applied topically to treat skin pain, capsaicin empties the stores of substance P from the nerve endings in the skin — this is the initial burning sensation. Capsaicin also prevents the nerve endings from making more substance P, and thus further pain signals from the skin are greatly diminished or completely eliminated. Capsaicin is the only compound known to block the transmission of substance P to the brain.

Substance P causes the brain to produce endorphins, morphine-like natural painkillers that give the body a sense of well-being. Some experts have suggested that by eating fiery foods, chile lovers are unconsciously stimulating the brain to release endorphins, which is why there are tales of people like us who are "addicted" to chile peppers.

A 1980 study by P. Rozin and P. Schiller concluded that people love chiles because they are receiving pleasure from a "constrained risk," or a thrill. Such people are risk-takers and eat chiles for the same reason they may climb mountains or skydive. "These benignly masochistic activities are uniquely human," Rozin and Schiller point out.

Dr. Andrew Weil believes that the chile eater experiences a "rush" similar to that produced by psychotropic drugs. "He knows that pain can be transformed into a friendly sensation whose strength can go into making him high," Weil writes. He theorizes that familiarity with eating hot chiles enables the chile eater to "glide along on the strong stimulation, experiencing it as something between pleasure and pain that enforces concentration and brings about a high state of consciousness. This technique might be called 'mouth surfing.'"

Other physiological changes caused by capsaicin include the draining of the sinuses and gustatory sweating. Since chile both stimulates the appetite and cools off the body, the combination of the two factors explains why the majority of chile is consumed by people living in the tropics.

A 1954 study by T. S. Lee of the Department of Physiology at the University of Malaya in Singapore examined the mechanics of gustatory sweating. Volunteers chewed up Chiltepin-type chiles that Lee called *Capsicum minimum* and held them in their mouths for five minutes. Then their perspiration amounts were measured, and the distribution of sweating over various parts of the body was recorded. Lee's method produced sweating in forty-five out of forty-six volunteers, and he discovered that the perspiration was symmetrical and confined to the head and neck. It was always accompanied by a flushing of the face, tears, and nasal secretions — now known as gustatory rhinitis. Although not related to thermal sweating, gustatory sweating increased when the body was warmed and decreased when it was cooled.

Thirty-five years after Lee's study, medical researchers at the National Institute of Allergy and Infectious Diseases have developed a nasal spray that stops gustatory rhinitis, that dreaded draining of the nasal passages caused by eating hot chiles. The condition, sometimes called the "salsa sniffles," is caused by nerves overstimulated by capsaicin and is unlike the runniness associated with head colds or allergies, which is triggered by a histamine reaction.

The *Journal of Allergy and Clinical Immunology* reported that volunteers sprayed an antispasmodic drug up their noses before eating a spicy meal. In 100 percent of the cases, the noses were kept dry with no adverse side effects. Interestingly enough, the drug used was atropine, extracted from the deadly nightshade *Atropa belladonna*, which belongs — as do chile peppers — to the family Solanaceae.

Measuring the Heat

Determining the precise pungency of the varieties of chiles and the foods prepared with them has long been a goal of cooks and researchers alike. In 1912, Wilbur L. Scoville, a pharmacologist with Parke Davis, the drug company using capsaicin in its muscle salve, Heet, developed the Scoville Organoleptic Test. This test used a panel of five human heat samplers who tasted and analyzed a solution made from exact weights of chile peppers dissolved in alcohol and diluted with sugar water. The pungency was recorded in multiples of one hundred "Scoville Units." A majority of three of the tasters had to agree before a value was assigned to a given chile or food; however, it is evident that the Scoville Test was highly subjective, and that is why the test was replaced by high technology.

In the past, when human taste tests were used, wide variations in the capsaicin levels occurred even in the same variety of chile, accounting for the wildly differing Scoville heat scales appearing in various publications. The technique for determining Capsicum pungency by high-pressure liquid chromatography (HPLC) was developed by James Woodbury of Cal-Compack Foods in 1980. This process dissolves the powdered chile sample in ethanol saturated with sodium acetate. The sample is then analyzed with a spectrofluorometer that measures the capsaicin levels in parts per million, which is then converted to Scoville Units, the standard industry measurement.

The test is sensitive to two parts per million — about thirty Scoville units — which means that testing individual chiles is now much more accurate. Home cooks wishing to test their chiles will need to buy an Altex Model 322 Liquid Chromatograph equipped with a solvent programmer and dual pumps.

Incidentally, pure capsaicin equals sixteen million Scoville Units. Included here are ratings based on various tests on chiles with HPLC as reported by the Texas Agricultural Experiment Station, New Mexico State University, and several chile-processing companies. Because of the variability in heat levels caused by misidentification, hybridization, local variation, and growing conditions, these ratings should only be considered a general guide. Cooks are advised to pretest chiles by tasting a minute amount to determine approximate pungency.

Despite the accuracy of HPLC testing, we should remember, as Dr. Ben Villalon of the Texas Agricultural Experiment Station points out, "Capsaicin can and is quantitatively measured by high-pressure liquid chromatography, to exactness for that particular pod only, that particular plant, that particular location, and that particular season only." Thus, chiles will sometimes deviate from our heat scale because of local conditions.

Official Chile Heat Scale

Rating	Approximate Scoville Units	Chile Varieties
10	100,000–300,000	Habanero, Bahamian
9	50,000–100,000	Santaka, Chiltepin, Thai
8	30,000–50,000	Ají, Rocoto, Piquin, Cayenne, Tabasco
7	15,000–30,000	de Arbol
6	5,000–15,000	Yellow Wax Hot, Serrano
5	2,500–5,000	Jalapeño, Mirasol
4	1,500–2,500	Sandia, Cascabel
3	1,000–1,500	Ancho, Pasilla, Española
2	500–1,000	NuMex Big Jim, NM 6-4
1	100–500	R-Naky, Mexi-Bell, Cherry
0	0	Mild Bells, Pimiento, Sweet Banana

Putting Out the Fire

It is senseless to serve or consume dishes that are too hot to eat with comfort. If the discernible flavors of both the meal and the chiles are unidentifiable, the pleasure of dining is gone. But sometimes accidents happen, and inexperienced diners get burned out.

In 1989, John Riley, editor-publisher of the quarterly journal *Solanaceae,* tested various remedies reputed to remove the heat of the capsaicin in chile peppers. In each test, a slice of Serrano chile was chewed for one minute, and then one of the remedies was applied. The amount of time until the burning sensation eased was measured and the results were recorded. As we always suspected, ordinary milk was the clear winner.

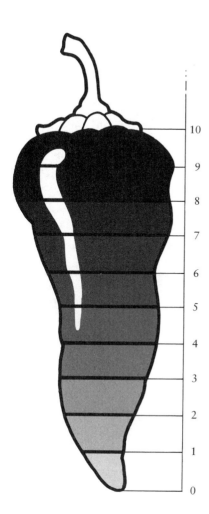

Official Chile Heat Scale

Remedy	Total Minutes
Rinse the mouth with water only	11
Rinse the mouth with one tablespoon olive oil	10
Drink one half cup heavy fruit syrup	10
Rinse mouth with one tablespoon glycerol	8
Drink one half cup milk, rinsing well	7

If a prepared recipe is too blistering, here are some ways to cool it down:

- Reduce the amount of chile in the recipe to begin with. More heat can always be added later.

- Remove the seeds and membranes (placental tissue) from the chile pods.

- Increase the amount of tomato products (if any) used in the recipe, such as tomato sauce, puree, or whole tomatoes.

- In appropriate recipes, such as enchiladas, add a side of sour cream or yogurt.

- If using canned chiles, rinse them well to remove the canning liquid.

- Soak the chiles in salted ice water.

- If making a sauce calling for green chiles, add pureed Bell peppers to dilute the heat.

- When buying crushed red chile, avoid products with yellow flakes, which indicate the presence of seeds and membrane.

Now, if anyone is literally burned out, here are some suggestions to cool down the mouth and throat:

- The best solution is the immediate consumption of dairy products such as sour cream, yogurt, or ice cream.

- Starchy foods such as bread or potatoes tend to absorb or dilute capsaicin. In New Mexico, we use sopaipillas with honey.

- Various cultures have their own cures. The Chinese use white rice, the Vietnamese suggest hot liquids such as tea, and East Indians utilize yogurt-based drinks and sauces.

- A Mexican cure says that if enough beer is consumed, no one will care how hot the chiles are!

An Undeservedly Bad Reputation

Because they are so hot, legend has held for centuries, *chiles must be dangerous.* Interestingly enough, they are reputed to aggravate some of the very conditions they are supposed to relieve, such as acid indigestion, cancer, dysentery, ulcers, and wounds.

We have demonstrated that capsaicin can cause burning of the skin and hands, a malady now known as "Hunan hand." Yet a topically applied, capsaicin-based cream is used to treat phantom-limb pain, a painful condition experienced by amputees. Another example of chiles as cause and cure is Jaloproctitis, a burning sensation that occurs during and after the elimination of Jalapeños. Yet red chiles are reputed to be a cure for hemorrhoids, as we detailed in Chapter 6.

Legend holds that chile peppers are murder on the human gastrointestinal system. They are accused of causing heartburn, gastritis, ulcers, and diarrhea among other maladies. Despite having such a bad reputation, medical evidence has repeatedly demonstrated that the capsaicin in chile peppers does little or no damage.

A 1988 study at the Veterans Administration Medical Center in Houston backs up the contention that chiles are safe to eat. As reported by the *Journal of the American Medical Association,* a team of doctors at Baylor College of Medicine in Houston conducted a unique experiment utilizing *videoendoscopy,* the high-tech procedure of inserting a fiber-optic tube and a miniature video camera into the stomach to inspect it visually.

The object of the experiment was to test the generally held

theory that capsaicin, the active heat chemical in chile peppers, damages the lining of the stomach. The research team, led by Dr. David Graham, subjected twelve volunteers (none were chile-lovers) to a series of test items — bland food, plain aspirin, "Mexican" food, and pizza. After each meal, the endoscope was inserted to determine if "gastric erosions" of the lining had occurred. By far, the most damaging meal was the bland one combined with aspirin.

Not believing their results, the research team then sprayed Tabasco sauce directly on the stomach lining. There was mucosal damage this time, but it was linked to the vinegar in the sauce. To further test capsaicin alone, the good doctors then injected thirty grams of freshly ground Jalapeños directly into the stomach. There was no visible mucosal damage.

Dr. Graham concluded in his study: "We found that ingestion of highly spiced meals by normal individuals did not cause endoscopically demonstrable gastric or duodenal mucosal damage." However, in an interview published in the *Los Angeles Times,* Dr. Graham admitted that chiles increase gastric acid secretion, but "they add to the flavor and enjoyment of eating and do not appear to cause stomach lining damage." In fact, some gastroenterologists suggest that capsaicin may actually protect the lining of the stomach from damage due to aspirin or alcohol.

Some medical researchers have suggested that capsaicin is both a cause and potential cure of some forms of cancer. According to one report, capsaicin has been linked to colon cancer through studies conducted among chile pepper eaters in India and Korea. In 1984, researchers at the Eppley Institute at the University of Nebraska reported that capsaicin had flunked the Ames Test — a quick bacterial assay used to screen possible carcinogens.

But additional research has indicated that the reputed carcinogenic properties of chile peppers have been highly exaggerated. During the same study, the Eppley research team also discovered that the antioxidant properties of the capsaicin may be capable of neutralizing harmful chemicals in the body responsible for some types of cancer. Investigator Peter Gannett stated that capsaicin prevents the formation of dimethylnitrosamine

(DMN) — a known animal carcinogen — by binding to and inactivating the enzymes that produce the chemical. In the liver, capsaicin is apparently transformed into a compound that soaks up chemicals called free radicals, which are thought to cause cancer.

"Some of the chemicals in hot peppers appear to be cancer-causing, but the same ones can protect against cancer," said Peter Gannett of the University of Nebraska Medical Center. "The overall effect depends upon how much you eat." Skeptics insist that the researchers are trying to scare us again with another potential carcinogen, just as they have in the past with the highly exaggerated dangers of coffee, sugar, and cranberries.

One critic calculated that a person would have to consume *two pounds* of capsaicin to see the effects the Nebraska research suggested. Since we can taste capsaicin in solutions as diluted as one part per million, there may only be a few pounds of capsaicin in the entire annual world crop of chiles!

Peppers as Panacea

It is now evident that the value of chile peppers as a nutritional food and a medicine far outweighs any supposed risk. A 1982 study of chile consumption in Thai people, conducted at the Siriraj Hospital in Bangkok, concluded: "Capsicum, a hot appetizer and seasoning, has been found to induce increased fibrinolytic activity and simultaneously cause hypocoagulability of the blood when ingested." Translated, the statement means that Thais have a lower risk of blood clots because they eat chiles!

Recently, capsaicin has been used in yet another medical application — to treat the intense pain caused by shingles. Shingles is an eruption of unpleasant skin blisters caused by *Herpes zoster,* the chicken-pox virus. Topically applied capsaicin depletes substance P, which carries pain impulses to the brain from nerves in the skin, thus effectively short-circuiting the agony. It is basically the same process that allows the chile lover to adapt to greater and greater amounts of hot chiles. The treatment for shingles is now available in an over-the-counter cream called

Zostrix that is also being tested for the relief of mastectomy pain, diabetic neuropathy, and phantom-limb pain.

More medical uses of capsaicin are being discovered each year. The British journal *Lancet* reported in 1988 that about 15 to 35 percent of the people who chew nicotine gum in an attempt to stop smoking become addicted to the gum. Researchers have been experimenting with placebo gums to help nicotine addicts kick the habit that helped them kick the habit.

But there is a catch — finding a substance that simulates the taste and effect of nicotine. After many studies, scientists have developed a nicotine-flavored placebo gum that seems to be working. Readers have by now probably figured out where this story is leading, but we will tell it anyway: capsaicin is the mystery ingredient in this placebo gum — yet another use for this incredibly versatile chemical.

Capsaicin may also help people who suffer from allergies. In 1989, researchers at the University of California at San Francisco began studying atmospheric conditions at the Gilroy Foods Gentry plant in Gilroy, California, to determine if workers who breathe air saturated with chile powder are healthier than those who do not. They conducted two types of tests on the employees, breathing capacity and the inhalation of a chile-based breath mist. The study, which is to be concluded in 1990, will try to determine if workers who breathe chile-laden air have a higher resistance to colds and allergies.

Undoubtedly, further medical uses of chile peppers and capsaicin will be found. We believe, however, that their greatest benefit to mankind is their addition to the foods we eat.

The Whole Chile Pepper Diet

Don't panic — this isn't one of those miracle fad diets that appear in the tabloids. We do not guarantee that readers will lose forty pounds of ugly fat with forty gourmet meals in forty days without any exercise. In fact, we use the word "diet" only in its most general sense, as simply the daily fare consumed by the human animal, so the Whole Chile Pepper Diet is intended to be a convenient method for chile pepper lovers to maximize the health benefits of the powerful pods.

The Whole Chile Pepper Diet is a simple regimen to follow: chile peppers are featured in *at least one meal eaten every day, 365 days a year.* Given such consumption, it is fair to assume that anyone following this diet would qualify as a chile pepper aficionado, or "chilehead" in the vernacular. Some skeptics might suggest that our regimen is more of an addiction than a diet. We counter with the argument that aside from their ability to burn us deliciously and make us perspire, hot peppers and the dishes cooked with them are a source of many dietary benefits.

We base the Whole Chile Pepper Diet on nothing less than the 1985 "Dietary Guidelines for Americans," established by the U.S. Departments of Agriculture and Health and Social Services. Each official guideline below is followed by a brief explanation of how hot peppers fit that criterion.

Eat a variety of foods. A condiment as well as a food, hot peppers are one of the most versatile recipe ingredients. All major world cuisines have dishes prepared with peppers; they are used in every imaginable recipe, from cocktails to dessert and every course in between. A variety of foods will, of course, ensure that one consumes a healthy amount of needed vitamins, minerals, and other nutrients.

Maintain desirable weight. Hot peppers contain few calories (37 per 100 grams of green chile, about three and a half ounces), and their heat can reduce the amount of food actually consumed.

Avoid too much fat, saturated fat, and cholesterol. Every 100 grams of green chile contains less than two-tenths of a gram of fat — a very low amount.

Eat foods with adequate starch and fiber. The fiber content of fresh hot chiles is fairly high (between 1.3 and 2.3 grams per 100 grams of chile), and many of the dishes prepared with them utilize starchy ingredients such as beans, pasta, and tortillas.

Avoid too much sugar. Any sugar in chiles is in the form of healthy complex carbohydrates, and few people eat sugary chile pepper desserts anyway.

Avoid too much sodium. Eating hot chiles is a perfect way to avoid salt; the pungency of the food confuses the taste buds and reduces the desire for salt; and fresh green chiles contain only 3.5 to 5.7 milligrams of sodium per 100 grams of peppers. Satisfy the taste buds with herbs, spices, and chile peppers rather than salt.

If one drinks alcoholic beverages, one should do so in moderate amounts. For the Whole Chile Pepper Diet we recommend reasonable quantities of any good chile pepper vodka, or readers can make their own by steeping whole small hot chiles in vodka.

Chiles As Calorie-Conquerors . . .

Stated in simple terms, the weight of any animal is a matter of balance: the intake of food versus the expenditure of energy. If we consume more calories than our bodies need for daily activity, the excess energy is stored as fat; if we consume fewer calories than we need, our bodies burn the stored fat.

The most efficient way to lose weight is to cut down on caloric intake while burning off excess calories through exercise. To lose one pound a week, we must decrease our daily food intake by 500 calories or burn 500 additional calories by exercise. But moderation is important; severe dieting or excessive excercise is not recommended. Since caloric and exercise levels vary dramatically from person to person depending on height, weight, gender, metabolic rate, and body frame, we suggest that persons who are severely overweight or need a special diet should consult with their physician or dietitian.

Because chiles are naturally low in calories, there is little worry about gaining weight while eating peppers. However, dieters should be careful about the foods they combine with hot peppers.

And believe it or not, new evidence has come to light indicating that chiles may indeed assist in burning calories. In 1986, researchers at Oxford Polytechnic Institute in England conducted an experiment in TEF, an acronym for "thermic effects of food." Twelve volunteers ate identical 766-calorie meals. On one day, 3 grams each of chile powder and mustard were added to the meals; on the next day, nothing was added. On the days chile and mustard were added, the volunteers burned from 4 to 76 additional calories, with an average of 45.

A possible explanation for the process is the fact that certain hot spices — especially chiles — temporarily speed up the body's metabolic rate. After eating, the metabolic rate increases anyway, a phenomenon known as "diet-induced thermic effect." But chiles boost that effect by a factor of 25 percent, which seems to indicate that increasing the amount of chile in a recipe could reduce the effective caloric content — provided, of course, that one does not drink more beer to counter the added heat.

Another intriguing possibility has been suggested by T. George Harris, who wrote in *American Health* magazine that chiles stimulate the taste buds but not the sense of smell. Thus they "perk up food without adding fat." Harris added that he formerly made jokes about the hot pepper diet; but now, "over the last couple of years, chile peppers have begun to emerge as the nutritional heroes of the future."

Our reduced calorie recipes include Low-Calorie Hot Salad Dressing, Low-Calorie Pepper Beef and Vegetables, and the exotic Thai Beef Salad.

. . . and Chiles As Cholesterol-Conquerors

Although cholesterol is necessary for the formation of hormones and cell membranes, the substance has been associated with coronary artery disease and other circulatory disorders, primarily because the human body manufactures its own cholesterol and consequently does not need the excess supplied by meats, poultry, seafood, and dairy products. Cholesterol is totally absent from plant tissue, and that is where hot peppers enter the picture.

In some cuisines, chiles have long been associated with high-cholesterol ingredients such as lard, dairy products, and fatty meats such as pork and beef. The Whole Chile Pepper Diet is designed to reverse this trend by utilizing low-cholesterol substitutions. Perhaps the most important substitution is the replacement of solid fats with nonsaturated oils, such as the use of margarine for butter — or, better still, vegetable oil for either. Soups and stews should be chilled so that solid fat can be skimmed off before serving. Another important low-cholesterol substitution in Mexican cooking calls for the replacement of hard cheeses (such as cheddar and jack) with cottage, pot, feta or skim milk ricotta cheeses. Low-fat or skim milk should replace whole milk and cream; egg yolks should be used sparingly, if at all. As protein sources, choose lean meat, fish, poultry, beans and peas.

Scientists are currently studying the effects of fish oil on reducing cholesterol and triglyceride levels in the blood. All the facts are not in, but many dietitians are recommending an increase in fish consumption to combat cholesterol. For the dieter interested in switching to spicy fish dishes, we suggest you try the seafood recipes in this book.

Here are some hints for reducing the cholesterol levels in our recipes:

- Limit the use of fats and oils by substituting unsaturated oils such as corn or safflower for lard, butter, and palm oil and coconut oil-based shortenings.

- Remove fat from meat and fatty skin from poultry and fish before cooking.

- Avoid frying or deep-frying foods; broil, bake, steam, or poach instead.

- Substitute chile pepper–based dressings (such as salsas) for fatty (mayonnaise-based) dressings.

Our reduced cholesterol recipes are Veal with Rosemary Chile Sauce and Broiled Salmon with Spicy Sauce Verde.

Fiery Fiber and Starch

For the Whole Chile Pepper Diet, we recommend the combination of chiles with starchy foods to provide needed fiber and starch without increasing the calories consumed.

Fiber is the part of the plant cell wall that cannot be totally digested by humans. The benefits of fiber in the diet, and in the treatment of colon cancer, heart disease, and diabetes are still under investigation, but most dietitians recommend consumption of a wide variety of vegetables, fruits, and whole grains.

Starch is a complex carbohydrate occurring naturally in foods such as beans, peas, corn, breads, cereals, and pasta. It is widely thought to be fattening, but starch provides a mere four calories per gram; what *is* fattening are the additional ingredients we add to starchy foods, such as putting butter on potatoes. The best chiles for high-fiber cookery are those that are used whole, with seeds and skins intact. In this category are pickled peppers and small hot chiles such as Serranos and Jalapeños used in salsas. Remember that fresh green chiles do not have to be peeled and seeded in all cases; for use in salsas and salads, they can simply be chopped up. For extra fiber, add chopped Bell peppers to recipes, mixed, of course, with the proper balance of hot chiles.

Our high-fiber recipes are Potatoes with Chile Colorado, Fiery Three-Bean Salad, and Roasted Corn and Chile Confetti Relish.

Low-Sodium Spiciness

One of the diets people have the most trouble following is one that is sodium-restricted. As the level of sodium is lowered, the meals become less tasty to the dieter accustomed to a high salt level. Also, the recipes become more difficult to prepare because of the varying sodium levels of the ingredients themselves. We suggest that chile peppers are very useful for the low-sodium dieter.

The substitution of hot peppers for salt makes gustatory sense because the pungency of the peppers counteracts the blandness of the meal resulting from salt restrictions. In other words, the heat masks the absence of salt. Fortunately, fresh or frozen chile peppers have an extremely low sodium content.

According to a study at New Mexico State University, "Even in a severely restricted diet, the sodium content of 3.7 to 5.7 milligrams per 100 grams found in fresh chile peppers is reasonable to include as a food choice." However, the study warns that canned green chile peppers should be avoided because of salt used in the canning process, which can be over a *hundred* times the amount in fresh or frozen chile pepper.

Our low-sodium recipes not only lack added salt, they utilize naturally low-sodium ingredients. And because of the heat and taste of the chiles, they do not need it! The Low-Sodium Chile Sauce and Low-Sodium Caldillo are alternatives to the Southwestern sauces and stews in Chapter 5, and the Herb Shaker is a very tasty and moderately hot salt substitute.

Of course, one is not limited to these recipes alone when using the Whole Chile Pepper Diet. Many of the other recipes in this book are healthy and can be made more so by following the guidelines in this chapter.

 # High "C" Salsa

Heat Scale: 6
Yield: 2 cups

4 to 6 green New Mexican chiles, roasted, peeled, stems and seeds removed, chopped
3 Jalapeño chiles, stems and seeds removed, chopped
4 tomatoes, chopped
1 medium red onion, chopped
1 clove garlic, minced
2 tablespoons chopped fresh cilantro or parsley
2 tablespoons vegetable oil
1 tablespoons fresh lime juice
1 teaspoon ground cumin
1/4 teaspoon ground cloves

This all-purpose "chunky" salsa is a good source of vitamin C, as well as being low in sodium. There are four sources of "C" in this recipe: the chiles, the tomato, the parsley, and the lime juice. Although vitamin C is affected by contact with the air, this salsa contains such a large amount that a single serving still meets the daily requirement.

Combine all the ingredients and allow them to sit for at least an hour before serving.

Serving Suggestions: This salsa can be served as a dip with chips, as a salsa over foods such as burritos or steaks, or over shredded lettuce as a salad dressing.

Walnut-Grapefruit Salad with Yellow Chiles

Heat Scale: 3
Serves: 4

4 Yellow Wax Hot chiles,
  stems and seeds removed,
  sliced in rings
2 tablespoons walnut oil
1 tablespoon balsamic
  vinegar
1 tablespoon lime juice
1 tablespoon chopped fresh
  parsley
2 teaspoons sugar
1 cup orange segments
1 cup grapefruit segments
1 cup diced jicama
1/4 cup chopped walnuts

Chiles and citrus fruits combine in a powerful combination of vitamin C and flavor. The heat of the chile complements the sweetness of the fruit.

Combine the chiles, oil, vinegar, lime juice, parsley, and sugar and allow them to sit for an hour to blend the flavors.

Toss the oranges, grapefruit, and jicima and place on a plate. Pour the dressing over the salad and top with the walnuts and serve.

Serving Suggestions: This salad goes especially well with fish and poultry dishes.

 # Monkfish with Chile Orange Oil

Heat Scale: 5
Serves: 4

Note: This recipe requires
advance preparation.

1/4 cup dried crushed red
  New Mexican chiles, seeds
  included
2 cups peanut oil
1 teaspoon sesame oil
zest of 3 oranges, finely
  minced
2 cloves garlic, finely minced
1 1/2 pounds monkfish
  fillets

The dried red chile used in this recipe provides an ample amount of vitamin A even when used as a marinade.

Heat the peanut oil to about 325° F. Remove from the heat and stir in the sesame oil, orange zest, garlic, and chile. Allow the oil to cool, add the fish, and marinate overnight in the refrigerator.

Grill the fish over charcoal until done, basting frequently with the marinade.

Apple-Jicama Salad with Green Chile Dressing

Heat Scale: 3
Serves: 4 to 6

The Dressing:

6 green New Mexican
  chiles, roasted, peeled,
  stems and seeds removed,
  chopped
2 cucumbers, peeled and
  seeded, chopped
1/4 cup chopped fresh
  cilantro or parsley
4 scallions, chopped,
  including the greens
1/4 cup vegetable oil
2 tablespoons cider vinegar
2 cloves garlic, chopped
1 cup plain yogurt

The Salad:

1 Poblano chile, stem and
  seeds removed, chopped
1 large Granny Smith apple,
  chopped
1 cup chopped jicama
1 cup mandarin orange
  sections
mixed salad greens such as
  radicchio, and butter or
  red leaf lettuce
1/4 cup piñon nuts or
  sesame seeds

Everyone knows that salads are healthy, providing roughage and fiber, as well as a good source of vitamins. What most people do not realize is that salad dressings are often high in fat, calories, and salt. Chiles play an important part in the following recipe, which is rich in the healthy attributes and low in the negative ones.

To Make the Dressing: Put the chiles, cucumbers, cilantro, scallions, oil, and vinegar in a blender and puree until smooth. Add the yogurt and mix well. Allow the dressing to sit for an hour or more to blend the flavors.

To Assemble the Salad: Mix together the Poblano chile, apple, jicama, oranges, and salad greens. Toss with only enough of the dressing to lighlty coat the lettuce, top with the nuts, and serve.

Low-Calorie Hot Salad Dressing

Heat Scale: 5
Yield: 1 1/3 cups

1 teaspoon ground Cayenne
2 green New Mexican chiles, roasted, peeled, stems and seeds removed, chopped
1/2 cup catsup
3/4 cup cider vinegar
1 tablespoon vegetable oil
1 teaspoon sugar
1/2 teaspoon dry mustard
2 cloves garlic, finely chopped
1 tablespoon chopped fresh parsley
freshly ground black pepper

Try this recipe in place of commercial low-calorie dressings, which may have up to 90 calories per tablespoon; this one has only 15 calories per tablespoon, and much less sodium.

Combine all the ingredients and refrigerate for at least an hour before serving.

Low-Calorie Pepper Beef and Vegetables

Heat Scale: 6
Serves: 4

The Marinade:

2 teaspoons dried crushed red chile, seeds included

1 tablespoon Sichuan peppercorns*, toasted and ground

3 tablespoons light soy sauce

1 tablespoon sesame oil

1 tablespoon rice wine

2 teaspoons finely chopped fresh ginger

2 cloves garlic, minced

1 teaspoon sugar

The Stir-Fry:

4 dried Piquin chiles, or other small dried red chiles

3 Serrano or Yellow Wax Hot chiles, stems and seeds removed, cut in rings

1 small Bell pepper, stem and seeds removed, cut in strips

1/2 pound flank steak, cut across the grain in 1/4-inch strips

2 cups broccoli flowerets

1 cup cauliflower flowerets

1 1/2 tablespoons Red Chile Oil (see recipe Chapter 2)

1/2 cup beef broth

4 scallions, chopped including the greens

This tasty stir-fry uses both hot and mild peppers as well as a variety of vegetables to flavor this "under 300-calorie" dish. Stir-frying is a very healthy method of preparation if done correctly, as the food absorbs very little of the oil. Try different vegetables to change the basic recipe.

Mix all the ingredients together for the marinade and marinate the beef for 30 minutes.

Blanch the broccoli, cauliflower, and Bell pepper for 2 minutes, then remove and drain.

Heat the Red Chile Oil in a wok or heavy skillet to 350° F, add the Piquins and simmer until the peppers start to sizzle.

Add the beef and marinade and stir-fry until the beef is done but still rare, about 2 minutes.

Add the vegetables and the broth to the wok, and cover and steam for 2 minutes. Garnish with the scallions and serve.

*Available in Asian markets.

Thai Beef Salad

Heat Scale: 5
Serves: 6

Note: This recipe requires advance preparation.

4 tablespoons dried crushed red chile, including the seeds
4 tablespoons soy sauce
2 tablespoons rice vinegar
2 tablespoons vegetable oil
1 tablespoon lime juice
1/2 teaspoon sesame oil
4 scallions, chopped, including the greens
3/4 pound boneless top round steak, cut in strips 1 1/4 inches long by 1/4 inch wide
1 large tomato, cut in wedges
12 fresh pea pods, blanched
1 large cucumber, peeled and sliced thin
1/2 cup broccoli, broken into flowerets
butter lettuce leaves
1 teaspoon sesame seeds
fresh mint leaves for garnish

People tend not to think of beef as being low in calories or cholesterol, but this entrée salad is both. It is high in complex carbohydrates, fiber, and vitamin A, and if a low sodium soy sauce is substituted, it is also low in sodium. It is a traditional snack in Thailand.

Combine the chile, soy sauce, rice vinegar, oils, lime juice, scallions, and beef and marinate in refrigerator for 6 hours or overnight.

Broil or grill the meat until rare, basting with the marinade.

Arrange the vegetables on the lettuce. Place the strips of meat on the lettuce, top with the sesame seeds, garnish with the mint leaves, and serve.

Veal with Rosemary Chile Sauce

Heat Scale: 1
Serves: 4

2 dried Ancho chiles, stems and seeds removed
2 tablespoons vegetable oil
4 veal cutlets, pounded between wax-paper sheets until 1/8 inch thick
flour for dredging
2 teaspoons chopped shallots or scallions
1/2 cup red wine
2 teaspoons chopped fresh rosemary
1/4 cup chicken stock
2 tablespoons cornstarch mixed with 2 tablespoons water
1 tablespoon chopped walnuts

Veal, which is low in cholesterol, is often covered with a heavy cream sauce that is high in fat and cholesterol. This recipe calls for a light glaze rather than a heavy sauce. Skinless chicken breasts can be substituted for the veal in this recipe.

Cover the chiles with hot water and let sit for 15 minutes until softened. Place the chiles in a blender along with 1 cup of the water they soaked in and puree until smooth.

Heat the oil in a skillet until almost smoking.

Lightly dredge the cutlets with the flour and sauté the veal until lightly browned, about 1 minute on each side or until done. Remove and keep warm.

Sauté the shallots in the oil until soft.

Deglaze the pan with the wine. Add the rosemary and simmer until reduced to 1/4 cup.

Add the stock and chile sauce and simmer. Thicken the sauce, if necessary, with the cornstarch.

Place the veal on plates, top with the sauce, garnish with the walnuts, and serve.

Broiled Salmon with Spicy Sauce Verde

Heat Scale: 4
Serves: 4

4 green New Mexican chiles, roasted, peeled, stems and seeds removed, chopped
1 tablespoon hot pepper sauce such as Habanero (see recipe Chapter 2)
2 teaspoons chopped scallions, including the greens
1 tablespoon margarine
3 tablespoons pickled green peppercorns, drained
2 teaspoons flour
1/2 cup dry white wine
1/4 cup skim milk
1 teaspoon dried dill
4 salmon steaks

The desire of Americans to cut down on cholesterol has led to a rise in fish consumption. However, fish does not have to be served plain to be healthful, as proved by this recipe. The sauce is low in sodium, fat, and calories. One thing to remember when cooking with wine is that the alcohol (with many of its calories) evaporates as it cooks.

Sauté the scallions in the margarine for 2 minutes. Add the green peppercorns and continue to sauté for an additional 2 minutes. Add the flour and cook for 2 minutes, stirring constantly. Stir in the wine and milk and blend well.

Add the green chile, pepper sauce, and dill. Bring to a boil, reduce the heat, and simmer until the sauce has been reduced and thickened.

Grill or broil the salmon until done.

Place some of the sauce on a plate, top with the fish, and serve.

Potatoes with Chile Colorado

Heat Scale: 3
Serves: 4

2 tablespoons dried crushed red chile, seeds included
1/4 cup chopped onions
1 tablespoon margarine
2 medium potatoes, cooked with the skins on, cubed

This easy, flavorful recipe is high in complex carbohydrates, low in sodium, while providing an outstanding source of vitamin A. One serving of these potatoes more than exceeds the daily requirement for this vitamin, supplied here by the dried red chile.

Sauté the onion and the chile in the margarine.

Toss the potatoes in the mixture and bake in a 350° F oven until heated through.

Serving Suggestions: These potatoes go well with broiled meats or baked chicken.

Fiery Three-Bean Salad

Heat Scale: 5
Serves: 6
Note: This recipe requires advance preparation.

This tasty salad is high in fiber and complex carbohydrates. The fiber comes from a number of sources in this recipe, not only from the chile but also from the three types of beans: kidney, green, and garbanzo, or chick-peas. The salad also provides a source of protein while being low in sodium.

The Salad:

4 Jalapeño chiles, stems removed, chopped
4 Yellow Wax Hot chiles, stems removed, chopped
1/2 cup garbanzo beans, cooked and drained
1/2 cup kidney beans, cooked and drained
1/2 cup green beans, cooked and drained
6 scallions, chopped, including the greens

The Dressing:

1/4 cup olive oil
3 tablespoons Hot Chile Vinegar (see recipe Chapter 2)
1 clove garlic, minced
2 tablespoons chopped fresh cilantro or parsley
1 tablespoon Dijon-type mustard
1 teaspoon ground cumin
freshly ground black pepper

While the beans are warm, combine them with the chiles and scallions.

Combine the dressing ingredients in a blender and mix until well blended.

Pour the dressing over the warm salad, toss well, and let sit for an hour or refrigerate overnight before serving.

Serving Suggestions: Serve on a bed of shredded lettuce garnished with Bell pepper rings or pimiento strips.

Roasted Corn and Chile Confetti Relish

Heat Scale: 4
Serves: 4 to 6

4 Jalapeño chiles, stems and
  seeds removed, chopped
1 Poblano chile, stem and
  seeds removed, chopped
1 small red Bell pepper,
  stem and seeds removed,
  chopped
5 ears of corn with the
  husks left on
1 tablespoon chopped
  scallions, including the
  greens
1 tablespoon chopped fresh
  oregano
1/2 cup finely chopped
  onion
2 tablespoons vegetable oil
2 tablespoons distilled white
  vinegar or Hot Chile
  Vinegar (see recipe
  Chapter 2)

This is a versatile recipe high in complex carbohydrates and starches from the fresh chiles and corn. It also provides a source of vitamin C from the chiles while being very low in sodium. It adds color to any plate, so serve it as side relish, an accompaniment salad, or warmed as a vegetable.

Soak the ears of corn in their husks in water for 30 minutes. Roast them by placing the ears on a hot grill and turning often until the corn is tender. Or place them in a 400° F oven and roast for 20 minutes. Cut the corn off the cobs.

Combine the chiles, corn, oregano, and scallions and toss well to mix.

Heat the oil and sauté the chopped onion until soft. Add the vinegar and bring to a boil. Pour the mixture over the corn and chiles and allow to sit for an hour to blend the flavors.

Variations: For a hotter relish, substitute Red Chile Oil (see recipe Chapter 2) for the vegetable oil.

Low-Sodium Chile Sauce

Heat Scale: 3
Yield: 2 cups
Note: This recipe requires
advance preparation.

5 teaspoons dried ground
  Pasilla chile or substitute
  ground red New Mexican
  chile
8 tomatoes, peeled and
  seeds removed, chopped or
  1 3-pound can low-sodium
  canned tomatoes

Use this low-sodium sauce in place of bottled "chili sauce," catsup, or commercial barbecue sauce that can contain up to 130 milligrams of sodium per tablespoon. This recipe has less than 5 milligrams of sodium per tablespoon. Experiment with the levels of spices to suit individual tastes.

Combine the chile, tomatoes, tomato juice, and onion in a non-aluminum pan and simmer for 15 minutes or until the tomatoes break down.

Add the remaining ingredients and simmer for 3 to 4 hours until the sauce is the consistency of thick catsup.

1 cup low-sodium tomato
  juice
1 large onion, chopped
1 cup cider vinegar
4 tablespoons brown sugar
1 teaspoon dry mustard
1/4 teaspoon ground
  cinnamon
1/4 teaspoon ground cloves
1/4 teaspoon ground nutmeg
1/4 teaspoon ground ginger
freshly ground black pepper

Store in the refrigerator for at least 24 hours before serving.
Serving Suggestions: Use in place of catsup in any recipe on sandwiches, or as a marinade when barbecuing.

 # Low-Sodium Caldillo

Heat Scale: 5
Serves: 6

6 green New Mexican
  chiles, roasted, peeled,
  stems and seeds removed,
  chopped
3/4 pound round steak, cut
  in 3/4-inch cubes
2 tablespoons vegetable oil
2 large potatoes, diced
1 small onion, chopped fine
2 stalks celery, chopped fine
4 cups low-sodium beef
  broth
1 teaspoon powdered cumin
1 teaspoon freshly ground
  black pepper
1 teaspoon chopped fresh
  cilantro

Caldillo *("light broth")* *is the Southwest's answer to beef and vegetable soup. The heat and taste of the chiles masks the lack of salt in the following soup. This recipe is low in calories, with each serving having less than 200. Serve with a crisp salad with Low-Calorie Hot Salad Dressing (see recipe this chapter) and a fruited yogurt for a complete, flavorful meal.*

Brown the meat in the oil, remove, and drain.

Add the potatoes, onions, and celery and sauté until the potatoes are browned.

Add the broth, chiles, cumin, and black pepper. Bring to a boil, reduce the heat, and simmer until the potatoes are done, about 35 minutes. Five minutes before serving, add the meat.

Top with the cilantro and serve.

Herb Shaker

Heat Scale: 7
Yield: 1/4 cup

3 teaspoons ground
   Cayenne
1 tablespoon garlic powder
1 teaspoon ground basil
1 teaspoon ground thyme
1 teaspoon ground parsley
   flakes
1 teaspoon ground savory
1 teaspoon ground mace
1 teaspoon onion powder
1 teaspoon ground black
   pepper
1 teaspoon ground sage
1 teaspoon marjoram

This recipe for a salt substitute is based on one from the American Heart Association. Reach for the chile instead of the sodium!

Combine all the ingredients in a salt shaker, label it "Herb Shaker," and use it to flavor meats, vegetables, starches, or anything that would usually need salt.

CHAPTER NINE

Asia Heats Up

Oh soul, come back! Why should you go so far away?
All your household have come to do you honor:
All kinds of good food are ready:
Bitter, salt, sour, hot, and sweet:
There are dishes of all flavors.

Chao Hun, ca. 200 B.C.

THIS ancient poem predicted the use of chile peppers in China twenty centuries before they arrived there. It is a fragment from "The Summons of the Soul," written in the third century B.C. by the Chinese poet Chao Hun, which illustrates an ideal of Asian cookery that persists to this day: the the merging of all possible taste sensations into a single dish, or over the course of the meal. Although the poem establishes the necessity of hot spices in Asian cooking, there was one slight problem: chile peppers did not exist in Asia at that time, so the "hot" flavors of good food could not be fully accomplished.

What spice fired up Asian cooking before chiles arrived on the scene? Most probably, the fruit of a thorny shrub called *fagara,* also known as prickly ash. The berries of this bush are called brown pepper or Chinese pepper and are pungent in a manner similar to peppercorns, ginger, or horseradish but are not truly hot like chiles. Yes, they assault the senses momentarily, but then quickly fade away because they lack the real burn of capsaicin. Alas, *fagara* was a modest flame compared to what was on the way.

Asians waited two thousand years for a truly hot ingredient to complement their other classic flavors and to fulfill the prophecy of Chao Hun's poem. They were finally rewarded in the sixteenth century, when the real heat arrived: chile peppers. Asian cuisines would never lack for heat again.

As often happens during the transfer of foods around the world, the New World origin of chile peppers was unknown or forgotten. European explorers and colonists assumed the plants were native to Africa or India because the natives they encountered so loved the hot fruits. In effect, chiles spread across the globe faster than history could keep track of them. The reason for this quick dissemination of chiles was simple: supply and demand. The traders and their customers simply loved the new hot spice.

Portuguese traders introduced the Capsicums into Thailand as early as 1511, probably from their trading base in Malacca, between the Malay Peninsula and Sumatra. Although hard evidence is lacking, ethnobotanists theorize that Arab and Hindu traders carried the Indian chile peppers to Indonesia around the late 1520s, and from there to New Guinea. In 1529, a treaty between Spain and Portugal gave the Spanish control of the Philippines and the Portuguese control of Malaysia. By 1550, chiles had become well established in the East Indies, probably spread both by birds as well as by human trade and cultivation.

Some theories hold that either Malay, Chinese, or Portuguese traders first introduced chiles to China through the ports of Macao and Singapore, although other scenarios suggest that the chiles in western China were imported from India. The expansion of chile agriculture into Asia was assisted by the Spanish, who had colonies in the Philippines by 1571, and had established trade routes to Canton, China, and Nagasaki, Japan.

From Manila in the Philippines, the Spanish established a galleon route to Acapulco, Mexico, by way of Micronesia and Melanesia, thus spreading chile peppers into the Pacific Islands. So by 1593, just a century after Columbus "discovered" them and brought them back across the Atlantic, chile peppers had encircled the globe. It is an ironic culinary fact that the imported chiles became more important than many traditional spices in Asian cuisines, thus illustrating how the pungency of chiles has combined with other flavors to win a fanatic following of devotees.

Although chile peppers are present to some extent in all Asian countries, they are particularly beloved in the cuisines of three distinct regions: Thailand and nearby Laos and Vietnam, Indonesia and Malaysia, and China. Chile peppers do appear as condiments and occasionally in recipes from the Philippines, Japan, and Korea, but they are less of a factor in those cuisines.

The Fiery Triangle: Thailand and Its Neighbors

The San Francisco Bay Area, with a total Thai population of about one thousand, has over a hundred Thai restaurants. The Los Angeles area, with fewer citizens of Thai heritage, has over two hundred Thai restaurants! It is for good reason that Thai cuisine has become a favorite of American fiery food aficionados — it is one of the hottest cuisines in the world, and also one of the most diverse in terms of the different varieties of chiles that are used. As Thai-food expert Jennifer Brennan described the process, chile peppers were "adopted by the Thai with a fervor normally associated with the return of a long-lost child."

Perhaps, then, it is no surprise that Bangkok is also in the running for the title of hottest city in the world. This beautiful city is populated, not only by the chile-loving Thais and Chinese but also by other ethnic groups that use them heavily in their cuisines: East Indians, Pakistanis, and Malays. Bangkok markets rival those of Mexico for the varieties of chiles (called *prik*) that are offered for sale. One of the most common chiles, *prik chee fa,* is fat and about four inches long and closely resembles a small version of the New Mexican pods. According to one source, the favorite chile of Thailand is *prik kee nu luang,* a small orange variety. Other chiles include a Wax-type chile; the long, thin "Thai" chiles, Cayenne or Piquin varieties such as the Japanese Santaka; and *Kashmiri* chiles, which are close relatives of the Jalapeños and Serranos.

The Kashmiri chiles are also called *sriracha,* or *siracha* chiles. They are so named because a sauce made from these chiles originated in the Thai seaside town of Sriracha as an accompaniment to fish, and it became so popular that it has been bottled and sold around the world.

Another popular Thai sauce is *nam prik,* which consists of a bewildering number of possible ingredients including fish sauce, chiles, garlic, sugar, lime juice, and even egg yolks. One of our featured recipes from Thailand is *nam prik kai gem,* or Nam Prik Egg Sauce, an extremely hot (8 on the Heat Scale) "pepper water" that spices up soups, rice dishes, or eggs. Fresh chiles also appear in Thai dishes, as evidenced by our recipe for Thai Green Mango and Pork Platter.

The same traders who brought the chile pepper to Thailand also spread the use of curries from India to all parts of the globe. Consequently, Thailand is a perfect example of a culinary collision of cultures; Indian curry spices were combined with the latest exotic import — chile peppers — to create some of the hottest curries on earth.

In fact, hot curries are staples in Thai cooking and take several forms. One form is curry pastes, which consist of onions, garlic, chiles, and curry spices such as coriander and cardamom, all pounded together with mortar and pestle until smooth. Commercially prepared curry pastes can be purchased in Asian markets, or made at home by utilizing a food processor or blender.

Another type of curry, *kaeng,* is a term for a bewildering variety of Thai curries. Some *kaengs* resemble liquid Indian curry sauces and are abundant with traditional curry spices such as turmeric, coriander, and cardamom. Another type of *kaeng* curry omits these curry spices and substitutes herbs like cilantro, but the chiles are still there. This second group of *kaeng* curries is said to be the original Thai curries, invented long before they were influenced by Indian spices. As with the curries of Sri Lanka, these *kaeng* curries are multicolored; depending upon the color of the chiles and other spices and the amount of coconut milk added, they range from light yellow to green to pale red.

Kaeng kari is yellow-colored because it contains most of the curry spices, including turmeric, and is fairly mild. One of the more pungent of these *kaeng* curries, *kaeng phed,* is made with tiny red chiles, coconut milk, and basil leaves, and is served with seafood. A tasty example of an "original" *kaeng* curry is our recipe for Chicken with Green Curry Paste, made with *krung kaeng keo wan,* which many Thais believe to be the hottest curry of all. Here, hidden within this seemingly innocent vichyssoise-like sauce, are the smallest and hottest green chiles available combined with fresh basil.

Such culinary deception illustrates yet another aspect of Thai cuisine: the presentation of the meal. "The Thais are as interested in beautiful presentation as the Japanese are," writes Jennifer Brennan. "The contrasts of color and texture, of hot and cold, of spicy and mild are as important here as in any cuisine in the world."

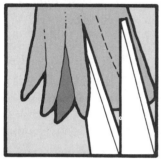

Carving chile flowers

Considering the emphasis on both heat and presentation in their cuisine, it is not surprising that the Thais love to garnish their hot meals with — what else? — hot chiles. Their adoration for the chile pepper extends to elaborately carved chile pod-flowers. They use multicolored, small chiles for the best flower effect, with colors ranging from green to yellow to red to purple. The procedure for creating chile pepper pod flowers is quite simple. Hold the chile by the stem on a cutting board and use a sharp knife to slice the chile in half, lengthwise, starting an eighth of an inch from the stem down to the point (or apex, for the botanically minded). Rotate the chile 180 degrees and repeat the procedure until the chile is divided into sixteenths or more.

The thinner the "petals," the more convincing the chiles will be as flowers when the chiles are soaked in water containing ice cubes, which is the next step. Immerse the chiles in ice water until the slices curl — a few hours — and then remove the seeds with the tip of a knife. The chile flowers are then arranged artistically on the platter and later devoured as a spicy salad condiment that accompanies the traditional Thai curries.

The influence of such curries, with all their multiple spices, did not extend into Laos, which borders Thailand to the northeast. Rather, fresh, small red and green chiles are used extensively in a number of chile pastes there. Jalapeño- and Serrano-type chiles are beaten with pestles in huge mortars, and locally available spices are added. Our favorite Laotian creation is a dish called *mawk mak phet*, Stuffed Chile Peppers, which is a delicious example of a fresh chile recipe from that country. It features Poblano or New Mexican chiles, which are stuffed with vegetables, spices, and white fish, and then steamed.

Fish combined with chiles also provides the essential flavor of the third country of our "fiery triangle." In Vietnam, where the heart of the chile cuisine coincides with the center of the country, principally in the city of Hue, a fish and chile sauce called *nuac cham* reigns supreme. It consists of fish sauce, lime, sugar, garlic, and fresh, small, red Serrano-type chiles and is featured here in a classic dish, Vietnamese Salad with Nuoc Cham Sauce. Another famous Vietnamese dish using hot chiles is illustrated with the recipe for Hot Pho, a beef and noodle soup with many fresh spices and Jalapeño-like chiles.

The Spiciest Islands: Indonesia, Malaysia, and Singapore

The spice trade was one of the primary motivating factors in European exploration of the rest of the world, so it is not surprising that many countries sought to control the output of the "Spice Islands." These islands, which now comprise parts of the countries of Indonesia and Malaysia, produced cinnamon, cloves, nutmeg, black pepper, and many other spices. What *is* surprising about the Spice Islands is that they were infiltrated and "conquered" by a New World spice — chile peppers.

After the Portuguese won control of the Strait of Malacca in 1511, it is probable that chile peppers were imported soon afterward by traders sailing to and from the Portuguese colony of Goa, India. Asian food authority Copeland Marks has observed that the cuisine of the region would be "unthinkable without them. . . . When the chile arrived in Indonesia it was welcomed enthusiastically and now may be considered an addiction."

In Indonesia, where chiles are variously called *cabe* or *lombok,* they are added to many dishes and often combined with coconut cream or milk. On the island of Java, sugar is added, making that cuisine a mixture of sweet, sour, and fiery hot. Some cooks there believe that the addition of sugar keeps the power of the chiles and other spices under control.

Perhaps the principal use of chiles in this part of Asia is in sauces that are spread over rice or are used as a dip for *sate,* barbecued small chunks of meat. Chiles are often combined with peanuts for the *sate* dips, as we illustrate in our recipe examples from Indonesia: Broiled Skewered Lamb Sate (*sate kambing*) with Peanut-Chile Sauce (*katjang saos*), accompanied by a complex salad called Gado Gado.

Other favorite hot chile sauces are the *sambals,* which are relishes made from lime juice, shallots or onions, garlic, and fresh chiles and are usually served over plain white rice. An Indonesian legend holds that even an ugly girl will find a husband if she can create a great *sambal.* On the island of Sumatra, cooks make *lado,* a *sambal* consisting of chiles, salt, tamarind, and shallots, which is stir-fried with seafood, hardboiled eggs, or

A heap of red chiles just harvested, Bangka Island, Indonesia (The Bettmann Archive)

vegetables. One of our favorite *sambals* is the recipe we include for Sambal Ulek, which combines chiles and shrimp paste.

One of the most interesting chile cuisines of Asia is the Nonya cooking of Singapore, which illustrates the collision of Chinese dishes with Malay spices such as curries and chiles. The Nonya are descendants of mixed marriages of Malay women and Chinese men, who insisted that their wives cook in the Chinese style. The necessity of using Malaysian rather than Chinese produce resulted in the addition of chile peppers to the recipes. Fiery Nonya dishes from Singapore and Malaysia include the famous Singapore Chile Crab; *bengkah sara*, a sponge cake laced with hot chiles; *nasi lemak*, a coconut-flavored rice with chile paste; and *otak-otak*, a mixture of cooked fish and chile paste. The recipe for *sambal timun* — Pineapple, Cucumber, and Chile Condiment, which combines Serrano or Jalapeño chiles, pineapple, and cucumber — is a good example of a condiment from the Nonya kitchens of Singapore.

In Malaysia and particularly Singapore, the uses of chiles appear to be endless, and there is an extensive range of chile pastes and sauces from hot to hottest, as well as curries and salads that can be equally fiery. As illustrations of some of the hotter Malaysian dishes, we have included the recipes for Fish in Curry Spice Paste, with the accompanying Malaysian Curry Paste, which rates a tongue-scalding 7 on the Heat Scale.

China and Beyond

Despite the recent popularity of Thai cooking in the United States, there is little doubt that the Asian reputation for hot chile cooking began with China, particularly the regions of Sichuan and Hunan. However, we should not ignore other parts of China. Although most current Chinese cookbooks are devoid of chile pepper recipes from Canton and other areas of south China, two members of the family *Solanaceae* eventually were adopted there. According to Chinese-food expert E. N. Anderson,

> Tomatoes and chiles not only transformed the taste of southern Chinese cooking, they also provided new and very rich sources of vitamins A and C and certain minerals, thus improving the diet of the south Chinese considerably. Easy to grow, highly productive, and bearing virtually year-round in the subtropical climate, these plants eliminated the seasonal bottlenecks on vitamin availability.

An example of the use of tomatoes and chiles in southern China is our recipe for Pork Strips and Three Peppers.

Cooks of the coastal regions of China often created seafood dishes in combination with chiles. Our recipe for Citrus Cashew Lobster, for example, uses both hot pods and powder with lobster and cashews to create a memorable dish that is both hot and sweet. Shrimp is heated up with both Piquins and chile oil in Hot and Pungent Shrimp, further proving that southern and eastern China have their fiery hot dishes.

But it was in the west where chiles really triumphed in Chinese cuisine, and there are at least two mysteries about the use of chiles in western China. The first question is, how did they get there? The second, why did the Chinese love them so much?

Some experts speculate that chiles were imported from Singapore, or carried inland from Macao, where hot dishes are more popular today than in neighboring Canton. More likely is the theory that chiles were introduced into Sichuan by sixteenth century Indian Buddhist missionaries traveling the "Silk Route" between India and China. After all, western Sichuan is closer to India than to either Macao or Singapore. No matter how they arrived in western China, chiles soon became enormously important to the food of the people.

E. N. Anderson, who has studied the chile situation in China extensively, described the effect of chiles on the cuisines of the Far East as "epochal." The use of the large varieties of *Capsicum annuum* called *la chiao* were important because of the addition of vitamins A and C to low-vitamin grains such as rice. In western China, chiles were easy to grow, simple to preserve, and soon became vital to life there.

The second mystery is why chiles were embraced with such fervor in western China. As usual, many theories have been advanced by ethnobotanists, anthropologists, and Asian studies experts. The three most likely theories are the Perennial Cool-Down Principle, the Food Preservation Scenario, and the Poetic Proposition.

The Perennial Cool-Down Principle holds that since New World cultures utilized chiles to cool down in hot climates, it makes sense that they would be put to the same use when introduced into other regions. Both Sichuan and Hunan are hot tropical inlands similar to regions in South America and Mexico, where chiles were first adopted into the human diet. In such regions with no freezes, chiles grow as perennials, so they are available all year long.

Another possible reason for the popularity of chiles in western China is the Food Preservation Scenario. Before salt was mined in the region, the Sichuanese utilized hot spices as a substitute. Later, chile peppers came into use as a food preservative in the form of chile pastes and chile oils. In Chapter 2, we have included our favorite hot oil recipe, Red Chile Oil, which tops the Heat Scale at a dangerous 9.

Perhaps the most persuasive theory for the popularity of chiles is the Poetic Proposition, which recalls Chao Hun's poem. According to author-chef Karen Lee, "The hot peppers stimulate the palate, causing a sensitivity that brings an awareness of the spectrum of flavors to follow: after the hot and spicy, the mild, mellow, sour, salty, sweet, aromatic, bland, bitter, and pungent flavors linger in the aftertaste." This theory echoes Chao Hun's "Summons of the Soul" because it utilizes the combination of multiple flavors in a single meal. Our recipe for Spiced Beef in Tangerine Sauce is excellent culinary evidence supporting the Poetic Proposition.

Sichuan and Hunan cooks depend mostly upon chile pastes and oils to provide the heat in their meals. Fresh peppers are more commonly used in Hunan than Sichuan, where small, dried Santaka-type chiles are commonly added whole, seeds and all, to stir-fry dishes. Other commonly used seasonings in the cooking of Sichuan and Hunan are sesame-seed paste, chile paste with garlic, and an aromatic chile vinegar.

Chile in such forms is often combined with ground rice, sesame seeds, and peanuts as a snack or a coating for grilled meats. The combination of chiles with nutty products like sesame seeds and peanuts is called *ma la* and is one of the essential flavors of western Chinese cooking. An example of these taste sensations can be found in our recipe for Hunan Strange-Flavored Chicken.

Contrary to popular belief, chefs cooking in the Sichuan or Hunan style are not trying to incinerate the people who eat their creations. Howard Hillman, an expert on world cuisines, has written of the way heat is applied in western China:

Even on the peasant level, the people prefer the dishes on the table to have degrees of hotness varying from mild to fiery. This is in contrast to the monotonous everything-as-hot-as-possible approach favored by many non-Chinese Sichuan restaurant-goers. Making one Sichuan dish hotter than another is not a measure of a chef's talent; all it takes is the addition of extra chile, a feat that could be performed by a trained monkey. Epicures judge a Sichuan chef by the subtly complex overtones of his sauces and whether they complement the other ingredients in his dishes.

Perhaps the most obscure fiery cuisine of Asia is that of Xinjiang, China's largest province. Located in the northwest part of the country, surrounded by Tibet, Russia, Mongolia, Afghanistan, and Pakistan, Xinjiang is the land of the Uygurs, the Mongols, the Tatars and other peoples related to Turkic central Asians. The capital of Xinjiang is Urumchi, the most inland city in the world. Here, where most of the population is Moslem, pork is replaced by lamb, which is commonly combined with chile peppers.

Our favorite lamb and chile dish from Xinjiang is *kao yang ruo chuan*, Xinjiang Lamb and Chile Barbecue, in which lamb kabobs are marinated in garlic, lemon, and an extremely hot chile oil sauce and then barbecued with Jalapeño-type chiles. Other lamb and chile dishes from the region include: a sliced lamb meal with onions and Jalapeño-type chiles; *la tiao-ze*, which combines noodles and lamb with a garlic and chile pepper sauce; and lamb-filled pot-stickers with hot chile-vinegar-soy sauce.

What does the future hold for China's ever-growing fascination with chile peppers? At first, the New World furnished chiles to China, which returned the favor by inventing great recipes for their use. But now Asia is selling us their chiles and thus starting a chile trade war that may eventually lead to a serious balance-of-chiles deficit.

In 1988, China was the second largest exporter of whole chile pods into the United States, shipping 2,400 metric tons that year. Ground red chile transported from Hong Kong contributed another 254 metric tons to the total. It seems that these days the Chinese are as interested in chile money as chile poetry, and although precise figures are not available, there is little doubt that the People's Republic of China is now the greatest producer and consumer of chile peppers in the world, surpassing even India, Mexico, and the United States.

Even the Japanese, who are not known for a fiery cuisine, are becoming more interested in and devoted to the chile pepper. Soon after the Portuguese arrived, the Japanese began cultivating a Cayenne-type variety called Santaka, which is one of the hottest chiles grown today. Japan even exports about fourteen metric tons per year of ground red chile into the United States! Although

Sorting red chiles, Japan, 1922 (UPI/Bettmann Newsphotos)

it has taken centuries, chiles have finally invaded Japanese food, although not in the classic cuisine. The fastest-growing fast-food chain in Japan during the late 1980s was Taco Time, which did not cater to traditional Japanese tastes but boldly advertised its food as the hottest around — and foreign as well.

Korea has quite a reputation for fiery foods, yet our research indicates that chiles are used principally as a condiment in that country. A very salty chile paste called *gochujang* fires up noodle dishes. Strips of dried red chile sliced thread-fine, called *silgochu*, are used widely as a hot spice in foods such as *kim chee*, the pickled or fermented cabbage concoction that is the national dish.

In 1988, South Korea exported eighty-eight metric tons of ground red chile, and about four metric tons of New Mexican–type chiles into the United States; however, precise production figures for the country are difficult to obtain. Because the Koreans also use green chiles in their cooking, we have included Korean Radish and Chile Salad prepared with the large, white *daikon* radish plus apples and green onions.

From eastern Asia, chiles were transferred to the Pacific Islands. How and when this dispersal occurred is the subject of much debate. Some experts theorize that after chiles were introduced into New Guinea, they were carried by native traders to Melanesia and then to Polynesia. Once there, the fiery fruits were adopted into the island cuisines and combined with both indigenous and imported foodstuffs such as fish, coconuts, and bananas — as in our recipe for Poisson Kokonada.

Other theorists believe that chiles were carried on Spanish galleons, leaving from Acapulco and bound for the Philippines. However, the main galleon route ran south of the Hawaiian Islands and north of the rest of Polynesia, and a landing at either island group would have been extremely unlikely considering the galleon captains were under orders not to change the route. In fact, the Pacific both north and south of the galleon route remained unexplored until Cook's voyages between 1768 and 1780.

A third theory, proposed by Pacific explorer Thor Heyerdahl, holds that chiles were introduced into Polynesia by pre-Columbian Indians such as the Incas. In 1964, Heyerdahl published an article in which he alleged that chiles were growing on Easter Island at the time of the arrival of Europeans, approximately 1768. Botanists, however, dispute Heyerdahl and point out that chiles are conspicuously absent from the plant lists of the Polynesian Islands compiled by the botanists aboard Cook's ships. Although it is exciting to think that the Incas were sailing the Pacific, or that pre-Columbian visits to the Americas were made by Polynesians and others, there is simply not enough scientific evidence to support such a theory.

So although we do not know precisely when or how they accomplished it, chile peppers crossed the Pacific and eventually appeared on the Galápagos Islands, which are only about six hundred miles from the South American coast. In fact, those islands have their own species of chile, *Capsicum galapagoense*.

However the final leg of the journey occurred, chiles in fact circumnavigated the globe and ended up very close to the nuclear region where they originated millennia before. In doing so, they forever fired up most of the important world cuisines.

 # Nam Prik Egg Sauce

Heat Scale: 8
Yield: 1/2 cup

8 to 10 Serrano or Jalapeño chiles, stems removed
4 cloves garlic
4 scallions or shallots, chopped, white part only
4 hard-cooked egg yolks
1 tablespoon fish sauce (*nam pla* or *nuoc nam**)
2 teaspoons sugar
3 tablespoons lime or lemon juice

Nam prik *literally means "pepper water," and that is a good description of these traditional sauces. Similar to* nuoc cham, *there are many, many varieties found on the tables of Thailand. Serve Nam Prik with raw vegetables as a type of salad; with soup, rice, and curries; or as a table sauce to add heat to any dish.*

Puree all the ingredients into a smooth sauce. Add more lime juice if necessary.

Serving Suggestions: Serve over scrambled eggs for a truly unique Asian breakfast.

*Available in Asian markets.

Thai Green Mango and Pork Platter

Heat Scale: 7
Serves: 4

6 Thai or Serrano chiles,
  stems and seeds removed,
  cut in strips
4 cloves garlic, coarsely
  chopped
1 tablespoon finely chopped
  fresh ginger
2 tablespoons oil, peanut
  preferred
1 pound boneless pork, cut
  in strips
1 tablespoon fish sauce
  (*nam pla* or *nuoc nam**)
1 teaspoon shrimp paste*
1 teaspoon sugar
1 cup water
2 cups diced mango
3 tablespoons roasted
  unsalted peanuts, crushed
3 tablespoons chopped fresh
  cilantro

Thai food is known for being some of the hottest in the world, but it is also a cuisine of complex flavors. Pork and other meats are costly, so this dish would be served only on special occasions. To provide a salty taste, the nam pla *sauce is used. The mangos should be slightly underripe.*

Stir-fry the chiles, garlic, and ginger in the oil for 2 minutes, being careful that they do not burn.

Add the pork strips and continue to fry until the pork is browned. Stir in the fish sauce, shrimp paste, sugar, and water. Cover the pan and simmer until the pork is tender and the sauce is reduced and thick.

Remove from the heat and stir in the mango and peanuts. Garnish with the cilantro and serve.

Serving Suggestions: Serve over steamed white rice.

Variations: For a hotter dish, substitute Red Chile Oil (see recipe Chapter 2) for the peanut oil.

*Available in Asian markets.

Green Curry Paste

Heat Scale: 8
Yield: 1 cup

10 Serrano or Jalapeño
chiles, stems removed
2 tablespoons chopped
garlic
1/4 cup chopped shallots, or
substitute 1/4 cup chopped
scallions, including the
greens
1 tablespoon finely chopped
fresh ginger
1/4 cup chopped fresh
cilantro
2 teaspoons whole coriander
seeds
2 teaspoons whole caraway
seeds
1 teaspoon whole black
peppercorns
1 teaspoon ground cumin
1 teaspoon ground nutmeg
1/4 teaspoon ground cloves
2 teaspoons grated lemon
rind
3 to 4 tablespoons vegetable
oil

Thai curry pastes are simple to prepare, can be made ahead of time, and can be refrigerated or frozen. This green curry, known as krung kaeng keo wan, *is the hottest of these pastes, but the heat can be adjusted by reducing the number of chiles.*

Puree the chiles, garlic, shallots, ginger, and cilantro in 1 tablespoon of the oil until it is a smooth paste.

Grind the seeds and peppercorns and add to the paste.

Add the remaining ingredients and puree to a thick paste, adding more oil if necessary.

 # Chicken with Green Curry Paste

Heat Scale: 6
Serves: 4

4 Serrano or Jalapeño chiles,
stems removed, thinly
sliced
1 cup Green Curry Paste
(see preceding recipe)

Appearances can be deceiving — this is not chicken in pesto sauce! This recipe combines the Thai's love of both chiles and herbs. Served over rice, this dish is a classic example of a kaeng *curry.*

Heat the curry paste and the fish sauce in one half of the coconut milk. Add the chicken and cook until just tender. Remove the chicken and keep warm.

1 tablespoon fish sauce
  (*nam pla* or *nuoc nam**)
1 1/2 cups unsweetened
  coconut milk
1 1/2 pounds chicken, skin
  removed, cut in 1-inch
  strips
1 tablespoon sugar
2 teaspoons lemon juice
1/2 cup chopped fresh basil
1/4 cup chopped fresh mint

Stir in the chiles, sugar, lemon juice, and remaining coconut milk. Bring to a boil, reduce the heat, and simmer for 10 minutes until the sauce is creamy and thickened.

Return the chicken and add the basil. Cook for an additional 5 minutes or until thoroughly heated.

Serving Suggestions: Serve with Korean Radish and Chile Salad (see recipe this chapter) and steamed white rice.

*Available in Asian markets.

Stuffed Chile Peppers

Heat Scale: 3
Serves: 4

8 Poblano or green New
  Mexican chiles, roasted
  and peeled
3/4 pound white fish fillets
  such as flounder or
  snapper, flaked
1/2 cup cooked rice
4 scallions, chopped,
  including the greens
2 cloves garlic, minced
1 tablespoon fish sauce
  (*nam pla* or *nuoc nam**)
1 teaspoon finely chopped
  fresh ginger
juice of 1 lemon

Stuffed chiles (mawk mak phet) *are steamed in banana leaves in Laos, but since the leaves are difficult to find, we steam ours in foil. Experiment with a variety of fillings such as ground pork, ground beef, and rice.*

Slit each chile from the stem to the tip, being careful not to cut completely through the chile to the other side. Remove the membrane and the seeds.

Combine the remaining ingredients and toss until thoroughly mixed. Stuff each chile with the mixture and wrap the chiles tightly in the aluminum foil, two to a package.

Place the packets in a bamboo steamer or colander over boiling water. Cover and steam for 20 to 25 minutes.

Serve the chiles with any juices from the foil poured over the top.

Serving Suggestions: Serve with Vietnamese Salad with Nuoc Cham Sauce (see recipe this chapter).

*Available in Asian markets.

Nuoc Cham Sauce

Heat Scale: 6
Yield: 1/2 cup

4 small dried red chiles or 4
  Serrano chiles, stems
  removed
1 clove garlic
2 teaspoons sugar
2 tablespoons fresh lime or
  lemon juice (include some
  of the pulp)
2 tablespoons fish sauce
  (*nam pla* or *nuoc nam**)
3 tablespoons water, more if
  necessary

This sauce is as common on a Vietnamese table as salt is on a Western table. The basis of the recipe is a fish sauce called nuoc nam *and chiles — two staples of Southeast Asian cuisine. Use this seasoning sparingly to begin with, or dilute it with additional water if it seems too strong at first; the taste does tend to "grow" on people.*

Puree or pound all the ingredients to a smooth sauce. This sauce can be stored in the refrigerator for up to 2 weeks.

   *Available in Asian markets.

Vietnamese Salad with Nuoc Cham Sauce

Heat Scale: 2
Serves: 6

4 tablespoons Nuoc Cham
  Sauce (see preceding
  recipe)
1/8 package rice stick
  noodles*
vegetable oil for frying
2 teaspoons peanut oil
1/2 pound cooked shrimp,
  shelled and deveined
1/4 head cabbage, shredded
2 carrots, shredded
1 cucumber, shredded
1/4 cup chopped scallions,
  including the greens
1/4 cup chopped fresh
  cilantro or mint leaves
  (optional)
2 tablespoons roasted
  peanuts, chopped

The ingredients for this spicy salad can be prepared ahead of time, but do not assemble until just before serving or the noodles will become soft and soggy. Vary this recipe by substituting cooked pork, chicken, or beef (cut into thin strips), for the shrimp.

Fry the noodles in the oil until crisp and browned. Remove and drain.

   Mix the peanut oil with the Nuoc Cham Sauce to make a dressing.

   Combine the shrimp and vegetables and toss with the dressing until well coated.

   To Serve: Arrange the salad on a serving platter, cover with the noodles, and top with the peanuts.

   *Available in Asian markets.

 # Hot Pho

Heat Scale: 4
Serves: 6

4 Jalapeño chiles, stems
  removed, sliced in thin
  rings
1 tablespoon Chile Paste
  (see recipe Chapter 2)
1 small onion, chopped
1 tablespoon finely chopped
  fresh ginger
1 2-inch stick whole
  cinnamon
1 stalk lemon grass*
1 quart beef broth
1 pound boneless lean beef
  such as sirloin, thinly sliced
  across the grain into 1-inch
  by 3-inch strips
1 teaspoon fish sauce (*nam
  pla* or *nuoc nam**)
1 pound dry rice noodles,
  cooked and drained
3 tablespoons chopped
  scallions, including the
  greens
1/4 pound bean sprouts
1 cup chopped fresh basil
1 cup chopped fresh
  coriander

This cross between a soup and a salad is a very common meal in Vietnam and is sometimes called Saigon Soup. The condiments are served in bowls and guests add them at the table.

Combine the chile paste, onion, ginger, cinnamon, lemon grass, and broth. Bring to a boil and simmer for an hour. Strain the broth and discard the solids.

Add the beef to the broth and simmer for 5 minutes to cook the meat. Remove the beef and keep warm.

Reheat the broth and add the Jalapeños and fish sauce.

To Serve: Divide the noodles into individual bowls and top with the meat. Pour the hot broth into the bowls, garnish with the chopped scallions, and serve with the sprouts, basil, and coriander in separate bowls. Guests can then add them to the soup as desired.

*Available in Asian markets.

Peanut-Chile Sauce

Heat Scale: 8
Yield: 1 to 1 1/2 cups

3 tablespoons dried crushed
  Piquin chile, seeds included
4 scallions, chopped, white
  part only
4 cloves garlic, minced
1 teaspoon finely chopped
  fresh ginger
1 tablespoon peanut oil
1 cup chicken broth
1 tablespoon soy sauce
2 teaspoons dark brown
  sugar
1/4 teaspoon ground cumin
1 tablespoon lime juice
1/2 cup crunchy peanut
  butter

This hot and spicy peanut sauce, katjan saos, *is a standard in Indonesia. It is not only used for* sates *but also as a basis for unusual curries and dipping sauces. It is traditionally prepared by pounding the peanuts into a paste before using. We have simplified the recipe by substituting crunchy peanut butter.*

Sauté the scallions, garlic, and ginger in the oil for 3 to 4 minutes until soft and transparent but not browned.

Add the chicken stock and bring to a boil. Reduce the heat and stir in the remaining ingredients. Simmer the sauce, uncovered, for 10 to 15 minutes until thickened.

Serving Suggestions: Combine with lamb as a *sate* (see following recipe) or use as a dip for crisp garden vegetables such as cauliflower, celery, carrots, and cucumbers.

Broiled Skewered Lamb Sate with Peanut-Chile Sauce

Heat Scale: 5
Serves: 8 as an appetizer

1/2 cup Peanut-Chile Sauce
 (see preceding recipe)
2 tablespoons lime juice
1 pound boneless lamb, cut
 in 1-inch cubes

These popular and versatile meat kabobs make excellent appetizers as well as a delicious entrée. They are consumed all over Indonesia as snacks from traveling street vendors, at curbside stands, or as part of a meal or feast. The meats can be pork, beef, chicken, or lamb depending on preference and religious taboos, but one thing is common — the kabobs never contain vegetables. The following lamb sate kambing *is excellent for an outdoor barbecue, and is wonderful when eaten hot off the grill.*

Combine the Peanut-Chile Sauce and lime juice. Toss the lamb cubes in the mixture until evenly coated. Marinate the meat at room temperature for 2 hours.

Thread the meat on skewers and broil or grill until done, basting once with the sauce. Serve with a side dish of the sauce for dipping.

Serving Suggestion: Serve as an appetizer to an outdoor meal of grilled chicken.

Gado Gado

Heat Scale: 4
Serves: 6 to 8

The Dressing:

2 tablespoons dried crushed
  red chile such as Piquin,
  seeds included
1/4 cup finely chopped
  onions
1 tablespoon finely chopped
  fresh ginger
1 clove garlic, minced
1 tablespoon oil, peanut
  preferred
1 1/4 cup unsweetened
  canned coconut milk
1/2 cup crunchy peanut
  butter
2 tablespoons soy sauce
2 tablespoons brown sugar
1 tablespoon lemon juice

The Salad:

2 fresh bean-curd cakes
2 cups shredded cabbage
2 large new (red) potatoes,
  boiled and cut in 1/4-inch
  thick slices
1/4 pound cooked green
  beans, cut into 3-inch
  pieces
2 cups bean sprouts
1 medium carrot, cut into 2-
  by 1/4-inch julienne strips,
  cooked
1 large cucumber, sliced
2 hard-cooked eggs, sliced
3 scallions, thinly sliced
  including the greens
1 cup chopped roasted
  peanuts

Indonesians love salads and have developed a variety of them, ranging from relatively simple to very elaborate. This popular salad from Java is composed of a wide array of raw and parboiled vegetables and is traditionally served in layers with a spicy peanut and coconut-milk dressing.

To Make the Dressing: Sauté the onions, ginger, and garlic in the oil until softened. Stir in the remainder of the ingredients. Bring to a boil, stirring constantly. Reduce the heat and simmer until thickened, about 10 minutes.

To Make the Salad: Poach the bean curd in simmering water for 10 minutes. Remove and drain. Cut into 1-inch cubes. Arrange the vegetables in layers, starting with the cabbage, then cucumbers, potatoes, green beans, bean sprouts, carrots, and bean curds. Place the egg slices around the side. Top with the scallions onions and chopped peanuts. Warm the dressing and either pour over the salad or serve in a bowl on the side.

Serving Suggestions: This salad can be served as a light entrée or as part of a more elaborate feast of chicken *sates*, rice, and fried plantains.

Sambal Ulek

Heat Scale: 8
Yield: 1/2 cup

1 cup dried red chiles such
  as Piquins or Cayennes,
  stems removed
6 cloves garlic, chopped
3 tablespoons lime juice
1 tablespoon sugar
1 teaspoon shrimp paste*
1 teaspoon peanut oil

Sambals are condiments used to flavor or to spice dishes throughout all of the Indonesian islands. They can be cooked or raw and are composed of a variety of ingredients including fruits, vegetables, meats, or fish. They may be simple, but the one ingredient that is common is chile. No meal in Indonesia would be served without a sambal.

Cover the chiles with hot water and let sit for 15 minutes until softened. Remove the chiles and drain.

Combine all the ingredients in a blender and puree to a sauce. Thin with more lime juice if necessary.

Serving Suggestions: Serve with grilled meats or poultry or put on the table as a condiment to be added to any food.

*Available in Asian markets.

Singapore Chile Crab

Heat Scale: 5
Serves: 4

4 hot red or green fresh
  chiles such as Serranos,
  stems removed
3/4 teaspoon ground
  Cayenne
2 teaspoons finely chopped
  fresh ginger
3 cloves garlic, chopped
3 tablespoons peanut oil
2 pounds lump crabmeat,
  cooked
2 tablespoons catsup
4 teaspoons lemon juice
2 teaspoons light soy sauce

This crab dish is as much a part of Singapore as the harbor and skyline. Traditionally made with live crabs, we have substituted lump crabmeat for those who prefer not to deal with catching and killing a crab.

Puree the chiles, ginger, and garlic into a paste.

Heat the oil and stir-fry the chile mixture for 2 to 3 minutes. Add the remaining ingredients, including the crab, and fry over high heat for an additional 2 minutes.

Add 1/2 cup water, cover, and simmer for 5 minutes or until thoroughly heated.

Serving Suggestion: Serve over rice and with crusty bread for dipping into the sauce.

Pineapple, Cucumber, and Chile Condiment

Heat Scale: 5
Yield: 4 cups

4 Serrano or Jalapeño chiles,
  stems removed, chopped
1/2 cup dried shrimp*
1/4 cup lime juice, fresh
  preferred
1/4 cup vinegar
4 teaspoons sugar
1 cucumber, cubed
1/2 cup pineapple chunks,
  fresh preferred
4 scallions, chopped,
  including the greens

This typical Nonya relish from Singapore demonstrates the combination of cultures — Malaysian fruit and Chinese dried shrimp. Serve this Oriental "salsa" with rice and curry dishes, or with any dish that needs a sweet and hot flavor.

Combine the chiles, shrimp, lime juice, vinegar, and sugar in a blender and puree until smooth.

Toss the remaining ingredients with the dressing and let sit for 2 to 3 hours to blend the flavors before serving.

  *Available in Asian markets.

Malaysian Curry Paste

Heat Scale: 7
Yield: 1 cup

6 dried Piquin or Cayenne chiles
1 tablespoon whole coriander seeds
1 tablespoon whole cumin seeds
1 teaspoon whole black peppercorns
1 1-inch stick whole cinnamon, or 1/4 teaspoon ground cinnamon
2 tablespoons lemon juice
1 small onion, chopped
2 cloves garlic
2 tablespoons cashews or almonds, chopped
1 teaspoon turmeric
1/4 cup unsweetened coconut milk
3 tablespoons white vinegar

Even though there are probably as many different curry pastes as cooks in Malaysia, we have narrowed our selection to one that goes well with fish. We have substituted cashews or almonds in the recipe for the local candlenuts, called buah keras, *which are virtually impossible to find. This curry paste will keep, under refrigeration, for up to 2 months. Put a little oil on the top of the paste to help prevent it from spoiling.*

Grind or pound the chiles, coriander, cumin, peppercorns, and cinnamon to make a powder.

Place the powder and all the remaining ingredients into a blender or processor, and puree into a smooth paste. Add more coconut milk or water if necessary.

Serving Suggestions: This spicy curry goes well with fish, beef, or pork.

Fish in Curry Spice Paste

Heat Scale: 5
Serves: 4

1/2 cup Malaysian Curry Paste (see preceding recipe)
2 1/2 to 3 pounds whole snapper, sea bass, mackerel, or other strong-tasting fish
2 tablespoons vegetable oil
1 cup unsweetened coconut milk

Malaysia's long coastline provides an abundance of fresh fish. The fish, when prepared with a hot and spicy curry paste, is the basis of a truly authentic Southeast Asian meal.

Make 4 or 5 deep incisions on each side of the fish and rub in a portion of the curry paste.

Heat the oil in a large pan and sauté the remaining paste for a couple of minutes. Slowly stir in the coconut milk to make a sauce. Place the fish on top of the sauce. Cover and simmer until the fish flakes easily, about 20 minutes.

Serving Suggestions: Place the fish on a bed of rice, top with some of the sauce, and garnish with fresh pineapple and melon wedges.

Pork Strips and Three Peppers

Heat Scale: 5
Serves: 4

6 Serrano chiles or other
  small green chiles, stems
  removed, cut into rings
4 small dried red chiles such
  as Piquins
1 small Bell pepper, stem
  and seeds removed,
  julienned
3 tablespoons Red Chile Oil
  (see recipe Chapter 2)
1 tablespoon soy sauce
1 tablespoon rice wine or
  dry sherry
1 tablespoon finely chopped
  fresh ginger
3 cloves garlic, minced
1 teaspoon five-spice
  powder*
2 teaspoons sugar
1 teaspoon cornstarch
1 pound lean pork cut
  across grain into thin strips
1/2 cup oil, peanut preferred
6 scallions, chopped,
  including the greens
2 tomatoes, cut in small
  wedges
1/2 cup chicken broth
1 tablespoon cornstarch
  mixed with 1/4 cup water

Three varieties of peppers, two hot and one mild, add not only heat but also color to this recipe from southern China. Traditional white rice and a "sweet and sour" dish or the following hot and sweet recipe for Citrus Cashew Lobster will complement this complex-flavored pork and tomato entrée.

Combine the Chile Oil, soy sauce, rice wine, ginger, garlic, five-spice powder, sugar, and cornstarch to make a marinade. Marinate the pork in this mixture for 2 to 3 hours. Remove and drain, reserving 1/4 cup of the marinade.

Heat the peanut oil until hot, add the dried chiles, and stir-fry for 2 minutes, being careful not to let them burn. Add the pork and stir-fry for 5 minutes or until the pork is lightly browned. Remove, drain, and keep warm.

Pour off all but 4 tablespoons of the oil. Add the scallions and stir-fry for 30 seconds. Add the chile rings and Bell pepper and stir-fry for an additional 1 minute (the vegetables should remain crisp).

Add the tomatoes, broth, and marinade. Bring to a boil and stir in just enough of the cornstarch and water mixture to thicken the sauce. Add the pork and heat until thoroughly hot.

*Available in Asian markets.

Citrus Cashew Lobster

Heat Scale: 6
Serves: 4

1 teaspoon ground Cayenne
8 small dried red chiles such
  as Piquins
3 tablespoons cornstarch
meat from 3 lobster tails,
  cut in 1-inch cubes
vegetable oil for frying
2 teaspoons finely chopped
  fresh ginger
2 teaspoons orange peel, cut
  in strips
1/3 cup orange juice
2 teaspoons rice wine or dry
  sherry
2 teaspoons rice vinegar
1 teaspoon soy sauce
1 teaspoon sugar
2 teaspoons cornstarch
  mixed with 3 teaspoons
  water
2 tablespoons roasted
  cashews

The cashew nuts add texture to this hot and sweet seafood dish from China. Any firm white fish or shrimp can be substituted for the lobster, and, for a change of pace, serve this dish with thin linguine instead of rice.

Mix the Cayenne with the cornstarch and toss the lobster cubes in the mixture.

Stir-fry the lobster in the hot oil for 2 minutes. Remove and drain.

Pour off all but 1 tablespoon of the oil.

Fry the chiles in the oil until they start to turn black and then remove.

Add the ginger and orange peel to the pan for 10 to 15 seconds; then add the orange juice, wine, vinegar, soy sauce, and sugar.

Bring the mixture to a boil and slowly stir in enough of the cornstarch mixture to thicken.

Return the lobster to the sauce, add the cashew nuts, heat, and serve.

Variation: Substitute shrimp or a firm white fish for the lobster.

Hot and Pungent Shrimp

Heat Scale: 6
Serves: 2

6 small dried red chiles such as Piquins
2 tablespoons Red Chile Oil (see recipe Chapter 2)
1 tablespoon finely chopped fresh ginger
1 teaspoon chopped garlic
3/4 pound shrimp, shelled and deveined
4 tablespoons rice vinegar
4 tablespoons sugar
1 tablespoon soy sauce
1 tablespoon dry sherry
2 tablespoons catsup
3 tablespoons cornstarch mixed with 3 tablespoons water
3 scallions, chopped, including the greens

Hotter Chinese food from Sichuan has been growing in popularity over the past few years. The heat of this dish can be adjusted by reducing or increasing the number of chiles, or by substituting peanut oil for the chile oil.

Heat the oil in a wok or heavy skillet to 350° F. Add the chiles and sauté until they start to turn black. Add the ginger and the garlic and stir-fry for an additional minute. Add the shrimp and cook until just done — the shrimp will turn pink and lose their translucency. Remove and keep warm.

Add the vinegar, sugar, soy sauce, sherry and catsup to the wok. Heat until boiling, and slowly add the cornstarch mixture until thickened.

Return the shrimp to the sauce and heat thoroughly. Garnish with the scallions and serve.

Serving Suggestions: Traditionally served with plain white rice.

Spiced Beef in Tangerine Sauce

Heat Scale: 5
Serves: 4 to 6

5 small dried red chiles such as Piquins
3/4 teaspoon Chile Paste (see recipe Chapter 2)
2 teaspoons ground Sichuan peppercorns*
2 eggs
4 tablespoons cornstarch
1 1/2 pounds beef (sirloin or top round), cut in thin strips

This recipe incorporates four distinctive Sichuan ingredients: chile paste, chile peppers, Sichuan peppercorns, and tangerines. It also illustrates a distinctive method of beef preparation. Crisply fried beef is dry and chewy and the flavor more concentrated, thus requiring a highly seasoned multiple-flavored sauce such as this. Pork and chicken are also delicious in this recipe, and, if tangerines are not available, substitute oranges.

Combine the eggs and cornstarch and toss the beef strips in the mixture until well coated. Stir-fry the beef for 1 to 2 minutes or until crispy. Remove and drain. Pour out all but 1 tablespoon of the oil.

2 teaspoons finely chopped
  fresh ginger
2 cloves garlic, minced
1/2 cup tangerine or orange
  juice
2 tablespoons dark soy
  sauce
1 tablespoon *hoisin* sauce*
1 teaspoon sugar
2 tablespoons tangerine or
  orange peel, cut in strips
1 teaspoon rice wine vinegar
oil for stir-frying, peanut
  preferred

Combine the chiles, peppercorns, ginger, and garlic in a bowl. In another bowl combine the juice, soy sauce, *hoisin* sauce, sugar, chile paste, and mix well.

Heat the oil and stir-fry the chile pepper mixture for 30 seconds. Add the peel and juice mixture and stir-fry for an additional 15 seconds. Return the beef to the wok or pan, add the vinegar, and continue to cook until heated.

*Available in Asian markets.

 # Hunan Strange-Flavored Chicken

Heat Scale: 3
Serves: 4 to 6

1 tablespoon Red Chile Oil
  (see recipe Chapter 2)
2 teaspoons ground Sichuan
  peppercorns*
1 tablespoon sesame oil
1 1/2 tablespoons peanut oil
2 tablespoons light soy
  sauce
2 tablespoons rice vinegar
1 tablespoon sesame paste*
  or substitute smooth
  peanut butter
1 tablespoon sugar
1 teaspoon finely chopped
  fresh ginger
1 pound cooked chicken,
  skin removed, diced
2 scallions, chopped,
  including the greens
1 cucumber, cubed
1/4 cup roasted cashew nuts
sliced cucumbers
shredded lettuce

This cold chicken salad is not really strange — just delicious! It gets its name from the sauce, which is salty, sweet, sour and hot . . . all in one dish. In the Chinese province of Hunan where the summers are hot, a cool yet pungent entrée is always welcome.

Combine the Red Chile Oil, peppercorns, sesame and peanut oils, soy sauce, vinegar, sesame paste, sugar, and ginger and blend well. Allow the dressing to sit for a couple of hours to blend the flavors. Toss the chicken, scallions, cubed cucumber, and nuts in the sauce.

To Serve: Make a bed of the lettuce, arrange the sliced cucumbers on the lettuce, and top with the chicken salad.

*Available in Asian markets.

Xinjiang Lamb and Chile Barbecue

Heat Scale: 6
Serves: 4

Note: This recipe requires advance preparation.

1/4 cup Red Chile Oil (see recipe Chapter 2)
8 whole Jalapeño chiles
1/2 cup fresh lemon juice
2 tablespoons rice wine
4 cloves garlic, minced
2 teaspoons ground Sichuan peppercorns*
1/4 teaspoon salt
1/4 teaspoon sugar
2 pounds lamb, cut in 2-inch cubes
4 sesame-seed buns
chopped scallions, including the greens
chopped fresh cilantro

Xinjiang, which borders Mongolia, is noted for its barbecued lamb even though lamb is rarely eaten in other parts of China. In fact, the Mongolian tribes introduced lamb to the rest of China. This simple barbecue could easily be prepared by the nomads on the plains of Xinjiang.

Combine the the Red Chile Oil, lemon juice, rice wine, garlic, peppercorns, salt, and sugar. Marinate the lamb and Jalapeños in the refrigerator overnight.

Thread the lamb on skewers, alternating with the Jalapeños. Barbecue or broil, basting frequently with the reserved marinade until done.

Serve the lamb and chiles in the buns with the chopped scallions and cilantro.

*Available in Asian markets.

Korean Radish and Chile Salad

Heat Scale: 5
Serves: 4

The Dressing:

5 small green chiles such as Serranos, stems removed, finely chopped
3 tablespoons distilled white vinegar
2 tablespoons light soy sauce

The cooking of Korea is a mixture of Chinese and Japanese styles. Since the winters can be very severe, Koreans tend to eat more meat and they do not spare the chiles. Daikon, the large white radish, is the type used in this spicy accompaniment salad, but if unavailable, any type of radish will do.

Combine all the ingredients for the dressing and let sit at room temperature to blend the flavors.

Toast the sesame seeds on a hot skillet until they start to crackle.

1 tablespoon vegetable oil
2 teaspoons sesame oil
2 teaspoons sugar
1 teaspoon finely chopped
 fresh ginger
1 clove garlic, minced
1 teaspoon salt

The Salad:

1 tablespoon sesame seeds
2 large *daikon* radishes, cut
 in strips the size of
 matchsticks, or substitute 1
 cup shredded radishes
1 Granny Smith apple, cut
 in strips the size of
 matchsticks
2 tablespoons lemon juice
1 cup shredded cabbage
3 scallions, thinly sliced
 including the greens

Sprinkle the lemon juice over the radish and apple slices to keep them from turning brown. Toss the mixture with the cabbage and dressing. Top with the sesame seeds and serve.

Serving Suggestions: This salad goes well with barbecued beef short ribs, sautéed green beans and mushrooms, and rice pudding.

Poisson Kokonada

Heat Scale: 2
Serves: 4 to 6 as an
appetizer

Note: This recipe requires advance preparation.

3 small green chiles such as
 Serranos, stems removed,
 chopped
1 pound firm white fish, cut
 in 1 1/2-inch cubes
1 cup lime juice
1/2 cup chopped onions
1 cup grated fresh coconut
1 small banana, chopped
1 cup chopped mango
1/4 cup unsweetened
 coconut milk

Coconut is "king" throughout the South Pacific. The meat is eaten or used to make coconut milk or cream, the liquid is used as a beverage, the oil is used for cooking, the shells make cups, and the husks are burned. Coconut also plays an important part in this raw fish appetizer that is a distant relative to the ceviche dishes served in Latin America. Popular throughout the Pacific islands, this version is from Fiji, where they add chiles to the dish.

Combine the lime juice and onions and pour over the fish. Marinate the fish in a ceramic or glass dish for 4 hours in the refrigerator. Turn occasionally, until the fish loses its translucency and turns opaque. Drain and gently squeeze the fish to remove any excess marinade.

Gently toss the fish, chiles, coconut, banana, and mango with the coconut milk and serve.

CHAPTER TEN

The Legend of the Chile Pepper

"The conquest is complete. Hot peppers have taken over the United States."

Jake Page, *Hippocrates*, 1987

WE have seen in Chapter 5 how chile peppers infiltrated the American Southwest and became firmly established there between the sixteenth and nineteenth centuries, even to the point of dominating the cuisines of the region. However, the Southwest was not the only part of the United States to embrace the pungent pods.

In colonial America, chiles were grown by Thomas Jefferson, who imported seeds from Mexico and planted them at Monticello in Virginia. George Washington grew "bird peppers" at Mount Vernon, along with other experimental plants such as palmettos and Guinea grass. But chiles never really became popular on the East Coast. They were, however, adopted with great fervor in Louisiana by way of Mexico.

While the early settlers of the Southwest were growing New Mexican–type chiles and cooking enchiladas, Mexicans were developing and cultivating many different strains of Capsicums. One such strain, *Capsicum frutescens,* was grown near the port of Tabasco on the Gulf of Mexico, which had regular trade with New Orleans. During the U.S. war with Mexico, American soldiers captured the port of Tabasco (which is now called San Juan Batista) in July 1847.

Although exact details are lacking, historians believe that chiles were imported into New Orleans by soldiers returning to that city for treatment of various tropical diseases. Somehow, seeds were transferred to a prominent banker and legislator, Colonel Maunsell White. By 1849, White was cultivating the chiles, which were then spelled "Tobasco," on his Deer Range Plantation. That year, the *New Orleans Daily Delta* printed a letter from a visitor to White's plantation who reported, "I must not omit to notice the Colonel's pepper patch, which is two acres in extent, all planted with a new species of red pepper, which Colonel White has introduced into this country, called Tobasco red pepper. The Colonel attributes the admirable health of his hands to the free use of this pepper."

Colonel White manufactured the first hot sauce from the Tobasco chiles and advertised bottles of it for sale in 1859. About this time, he gave some chiles and his sauce recipe to a friend named Edmund McIlhenny, who promptly planted the seeds on his plantation on Avery Island. McIlhenny's horticultural enterprise was interrupted by the Civil War and invading Union troops from captured New Orleans. In 1863, McIlhenny and his family abandoned their Avery Island plantation to take refuge in San Antonio, Texas.

When the McIlhenny family returned to Avery Island in 1865, they found their plantation destroyed and their sugarcane fields in ruin. However, a few volunteer chile plants still survived, providing enough seeds for McIlhenny to rebuild his pepper patch. Gradually, his yield of pods increased to the point where he could experiment with his sauce recipe, in which mashed chiles were strained, and the resulting juice was mixed with vinegar and salt and aged in fifty-gallon white oak barrels. In 1868, McIlhenny packaged his aged sauce in 350 used cologne bottles and sent them as samples to likely wholesalers. The sauce was so popular that orders poured in for thousands of bottles priced at a dollar each, wholesale.

In 1870, McIlhenny obtained a patent on his Tabasco (as it was now called) brand hot pepper sauce and by 1872 had opened an office in London to handle the European market. The increasing demand for Tabasco sauce caused changes in the packaging of the product as the corked bottles sealed with green wax were replaced by bottles with metal tops. In 1885, the product won a gold medal for excellence at the World's Industrial and Cotton Centennial Exposition in New Orleans. By 1886, completion of the nationwide railway network greatly assisted the distribution of Tabasco sauce.

After the death of Edmund McIlhenny in 1890, the family business was turned over to his son John, who immediately inherited trouble in the form of a crop failure. John attempted to locate Tabasco chiles in Mexico but could not find any to meet his specifications. Fortunately, his father had stored sufficient reserves of pepper mash, so the family business weathered the crisis. However, that experience taught the family not to depend solely upon Tabasco chiles grown in Louisiana. Today, Tabascos are grown under contract in Colombia and other Central and South American countries, and the mash is imported into the United States in barrels.

John McIlhenny was quite a promoter and traveled all over the country promoting his family's sauce. "I had bill posters prepared," he once said, "and had large wooden signs in the fields near the cities. I had an opera troupe playing a light opera. At different times I had certain cities canvassed by drummers, in a house-to-house canvass. I had exhibits in food expositions, with demonstrators attached. I gave away many thousands of circulars and folders, and miniature bottles of Tabasco pepper sauce."

All of this promotion did not go unnoticed by the competition. In 1898, another Louisiana entrepreneur named B. F. Trappey began growing Tabasco chiles from Avery Island seed. He founded the company B. F. Trappey and Sons and began producing his own sauce, which was also called "Tabasco." The McIlhenny family eventually responded to this challenge by receiving a trademark for their Tabasco brand in 1906. The two companies competed with identically named sauces until 1929, when the McIlhenny family won a trademark-infringement suit against the Trappeys. From that time on, only the McIlhenny sauce could be called "Tabasco," and competitors were reduced to merely including Tabasco chiles in their list of ingredients.

The rise of Louisiana hot sauces greatly influenced the two related cuisines in the area, Creole and Cajun. The Creoles are descendants of the original French settlers of Louisiana, while the Cajuns are descended from French-speaking immigrants from Nova Scotia, which was originally called Acadia. (The term "Cajun" is a corrupt form of "Acadian.") Although Creole cooking is basically a localized, urban version of French cooking, and Cajun cuisine is a countrified mélange of French, African, and Indian cooking, both styles share similar ingredients and recipes.

Some food historians speculate that Creole and Cajun food

was first spiced up by Cayenne chiles brought from Africa by slaves and grown in plantation gardens but never commercially cultivated until the twentieth century. Today, both Cayenne and Tabasco chiles are grown in Louisiana, but not in great amounts — only about 230 acres of chiles are cultivated in the state. However, imported Cayenne powder, locally bottled Cayenne hot sauces, and many brands of Tabasco-based hot sauces are readily available to spice up Cajun and Creole dishes. As an indication of the growing popularity of hot sauces, between 1985 and 1987 the McIlhenny Company increased its yearly production of Tabasco pepper mash from 10,221 barrels to 16,470 barrels.

Although Cayenne- and Tabasco-based sauces are used as ingredients in the recipes, they are also the principal condiments of the region. In virtually every restaurant or home dining room, a selection of different brands of hot sauces is available to add even more heat to the already fiery foods.

Our collection of Creole and Cajun recipes provides a sampling of the flavors and styles of cooking in the region. The seafood orientation is evident in the classic dish Crayfish Étouffée. Tabasco Sauce dominates traditional Southern fried chicken in Louisiana Spiced Fried Chicken. Red Beans and Rice is a staple in Louisiana and features the combination of Tabasco and Cayenne.

Another Louisiana classic, Shrimp Creole, again combines both chiles of the region, this time with many vegetables and spices. The Cajuns love hot sausages, as evidenced by the recipe for Andouille Jambalaya. (Incidentally, the word *jambalaya* is a combination of the French *jambon* — ham — and an African word for rice, *ya*.) Fiery Seafood Gumbo is an elaborate stew that is well worth the effort to prepare.

The popularity of chiles in Louisiana and the Southwest led to a greater awareness of them in the rest of the United States, and by the latter half of the nineteenth century a number of varieties were available to the general gardening public. The Burpee Seed Company's 1888 *Farm Annual* offered some twenty varieties, including the Celestial, the Red Squash (of Massachusetts origin and "handsome appearance"), the Spanish Monstrous (six to eight inches long), the Red Chili ("the best for pepper sauce"), the Long Yellow, and the Cranberry, said to resemble one.

In 1896 Emilio Ortega, a California rancher, took chile seeds from New Mexico to Oxnard, California, and began cultivation. He was so successful and the chiles were so popular that he opened the first chile cannery, near Anaheim, in 1900, and that is why the long green type of chile became known as "Anaheim." However, that name is a misnomer, and today this pod type is called "New Mexican."

In 1907, Fabian Garcia, a horticulturist at the Agricultural Experiment Station at the New Mexico College of Agriculture and Mechanical Arts (now New Mexico State University) began his first experiments in breeding more standardized chile varieties, and in 1908 published *Chile Culture*, the first chile bulletin from the Agricultural Experiment Station. In 1913, Garcia became director of the Experiment Station and expanded his breeding program.

Finally, in 1917, after ten years of experiments with various strains of Pasilla chiles, Garcia released New Mexico No. 9, the first attempt to grow chiles with a dependable pod size and heat level. The No. 9 variety became the chile standard in New Mexico until 1950, when Roy Harper, another horticulturist, released New Mexico No. 6, a variety that matured earlier, produced higher yields, was wilt resistant, and was less pungent than No. 9.

The New Mexico No. 6 variety was by far the biggest breakthrough in the chile breeding program. According to Roy Nakayama, who succeeded Harper as director of the New Mexico Agricultural Experiment Station, "The No. 6 variety changed the image of chile from a ball of fire that sent consumers rushing to the water jug to that of a multi-purpose vegetable with a pleasing flavor. Commerical production and marketing, especially of green chiles and sauces, have been growing steadily since people around the world have discovered the delicious taste of chile without the overpowering pungency."

In 1957, the New Mexico No. 6 variety was modified, made less pungent again, and the new variety was called "New Mexico No. 6-4." The No. 6-4 variety became the chile industry standard in New Mexico and over thirty years later is still the most popular chile commercially grown in the state. Other chile varieties such as Big Jim and New Mexico R-Naky have been developed but became popular mostly with home gardeners.

The chile breeding program at New Mexico State University has resulted in New Mexico becoming the largest producer of hot peppers in the United States. In 1988, the state harvested 36,202 dry equivalent tons of pods worth $38.6 million on 22,210 acres. In just ten years, New Mexico chile production has increased nearly 100 percent, which is ample evidence of the growing popularity of chiles.

Of Festivals, Cookoffs, and Contests

During the second half of the twentieth century, the legend of the chile pepper began to explode as enthusiasts began to glorify its fiery nature with celebrations in various parts of the country. Some of the earliest celebrations were pepper-eating contests, which apparently originated in Louisiana. In 1956, *Newsweek* magazine reported such a contest in the Bayou Teche country near New Iberia. The contestants were required to munch their way through progressively hotter chiles and were penalized if they winced, shuddered, or flinched. It is interesting to note that the magazine stated that Jalapeños were "the hottest pepper known," which we now know is not true. The winner of that contest, Ed (Hot Mouth) Taylor, "munched his way right through the Jalapeño as nonchalantly as if he had been eating turnip greens," reported the magazine.

Chile-eating contests are now commonplace throughout the Southwest and occasionally occur in other parts of the country, with Jalapeños still the chile of choice. In 1988, John Espinosa of San Antonio, Texas, gulped his way into the *Guinness Book of World Records* by consuming an amazing *twenty-nine* Jalapeños in two minutes flat! It should be noted that the authors of this book neither endorse nor encourage hot pepper–eating contests because of the danger of capsaicin burns and other medical complications.

The 1950s also witnessed the beginning of chili con carne cookoffs, which are now the largest celebrations in the country involving chile peppers. The Chili Appreciation Society was formed in 1951 by George Haddaway and Jim Fuller to "improve the quality of chili in restaurants and broadcast Texas-style recipes all over the earth." The organization was head-quartered in Dallas, and when chapters began to form in other countries the "International" was added to the name.

The Chili Appreciation Society, International (CASI), was a non-dues-paying organization, and members did their own sec-retarial work. Their bible was *With or Without Beans* by Joe Cooper of Dallas, which is no longer in print. The Society slogan was, "The aroma of good chili should generate rapture akin to a lover's kiss."

The Society's chapters had luncheon or dinner meetings about once a month over steaming "bowls of red." Their "missionary endeavors" were debated and members spent a lot of time an-swering letters from all over the world and sending out "ap-proved" recipes to those who requested them. Vats of chili were even packed in dry ice and shipped to chili-starved members in Europe. By 1964, Haddaway and his buddies headed for Los Angeles to establish a California chapter, which was duly in-stalled at the Airport Marina Hotel. The Californians liked the chili and the Society, but warned the inexperienced: "Real chili con carne is not for sissies. Fowler's Four-Alarm Chili is reputed to open 18 sinus cavities unknown to the medical profession."

The first Terlingua, Texas, cookoff, held in 1967, was a promotion for Frank X. Tolbert's book *A Bowl of Red,* and featured a cookoff between Wick Fowler, inventor of Four-Alarm Chili Mix, and humorist H. Allen Smith, author of the article "Nobody Knows More About Chili Than I Do," which appeared in a 1967 issue of *Holiday* magazine. Because of the remoteness of the Terlingua cookoff, no one thought very many chili fans would show up, but 209 chapters of CASI were rep-resented and over a thousand spectators attended. The contest ended in a draw between Fowler and Smith. In 1968, the second cookoff at Terlingua was also declared a draw by Tolbert. But, of course, he had no choice, since the ballot box was stolen by masked men with guns. These desperadoes threw it into an out-house located over a mine shaft!

By 1970, over five thousand spectators trekked to Terlingua, and it was evident that a major event had been created. CASI started to get organized, and local "Pods" were formed to hold preliminary cookoffs. The number of contests grew and eventually "chiliheads," as they were called, developed such a listing of cookoffs that competition cooking is now similar to a professional sports circuit. Most members of CASI belong to Pods, and cooks are given points for placing at sanctioned cookoffs throughout the year: four points for winning, three for second, two for third, and one for fourth. At the end of the year, all cooks having enough points to qualify are invited to cook at Terlingua, always the first Saturday in November.

The Terlingua cookoff can no longer legally be called the "World Championship" because that phrase has been trademarked by the International Chili Society (ICS). The International Chili Society was booted out of Texas in 1974 and was reborn in California. During the 1974 Terlingua cookoff, CASI celebrities C. V. Wood and Carroll Shelby flew a network-television crew in to cover the festivities. Of course, it was only natural that the media people would interview the people who had provided the transportation, but Frank Tolbert did not appreciate the promotion. After standing around on the sidelines and not receiving any attention from the TV crew, he became angry. In a letter to Wood and Shelby, he invited them to promote their own chili cookoff in California and "save the freight." So they did.

They formed the International Chili Society and made plans for a major cookoff. After searching for a suitable location for the ICS cookoff in California, the Tropico Gold Mine, located three miles west of Rosamond in the Mohave Desert was selected. The International Chili Society also thumbed its nose at CASI by trademarking the phrase "World Championship Chili Cookoff."

The first Championship Chili Cookoff held in California was twice as big as expected — about 20,000 people attended. Perhaps some of them were star-struck by the celebrity judges: William Conrad, Robert Mitchum, Ernest Borgnine, Peter Marshall, Dale Robertson, and John Derek. The "Miss Chile Pepper" was Diana House, who went on to spice up *Playboy* magazine.

Meanwhile, back in Texas, Frank Tolbert was busy organizing CASI and promoting the Terlingua cookoff. Although relations between the two societies seemed to be "heated," they were in constant communication with each other. Early in 1976, ICS began to get organized by finding corporate sponsors. Pepsi, Budweiser, Hunt-Wesson, Tabasco Brand, the American Spice Trade Association, and Tequila Sauza came on board to help raise money for various charities. By 1977 the turnout at Tropico Gold Mine for the championship exceeded 35,000. That year Tommy Lasorda, Leslie Uggams, Andy Granatelli, and Bobby Unser were added to the celebrity judging staff, and by the end of the fourth championship, over $50,000 had been raised for charity.

Cash prizes were growing as well. In 1978, the World's Champion Chili Cook, LaVerne "Nevada Annie" Harris, picked up $14,000 — which was great pay for three hours of cooking. Ten years later, the 1988 Championship was held on October 30 in Tropico with over $35,000 in cash prizes and awards. Since 1975 ICS has raised over $10 million for charities and nonprofit organizations. There are nearly 15,000 members worldwide who sanction about 350 cookoffs every year with nearly 10,000 contestants and 5,000 judges. Obviously, chili cookoffs today are no longer off-the-wall events, but rather, viable fund-raising efforts.

In addition to raising money, ICS also has a lot of fun, which is demonstrated by some of the events at the Tropico Gold Mine cookoff. In 1988, the Tulsa, Oklahoma, Jaycees built the World's Largest Pot of Competition-Style Chili. The 750 gallons of chili was made with 75 pounds of bacon, 3,000 pounds of chili-grind meat, 1,500 pounds of onions, 1,200 cloves of garlic, nearly 30 pounds of spices — and, of course, over 50 pounds of fresh chiles. The concoction, based on a recipe called "Chili from Hell," was served to more than 20,000 chiliheads at Tropico in a benefit for the St. Jude's Children's Hospital in Memphis.

Chili lovers are never satisfied. Despite the fact that the Bowl o' Red is the Texas state dish, a movement has begun to have Congress declare chili con carne America's Official Food. Led by self-proclaimed World Chili Ambassador Ormly Gumfudgin, and supported by the International Chili Society and Maximum Strength Pepto-Bismol, the movement hopes to obtain the signatures of *one million* chiliheads on a petition to support passage of the bill, which is already before Congress. Considering the fact that over 750,000 people attend chili cookoffs each year, perhaps this goal is reachable.

For our examples of cookoff-type chili con carne recipes, we have analyzed the most commonly used ingredients in both CASI and ICS top cookoff recipes over the past decade and then created our versions of them. Now, we are not claiming we can win any cookoffs with CASI-Style Chili and ICS-Style Chili, but at least they are typical of the philosophies of the two societies and illustrate the differences in ingredients and techniques.

There seems to be no end to the ever-growing number of other festivals celebrating the chile pepper. Laredo, Texas, holds a Jalapeño Fiesta each year; while tiny Hatch, New Mexico, draws over 10,000 people to its Hatch Chile Fiesta, held every year over the Labor Day weekend. Tucson, Arizona, holds its Fiesta de los Chiles in mid-October at the Tucson Botanical Gardens, complete with a chile rap song performed by a puppeteer. Las Cruces, New Mexico throws an annual Enchilada Fiesta, at which they create the World's Largest Enchilada, nearly eight feet in diameter.

The latest chile contest craze has Southwestern cities competing for the title of "Mexican Food Capital" by way of a cookoff challenge. In 1987, Tucson Mayor Lew Murphy proclaimed his city to be the "Mexican Food Capital" of the World and Elsewhere." In a blistering letter to the mayors of San Antonio, El Paso, Los Angeles, Dallas, San Diego, Phoenix, Santa Fe, and Albuquerque, Murphy challenged those cities to a chile-cooking contest in Tucson. "It's time to put your Mexican menu where our mouth is," Murphy dared them.

Such a cavalier attitude produced fumes from Santa Fe's Mayor Sam Pick, who retorted: "We've been eating chile here in Santa Fe before Tucson was even thought of." Pick was alluding to the fact that Santa Fe was founded 165 years before Tucson, and added: "Everyone knows that Santa Feans are bred on red and weaned on green." Eventually, the cities of Phoenix, El Paso, Albuquerque, and Santa Fe collided with Tucson in early December 1987, to give a heated response to the chile challenge. The event was called, improbably enough, "The Great

American Mexican Food Cook-Off." The judges of the contest were all Mexicans — not Hispanics, mind you, but real Mexican chile aficionados imported from Tijuana. One of them was the president of the Tijuana restaurant owners' association.

The results of the contest proved that Tucson's claim to be the capital of Mexican Food was invalid. Overall winners were, in order: Santa Fe, Phoenix, and Albuquerque. The following year, Santa Fe chefs and cooks again seized control of the title of "Mexican Food Capital of the World and Elsewhere" at the 1988 Mayor's Chile Challenge held in Santa Fe.

Such contests inevitably bring up questions. What city is America's spiciest? Which state offers the greatest wealth of fiery food? In 1988, *The Whole Chile Pepper* magazine conducted a study based upon a compilation of nationwide Yellow Page classifications. The listings of over 2,800 Mexican-food restaurants and Mexican-food retail-product producers were analyzed. Since Mexican food contains one of the highest percentages of chile peppers of any cuisine, it was regarded as a prime indicator for the popularity of fiery foods in general.

The data were examined on a state-by-state and city-by-city basis, then compared to the population of each area to determine the number of people per Mexican-food retailer, thus giving a good indication of the demand for fiery food in each region. The study of the states indicated — not unexpectedly — that New Mexico and Texas ranked at the top of per capita consumption of Mexican food. New Mexico was the hottest state with one retailer per 11,900 residents. Texas was close behind with one outlet for every 13,700 Texans. California, despite its proximity to Mexico, ranked a weak eleventh, with only one retailer for every 53,000 residents. The southern area of that state was stronger than the northern part, as might be expected. Surprisingly, Kansas ranked third, with one retailer for every 17,200 people.

In the city-by-city study, two New Mexico cities took the top spots. Santa Fe ranked as the top fiery-food city in the country, with one retailer for every 4,890 residents. Las Cruces was close behind, with one outlet per 5,000 people. Austin, Texas, came in third with one hot retailer per 6,700 residents.

It should be pointed out that the data are not complete. To

compile a truly comprehensive study of the geography of fiery-food markets, it would be necessary to go beyond Mexican-food retailers and include Thai restaurants, East Indian restaurants and products, Hunan and Sichuan restaurants and markets, Caribbean and Cajun food, and "New Southwestern" restaurants and products. Although Mexican food currently constitutes the largest share of the chile pepper market, the other spicy cuisines are becoming quite popular as well.

New Southwest Cuisine

California restaurants have led the way in the development of what is called "New Southwest" cuisine. Some of the tenets of this style of cooking are the use of fresh, locally produced ingredients, the elimination of fattening or high-cholesterol ingredients, the regular appearance of more exotic chiles (rather than just the usual New Mexican varieties), and a dedication to the beautiful presentation of the meal. New Southwest chefs rarely use canned, frozen, or otherwise prepared foods.

Perhaps the most famous of these restaurants is Chez Panisse, which opened in 1971 in Berkeley and featured Alice Waters's French-California specialties, such as Corn Soup with Roasted Poblano Chiles and Charcoal-Grilled Veal with Mustard Herb Butter. Our recipe for Juniper Lamb Chops is in this style.

John Sedlar's St. Estephe Restaurant in Manhattan Beach is renowned for its artistic presentation of New Southwest dishes, and the Fourth Street Grill in Berkeley loves chile peppers so much that once a year it features "A Culinary Celebration of the Chile Pepper." This two-week-long celebration offers all-chile dinners such as Mesquite-Grilled Hawaiian Tuna with Mango, Serrano, and Pineapple Chutney and Chile Braised Pork with Small Squashes and Flowers.

Gradually, this New Southwest cuisine moved east. Arizona has its representative restaurants, such as The Rancher's Club and Cafe Terra Cotta in Tucson and the Piñon Grill in Scottsdale. In Texas, Houston's Cafe Annie (which offers Rabbit with Poblano Maple Sauce) and Dallas's Routh Street Cafe (famous for its Roast Tenderloin of Beef with Ancho Chile Tamarind Sauce) are the leaders in New Southwest cuisine. Our recipe for Beef

Fillet in Cracked Pepper Chipotle Sauce is an example of the elegant — and spicy — treatment of a standard cut of meat.

One California transplant (from Chez Panisse), Mark Miller of Santa Fe's Coyote Cafe, creates recipes that epitomize New Southwest cuisine. A former anthropologist, Mark believes in a sort of culinary evolution, where cookery must move forward. "Southwestern cuisine today is frozen in time," he says. "It neither looks to the past nor progresses into the future. In New Mexico, for instance, the 'traditional' foods can be traced back only a few generations to the Spanish, when in reality the food tradition extends all the way back to the ancient Anasazi culture."

As a culinary anthropologist, Mark is often accused of corrupting traditional foods by preparing such dishes as Wild Mushroom Tamales. "Indigenous cultures cooked with what they found around them," he insists. "Tradition in this case means the native larder, and Indians consumed both corn and mushrooms. Since we can assume the same level of sophistication occurred in both their pottery and their cookery, wild mushroom tamales are not only traditional, they are logical re-creations of what the ancient Southwest Indians probably ate."

Although disconcerting to some, the innovations of the New Southwest chefs are fully in keeping with historical tradition — the interaction of various cultures with different ideas of what constitutes Southwest cookery. In our collection of Southwestern recipes, cooks may take their choice from a wide variety of recipes from all over the region.

Jalapeño Pasta with Garlic Butter Sauce reverses the usual trend of the chile-based sauce; here the chiles are in the pasta and the sauce is mild. Our recipe for Blue Corn Enchiladas with Crab in Chile Cream combines traditional styles of preparation with unusual ingredients. The Grilled Marinated Chicken Breast with Fruit Salsa was inspired by the mixture of fruit and chiles that originated in the Caribbean and Central America but is now showing up all over the Southwest. For holiday celebrations, we offer our version of New Southwest turkey, Smoked Turkey with Orange Cascabel Chile Oil.

To complete our collection of New Southwest recipes, we offer an eclectic menu consisting of Cream of Jalapeño Soup with Roasted Pepper Sauce, Marinated Shrimp and Summer Fruit Salad, Roulade of Pork with Green Chile and Cilantro, and our only chile dessert, Citrus Pepper Sorbet.

Chiles As a Trend, Not a Fad

It is now possible to wake up in the morning, put on a pair of chile pepper underpants, dress in a chile pepper T-shirt or skirt, drink coffee from a chile pepper cup, eat breakfast from plates emblazoned with red chiles, check a chile pepper wind sock for wind direction, address a chile pepper greeting card to a friend, and then drive into town to visit a chile pepper specialty shop to buy even more chile pepper food and nonfood items.

Since there are now dozens — if not hundreds — of nonfood products based on chile peppers, speculation has arisen that we are experiencing a fad that will soon fade away. People still remember Hula-Hoops, coonskin caps, and Nehru jackets, and some skeptics think that chile peppers fall into the same category. We believe that the confusion about chile peppers (and, by extension, fiery foods) being fads arises from the fact that chile peppers have the *trappings* of a fad.

Within just a few years, chiles became enormously popular in the United States. The phenomenon was sparked by media attention and was driven by vehicles such as *The Whole Chile Pepper* magazine. Suddenly, it seemed, everyone was talking about, writing about, cooking with, and eating chile peppers. But unlike typical fads, such media attention came *after* the fact, not before it, because chile peppers were already firmly established in the cuisines of the Sunbelt states from Louisiana west to California. The media attention did not create the popularity of chile peppers as it did that of the Hula-Hoop; it merely reported what was already happening.

The other trapping that makes chile peppers appear to be a fad is the "warm fuzzy" concept. "Warm fuzzy" is a marketing expression for a "cute" product that is popular because it stimulates several senses simultaneously. An example of a "warm fuzzy" is the cartoon cat Garfield, which is embraced by sight in comic strips and television and by touch when a stuffed toy is cuddled. Chile peppers, because of their shape, color, heat, and fragrance, embrace the sensations of sight, taste, and smell simultaneously, and thus have become warm fuzzies in the perception of consumers.

The shape and color of chile pods are visually pleasing, and they are easy to caricature. Red chile *ristras*, which originated as a preservation method, are now a home decoration. They are not only symbolic of the Southwest but also are now popular all over the country. In New Mexico, the aroma of roasting green chile is associated with the changing of the seasons from summer to fall and is so traditional that it conjures up nostalgic emotions in those who inhale the fragrant fumes. The beloved heat of chiles — and the near addiction it causes in those people who consume them regularly — has been detailed in Chapter 8.

The "warm fuzzy" concept has caused chile peppers to be plastered over every product imaginable because the public loves *everything* about the chile pepper. Chiles appear to be a fad, but they are not. First, they have been around a long time in the human diet — since about 7500 B.C. Second, they have penetrated into most of the world's regions and cuisines, and it is estimated that three-fourths of the world's population uses chile peppers as a regular part of their diet.

Third, for additional evidence supporting our contention that chile peppers — and fiery foods in particular — are a trend, not a fad, we have collected some interesting statistics. Sales of Mexican food in grocery stores rose 230 percent between 1980 and 1987, and well over a hundred new gourmet brands of fiery foods now enter the marketplace each year. Sales of Texas picante sauces and salsas have increased at the rate of 25 percent a year, and Mexican sauces in general now are the biggest sellers of all sauce and gravy products, with a 16 percent share.

In 1988, Mexican food became the most popular ethnic cuisine in the United States, with total restaurant sales surpassing those of Italian food (excepting pizza), according to the research firm of SAMI-Burke. Even McDonald's, that bastion of bland burgers and fries, is test marketing breakfast burritos with green chile and Quarter-Pounders *ranchero-style!*

One of the most impressive statistics comes from the fiery-foods industry — those whose products contain chile peppers. Estimated annual sales for the industry in 1989 were $1.7 billion.

This figure leads to the inescapable conclusion that chile pepper—based food and nonfood products comprise a large, rapidly growing industry. The forces driving this growth are an ever-increasing demand from the American public for more hot and spicy foods and a growing love affair with chile peppers themselves. Chile peppers are now firmly entrenched in the diet of tens of millions of Americans, through the enjoyment of fiery cuisines such as Mexican, New Mexican, Tex-Mex, Cajun, Thai, Sichuan, East Indian, and Caribbean.

With chile peppers and fiery foods becoming solidly entrenched in the mainstream American diet, what developments can we expect to see? We believe that fiery foods — and especially Mexican food — will continue to show solid growth in all segments of the industry. Chile peppers and food products will continue their penetration of eastern and midwestern markets, and new packaging techniques will increase the shelf life for fresh green chiles in produce departments, leading to the availability of New Mexican varieties of chile all over the country. Exotic chiles, particularly the hotter varieties such as Habaneros and Ajís, will increase in popularity.

An increased number of locally produced salsas and hot sauces will be introduced, despite the fact that there are over 165 different brands already. More sales will be seen by pepper-oriented products prevalent in cuisines other than just Mexican and Southwestern; some examples are hot Asian oils, Serrano sauces, Caribbean sauces and marinades, and East Indian condiments.

Fiery food and New Southwest restaurants will increase in number and will develop their own gourmet product lines, as evidenced by the fact that the East Coast Grill in Cambridge, Massachusetts, has produced a Habanero chile and mustard sauce called Inner Beauty.

Throughout this book, we have shown how chiles have conquered nations; therefore, we advise chile lovers to take pity on those skeptics who say the pungent pods are just a fad. Simply serve them some of the recipes contained in this book, and, while they are sweating, tell them that if chiles are a fad, they have been so for about ten thousand years.

 # Crayfish Étouffée

Heat Scale: 3
Serves: 4

4 teaspoons Louisiana-type hot sauce
1 small Bell pepper, diced
1/3 cup vegetable oil
1/4 cup flour
1 medium onion, chopped
2 cloves garlic, minced
2 stalks celery, diced
2 medium tomatoes, peeled and chopped
1 cup fish stock or clam juice
1/2 teaspoon basil
1/4 teaspoon thyme
1 bay leaf
freshly ground black pepper
1 pound crayfish, peeled
1/2 cup chopped scallions, including the greens

The word étouffée *comes from the French word for "smother," and in this recipe, it refers to being smothered by a sauce. This dish, as with all traditional Cajun dishes, begins with a roux — or the browning of flour in a fat or oil for use as a thickening agent.*

To make the roux: Heat the oil in a heavy skillet until hot. Gradually stir in the flour and stir constantly until the mixture turns brown. Be very careful that the roux does not burn.

Sauté the onions, garlic, celery, and Bell pepper in the roux for 5 minutes.

Add the tomatoes, stock, basil, thyme, and bay leaf. Bring to a boil, stirring constantly. Reduce the heat and simmer for 15 minutes or until it thickens to a sauce.

Add the hot sauce, crayfish, and scallions and simmer for an additional 5 minutes or until the crayfish are done. Remove the bay leaf and serve.

Serving Suggestions: Serve with celery seed coleslaw, green beans, and corn bread.

Variations: Use shrimp or lobster meat in place of the crayfish.

Louisiana Spiced Fried Chicken

Heat Scale: 4
Serves: 2
Note: This recipe requires advance preparation.

3 tablespoons Louisiana-
   type hot sauce
2 tablespoons dried ground
   red New Mexican chiles
2 chicken breasts
1/2 cup flour
1 teaspoon onion powder
1/2 teaspoon garlic powder
1/2 teaspoon freshly ground
   black pepper
1 cup heavy cream
vegetable oil for deep-frying

Try this variation of traditional Southern fried chicken — one with a bite. Made popular by Popeye's, a fast-food chain, this spicy chicken is delicious served hot or cold.

Pour the Tabasco sauce over the chicken and marinate in the refrigerator for 3 to 4 hours.

Combine the flour, ground chile, and spices in a brown paper bag. Add the chicken and coat evenly. Dip the chicken in the cream and then back in the seasoned flour.

Deep-fry the chicken breasts in 350° F oil for 10 minutes or until they are evenly browned. Drain on paper towels. Place on a rack on a baking pan and bake for 30 minutes at 325° F or until done.

Serving Suggestions: Coleslaw, steak-fry potatoes, and buttermilk biscuits go well with the chicken.

Red Beans and Rice

Heat Scale: 4
Serves: 4 to 6
Note: This recipe requires advance preparation.

2 teaspoons ground
   Cayenne
1 1/2 tablespoons Louisiana-
   type hot sauce
1 Bell pepper, stem and
   seeds removed, chopped
1/2 pound dried red beans,
   sorted and rinsed
1/2 pound Andouille
   sausage, or substitute
   smoked sausage, cut into
   cubes
1/2 pound smoked ham
   shank

A staple thoughout the South, these beans are served as both a side dish and a main dish. In New Orleans it is a Monday luncheon favorite. It is not only easy to prepare but also wonderfully tasty.

Cover the beans with water and soak them overnight.

Add 1 tablespoon of the hot sauce, the Bell pepper, sausage, ham shanks, onion, celery, garlic, thyme, black pepper, sage, and bay leaf to the beans and bring to a boil. Reduce the heat, and simmer until the beans are tender, about 2 to 2 1/2 hours. Add more water if necessary.

Discard any ham bones and the bay leaf. Remove 1/4 cup of the beans from the pot and mash into a paste, and then add the mashed mixture back to the pot.

Add the Cayenne and the remainder of the hot sauce and simmer for 15 minutes. Serve over the hot rice with extra hot sauce served on the side.

1 large onion, chopped
2 stalks celery, chopped
2 cloves garlic, minced
1 teaspoon dried thyme
1 teaspoon freshly ground
  black pepper
1/2 teaspoon ground sage
1 bay leaf
4 cups cooked rice

Serving Suggestions: Serve with a tossed garden salad and corn bread.

 # Shrimp Creole

Heat Scale: 3
Serves: 4 to 6

2 teaspoons ground
  Cayenne
2 teaspoons Louisiana-type
  hot sauce
2 medium Bell peppers,
  stems and seeds removed,
  chopped
1 large onion, chopped
4 cloves garlic, minced
2 stalks celery, chopped
1/4 cup vegetable oil
2 large tomatoes, peeled and
  seeds removed, and
  chopped
1 cup red wine (optional)
2 cups shrimp stock or
  substitute bottled clam
  juice
2 large bay leaves
1 tablespoon dried thyme
1 1/2 teaspoons dried basil
1/2 teaspoon freshly ground
  black pepper
1 1/2 pounds uncooked
  medium shrimp, peeled
  and deveined
2 cups cooked rice
6 scallions, chopped,
  including the greens

Creole cooking began in New Orleans as a mixture of French and Spanish styles and is more sophisticated than the country, or Cajun, type of cooking. Known the world over, this dish is a delicious example of that blend.

Sauté the Bell peppers, onion, garlic, and celery in the oil until soft.

Add the tomatoes and wine and simmer the sauce until it has been reduced by one half. Add the Cayenne, hot sauce, stock, bay leaves, thyme, basil, and black pepper. Simmer the sauce for 30 minutes.

Add the shrimp and cook for 5 to 7 minutes or until the shrimp is done.

Place the rice on a plate, pour the Shrimp Creole on top, garnish with the chopped scallions, and serve.

Andouille Jambalaya

Heat Scale: 2
Serves: 4

1 1/2 teaspoons ground Cayenne
1 small Bell pepper, stem and seeds removed, chopped
1 tablespoon Louisiana-type hot sauce
1 pound Andouille or smoked sausage, diced
1 large onion, chopped
1 cup chopped celery
2 cloves garlic, minced
3 tablespoons margarine or vegetable oil
1 1/2 cups rice
2 medium tomatoes, peeled and diced
1/2 teaspoon dried thyme
3 cups chicken stock
3/4 pound ham, diced
6 scallions, chopped, including the greens
2 tablespoons minced fresh parsley

One-pot meals are typical of bayou or Louisiana cooking. This dish may have originated with the Spanish as a paella. It differs from Cajun cooking, as no roux is used. Andouille is a favorite Cajun sausage; if it is not available, substitute any smoked sausage for this recipe. (Actually, any beef, ham, pork, poultry, sausage, or seafood can be used, so whatever is on hand is fine.)

Sauté the Bell pepper, sausage, onion, celery, and garlic in the margarine or oil until the onions are soft. Add the rice and sauté, stirring constantly, until browned.

Stir in the Cayenne, hot sauce, tomatoes, thyme, stock, and ham. Bring to a boil, reduce the heat, and simmer for 30 minutes or until the rice is done.

Before serving, stir in the green onions and parsley.

Serving Suggestions: Serve with a crisp tossed salad and crusty French bread.

Fiery Seafood Gumbo

Heat Scale: 5
Serves: 6 to 8

1 tablespoon dried crushed
red chile, seeds included
2 teaspoons ground
Cayenne
1 cup chopped Bell pepper
1 pound raw shrimp
1 quart chicken stock
1/2 cup bacon drippings or
vegetable oil
1/2 cup flour
1 large onion, chopped
2 stalks celery, chopped
4 cloves garlic, minced
1/2 pound okra, cut
crosswise into rounds
1 teaspoon distilled white
vinegar
1 tablespoon vegetable oil
1 medium tomato, peeled
and chopped
2 tablespoons Pickapeppa
Sauce (optional)
2 bay leaves, crumbled
1/2 teaspoon ground thyme
1/4 teaspoon ground
oregano
1/2 pound fish fillets, cut
into 3/4-inch chunks
1/2 pound lump crabmeat
3 cups cooked rice
chopped fresh parsley for
garnish

A gumbo is a Cajun soup that has a roux as a base and uses file *(sassafras leaves) and/or okra as a thickening agent. This dish has African origins, as the Bantu word for okra is* gumbo! *Often served as a main dish, this "soup" may contain chicken, beef, or ham in addition to vegetables, tomatoes, and spices.*

Poach the shrimp in the chicken stock until they turn pink, about 4 minutes. Remove the shrimp, save the broth, and shell and devein the shrimp. Keep the shrimp cool until ready to add back into the gumbo.

Melt the bacon drippings and stir in the flour. Heat the roux, stirring constantly, until it is a very dark brown color, being careful that it does not burn. Add the onions, celery, and garlic and continue to heat for a couple of minutes to soften the vegetables. Remove from the heat so that the roux does not continue to brown.

Heat the okra and vinegar in the vegetable oil for 20 minutes or until the okra is no longer stringy, stirring occasionally.

Reheat the broth to boiling and slowly stir the roux mixture into the liquid. Add the chile, Cayenne, okra, tomato, Pickapeppa sauce, bay leaves, thyme, and oregano. Then reduce the heat and simmer for a couple of hours until thick.

Add the fish and crabmeat and heat for 5 minutes.

Remove from the heat and add the shrimp. Allow to sit for a couple of minutes before serving.

To Serve: Place some of the cooked rice in the bottom of a bowl, pour the gumbo over the top, and garnish with the parsley.

Serving Suggestions: Serve with potato salad and sourdough bread.

Note: Gumbo can be prepared ahead of time. Prepare the gumbo up to the point where the fish is added. Refrigerate until ready to heat and serve.

CASI-Style Chili

Heat Scale: 4
Serves: 6

4 Jalapeño chiles, stems and
   seeds removed, sliced in
   half
4 tablespoons Chili Powder,
   either commerical or
   homemade (see recipe
   Chapter 2)
1 tablespoon ground
   Paprika
2 pounds beef chuck, cut
   into 1 1/2-inch cubes
1 medium onion, chopped
2 tablespoons chopped
   kidney fat, or substitute
   vegetable oil
1 8-ounce can tomato sauce
1 12-ounce can beer
2 cups beef stock
3 teaspoons ground cumin
2 teaspoons garlic powder
1 teaspoon freshly ground
   black pepper
1/4 cup *masa*

*CASI chili-cookoff winners tend to use blended chili powder and
also Jalapeño chiles, which are usually removed before serving.
The beef is cubed, and* masa, *which is a flour made from ground
dried corn and available in Latin markets, is used to thicken the
chili.*

Brown the meat and onions in the oil or fat.

Add the tomato sauce, beer, beef stock, chiles, cumin, garlic,
black pepper, and 2 tablespoons of the Chili Powder. Simmer
the chili over a low heat for 2 hours until the meat is tender.

To thicken, make a thin paste of the masa and water. Quickly
stir this into the chili — if done too slowly it will lump.

Add the remaining Chili Powder and Paprika. Simmer for an
additional 15 minutes. Remove the Jalapeños and serve.

 # ICS-Style Chili

Heat Scale: 4
Serves: 6 to 8

3 tablespoons dried ground
   red New Mexican chile
1 7-ounce can diced green
   New Mexican chile
2 teaspoons ground
   Cayenne, or more for
   added heat

*The ICS chili cooks use more New Mexican chile powder and
add diced green New Mexican chiles. The meat is cubed or
coarsely ground and different spices such as tarragon, turmeric,
allspice, and even curry powder are added.*

Brown the beef in the oil. Add the onion, celery, and garlic and
sauté until soft.

2 pounds beef sirloin, either coarsely ground or cut in cubes
2 tablespoons vegetable oil
2 medium onions, chopped
2 stalks celery, chopped
3 cloves garlic, minced
1 16-ounce can tomatoes, chopped
1 tablespoon ground cumin
1 teaspoon ground oregano

Add the remaining ingredients and enough water to cover and simmer for about 2 to 3 hours or until the meat is tender. Add more water if necessary.

 # Juniper Lamb Chops

Heat Scale: 5
Serves: 2

5 dried Chiltepin chiles or other small dried red chiles
3 teaspoons juniper berries*
1 teaspoon whole white peppercorns
2 cloves garlic
2 loin lamb chops
1/2 cup dry white wine
2 tablespoons margarine
1 tablespoon vegetable oil
1/2 cup heavy cream

For a stronger juniper taste, substitute gin for the wine in this recipe.

Coarsely grind the chiles, juniper berries, peppercorns, and garlic. Pound the mixture into both sides of the lamb chops. Place the chops in a glass or ceramic pan, pour the wine over the top and marinate for at least an hour. Remove the chops and reserve the marinade.

Heat 1 tablespoon of the margarine with the oil. Brown the chops on both sides and cook to desired doneness. Remove and keep warm.

Add the remaining tablespoon of margarine and the marinade to the pan. Bring to a boil, scraping down any pan drippings. Add the cream and continue to boil until the sauce is reduced by one half.

Serve the chops with the sauce poured over the top.

*Available in gourmet stores.

Beef Fillet in Cracked Pepper Chipotle Sauce

Heat Scale: 4
Serves: 2

The Sauce:

2 canned Chipotle chiles in adobo sauce, reserve sauce
1 large dried Ancho chile, stem and seeds removed, torn in pieces
2 tablespoons clarified butter or vegetable oil
2 tablespoons chopped onion
2 cloves garlic
1 cup beef stock
1/2 cup dry red wine
2 teaspoons adobo sauce (from the canned Chipotles)
1 teaspoon freshly ground black pepper
2 teaspoons chopped fresh rosemary
1 teaspoon sugar

The Fillets:

2 6-ounce beef fillets
2 tablespoons olive oil
1 teaspoon green peppercorns, cracked
1 teaspoon black peppercorns, cracked
1 teaspoon white peppercorns, cracked

The name chipotle *comes from the Aztec (Nahuatl) words for* chile (chil) *and* smoked (poctli), *and together they describe the process of smoke-drying Jalapeños to produce this chile. The flavor they impart is smoky and hot, which is different from any other chile. Chipotles are sold in the dry form or canned in a tomato-based adobo sauce; this recipe calls for the latter.*

To Make the Sauce: Heat the butter and add the Ancho to soften. Add the onion and garlic and sauté until browned. Stir in the remaining ingredients. Cover and simmer until reduced by one half.

Place all the ingredients in a blender and puree until smooth. Then strain the sauce.

To Make the Fillets: Sauté the beef fillets in the olive oil to desired doneness. Remove and keep warm.

Heat the chile sauce and stir in the peppercorns.

Place the sauce on heated plates, slice the beef diagonally into strips, and place on the sauce.

Serving Suggestions: Serve with wild rice and asparagus.

Jalapeño Pasta with Garlic Butter Sauce

Heat Scale: 3
Serves: 6

The Pasta:

10 Jalapeño chiles, stems
  and seeds removed,
  chopped
1/2 cup fresh parsley leaves
1 tablespoon vegetable oil
2 large eggs
2 cups flour
water

The Sauce:

1/4 pound butter
8 cloves garlic, minced
grated Romano cheese

For differently flavored and colored pastas, use this basic recipe and replace the Jalapeños with fresh red or green chile or the favorite chile of choice. Simple sauces allow the flavor and heat of the pastas to stand out.

To Make the Pasta: Place the chiles, parsley, and oil in a blender and puree until smooth. Add the eggs to the mixture and mix well.

If mixing by hand, place the flour on a board or in a bowl. Make a well in the center and pour in the chile puree. Stir with a fork until well mixed and crumbly. Form a ball and knead on a lightly floured board until smooth and elastic. Add some water if necessary and just enough flour to prevent the dough from sticking to the board.

If using a pasta machine, follow the manufacturer's directions.

Roll out the dough and cut into linguine strips. The pasta can be made ahead of time and stored in the refrigerator for up to 2 days.

To Make the Sauce: Sauté the garlic in the butter for 5 minutes, being careful that it does not burn.

Heat 2 quarts of water to a rolling boil. Add salt and stir in the pasta. Cover until water comes to a boil again, remove the cover, and cook until done but still firm (al dente), about 2 to 3 minutes. Remove and drain. (Please don't add oil to the water — it is not necessary if the water is boiling!)

Toss the pasta with the garlic butter, top with the cheese, and serve.

Blue Corn Enchiladas with Crabmeat in Chile Cream

Heat Scale: 3
Serves: 6

6 green New Mexican
  chiles, roasted, peeled,
  stems and seeds removed,
  chopped
1 tablespoon dried ground
  red New Mexican chile
3 tablespoons chopped
  onion
2 cloves garlic, minced
2 tablespoons butter or
  margarine
2 tablespoons flour
1 teaspoon ground cumin
1 cup dry white wine
1 cup heavy cream
1/2 cup sour cream
6 scallions, chopped,
  including the greens
1 pound cooked lump
  crabmeat
2 cups grated Monterey
  Jack cheese
6 blue corn tortillas
chopped fresh cilantro for a
  garnish

The nutty flavor of blue corn tortillas complements the rich and spicy cream sauce in this recipe. Additionally, the combination of crabmeat with tortillas reflects the New Southwestern style of mixing unusual ingredients with the traditional.

Sauté the onion and garlic in the butter until soft. Add the green chiles. Stir in the flour and cumin and heat for 3 minutes.

Stir in the wine and simmer until the sauce is smooth. Add the heavy cream and chopped scallions and simmer for 3 to 5 minutes or until the sauce is thick. Remove from the heat and stir in the sour cream.

Mix the crabmeat with 1 cup of the sauce and 1 cup of the cheese.

Soften the tortillas in a damp towel in the oven, and butter a baking dish. Place one of the tortillas in the dish, put a couple of tablespoons of the crab mixture on the tortilla, and roll it up, making sure that the open end of the tortilla is on the bottom of the casserole (so the enchilada will stay together). Continue the process for each of the tortillas until the dish is filled.

Pour the remaining sauce over the tortillas and top with more grated cheese. Heat in a 350° F oven just long enough to heat through, about 15 minutes.

Garnish with the cilantro before serving.

Grilled Marinated Chicken Breast with Fruit Salsa

Heat Scale: 4
Serves: 4

Note: This recipe requires advance preparation.

The Marinade:

5 Serrano chiles, stems and
  seeds removed, finely
  chopped
1/2 cup orange segments
3 tablespoons lime juice
4 tablespoons vegetable oil
2 tablespoons tequila

The Salsa:

4 Serrano chiles, stems and
  seeds removed, finely
  chopped
1 cup chopped fresh
  pineapple
1/2 cup chopped fresh
  orange segments
1/2 cup diced cantaloupe or
  honeydew melon
2 tablespoons lime juice
2 tablespoons chopped fresh
  cilantro
1 tablespoon vegetable oil
2 teaspoons finely chopped
  fresh ginger
1 teaspoon sugar
4 boneless chicken breasts,
  skin removed

Fruit and chiles combine to add an exotic flavor to otherwise bland chicken breasts.

Combine all the ingredients for the marinade in a blender and puree until smooth.

Make 1/4-inch deep crosshatch gashes in the chicken. Rub in the marinade and marinate overnight in the refrigerator.

Combine all the ingredients for the salsa and allow to sit at room temperature for a couple of hours to blend the flavors.

Grill or broil the chicken breasts, basting frequently with the marinade.

To Serve: Place the chicken on a plate and garnish with the salsa.

Smoked Turkey with Orange Cascabel Chile Oil

Heat Scale: 3
Serves: 4 to 6

6 dried Cascabel chiles,
   stems and seeds removed,
   crushed
2 dried red New Mexican
   chiles, stems and seeds
   removed, crushed
1/2 cup oil, peanut preferred
4 cloves garlic, minced
2 tablespoons finely
   chopped onion
2 tablespoons orange zest
2 teaspoon finely chopped
   fresh ginger
coarsely ground black
   pepper
1 10-pound turkey

This recipe has an Oriental taste due to the addition of fresh ginger. It is simple to prepare and great for an outdoor summer barbecue. The smoker used is a barbecue smoker, that is, one with a removable top.

Heat the oil to 325° F and sauté the chiles, garlic, onion, orange zest, and ginger for 2 minutes. Remove from the heat, place in a blender, and puree to a sauce. Stir in the black pepper.

Split the turkey in half by cutting through the breast and backbone. Brush the chile oil mixture over the turkey and marinate for a couple of hours in the refrigerator.

Place the turkey, breast-side up, on a grill in a smoker and smoke over charcoal with mesquite chips. Baste the turkey with the oil every half hour until the turkey is done, approximately 4 hours.

Serve the turkey with the chile sauce on the side.

Serving Suggestions: Serve with warmed flour tortillas, chile Quelites (see recipe Chapter 5), grilled onions, and a salsa.

Cream of Jalapeño Soup with Roasted Pepper Sauce

Heat Scale: 5
Serves: 6 to 8

The Soup:

4 Jalapeño chiles, stems and
   seeds removed, finely
   chopped
6 tablespoons butter or
   margarine
1 large onion, chopped fine
2 large carrots, peeled and
   diced
3 cups chicken stock
3 tablespoons flour
1 cup light cream
1 cup grated Monterey Jack
   cheese

The Sauce:

6 Serrano chiles, which have
   been roasted, stems
   removed
4 tablespoons olive oil
3 tablespoons Hot Chile
   Vinegar (see recipe Chapter
   2)
3 tablespoons chopped fresh
   cilantro

The heat of this rich and creamy soup makes it a good accompaniment to a basic broiled entrée and simple vegetable or salad. Serve the pepper sauce on the side so that guests may add it to their taste.

To Make the Soup: Melt 3 tablespoons of the butter and sauté the chiles, onion, and carrots for 5 minutes or until the vegetables are softened. Add 1 cup of the stock and simmer until the vegetables are very soft. Puree the vegetables until smooth.

Melt the remaining butter, add the flour and heat for 3 to 4 minutes, being careful not to let the roux brown. Stir in the remaining chicken stock and the cream. Bring to a boil, stirring constantly. Reduce the heat and simmer for 10 minutes until thickened.

Stir in the cheese and vegetable puree and heat until the cheese melts, stirring constantly.

To Make the Sauce: Place all the ingredients in a blender and puree until smooth. Add more oil if necessary. Simmer the sauce in a pan for 5 minutes to blend the flavors.

Marinated Shrimp and Summer Fruit Salad

Heat Scale: 5
Serves: 4

Note: This recipe requires advance preparation.

The Marinade:

2 tablespoons Habanero Pepper Sauce, either commercial or homemade (see recipe Chapter 2)
1/4 cup peach syrup, from drained peaches
1/4 cup orange juice
1/4 cup peanut oil
1/4 teaspoon ground cumin

The Salad:

1 pound shrimp, shelled and deveined
1 cup sliced peaches, drained
1 cup orange segments
1 cup melon cubes
mixed salad greens — butter, romaine, leaf
lime juice
vegetable oil
chopped pistachios for garnish

This is an excellent dish for a summer barbecue. Marinate the shrimp the day before. Eat this dish while the shrimp are still warm.

Combine the Habanero Pepper Sauce, peach syrup, orange juice, oil, and cumin. Marinate the shrimp in the mixture overnight in the refrigerator. Grill or sauté the shrimp, basting frequently with the marinade.

Toss the greens with a little lime juice and oil and place on separate plates. Arrange the fruits on the lettuce beds and top with the shrimp, garnish with the nuts, and serve.

Roulade of Pork with Green Chile and Cilantro

Heat Scale: 3
Serves: 6

3 cups chopped green New Mexican chile, roasted, peeled, stems removed
1 medium onion, chopped
6 cloves garlic, chopped
1 small Granny Smith apple, cored and chopped
1/2 cup chopped fresh cilantro
3 tablespoons butter or margarine
3 pound pork roast, boned
flour for dredging
2 cups white wine
2 tablespoons flour mixed with 1/4 cup water

This simple-to-prepare pork roast makes a dramatic presentation when it is carved at the table. Serve it with applesauce, sour cream–whipped potatoes, and a vegetable of your choice.

Preheat the oven to 450° F.

Sauté the onions, garlic, and apple in the butter until soft. Add the chile and cilantro. Spread the mixture on the pork, roll it up, and tie the roast in 4 to 6 places to hold it together. Lightly dust the pork with flour.

Place the pork on a rack in a roasting pan, reduce the heat to 350° F and roast, uncovered, until done, usually 35 minutes per pound. The internal temperature should be 185° F.

Remove the pork and keep warm. Deglaze the pan with wine and strain the drippings. Place the strained wine in a saucepan, bring to a boil, and slowly pour the flour mixture into the drippings to thicken and form a glaze. Add more wine to thin, if necessary.

To Serve: Carve the pork and serve with the wine sauce on the side.

Citrus Pepper Sorbet

Heat Scale: 2
Serves: 6 to 8

3 Yellow Wax Hot peppers, stems and seeds removed, chopped
1 3/4 cups water
1 1/4 cups sugar
3 large oranges, peeled and chopped
2 tablespoons dark rum
4 tablespoons fresh lemon or lime juice
3 tablespoons light corn syrup

Sorbets can be served either as a dessert or as a refresher between courses. The addition of peppers to the recipe adds just a little heat to the frozen fruit juices.

Combine 1 1/4 cups of water with the sugar and heat until the sugar dissolves. Bring to a boil, remove from the heat, and cool to room temperature. Cool in the refrigerator for 2 hours.

Puree the remaining ingredients with 1/2 cup water and refrigerate for 2 hours.

Stir the sugar mixture into the fruit. Pour the mixture into an ice-cream maker and follow the directions for making ice cream.

APPENDIX 1
SEED SOURCES

AS we discussed in Chapter 2, chile peppers are notorious cross-pollinators, so seed producers must grow their chile plants in isolation for the seeds to be "true." Unfortunately, some seed companies do not take enough care to prevent cross-pollination and as a result their seeds produce many hybrids.

The companies on the following list have supplied reliable chile seeds. We know this is true because we have either used the seeds or heard reports about them from other gardeners. However, since chiles hybridize so easily, there is no guarantee that a new variety will not crop up every once in a while, despite the best of care.

Alfrey Seeds, P.O. Box 415, Knoxville, TN 37901
    Varieties include Poblano, and the following Ornamentals: Peter Pepper, Purple Pepper, Rat Turd, Squash, Black Plum, Kisser.
Horticultural Enterprises, P.O. Box 810082, Dallas, TX 73581
    More than thirty varieties, including Poblano, Pasilla, Jalapeño, Banana, Cayenne, Serrano, Big Jim.
Native Seeds/SEARCH, 2509 North Campbell Avenue #325, Tucson, AZ 87545
    Varieties include Chiltepin, de Arbol, Coban, Mirasol.
Plants of the Southwest, 1812 Second Street, Santa Fe, NM 87501

Varieties include Poblano, Big Jim, Cayenne, Chimayo, Habanero, Mirasol, Sandia, Serrano.

Porter and Son, Seedsmen, 1510 East Washington Street, Stephenville, TX 76401

Varieties include Jalapeño, Cherry, Peperoncini, Tabasco, Habaneros, and several Ornamentals.

Tomato Growers Supply Company, P.O. Box 2237, Fort Myers, FL 33902

Varieties include Hungarian Wax, Cayenne, Mexi-Bell, Serrano, TAM Jalapeño.

Note: In addition to the above companies, all of the major seed companies such as Burpee, Gurney, Park, and Stokes carry seeds for at least a couple of varieties and can be trusted to provide reliable seed.

APPENDIX 2
MAIL-ORDER CHILE
SOURCES

THE following mail-order companies have been in business for years and are dependable suppliers.

Old Southwest Trading Company, P.O. Box 7545, Albuquerque, NM 87195
  Products include dried exotic and New Mexican chiles, fresh green New Mexican chiles during the season, Southwestern ingredients and spices.
Casados Farms, P.O. Box 1269, San Juan Pueblo, NM 87566
  Products include New Mexican chiles, Southwestern ingredients.
Green Chili Fix Company, P.O. Box 5463, Santa Fe, NM 87502
  Products include green chile powder, dried green chile, and green chile mixes.
Pecos Valley Spice Company, 500 East Seventy-seventh Street, Suite 2324, New York, NY 10162
  Products include chiles, chili fixings, salsas, Southwestern ingredients.
Santa Cruz Chili and Spice Company, P.O. Box 177, Tumacacori, AZ 65640
  Products include chiles, chile products, and salsas.
Pendery's, 304 East Belknap Street, Fort Worth, TX 76102
  Products include herbs, spices, chiles, and chile powders.

BIBLIOGRAPHY

Part 1: General History

This section includes nomenclature, anecdotes, legend and lore, sociological and social aspects, and fiestas and other celebrations.

Acosta, José D.
    1979. *The Natural and Moral History of the Indies.* Ed. C. R. Markham. New York: Lenox Hill Publishing Company. Reprint of 1880 edition of Acosta's 1590 work.
Andrews, Jean
    1984. *Peppers: The Domesticated Capsicums.* Austin: University of Texas Press.
    1988. "Around the World with the Chili Pepper: Post-Columbian Distribution of Domesticated Capsicums." *Journal of Gastronomy* 4 (Autumn): 21.
Anon.
    1956. "Some Like Them Hot (Hot Pepper–Eating Contest)." *Newsweek,* 48 (Oct. 22): 41.
    1982. "Hot Topic for a NM Film." *Santa Fe New Mexican,* Oct. 6.
    1984. "Here and There: The Grandaddy Chili Fest (Terlingua, TX)." *Travel-Holiday* 162 (Oct.): 102.
    1984. "Chile Pepper Becoming Food Dye Replacement." *Santa Fe New Mexican,* Nov. 27.
    1985. "Chiles, the Top 7." *Health* 17 (Feb.): 42.
    1985. "Chile or Chili?" *Albuquerque Tribune,* June 14.
    1985. "A Family Heritage (McIlhenny's Tabasco)." *Chili* (Oct.): 28.

1986. "Record Ristra." *Albuquerque Journal,* Oct. 9.

1987. "Burning Peppers Send Shoppers to Hospital." *Albuquerque Journal,* Mar. 18.

1987. "Killing of Chile-Eating Deer OK'd." *Albuquerque Journal,* Sept. 2.

1987. "Pepper-Eating Champ Downs 27." *Albuquerque Tribune,* Sept. 28.

1987. "Mayor Ticked at Tucson Chile Challenge." *Albuquerque Tribune,* Oct. 29, A3.

1987. "Tabasco Sauce Factory Can Be One Hot Tour." *Albuquerque Tribune,* Nov. 6.

1987. "Santa Fe Food Quiets Tucson." *Albuquerque Tribune,* Dec. 7, A2.

1988. "Terrific Tabasco." *NASFT Showcase Magazine,* (July–Aug.).

1989. "Salt and Pepper Flavor This Island." *Southern Living* 24 (Mar.): 34.

Baker, Kathryn
1985. "Chili or Chile? Texas vs. NM in Hot Issue." *Santa Fe New Mexican,* June 14, A1.

Benner, Susan
1987. "Chiles: Pungent, Sweet and Rich." *New York Times,* Sept. 27.

Benson, Elizabeth P.
1967. *The Maya World.* New York: Thomas Y. Crowell Co.

Bird, J.
1948. "America's Oldest Farmers." *Natural History* 57:296.

Blooston, George
1988. "The Heat Parade." *Savvy* 9 (Sept.): 98.

Bork, Robert H.
1985. "Give Me a Bowl of Texas Chili." *Forbes* 136 (Sept.): 184.

Brothwell, Don and Patricia
1969. *Food in Antiquity.* London: Thames & Hudson.

Cobo, Father Bernabe
1979. *History of the Inca Empire.* Trans. Roland Hamilton from the 1653 work. Austin: University of Texas Press.

Conoway, James
1984. "On Avery Island, Tabasco Sauce Is the Spice of Life." *Smithsonian* 15 (May): 72.

Crea, Joe
1989. "Taste Sensations: Lively Flavors Have Captured U.S. Taste Buds." *Kansas City Star,* Aug. 30, D1.

Crenshaw, John
1976. "New Mexico's Fiery Soul." *New Mexico Magazine* (May): 33.

1984. "A Few Hot Facts." *New Mexico Magazine* (Mar.): 42.

Croft, Jeanne

    1981. "Chile Cookoff — Adoration of a Fiery God." *New Mexico Magazine* (Oct.): 67.

    1984. "Chile!" *New Mexico Magazine* (Mar.): 38.

Crosby, Alfred W., Jr.

    1972. *The Columbian Exchange: Biological and Cultural Consequences of 1492.* Westport, CT: Greenwood Press.

de la Vega, Garcilaso (El Inca)

    1966. *Royal Commentaries of the Incas.* Trans. Harold V. Livermore from the 1609 work. Austin: University of Texas Press.

DeWitt, Dave

    1980. "New Mexico Chiles." *Viva New Mexico Magazine* (March–April): 83.

    1986. "Let's Burn a Hole in Those Laughable Chile Myths." *Albuquerque Tribune,* June 5, B1.

    1988. "Confessions of a Chile Addict." (Pseud., "Stu Burns") *The Whole Chile Pepper* 2 (Summer): 26.

DeWitt, Dave, ed.

    1987. *The Whole Chile Pepper.* Albuqerque: Out West Publishing.

DeWitt, Dave, and Nancy Gerlach

    1985. "Even in Earliest Roots, Chile Peppers a Hot Item." *Albuquerque Tribune,* Sept. 19, B1.

    1985. "Indians Get Credit for Spreading Chile Farming." *Albuquerque Tribune,* Sept. 26, B1.

    1985. "Chile Blazed World-Wide Path." *Albuquerque Tribune,* Oct. 3, B1.

    1985. "Red and Green: Chile Dominates New Mexico Holiday Color Scheme." *Albuquerque Journal,* Dec. 12, B1.

    1986. "Chilies: The Good, the Bad, and the Spicy." *San Diego Tribune,* Jan. 22, Food-1.

    1987. *The Whole Chile Pepper Catalog.* Albuquerque: Out West Publishing.

    1987. "Chile Quiz." *Albuquerque Living* (Nov.): 13.

Diven, Bill

    1988. "Chile Pioneer Roy Nakayama Dies." *Albuquerque Journal,* July 13, D1.

Domenici, Peter

    1983. "The Correct Way to Spell Chile." *Congressional Record* 129 (Nov. 3).

Everett, Thomas H.

    1981. "Capsicum." In *New York Times Illustrated Encyclopedia of Horticulture,* 609. New York: Garland Publishing.

Flores, Camille

    1988. "It's Hot, Hot, Hot: Chile Time in Hatch." *New Mexico Magazine* (Sept.): 36.

Forsythe, Michael

    1987. "Some Like It Hot (Louisiana Hot Sauce)." *New Orleans Magazine* 21 (July): 72.

Fuchs, Leonhard

    1542. *De Historia Stirpium Commentarii Insignes.* Basel.

Githens, Thomas S., and Carroll E. Wood, Jr.

    1943. *The Food Resources of Africa.* Philadelphia: University of Pennsylvania Press.

Halasz, Zoltan

    1963. *Hungarian Paprika Through the Ages.* Budapest: Corvina Press.

Heiser, Charles B.

    1951. "Some Like It Hot." *Natural History* 61 (Sept.): 307.

Helms, Mary W.

    1976. *Ancient Panama.* Austin: University of Texas Press.

Heyerdahl, Thor

    1964. "Plant Evidence for Contacts with America Before Columbus." *Antiquity* 38:120.

Hirth, Kenneth G.

    1984. *Trade and Exchange in Early Mesoamerica.* Albuquerque: University of New Mexico Press.

Holbrook, Carey

    1938. "A Bowl of Red . . ." *New Mexico Magazine* (Nov.): 17.

Holmes, Sue Major

    1987. " 'Mr. Chile' Peppers Market with Improved Plants." *Albuquerque Journal,* Mar. 22, C3.

Horton, Jo Ann

    1989. "The Chili Appreciation Society, International — a History, Sorta." *The Whole Chile Pepper* 3 (Winter): 22.

Irvin, Kelly L.

    1988. "Chili: Some People Say They Just *Have* to Have It." *El Paso Times,* July 27, D1.

Long-Solis, Janet

    1986. *Capsicum y Cultura: La Historia del Chilli.* México, D.F.: Fondo de Cultura Económica.

McDonald, Sue

    1980. "Chili Pepper Study Isn't Just Hot Air." *Cincinnati Enquirer,* Feb. 13.

Meilink-Koelofsz, M. A. P., and V. M. Godinho

    1962. *Asian Trade and European Influence in the Indonesian Archipelago, 1500–1630.* The Hague: Martinus Nijhoff.

Nabhan, Gary

    1978. "Chiltepines!" *El Palacio* (Museum of New Mexico) 84:30–34.

1985. "For the Birds: The Red-Hot Mother of Chiles." In *Gathering the Desert*. Tucson, AZ: University of Arizona Press.

1985. "The Red Hot Mother of Chiles." *Albuquerque Journal Impact*, Nov. 19, 3.

Nabhan, Gary, et al.

1989. "New Crops for Marginal Peoples in Marginal Lands: Wild Chiles as a Case Study." In *Agroecology and Small Farm Development*, ed. Miguel Altieri and Susanna Hecht. Phoenix: CRC Press.

National Research Council

1989. *Lost Crops of the Incas*. Washington, D.C.: National Academy Press.

Neary, John

1977. "The Big Chile." *Horticulture* 55 (Mar.): 69.

Nickell, Judy

1987. "Some Like It Hot." *Albuquerque Tribune*, Aug. 26, B10.

1987. "Hot Fun in the Sun, Or How to Make Chile Ristras." *Albuquerque Tribune*, Oct. 19, B1.

Patiño, V. M.

1964. *Plantas Cultivadas y Animales Domésticos en America Equinoccial*. Tomo II. *Plantas Alimenticias*. Cali, Colombia: Imprenta Departmental.

Pfefferkorn, Ignatz

1794. *Sonora: A Description of the Province*. Trans. Theodore Treutlein. Albuquerque: University of New Mexico Press, 1949.

Price, Jess

1986. "Peppers Take Off." *Southwest Airlines Spirit* (Oct.): 108.

Reid, Dixie

1983. "Mister Chili." *Albuquerque Journal Impact*, Nov. 1, 4.

Ridley, Henry N.

1930. *The Dispersal of Plants Throughout the World*. Ashford (Kent), England: L. Reeve & Co.

Ries, M.

1968. *The Hundred Year History of Tabasco*. Avery Island, LA: McIlhenny Co.

Robbins, Catherine C.

1987. "Hordes of Chili Addicts Stock Up for Long, Cold Winter." *New York Times*, Sept. 27.

Salaz, Fernando

1947. "That Good Chile." *New Mexico Magazine* (Dec.): 21.

Schweid, R.

1980. *Hot Peppers* (Tabasco). Seattle: Madronna Publishing.

Sharpe, Patricia

1987. "The Chilipiquin." *Texas Monthly* 15 (Nov.): 145.

Sherratt, Andrew, ed.
 1980. *The Cambridge Encyclopedia of Archaeology.* New York: Crown.

Sokolov, Raymond
 1974. "Some Like It Hot." *Natural History* 83 (Apr.): 65.
 1985. "Hot Stuff: Why Has It Taken Half a Millennium for Chiles to Take Hold in Anglo-Saxon Cultures?" *Natural History* 94 (Aug.): 74.

Sterba, James P.
 1975. "An Authority on Chilies, from the Innocuous to the Incendiary." *New York Times,* Sept. 14, L46.

Stewart, John
 1935. "Chile for the Nation." *New Mexico Magazine* (May): 26.

Stiger, Susan
 1988. "Share New Mexico's Good Taste (Mail-Order Companies)." *Albuquerque Journal,* Nov. 17, B1.
 1988. "Santa Fe Wins Chile Challenge." *Albuquerque Journal,* Nov. 20, F7.

Stockton, William
 1985. "Hunt for Perfect Mole Leads to Rich Delights." *Albuquerque Tribune,* Dec. 12, B6.

Stoneback, Diane
 1988. "Louisiana's Legendary Tabasco Scavenged from Civil War Ruins." *Albuquerque Journal,* Mar. 3, B3.

Swift, Bob
 1988. "The Heat Is On: Chilies Are Our Latest Food Fad." *Miami Herald,* Dec. 3, B2.

Tannahill, Reay
 1988. *Food in History.* New York: Crown.

Thompson, Mark
 1985. "Avery Island's Spicy Tradition." *Islands* (Nov.–Dec.): 62.

Tolbert, Frank X.
 1962. "That Bowl of Fire Called Chili." *Saturday Evening Post* 235 (Nov. 24): 38.
 1972. *A Bowl of Red.* New York: Doubleday.

Tozer, Eliot
 1988. "Quest for Fire." *National Gardening* (May): 35.

Valcárcel, L. E.
 1925. *Del Ayllu al Imperio.* Lima.

Vietmeyer, Noel
 1989. "Here Comes the Hot Stuff." *International Wildlife* 19 (July–Aug.): 14.

Villalon, Benigno.
 1989. "Chile + Chili + Chilli + Axi = Pepper." *The Whole Chile Pepper* 3 (Spring): 24.

Vogt, Evon Z., ed.

    1969. *Handbook of Middle American Indians.* Vol. 7, *Ethnology.* Austin: University of Texas Press.

von Humboldt, Friedrich Alexander

    1814. *Political Essay on the Kingdom of New Spain, Vol. 1.* Trans. J. Black. London: Longman, Murat, Rees, Orms, and Brown.

Ward, Ed

    1980. "Chile Peppers: Some Like It Hot." *High Times* (May): 63.

    1981. "Some Like Them Hot." *Reader's Digest* 118 (Feb.): 135.

Wear, Ben

    1988. "Restaurants Confirm Heat Wave — Chile's Sting Blamed on Year's Heavy Rains." *Albuquerque Journal*, Oct. 14, A1.

Weatherford, Jack

    1988. *Indian Givers: How the Indians of the Americas Transformed the World.* New York: Crown.

West, Jim

    1989. "The International Chili Society." *The Whole Chile Pepper* 3 (Winter): 25.

Part Two: From Plant to Product

This section includes chile pepper anatomy, taxonomy, physiology, chemistry, ecology, geography, genetics, cytology, ethnobotany, home and commercial cultivation, food science, and product marketing.

Abid, M. Sami Khan

    1979. "Marketing of Chillies." In *Marketing Infra-Structure, Margins and Seasonal Price Variation of Selected Agricultural Commodities in Sind Province of Pakistan. Final Report: Vegetables.* Tando Jam, Pakistan: Sind Agricultural University.

Anon.

    1940. "Domestic Paprika: Raising Peppers." *Business Week*, Dec. 7, 48.

    1963. "Chile, One of New Mexico's Agricultural Specialty Products." *New Mexico Agricultural Extension Service News* 43 (Summer).

    1968. "Capsaicin Content of *Capsicum* Fruits at Different Stages of Maturity." *Lloydia* 31 (Sept.): 272.

    1976. *Growing Peppers in California.* University of California Agricultural Leaflet 2676.

    1978. "Peppers." *Consumer Guide* 222 (Spring): 120.

    1978. "How to Dry Your Hot Peppers." *Flower and Garden* 22 (Aug.): 28.

1979. "Tips on Choosing Peppers." *Southern Living* 14 (Apr.): 196.

1981. "Green Peppers." *Horticulture* 59 (Apr.): 22.

1981. "Reflected Light for Better Peppers." *Organic Gardening* 28 (Aug.): 62.

1981. "White Mulch Yields More Peppers." *Organic Gardening* 28 (Aug.): 63.

1982. "Direct-Sowing of Tomatoes and Peppers." *Organic Gardening* 29 (Jan.): 73.

1982. "New Mild Chile Gets Warm Welcome." *Albuquerque Tribune*, Jan. 28, B8.

1983. "Homegrown Hot Sauce." *Organic Gardening* 30 (Mar.): 116.

1983. "A Chile for Every Taste." *Organic Gardening* 30 (Mar.): 64.

1984. "Why Not a Purple Pepper? Or Golden . . . as Well as Green, Red." *Sunset* 173 (Oct.): 106.

1984. "Ornamental Peppers Display Their Colorful Fruit Throughout the Winter." *Sunset* 173 (Dec.): 220.

1985. "How Hot Is That Pepper in the Garden?" *Yankee* 49 (Jan.): 111.

1985. *Hidalgo: A New Multiple Virus Resistant Pungent Serrano Pepper.* College Station, TX: Texas Agricultural Experiment Station Pamphlet L-2171 (Dec.).

1985. "Seed Time for a Hot Pepper Summer." *Sunset* 174 (Mar.): 238.

1985. "New Type of Green Chile is Well-Suited to This Area." *Santa Fe New Mexican*, Sept. 4.

1987. "Chile Production Set Record in '86." *Albuquerque Tribune*, Apr. 8.

1987. "Chile Industry Growth Points to a Hot Crop for New Mexico." *Enchantment* 38 (May): 2.

1988. "Cool Peppers for Higher Yields." *Organic Gardening* 35 (Feb.): 20.

1988. "Chile Production Up 6 Percent, Sets Price Record During '87." *Albuquerque Journal*, Mar. 27.

1988. "Where to Get Seeds of the More Uncommon Chili Peppers." *Sunset* 100 (Mar.): 224.

1988. "Wimpy to Fiery, Is There a Chili Pepper for You?" *Sunset* 100 (Mar.): 120.

1988. "Hot Days Needed to Make Chile Sizzle." *Albuquerque Journal*, Aug. 21, C7.

1989. "N.M. Chile Crop Shows 3 Percent Increase over 1987." *Albuquerque Journal*, Mar. 19, C7.

1989. "What Is 'Hot Pepper Cream' and What Are Its Uses?" *U.S. Pharmacist*, Apr., 28.

1989. "Chile Picker Developed for Special Crop." *Las Cruces* (NM) *Sun-News,* May 28, A7.

Askey, Linda C.

1984. "Fire Up the Season with Red Peppers." *Southern Living* 19 (Dec.): 84.

Associated Press

1987. "Sauce Firm Enters 40th Year with Winning Pace." *Albuquerque Journal,* Feb. 1, C7.

1988. "Canned Product Angers Some Hatch Valley Chile Farmers." *Albuquerque Journal,* Apr. 13, D1.

Bosland, Paul W., and J. Iglesias

1988. *Chile Pepper Breeding Program 1988 Report.* Las Cruces, NM: New Mexico State University.

Bosland, Paul W., et al.

1988. *Capsicum Pepper Varieties and Classification.* Las Cruces, NM: New Mexico State University Cooperative Extension Circular 530.

Bravo, Helia H.

1934. "Estudio Botanico Acerca de las Solanaceas Méxicanas del Genero *Capsicum.*" México, D.F.: *Anales del Instituto de Biologia* 5:303–21.

Caplan, Karen, et al.

1988. "On the Rise (Mexican-Food Marketing)." *Fortune* 118 (Aug.): 220.

Cochran, H. L.

1932. "Factors Affecting Flowering and Fruit Setting in the Pepper." *American Society of Horticultural Science* 33:434.

1935. "Some Factors Which Affect the Germination of Pepper Seeds." *American Society of Horticultural Science* 33:477.

1938. "Flower and Seed Development in Pepper." *American Society of Horticultural Science Proceedings* 77:449.

1940. "Characters for the Classification and Identification of Varieties of *Capsicum.*" *Bulletin of the Torrey Botanical Club* 67–8:710.

Corchado, Alfredo

1989. "Food Industry's War of the Salsas Is Getting Fierce." *Wall Street Journal,* Apr. 11, B1.

Cotter, D. J.

1980. *A Review of Studies on Chile.* New Mexico Agricultural Experiment Station Bulletin 673, April.

D'Arcy, W. G. and W. H. Eshbaugh

1973. "The Name for the Common Bird Pepper." *Phytologia* 25:350.

1974. "New World Peppers (*Capsicum,* Solanaceae) North of Colombia: A Resume." *Baileya* 19:93.

Davenport, W. A.

    1970. "A Progress Report on the Domestication of *Capsicum*." *Proceedings of the Association of American Geographers* 2:46.

Deb, D. B.

    1979. "The Solanaceae in India." In *The Biology and Taxonomy of the Solanaceae*, ed. J. G. Hawkes, R. N. Lester, and A. D. Skelding, 109–10. New York: Academic Press.

de Schlippe, Pierre

    1956. *Shifting Cultivation in Africa*. London: Routledge & Kegan Paul.

DeWitt, Dave

    1988. "Fiery Foods: Heating Up Profits." *Gourmet Retailer* 9 (Nov.): 10.

    1989. "Fiery Foods: Sales Are Sizzling." *Fancy Food* 6 (Feb.): 35.

DeWitt, Dave, and Jeff Gerlach

    1989. "In Search of the Ultimate Chile Patch." *Albuquerque Journal*, Feb. 8, B1.

    1989. "The Ultimate Chile Patch." *The Whole Chile Pepper* 3 (Spring):14.

Diven, Bill

    1987. "Floods Damage Sizable Chile Chunk." *Albuquerque Journal*, Aug. 30, C7.

    1988. "Chile Farmer Urges State to Establish Commission." *Albuquerque Journal*, June 22.

    1989. "Expert Calls Rise of Chile Virus Mysterious." *Albuquerque Journal*, Feb. 9, C1.

    1989. "Chile Pest Tracked to Winter Hideout." *Albuquerque Journal*, May 21, C1.

    1989. "Stronger Strain of N.M. Chile Can Resist Wilt." *Albuquerque Journal*, Sept. 22, B5.

    1989. " 'Designer Chiles' Update a Classic." *Albuquerque Journal*, Oct. 8, C1.

Eshbaugh, W. Hardy

    1968. "A Nomenclatural Note on the Genus Capsicum." *Taxon* 17:51–2.

    1970. "A Biosystematic and Evolutionary Study of *Capsicum baccatum* (Solanaceae)." *Brittonia* 22:31–43.

    1975. "Genetic and Biochemical Systematic Studies of Chili Peppers." *Bulletin of the Torrey Botanical Club* 102:396–403.

    1978. "The Taxonomy of the Genus *Capsicum* — Solanaceae." *Acta Horticulture* 15:153–66.

    1979. "Biosystematic and Evolutionary Study of *Capsicum pubescens* Complex." *National Geographic Society Research Reports* 1970:143–62.

1980. "The Taxonomy of the Genus *Capsicum* (Solanaceae)." *Phytologia* 47:153.

1980. "Chili Peppers in Bolivia." *Plant Genetics Research Newsletter* 43:17–19.

Eshbaugh, W. Hardy, and P. G. Smith

1983. "The Origin and Evolution of Domesticated *Capsicum* Species." *Journal of Ethnobiology* 3:49–54.

Flores, I.

1966. *Taxonomia y Distribución Geográphica de los Chiles en México.* México, D.F.: Instituto Nacional de Investigaciones Agricolas.

Garcia, Fabian

1908. *Chile Culture.* Las Cruces, NM: College of Agriculture and Mechanics Bulletin 67.

1921. *Improved Variety No. 9 of Native Chile.* Las Cruces, NM: College of Agriculture and Mechanics Bulletin 124.

Greenleaf, W. H.

1975. "The Tabasco Story." *HortScience* 10:98.

Hamel, Ruth, and Tim Schreiner

1988. "Chile Pepper Market." *American Demographics* 10 (Aug.): 54.

Harper, R. E.

1950. "Improved Variety of Chile for New Mexico." *New Mexico Agricultural Experiment Station Bulletin 1041.*

Hawkes, J. G., Lester, R. N., and A. D. Skelding, eds.

1979. *The Biology and Taxonomy of the Solanaceae.* New York: Academic Press.

Hawkins, J. G.

1982. "Capsicums." *American Horticulture* 61 (Feb.):56.

Heiser, Charles B.

1976. "Peppers: *Capsicum* (Solanaceae)." In *Evolution of Crop Plants,* ed. N. W. Simmonds, 265–8. London: Longman.

1987. *The Fascinating World of the Nightshades.* Mineola, NY: Dover Books. Reprint of *Nightshades, the Paradoxical Plants* (1969).

Heiser, Charles B., and Barbara Pickersgill

1969. "Names for the Cultivated Capsicum Species (Solanaceae)." *Taxon* 18:277–83.

1975. "Names for the Bird Peppers (*Capsicum* — Solanaceae)." *Baileya* 19:151–6.

Heiser, Charles B., and P. G. Smith

1948. "Observations on Another Species of Cultivated Pepper, *C. pubescens R. and P.*" *Proceedings of the American Society of Horticultural Science* 52:331–5.

1953. "The Cultivated *Capsicum* Peppers." *Economic Botany* 7:214–27.

1958. "New Species of *Capsicum* from South America." *Brittonia* 10:194–201.

1974. "A Spontaneous Hybrid of *Capsicum annuum* var. *minimum* and *Capsicum frutescens*." *Proceedings of the Indiana Academy of Sciences* 83:397–8.

International Board for Plant Genetic Resources

1983. *Genetic Resources of* Capsicum. Rome: IBPGR Secretariat.

Kaiser, S.

1935. "Factors Governing Shape and Size in *Capsicum* Fruits: A Genetic and Developmental Analysis." *Bulletin of the Torrey Botanical Club* 62:433–54.

Laborde, J. A., and Octavio Pozo Campodonico

1982. *Presente y Pasado del Chile en México*. México, D.F.: Instituto Nacional de Investigaciones Agricolas.

Lantz, E. M.

1943. "Home Dehydration of Chili Peppers." *Journal of Home Economics* 35 (Apr.): 222.

Lego, Mary C.

1984. "HPLC in the Flavor/Spice Trade." *Food Technology* 38 (April): 84.

Matta, F. B., and R. M. Nakayama

1984. " 'Española Improved' Chile Pepper." *HortScience* 19 (June): 454.

McLeod, M. J., et al.

1979. "A Preliminary Biochemical Systematic Study of the Genus *Capsicum* — Solanaceae." In *The Biology and Taxonomy of the Solanaceae*, ed. J. G. Hawkes, R. N. Lester, and A. D. Skelding, 701–13. New York: Academic Press.

1982. "Early Evolution of Chili Peppers." *Economic Botany* 36:361–8.

Meeker, John

1986. "Pickling Peppers: Sweet or Hot?" *Rodale's Organic Gardening* 33 (Sept.): 66.

Morgenthaler, Eric

1975. "Walter McIlhenny Makes Tabasco Sauce in Milieu of Old South." *Wall Street Journal,* Jan. 10.

Nakayama, Roy M., and F. B. Matta

1985. " 'NuMex R Naky' Chile Pepper." *HortScience* 20 (Oct.): 961.

National Pepper Conference

1984. *Newsletter: San Miguel de Allende Conference* (Jan.).

Neary, J.

    1977. "Big Chile (Interview with R. Nakayama)." *Horticulture 55* (Mar.): 68.

Pickersgill, Barbara

    1969. "The Archaeological Record of Chili Peppers (*Capsicum* spp.) and the Sequence of Plant Domestication in Peru." *American Antiquity* 34:54–61.

    1969. "The Domestication of Chili Peppers." In *The Domestication and Exploitation of Plants and Animals*, ed. P. J. Ucko and G. W. Dimbleby, 443. London: Gerald Duckworth.

    1971. "Relationships Between Weedy and Cultivated Forms in Some Species of Chili Peppers (Genus *Capsicum*). *International Journal of the Origin of Evolution* 25:683–91.

    1972. "Cultivated Plants as Evidence for Cultural Contacts." *American Antiquity* 37:97–104.

    1984. "Migration of Chili Peppers, *Capsicum* spp., in the Americas." In *Pre-Columbian Plant Migration*, ed. Doris Stone, 106–22. Cambridge, MA: Peabody Museum of Archaeology and Ethnology, Harvard University.

Pickersgill, Barbara, and A. H. Bunting

    1969. "Cultivated Plants and the Kon Tiki Theory." *Nature* 222:225–7.

Pickersgill, Barbara, et al.

    1979. "Numerical Taxonomic Studies of Variation and Domestication in Some Species of *Capsicum*. In *The Biology and Taxonomy of the Solanaceae*, ed. J. G. Hawkes, R. N. Lester, and A. D. Skelding, 679. New York: Academic Press.

Pinto Cortes, Benito

    1969. "El Cultivo del Chile." Chapingo, Mex.: *Novedades Horticolas* 14:4.

Proulx, E. A.

    1985. "Some Like Them Hot." *Horticulture* 63, (Jan.): 46.

Rupp, Rebecca

    1987. "Peppers." In *Blue Corn and Square Tomatoes*, 33. Pownal, VT: Garden Way.

Sapers, G. M., et al.

    1980. "Factors Affecting the pH of Home-Canned Peppers." *Journal of Food Science* 45 (May–June): 726.

Shannon, Emroy

    1989. *Chile Disease Control*. Las Cruces, NM: New Mexico State University Cooperative Extension Service Guide H-219.

Shinners, L. H.

    1956. "Technical Names for the Cultivated *Capsicum* Peppers." *Baileya* 4:81–3.

Smith, P. G.

 1950. "Inheritance of Brown and Green Mature Fruit Colors in Peppers." *Journal of Heredity* 41:138.

 1951. "Deciduous Ripe Fruit Characters in Peppers." *Journal of the American Society of Horticultural Science* 47:343.

 1966. "Peppers of Peru: A Report to AID." *North Carolina Bulletin 306,* Chapel Hill: University of North Carolina.

Smith, P. G., and C. B. Heiser

 1951. "Taxonomic and Genetic Studies on the Cultivated Peppers *C. annuum* and *C. frutescens.*" *American Journal of Botany* 38:367.

 1957. "Breeding Behavior of Cultivated Peppers." *American Society of Horticultural Science* 70:286.

 1957. "Taxonomy of *Capsicum sinense* Jacq. and the Geographic Distribution of the Cultivated *Capsicum* Species." *Bulletin of the Torrey Botanical Club* 84:413.

 1972. "Cultivated Plants as Evidence for Cultural Contacts." *American Antiquity* 37:97.

Smith, P. G., et al.

 1951. "*Capsicum pendulum* Will'd.: Another Cultivated Pepper from South America." *American Society of Horticultural Science* 57:339.

 1987. "Horticultural Classification of Peppers Grown in the United States." *HortScience* 22 (Feb.): 11.

Spiegel, Robert

 1988. "Spiciest City, State Determined." *Gourmet Retailer* 9 (Nov.): 13.

Stiger, Susan

 1988. "Power to the Pod: Hottest Show on Earth Features Chiles." *Albuquerque Journal,* Sept. 15, B1.

Tanksley, S. D.

 1984. "High Rates of Cross-Pollination in Chile Pepper." *HortScience* 19 (Aug.): 580.

Tozier, Eliot

 1988. "Quest for Fire." *National Gardening* (May): 36.

Trejo-Gonzalez, A., and C. Wild-Altamirano

 1973. "A New Method for the Determination of Capsaicin in *Capsicum* Fruits." *Journal of Food Science* 38 (Feb.): 342.

van Harten, A. M.

 1970. "Melegueta Pepper." *Economic Botany* 24:208.

Villalon, Ben

 1975. "Virus Diseases of Bell Peppers in South Texas." *Plant Disease Report* 59:859–62.

 1981. "Breeding Peppers Resistant to Virus Diseases." *Plant Diseases* 65 (July): 557.

1983. "Tam Mild Jalapeño Pepper." *HortScience* 18 (June): 492–3.

1986. "Tambel-2 Bell Pepper." *HortScience* 21 (Apr.): 328.

1986. " 'Hidalgo' Serrano Pepper." *HortScience* 21 (June): 540.

1986. " 'Tam Mild Chile-2' Pepper." *HortScience* 21 (Dec.): 1468.

Villalon, Ben, et al.

1987. *Development of a Multiple Virus Resistant "Tam Mild Chile-2."* College Station, TX: Texas Agricultural Experiment Station.

Part 3: Nutrition and Medicine

Reputed chile cures, properties of capsaicin, and vitamin and mineral research are included in this section.

Anon.

1956. "Vitamin in Peppers." *Today's Health* 34 (Sept.): 6.

1983. "Hot Peppers and Substance P." *The Lancet*, May 28.

1983. "Some Like It Hot: Peppers May Protect Against Blood Clots." *Prevention* 35 (July): 80.

1983. "Hot Pepper Pain Clue." *Science Digest* 91 (Sept.): 81.

1985. "Pepper Research Heats Up." *Journal of the American Dietetic Association* 85 (July): 798.

1986. "Metabolism and Toxicity of Capsaicin." *Nutrition Reviews* 44 (Jan.): 20.

1986. "Spicy Food Takes Its Toll on the Mouth." *Albuquerque Tribune*, May 8, B4.

1988. "Hot Pepper for Shingles." *Prevention* (Mar.): 10.

1988. "The Hot Side of Chiles." *Science News* 134 (July 16): 41.

1988. "When Hot May Be Carcinogenic." *Science News* 134 (July 16): 41.

Bennett, D. J., and G. W. Kirby

1968. "Constitution and Biosynthesis of Capsaicin." *Journal of the American Chemical Society* 442.

Brody, Jane

1983. "Eating Spicy Food: What Are the Effects?" *New York Times*, Sept. 21, C1.

1983. "Burning Mystery: Are Hot Peppers Good or Bad?" *Albuquerque Tribune*, Oct. 26, D4.

Clark, Joe M.

1941. "Chile for Health." *New Mexico Magazine* (Sept.): 14.

DeBenedette, Valerie

1985. "The Burning Question." *Health* 17 (Dec.): 9.

Diehl, A. K., and R. L. Bauer
  1978. "Jaloproctitis." *New England Journal of Medicine* 229:1137–38.

Duner-Engstron, M., et al.
  1986. "Autonomic Mechanisms Underlying Capsaicin-Induced Oral Sensation and Salivation in Man." *Journal of Physiology* 373 (Apr.): 87.

Franklin, D.
  1984. "Heated Research of Pepper Pain." *Science News* 126 (Sept.): 132.

Fuller, R. W., et al.
  1985. "Bronchoconstrictor Response to Inhaled Capsaicin in Humans." *Journal of Applied Physiology* 58 (Apr.): 1080.

Gergley, Lisa
  1988. "Vegetable Superstars." *Health* 20 (Sept.): 58.

Graham, David Y., et al.
  1988. "Spicy Food and the Stomach: Evaluation by Videoendoscopy." *Journal of the American Medical Association* 260 (Dec. 16): 3473.

Harris, T. George
  1987. "The Healthy News About Hot Peppers." *American Health* (Jan.–Feb.).

Haxton, H. A.
  1948. "Gustatory Sweating." *Brain* 71:16–25.

Hoskins, Mercedes
  1976. "Sodium, Potassium, and Caloric Composition of Green Chile Peppers: Dietetic Considerations." Las Cruces, NM: New Mexico State University Agricultural Experiment Station.

Huffman, V. L., et al.
  1982. "Volatile Components and Pungency in Fresh and Processed Jalapeño Peppers." *Journal of Food Science* 43:1809.

Kawada, T., et al.
  1986. "Effects of Capsaicin on Lipid Metabolism in Rats Fed a High Fat Diet." *Journal of Nutrition* 116 (July): 1272.

Lang, Les
  1987. "Hot Pepper Pickle (Cancer Link)." *Health* 19 (Sept.): 15.

Lantz, E. M.
  1945. "Some Factors Affecting the Ascorbic Acid Content of Chile (*Capsicum annuum*)." *New Mexico Agricultural Experiment Station Bulletin 324.*
  1946. "Effects of Canning and Drying on the Carotene and Ascorbic Acid Content of Chiles." *New Mexico Agricultural Experiment Station Bulletin 327.*

Law, M. W.
  1983. "High-Pressure Liquid Chromatographic Determination of

Capsaicin in Oleoresin and Personal Protection Aerosols." *Journal of the Association of Official Analytical Chemists* 66 (Sept.).

Lee, T. S.

1954. "Physiological Gustatory Sweating in a Warm Climate." *Journal of Physiology* 124:528–42.

Lunberg, Jan M., and Alois Saria

1983. "Capsaicin-Induced Desensitization of Airway Mucosa to Cigarette Smoke, Mechanical and Chemical Irritants." *Nature* 302:291.

Masada, Y., et al.

1971. "Analysis of the Pungent Principles of *Capsicum annuum* by Combined Gas Chromatography-Mass Spectrometry." *Journal of Food Science* 36 (Sept.): 858.

McClure, S. A.

1982. "Parallel Usage of Medicinal Plants by Africans and Their Caribbean Descendants." *Economic Botany* 36:291–301.

Montez, Abel

1986. "Chili Burn Treatments Sought by Researcher." *New Mexico Daily Lobo*, University of New Mexico, Mar. 13, 6.

Moskow, Shirley

1987. *Hunan Hand and Other Ailments*. Boston: Little, Brown.

Naj, Amal K.

1986. "Hot Topic: Chiles Cause Pleasant Pain, Even Mild Euphoria." *Wall Street Journal*, Nov. 25, 1.

Nelson, E. K.

1919. "The Constitution of Capsaicin, the Pungent Principle of *Capsicum*, II." *Journal of the American Chemical Society* 41:1115.

1920. "The Constitution of Capsaicin, the Pungent Principle of *Capsicum*, III." *Journal of the American Chemical Society* 42: 597–9.

Orellana, Sandra L.

1987. *Indian Medicine in Highland Guatemala*. Albuquerque, NM: University of New Mexico Press.

Page, Jake

1987. "Taste Bud Burnout." *Hippocrates* (May–June): 16.

Parachini, Allan

1988. "Spicy Foods No Sweat for the Stomach." *Los Angeles Times* (Orange County Edition), Dec. 20, V1.

Pauling, Linus

1977. "Albert Szent-Gyorgyi and Vitamin C." In *Search and Discover: A Tribute to Albert Szent-Gyorgyi*, ed. B. Karminer, 43–53. New York: Academic Press.

Perry, Charles

1988. "Hot News About Eating Chile Peppers." *Los Angeles Times Calendar*, July 3, 89.

Rabinovitz, Jonathan
   1989. "Doctors Research a Hot Idea." *Gilroy (CA) Dispatch*, July 12, A1.
   1989. "Those Hot Peppers That Make You Cough May Be Good for You." *Modesto (CA) Bee*, Aug. 3.
Reddy, B., and G. Sarojini
   1987. "Chemical and Nutritional Evaluation of Chili (*Capsicum annuum*) Seed Oil." *Journal of the American Chemists' Society* 64 (Oct.): 1419.
Robotham, H.
   1985. "Capsaicin Effects on Muscularis Mucosa of Opossum Esophagus: Substance P Release from Afferent Nerves?" *American Journal of Physiology* 248 (June): 655–62.
Rozin, Paul, and P. Schiller
   1980. "The Nature and Aquisition of a Preference for Chile Peppers by Humans." *Motivation and Emotion* 4:77–101.
Rozin, Paul, et al.
   1982. "Some Like It Hot: A Temporal Analysis of Hedonic Responses to Chili Pepper." *Appetite* 3 (March): 13.
Sanchez-Palomera, E.
   1951. "The Action of Spices on the Acid Gastric Secretion, on the Appetite, and on the Caloric Intake." *Gastroenterology* 18:254–68.
Sanna, Lou, and Robert Swientek
   1984. "HPLC Quantifies Heat Levels in Chili Pepper Products." *Food Processing* (Oct.).
Shertel, E. R., et al.
   1986. "Rapid Shallow Breathing Evoked by Capsaicin from Isolated Pulmonary Circulation." *Journal of Applied Physiology* 61 (Sept.): 1237.
Stasch, A. R., and M. M. Johnson
   1970. "Antioxidant Properties of Chile Pepper." *Journal of the American Dietetic Association* 56 (May): 409.
Stevenel, L.
   1956. "Red Pepper, A Too Much Forgotten Therapeutic Agent Against Anorexia, Liver Congestion, and Vascular Troubles." *Bull. Soc. Path. Exot.* 49:841–43.
Szent-Gyorgyi, A.
   1939. *On Oxidation, Fermentation, Vitamins, Health, and Disease.* Baltimore: Vanderbilt University.
   1978. "How New Understandings About the Biological Function of Ascorbic Acid May Profoundly Affect Our Lives." *Executive Health* 14.
Tominack, R. L., and D. A. Spyker
   1987. "Capsicum and Capsaicin — A Review: Case Report on the

Use of Hot Peppers in Child Abuse." *Journal of Toxicology and Clinical Toxicology* 25:591.

Viehoever, A. and Cohen, I.
  1938. "Mechanism of Action of Aphrodisiac and Other Irritant Drugs." *American Journal of Pharmacology* 110:226–49.

Viranuvatti, V., et al.
  1972. "Effects of *Capsicum* Solution on Human Gastric Mucosa as Observed Gastroscopically." *American Journal of Gastroenterology* 58:225–32.

Visudhiphan, S., et al.
  1982. "The Relationship Between High Fibrinolytic Activity and Daily Capsicum Ingestion in Thais." *American Journal of Clinical Nutrition* 35:1452–8.

Von Blaricom, L. O., and J. A. Martin
  1947. "Permanent Standards for Chemical Tests for Pungency in Peppers." *Journal of the American Society of Horticultural Science* 50:297.

Weil, Andrew
  1980. "Eating Chilies." In *The Marriage of the Sun and the Moon.* Boston: Houghton Mifflin Co.

White, B. H., and V. R. Goddard
  1948. "Green Chili Peppers as a Source of Ascorbic Acid in the Mexican Diet." *Journal of the American Dietetic Association* 24:666–9.

Woodbury, James E.
  1980. "Determination of Capsicum Pungency by High-Pressure Liquid Chromatography and Spectrofluorometric Detection." *Journal of the Association of Official Analytical Chemists* 63:556.

Part 4: Culinary Arts

International chile pepper cuisines, cooking, recipes, and decoration are included in this section.

Aaron, Jan, and Georgine Salom
  1982. *The Art of Mexican Cooking.* New York: New American Library.

Anderson, E. N.
  1988. *The Food of China.* New Haven: Yale University Press.

Andresen, Katy
  1985. "Hot Stuff: Fajitas Are All the Rage Even on the Poshest Menus." *Albuquerque Tribune,* May 30, B2.

Anon.

   1916. "New Mexico Chile and How to Prepare It." In *New Mexico Cookery*. State Land Office.

   1956. "Green Chili Peppers for Your Freezer." *Sunset* 117 (Aug.): 131.

   1973. "Your Own Red Chile Sauce from Your Own Dried Red Chiles." *Sunset* 151 (Oct.): 160.

   1974. "Tex-Mex Means Good and Spicy." *Southern Living* 19 (Feb.): 178.

   1977. "Devil's Food." *Esquire* 87 (Feb.): 72.

   1977. "Chiles Mild to Wild." *Sunset* 159 (Sept.): 82.

   1983. "Tex-Mex: A Series on Regional Cooking." *Life* 6 (Mar.): 52.

   1983. "Handling Hot Peppers." *Cuisine* 12 (Sept.): 62.

   1983. "Ole! (Hot Pepper Arranging)." *Flower and Garden* 27 (Sept.): 22.

   1984. "Thai Cooks Heat Up Things with Curry Paste." *Sunset* 173 (Dec.): 232.

   1987. "News of the Big Chile." *Cook's* (Sept.): 12.

   1989. "African Specialties." *Prepared Foods* (June): 75.

Bloom, Leslie

   1988. "Adding Fuel to the Taste for Fiery Foods." *New York Times* Sept. 21, C1.

Brennan, Georgeanne, and Charlotte Glenn

   1988. *Peppers Hot and Chile*. Reading, MA: Aris Books.

Brennan, Jennifer

   1986. "Tantalizing Thai Curries." *Food and Wine* (May): 77.

Bridges, Bill

   1981. *The Great American Chili Book*. New York: Rawson, Wade.

Brissenden, Rosemary

   1970. *South East Asian Food*. Middlesex, England: Penguin.

   1982. *Asia's Undiscovered Cuisine: Recipes from Thailand, Indonesia, and Malaysia*. New York: Pantheon.

Brown, Bob, et al.

   1971. *South American Cookbook*. New York: Dover.

Brown, Dale

   1968. *American Cooking*. New York: Time-Life Books.

Brown, Ellen

   1987. *Southwest Tastes: From the PBS Television Series "Great Chefs of the West."* Tucson: HP Books.

Butel, Jane

   1980. *Chili Madness*. New York: Workman.

   1980. *Jane Butel's Tex-Mex Cookbook*. New York: Harmony.

   1985. "The Big Chili Controversy." *Woman's Day*, Feb. 5, 104.

   1985. "Southwest Christmas." *Cook's* (Nov.): 52.

1987. *Hotter Than Hell.* Tucson: HP Books.

1987. *Fiesta!* New York: Harper & Row.

1988. "Traditional Christmas Eve Supper, New Mexico Style." *The Whole Chile Pepper* 2 (Fall): 10.

Cadwallader, Sharon

1987. *Savoring Mexico.* San Francisco: Chronicle Books.

Cameron, Sheila

1978. *The Best from New Mexico Kitchens.* Santa Fe: New Mexico Magazine.

1983. *More of the Best from New Mexico Kitchens.* Santa Fe: New Mexico Magazine.

Carter, Sylvia

1984. "American Cooks Are Hot on Chile." *Albuquerque Journal,* Oct. 18, B1.

1985. "How Does Your Pepper Measure Up?" *Newsday,* Jan. 30.

Chang, Ginger

1987. "The Szechwan Difference." *Bon Appetit* (Mar.): 80.

Childress, M. and C.

1978. *Adventures in Mexican Cookery.* San Francisco: Ortho Books.

Claiborne, Craig, and Pierre Franey

1984. "Peppers in Every Pot." *New York Times Magazine,* Sept. 23, 61.

Cockburn, Alexander

1986. "Fire and Rice: Cajun Cooking and the Hot Spice of History." *House and Garden* 158 (Aug.): 42.

Condon, Richard and Wendy

1988. *Ole Mole!* Dallas: Taylor Publishing.

Connors, Jill

1984. "Fired Up by Chili." *Americana* 12 (July–Aug.): 12.

Cranwell, John Phillips

1975. *The Hellfire Cookbook.* New York: Quadrangle.

Davidson, Alan

1982. "The Traditions of Laos." *Cuisine* (May): 43.

de Benitez, Ana M.

1974. *Pre-Hispanic Cookbook (Cocina Prehispanica).* Mexico, D.F.: Ediciones Euroamericanas Klaus Thiele.

De Groot, Roy Andries

1983. "What Wine With Spicy Food?" *Food and Wine* (June): 49.

Dent, Huntley

1985. *The Feast of Santa Fe.* New York: Simon & Schuster.

DeWitt, Dave

1989. "Chili Chic: Slimming with Sizzle." *St. Louis Post-Dispatch,* Mar. 6 , FN1.

1989. "Firewater." *The Whole Chile Pepper* 3 (Fall): 38.

DeWitt, Dave and Nancy Gerlach

    1984. *The Fiery Cuisines*. New York: St. Martin's Press.

    1984. *Fiery Cuisines: A Hot and Spicy Food Lover's Cookbook*. Chicago: Contemporary Books.

    1985. *Fiery Cuisines*. London: Macdonald and Co.

    1986. *Fiery Appetizers*. New York: St. Martin's Press.

    1987. *The Whole Chile Pepper Catalog*. Albuquerque: Out West Publishing.

    1988. "How the World Cooks Spicy Seafood." *The Whole Chile Pepper* 2 (Spring–Summer): 33.

    1988. "The Whole Chile Pepper Diet." *The Whole Chile Pepper* 2 (Spring–Summer): 15.

    1988. "Asia Heats Up." *The Whole Chile Pepper* 2 (Summer): 15.

    1988. "Ole to Mole and Posole." *The Whole Chile Pepper* 2 (Fall): 15.

    1989. "The Evolution of Chile Con Carne." *The Whole Chile Pepper* 3 (Winter): 14.

    1989. "Expedition to Belize." *The Whole Chile Pepper* 3 (Summer): 38.

Dille, Carolyn, and Susan Belsinger

    1984. "Chili Peppers." *Gourmet* 44 (June): 48.

    1985. *New Southwest Cooking*. New York: Macmillan.

Duncan, Geraldine

    1985. *Some Like It Hotter*. San Francisco: 101 Productions.

Eckhardt, Linda West

    1981. *The Only Texas Cookbook*. Austin: Texas Monthly Press.

Ferguson, Erna

    1965. *Mexican Cookbook*. New York: Doubleday.

Ferretti, Fred

    1986. "The Nonya Kitchen of Singapore." *Gourmet* 46 (Sept.): 50.

Fischer, A.

    1978. *A Chili Lover's Cookbook*. Phoenix: Golden West Publishers.

Freiman, Jane

    1984. "Fueling the Fire." *Cuisine* 13 (July): 38.

Gader, June

    1982. "A Taste of Thailand." *Bon Appetit* (Oct.): 79.

Gerlach, Nancy

    1988. "Fiery Fare." *The Whole Chile Pepper* 2 (Summer): 33.

    1988. "Fiery Fare: Spicy Soups." *The Whole Chile Pepper* 2 (Fall): 29.

    1989. "Powerful Pastas." *The Whole Chile Pepper* 3 (Winter): 35.

    1989. "Too Many Peppers." *The Whole Chile Pepper* 3 (Spring): 26.

    1989. "Spicy Salads." *The Whole Chile Pepper* 3 (Spring): 35.

    1989. "Sizzling Sandwiches." *The Whole Chile Pepper* 3 (Summer): 22.

1989. "Blistering Appetizers." *The Whole Chile Pepper* 3 (Fall): 15.

1989. "Red and Green for the Holidays: A Seasonal Buffet." *The Whole Chile Pepper* 3 (Fall): 8.

Gilbert, Fabiola C. de Baca

1942. *Historic Cookery*. Las Cruces, NM, College of Agriculture and Mechanic Arts Extension Circular 161.

Gins, Patricia, ed.

1977. *Great Southwest Cooking Classic*. Albuquerque: The Albuquerque Tribune.

Goodman, Michael, et al.

1987. *Totally Hot: The Ultimate Hot Pepper Cookbook*. New York: Doubleday.

Greer, Anne L.

1983. *Cuisine of the American Southwest*. New York: Cuisinart Cooking Club and Harper & Row.

1984. "Flavors of the American Southwest." *Gourmet* 44 (Nov.): 62.

1985. *Creative Mexican Cooking*. Austin: Texas Monthly Press.

Grunes, Barbara, and Phyllis Magida

1987. *The Southwest Sampler*. Chicago: Contemporary Books.

Hale, Sophie

1987. *The Hot and Spicy Cookbook*. Seacaucus, NJ: Chartwell.

Hanle, Zack

1986. "The New Texas Cuisine." *Bon Appetit* (Sept.): 48.

Hansen, Barbara

1981. *Mexican Cookery*. New York: Dell.

1988. "Traditional Mexican Foods Given East Indian Twist." *Albuquerque Journal*, June 23, B4.

Harris, Jessica B.

1986. *Hot Stuff: A Cookbook in Praise of the Piquant*. New York: Ballantine.

1987. "A Taste of the Islands: Spicy, Sweet, and Savory." *Black Enterprise* 17 (May): 47.

Hatchen, Harva

1970. *Kitchen Safari*. New York: Atheneum.

Hesse, Zora

1973. *Southwestern Indian Recipe Book*, Vol. 1. Palmer Lake, CO: The Filter Press.

Hillman, Howard

1979. *The Book of World Cuisines*. New York: Penguin.

Hodgson, Moira

1977. *The Hot and Spicy Cookbook*. New York: McGraw-Hill.

Holt, Paula, and Helene Juarez

1984. *Authentic Mexican Cooking*. New York: Simon & Schuster.

Hughes, Phyllis
    1972. *Pueblo Indian Cookbook.* Santa Fe: Museum of New Mexico
        Press.
Hultman, Tami, ed.
    1985. *The Africa News Cookbook.* New York: Penguin.
Hutson, Lucinda
    1987. *The Herb Garden Cookbook.* Austin: Texas Monthly Press.
Hyun, Judy
    1983. *The Korean Cookbook.* New York: Hollym Intl.
Jaffrey, Madhur
    1978. "Tastes of Thailand." *Gourmet* 38 (Oct.): 19.
    1986. "A Taste of India: Kerala." *Gourmet* 46 (Apr.): 68.
Jaramillo, Cleofas M.
    1942. *The Genuine New Mexico Tasty Recipes.* Santa Fe: The Seton
        Village Press. Reprint of 1939 edition.
Johnrae, Earl, and James McCormick
    1972. *The Chili Cookbook.* Los Angeles: Price/Stern/Sloan.
Johnson, M. M.
    1977. *Freezing Green Chile.* Las Cruces, NM: New Mexico State
        University Cooperative Service Guide 400E-311.
    1977. *Canning Green Chile Sauces.* Las Cruces, NM: New Mexico
        State University Cooperative Service Guide E-312.
Johnson, Ronald
    1968. *The Aficionado's Southwest Cooking.* Albuquerque: Univer-
        sity of New Mexico Press.
Kafka, B.
    1985. "After Tex-Mex: Blistering Cajun." *Vogue* 175 (July): 92.
Karoff, Barbara
    1989. "Hot Items." *USAir Magazine* (May): 108.
    1989. "Chilies." *Gourmet* 49 (Oct.): 115.
Kasper, Lynne
    1981. "Hot Chilies and Sweet Peppers." *Gourmet* 41 (Aug.): 71.
Kaufman, William I.
    1964. *The Wonderful World of Cooking: Recipes from the Carib-
        bean and Latin America.* New York: Dell.
Keegan, Marcia
    1977. *Pueblo and Navajo Cookery.* Santa Monica, CA: Earth Books.
Kennedy, Diana
    1972. *The Cuisines of Mexico.* New York: Harper & Row.
    1975. *The Tortilla Book.* New York: Harper & Row.
    1978. *Recipes from the Regional Cooks of Mexico.* New York:
        Harper & Row.
Lee, Karen
    1984. *Chinese Cooking Secrets.* New York: Doubleday.

Leonard, Jonathan
    1968. *Latin American Cooking*. New York: Time-Life Books.
Lesberg, Sandy
    1971. *The Art of African Cooking*. New York: Dell.
Lombardo, Dorothea
    1978. *Some Like It Hot*. Pasadena, CA: Ward Ritchie Press.
Lomelí, Arturo
    1986. *El Chile y Otros Picantes*. México, D.F.: Asociación Méxicana
        de Estudios para La Defensa del Comsumidor.
Marks, Copeland
    1979. "Indonesian Cookery." *Gourmet* 39 (Nov.): 50.
    1985. *False Tongues and Sunday Bread: A Guatemalan and Mayan
        Cookbook*. New York: M. Evans & Co.
McLaughlin, Michael
    1980. *The Manhattan Chili Company's Southwest American Cook-
        book*. New York: Crown.
    1988. "Bold and Spicy Southwest Food." *Food and Wine* (April):
        54.
McMahan, Jacqueline
    1987. *The Salsa Book*. Lake Hughes, CA: Olive Press.
    1987. *Red and Green Chile Book*. Lake Hughes, CA: Olive Press.
Morgan, Jinx
    1983. "In the Chinese Tradition." *Bon Appetit* (Jan.): 45.
Morphy, Countess
    1935. *Recipes of All Nations*. New York: William Wise & Co.
Neely, Martina and William
    1981. *The International Chili Society Official Chili Cookbook*. New
        York: St. Martin's Press.
Negre, Andre
    1978. *Caribbean Cooking*. Papeete, Tahiti: Les Editions du Paci-
        fique.
Ortiz, Elizabeth Lambert
    1968. *The Complete Book of Mexican Cooking*. New York: Ban-
        tam.
    1973. *The Complete Book of Caribbean Cooking*. New York: M.
        Evans & Co.
    1978. "Picking a Peck of Peppy Peppers." *Saturday Review* 5 (Oct.):
        38.
    1979. *The Book of Latin American Cooking*. New York: Knopf.
    1985. "The Cuisine of Mexico: Dried Chili Peppers." *Gourmet* 45
        (Jan.): 54.
    1985. "The Cuisine of Mexico: Fresh Green Peppers." *Gourmet* 45
        (Mar.): 58.
    1985. "The Cuisine of Mexico: Corn Tortilla Dishes." *Gourmet* 45
        (May): 62.

1985. "The Cuisine of Mexico: Tamales." *Gourmet* 45 (July): 50.

1985. "The Cuisine of Mexico: Soups." *Gourmet* 45 (Sept.): 60.

Owen, Sri

1980. *Indonesian Food and Cookery.* London: Prospect Books.

Pendergrast, Sam

1989. "Requiem for Texas Chili." *The Whole Chile Pepper* 3 (Winter): 28.

Peterson, Marge

1989. "Paprika Power: The Spicy Cooking of the Danube." *The Whole Chile Pepper* 3 (Summer): 31.

Piper, Marjorie

1969. *Sunset Mexican Cookbook.* Menlo Park, CA: Lane Books.

Quintana, Patricia

1986. *The Taste of Mexico.* New York: Stewart, Tabori, and Chang.

Prudhomme, Paul

1984. *Chef Paul Prudhomme's Lousiana Kitchen.* New York: William Morrow & Co.

Root, Waverly

1980. *Food.* New York: Simon & Schuster.

Rau, Santha Rama

1969. *The Cooking of India.* New York: Time-Life Books.

Sahni, Julie

1984. "An Indian Spice Sampler." *Gourmet* 44 (May): 42.

1985. "Special Feast from India." *Bon Appetit* (Oct.): 102.

1987. "Playing with Fire." *New York Times Magazine,* Oct. 11, 93.

Sanchez, Irene B., and Gloria Yund

1985. *Comida Sabrosa: Home-Style Southwestern Cooking.* Albuquerque: University of New Mexico Press.

Schlesinger, Chris

1989. "Equatorial Cuisine: A Hot Love Story." *The Whole Chile Pepper* 3 (Summer): 15.

Schrecker, Ellen

1976. *Mrs. Chang's Szechwan Cookbook.* New York: Harper & Row.

Singh, Dharmjit

1970. *Indian Cookery.* Middlesex, England: Penguin Books.

Smith, H. Allen

1969. *The Great Chili Confrontation.* New York: Trident Press.

Sokolov, Raymond

1979. "Chili con Blarney." In *Fading Feasts* (New York: Farrar, Straus and Giroux), 203.

1985. "Cold Spirits." *Natural History* 94 (July): 70.

Solomon, Charmaine

1976. *The Complete Asian Cookbook.* New York: McGraw-Hill.

Spaeth, Anthony
  1988. "In Guntur, India, Even at 107 Degrees, It's Always Chili, Chili and More Chili." *Wall Street Journal,* June 30.
Spieler, Marlena
  1985. *Hot and Spicy.* Los Angeles: Jeremy P. Tarcher.
Steele, Louise
  1987. *The Book of Hot and Spicy Foods.* Tucson: HP Books.
Stiger, Susan
  1987. "Rival Cities Pepper Mexican Cook-Off." *Albuquerque Journal,* Dec. 10, D1.
  1987. "The Heat is On as Chefs Make Specialties." *Albuquerque Journal,* Dec. 10, D1.
Tolbert, Frank X.
  1972. *A Bowl of Red.* New York: Doubleday.
Van de Post, Laurens
  1970. *African Cooking.* New York: Time-Life Books.
Villella, Lynn, and Patricia Gins, eds.
  1974. *Great Green Chili Cooking Classic.* Albuquerque: The Albuquerque Tribune.
Wolfe, Linda
  1970. *The Cooking of the Caribbean Islands.* New York: Time-Life Books.
Wormser, Richard
  1969. *Southwest Cookery, or, At Home on the Range.* New York: Garden City.
Yturbide, Teresa Castello
  1986. *Presencia de la Comida Prehispanica.* México, D.F.: Banamex.
Zamora, Susan
  1988. "The Hottest Thanksgiving Ever." *The Whole Chile Pepper* 2 (Fall): 35.

Part 5: Other Capsicum Bibliographies

Andrews, Jean
  1984. "Bibliography." In *Peppers: The Domesticated Capsicums,* 155–66. Austin: University of Texas Press.
Casili, V. W. D.
  1970. *Pigmentao e Pimenta* (Capsicum sp.), *Bibliograffia Brasileira Comentada.* Vicosa, Brasil: Universidade Federal de Vicosa, Ser. Técnica, Bol. 23.
Commonwealth Bureau of Horticultural and Plantation Crops
  1964–73. *Annotated Bibliographies on Capsicum Growing and Cultivars in the Tropics and Other Countries.* East Malling, England: Query Files 4777, 5891, 6159.

Commonwealth Bureau of Soils
    1969. "Bibliography on Peppers: Soils, Fertilizers, and Nutrition."
        East Malling, England: Bibliography No. 1324. (15 pp.)
DeWitt, David A.
    1989. *Chile Peppers: A Selected Bibliography of the Capsicums.*
        Albuquerque: Sunbelt Books.
Ferrari, J. P., and G. Ailluad
    1971. "Bibliography of the Genus *Capsicum.*" *J. d'Agric. Trop. et
        Bot. Appl.* 18:385–479.
Gallardo, Pablo Velásquez, and J. Alberto Arellano Rodríguez
    1984. *Bibliografía Mundial de Chile,* Capsicum spp. *(1965–1982).*
        México, D.F.: Instituto Nacional de Investigaciones Agrícolas
        México. (6,107 citations)
Health, H.
    1973. "Herbs and Spices, A Bibliography." *Flavour Industry* 4.
Long-Solis, Janet
    1986. "Bibliografía Citada." In *Capsicum y Cultura: La Historia
        del Chilli.* México: Fondo de Cultura Económica.

INDEX